For
such a
time
as this

Edited by Steve Brady & Harold Rowdon
Foreword by Sir Cliff Richard

For such a time as this

Perspectives on evangelicalism, past, present and future

SCRIPTURE UNION

Evangelical Alliance, Whitefield House,
186 Kennington Park Road, London, SE11 4BT.

Scripture Union, 207–209 Queensway,
Bletchley, Milton Keynes, MK2 2EB, England.

© Evangelical Alliance 1996

First published 1996

ISBN 1 85999 034 7

The right of Robert Amess, Michael Baughen, David Bebbington, Fran Beckett,
Steve Brady, Clive Calver, Donald Carson, Steve Chalke, Gerald Coates, Ian
Coffey, Peter Cotterell, Rosemary Dowsett, Colin Dye, Joel Edwards, Donald
English, Roger Forster, Rob Frost, Alan Gibson, Ken Gnanakan, Tom Houston,
Ken Hylson-Smith, R T Kendall, Steve King, Peter Lewis, Howard Marshall, Roy
McCloughry, Dave Pope, Ian Randall, Chris Seaton, John Stott, Derek Tidball,
Jun Vencer and Phil Wall to be identified as authors of this work has been asserted
by them in accordance with the Copyright, Designs and Patents Act 1988.

British Library Cataloguing-in-Publication Data
A catalogue record for this book is available from the British Library.

Cover design by Mark Carpenter Design Consultants.
Cover photograph: copyright © Tony Stone Images, London.

Phototypeset by Intype London Ltd.
Printed and bound in Great Britain by Mackays of Chatham.

CONTENTS

Where are we heading?

FOREWORD

I guess we're all able to point to new and life-enhancing experiences during the years following our commitment to Christ. Our new riches are many and varied, and we probably enjoy and appreciate them to a greater or lesser extent, depending on our needs. For me, one of the greatest discoveries was the remarkable galaxy of men and women of God who seemed to radiate Christian goodness, and who became inspirational role models. I recall listening to the preaching of Christian leaders and not only being able to identify with what they said but also to sense an almost tangible personal and family bond. Gilbert Kirby was just such a man who made a lasting impression.

He conveyed to this young and hungry Christian the essential ingredient of the new nature – a Christlikeness which was appealing. I knew nothing of the finer points of his theology, nor his opinions on political or social issues of the day. I didn't even know whether he liked rock 'n' roll! And it didn't matter a jot. Somehow this senior, highly-respected minister (with a great line in humour!) and the naive young pop singer were brothers in Christ. Not just jargon; I knew and felt it was for real.

How appropriate then that this book of essays on evangelical unity is linked so closely with Gilbert. For surely it's our Christlikeness which is at the heart – which *is* the heart – of our witness. We do and will disagree over our interpretations and our politics, and we probably still have much to learn about disagreeing without being disagreeable, but disunity among evangelicals is tantamount to a contradiction in terms. I remember, many years ago in a Crusader Bible Class, singing the old CSSM chorus 'Let the beauty of Jesus be seen in me'. Surely that's our starting point.

And, by the way, thanks, Gilbert.

Sir Cliff Richard

PREFACE

The origin of this book is to be found in different but related events: the 150th anniversary of the Evangelical Alliance (1846–1996) and the 80th birthday of one of the world's evangelical elder statesmen, Gilbert Kirby. What relates these two epochs is the fact that both EA and Gilbert have, over many decades, been concerned for the same issues: the historic Christian gospel, with its emphasis on conversion; the centrality of Jesus Christ and his cross; a passionate desire for holy activism in the proclamation of that gospel, both in words of truth and works of mercy; and a deep conviction that the unity for which Jesus prayed in John chapter 17 should be demonstrated across the spectrum of believers who call themselves 'evangelical'.

In some small way this book is itself a demonstration of such unity. As the list of contributors illustrates, a variety of authors from different evangelical traditions and cultures have contributed to this volume. Their contributions have passed through our editorial hands, though the emphases, 'burdens' and 'heart-cries' are their own, having received as little editorial 'pruning' as possible. Nevertheless, we believe, there is an inner coherence to be found in the wide variety of essays contributed. We are thankful to each contributor and to the secretarial staff at EA, ably co-ordinated by Rebecca Teller. Our special thanks are due to Clive Calver, EA's director general. Without his involvement as consulting editor at the genesis of this project, and his encouragement throughout, this book would not have been possible. Thank you, Clive.

Readers of a more practical orientation may wish to turn immediately to the 'Where are we heading?' section towards the end of the volume; those who believe that knowledge of the past is indispensable to both the present and the future may head for the 'Where we come from' division; and so on. We believe there is much within these pages of real value to the evangelical community 'for such a time as this' (Esther 4:14).

It is the prayer of the editors and contributors that God may use this collection of essays to encourage his people, to stimulate mission and hasten the day of our Lord Jesus Christ. To him be the glory!

Steve Brady & Harold Rowdon

THE CONTRIBUTORS

Robert Amess is the senior minister of Duke Street Baptist Church, Richmond, Surrey. He is on the council and executive of the Evangelical Alliance and various other Christian societies. He is married, with four daughters.

Michael Baughen was vicar and then rector of All Souls, Langham Place for twelve years before becoming Bishop of Chester in 1982. Married with three grown-up children and seven grandchildren, he is deeply concerned for evangelical unity and has considerable involvement in Christian music as an author and composer. He is a lover of travel and railways.

David Bebbington is Reader in History at the University of Stirling. He is author of several books including *Patterns in History* (1979), *Evangelicalism in Modern Britain* (1989), *Victorian Nonconformity* (1992) and *William Ewart Gladstone* (1993).

Fran Beckett is the newly appointed chief executive of the Shaftesbury Society. She lives in South London and has many years' experience in Christian social and community work. She is the author of *Called to Action* (1989) and is one of the core leadership team of Ichthus Christian Fellowship (Peckham & Dulwich).

Steve Brady is senior minister of Lansdowne Baptist Church, Bournemouth. He is married, with two children, hates gardening and is an ardent Everton supporter. He serves on the board of Moorlands College, Sopley.

Clive Calver is director general of the Evangelical Alliance and one of the founders of Spring Harvest. He is author of a number of books, co-author of the annual Spring Harvest seminar material, and much in demand as a speaker, teacher and evangelical spokesperson to the media. He is married, with four children.

Donald Carson is a Baptist minister and Research Professor of the New Testament at the Trinity Evangelical Divinity School in the USA. His many publications include major commentaries on Matthew and John. He is married, with two children.

Steve Chalke is general director of Oasis Trust, a charitable trust involved in church and social work in Britain and abroad. He is also a regular TV presenter. He is the author of several books and is married, with four children.

Gerald Coates is the director of Pioneer, a network of churches and ministries across the UK and beyond. He also leads Pioneer People, a church based in Cobham, Surrey. He is married and has three grown-up sons.

Ian Coffey is senior minister of Mutley Baptist Church, Plymouth, and a member of the council of management of the Evangelical Alliance. He is married, with four sons.

Peter Cotterell, an identical twin, was a missionary with SIM International in Ethiopia from 1957 to 1976. He has been a lecturer (1976–89) and principal (1989–95) at London Bible College. He has authored fourteen books, including *Mission and Meaninglessness* (1990). He is married, with two daughters.

Rosemary Dowsett is a missionary with OMF International, on loan to Glasgow Bible College where she lectures in World Christianity. She is a member of the Evangelical Alliance (Scotland) executive, and of the UK Evangelical Alliance council.

Colin Dye is senior minister of Kensington Temple, London, a large and growing Elim Church. He is married and is author of *Building a City Church* (1993). He exercises an international preaching and teaching ministry, having a special burden for Africa and South America, alongside his UK commitments.

Joel Edwards spent three years at London Bible College before working for the Inner London Probation Service. He then became the general secretary for the African Caribbean Evangelical Alliance and is currently EA's UK director.

Donald English, a Methodist minister, is a writer, broadcaster, scholar, ecumenical leader and missioner. Until July 1995 he was general secretary of the Home Mission Division of the Methodist Church, and is chairman of the World Methodist Council.

Roger Forster is the founder of and a leader in the Ichthus Christian Fellowship, London, and is an honorary vice-president of both EA and Tear Fund. He has written a large number of papers and booklets, and authored eight books including *God's Strategy in Human History* (1973) and *Christianity, Evidence and Truth* (1995). He is married, with three children and two grandchildren.

Rob Frost is a Methodist national evangelist. He is the leader of the annual holiday event, Easter People, and Seed Teams, an evangelistic programme with teams in France, Poland, Estonia and all over the UK.

His productions, *Burning Questions, Gospel End, Breaking Bread, Visions* and *Daybreak*, have been seen by audiences totalling hundreds of thousands.

Alan Gibson spent twenty-four years as a pastor among Evangelical Free Churches before becoming the general secretary of the British Evangelical Council in 1982. He is married, with three children and five grandsons.

Ken Gnanakan studied in London and is now general director of ACTS Ministries and general secretary of the Asia Theological Association. He is an educationalist and environmentalist based in Bangalore, India, with his wife and two children.

Tom Houston is minister-at-large of The Lausanne Committee for World Evangelization and pastor emeritus of the Nairobi Baptist Church, Kenya. He has served as executive director of the British and Foreign Bible Society, and president of World Vision International.

Ken Hylson-Smith is the author of *Evangelicals in the Church of England* (1989) and *High Churchmanship in the Church of England* (1993). He is bursar and a fellow of St Cross College, Oxford.

R T Kendall has been minister of Westminster Chapel, London, since 1977. He is married, with two children, is the author of several books and well-known as a speaker at Keswich and Spring Harvest.

Steve King was born and brought up in East London. He now works as a pastor and church planter with Cranleigh Community Church in Bournemouth. He is married, with three daughters.

Peter Lewis has been pastor of the Cornerstone Evangelical Church, Nottingham, for twenty-six years. He is author of *The Glory of Christ* (1992) and *The Lord's Prayer* (1995). He serves on the EA council and is a member of World Evangelical Fellowship Theological Commission.

Howard Marshall is Professor of New Testament Exegesis in the University of Aberdeen and a member of the Scottish Council of the Evangelical Alliance. He is the author of many articles, several commentaries and other books on the New Testament.

Roy McCloughry is director of Kingdom Trust, a consultancy on applied social ethics, and also lectures at St John's College, Nottingham. He has written several books, including *The Eye of the Needle* (1990) and *Men and Masculinity* (1992).

Dave Pope is the founder and a director of the Saltmine Trust, and a member of the Spring Harvest executive with particular responsibilities for worship. He also serves as the director of Trailblazers, an initiative designed to raise the profile of Christian service and mission. He is single and lives in the West Midlands.

Ian Randall, a Baptist minister, lectures in church history and is college chaplain at Spurgeon's College, London. His research and writing have been mainly on aspects of evangelicalism and he is currently studying movements of evangelical spirituality in England in the 1920s and '30s. He is married, with two daughters.

Harold Rowdon, born of missionary parents, was for many years senior lecturer in church history at the London Bible College. He has served on numerous boards of missionary and other societies, and his publications include *The Origins of the Brethren* (1967). He is currently editor of Partnership Publications.

Chris Seaton trained and worked as a solicitor before taking a full-time leadership role in Revelation (a Pioneer church) in 1987. He lives in Bognor Regis with his wife and two children. Apart from writing and preaching Chris enjoys cricket, golf and bird-watching.

John Stott was rector of All Souls, Langham Place, from 1950 to 1975 when he became rector emeritus. He is also president of Christian Impact. In addition, he travels widely and has written many books.

Derek Tidball is principal of the London Bible College and a vice-president of the Evangelical Alliance. He has previously served as a pastor and denominational executive. He was president of the Baptist Union of Great Britain, 1990–91. He is author of *Who are the Evangelicals?* (1994) and is married, with one son.

Augustin 'Jun' Vencer is the international director of the World Evangelical Fellowship. He was formerly the general secretary of the Philippine Council of Evangelical Churches, and of the Philippine Relief and Development Services. He has served as a pulpit minister of the Alliance Fellowship Church.

Phil Wall works as national youth evangelist for the Salvation Army and is also involved in church planting in South-west London. He is particularly involved in training and equipping young leaders.

Chapter 1

GILBERT KIRBY, AN EVANGELICAL STATESMAN: A TRIBUTE AND PROFILE

Steve Brady

I remember once I was sitting beside him on the platform, and I had not prepared my sermon very well and was terribly tense and nervous about it. He put his hand on my leg and said, 'God will be with you. Don't worry about what anyone else thinks.' I thought: how like Gilbert![1]

How like Gilbert Kirby (GWK) indeed. For over fifty years he has been encouraging congregations of 'ordinary' Christians, fellow pastors and preachers, students and internationally-known Christians like the author of the above statement, Dr Billy Graham.

'If you wish to honour a man, honour him while he is alive,' said a wise, unknown author. All too often, compliments about a man are reserved for his funeral oration. I am therefore grateful for the opportunity to write this profile in honour of someone who, twenty-five years ago, was my college principal and subsequently officiated at my marriage to Brenda (née Donaldson), his secretary for four years (1971–1975) at the London Bible College (LBC). Over the past twenty years, Brenda and I have lost count of the many kindnesses and the personal enrichment that both GWK and Connie, his dear and devoted wife, have bestowed upon us and our children. Moreover, I am delighted that my contribution qualifies under the category of 'biopsy' not 'autopsy', since GWK is very much 'still living by faith' (Hebrews 11:13). The desire of all his friends is that he will continue to 'hang on in' with us for a good while longer!

Perhaps, at this point, a word of explanation is in order, for there are others who are better qualified than I to write this tribute. Some have known him for over half a century (ask Connie!). Others have been his colleagues at the Evangelical Alliance (EA), the World Evangelical Fellowship (WEF) and LBC during his principalship, or have been members and 'right hand men and women' of the churches he has served as pastor. So why is it my privilege to contribute this tribute?

In 1992 I wrote to Gilbert's daughter, Ruth, and son-in-law, Clive Calver, director general of EA, suggesting that 1994 would be a significant year for GWK as he would be celebrating his eightieth birthday and, with Connie, a golden wedding anniversary. 'It strikes me that that would be an ideal time to bring out some kind of *festschrift*' [a book written to mark a special occasion in a distinguished person's life]. I added, 'I realize that as you are somewhat related to him [!] it may seem difficult for you to initiate. On the other hand, I am making the suggestion so you can honestly say it wasn't your idea! . . . However, I do think that GWK has made such an outstanding contribution to the evangelical life of this country that it would be a shame to miss such an opportunity.'[2]

So the 1994 opportunity was missed? Not quite! Those of you who are acquainted with Clive Calver know him to be a man of vision, always ready to 'kill two birds with one stone'. Early in 1993, when we met to discuss the project, he had an idea. 'It just so happens', he casually remarked, 'that EA will be celebrating its 150th anniversary a mere two years later!' He suggested that we 'produce something really worthwhile, which would bless the Body of Christ, and be a statement of affection and tribute to a man so many of us deeply esteem'.[3]

Many do indeed esteem GWK. Allow me to introduce to you a wise Christian, a godly pastor and an internationally known and respected evangelical statesman.

The early years

GWK was born in Forest Hill, a suburb of South-east London, a few weeks before the outbreak of the First World War, the only child of a textile agent and a mother who was a day-school teacher, both regular churchgoers. A move to nearby Sydenham and attendance at an inter-denominational Sunday school provided four-year-old GWK with his first line in humour – the chorus 'When mother was a sailor', his individual rendition of 'When mothers of Salem'!

After attending Bromley County School for boys, GWK entered Eltham College in 1926, the year of the General Strike. The school had been founded for the sons of missionaries, one of whom, Eric Liddell, had caused a stir at the 1924 Olympic Games by refusing to run on a Sunday.[4] Gilbert confesses that at school 'I was neither a brilliant scholar nor an outstanding sportsman but I managed to acquit myself quite well'.[5] This is most definitely an understatement, for he not only later passed an entrance examination for Cambridge University but also became a hockey 'half blue', captaining Fitzwilliam's First Eleven.

Being an Eltham pupil 'entitled' GWK to attend Bromley Crusaders which, in those days, only 'public and private schoolboys' were allowed to join. It was here, in the providence of God, that he was converted and received a good grounding in the evangelical faith. Dr R B Coleman ('Docco') – the senior leader, himself a former missionary and the family's GP – led a weekly Bible study, 'Keenites', which influenced successive generations of youngsters, not least GWK. Upon leaving Eltham College in 1933, he was offered a place at King's College, London, to study French with a view to becoming a teacher of modern languages. However, GWK had a growing conviction by this time that 'I should enter the Christian ministry and this was eventually confirmed to me from scripture (2 Timothy 4:1–6)'.[6]

'Docco' was a lay reader at Christ Church, Bromley, which GWK always attended on Sunday evenings. It was here that he first met Maurice Wood, later Bishop of Norwich, whose father and brother, Arthur and Frederick, had founded the National Young Life Campaign which at that time was in its heyday. However, since Gilbert's parents were members of Bromley Congregational Church, they suggested that he should speak to its minister, O G Whitfield, regarding training for the ministry. Cambridge now beckoned.

Student days

Cheshunt College, Cambridge, had been founded in the eighteenth century by Selina, Countess of Huntingdon, for the training of men for the Protestant ministry generally.[7] By 1933, however, its training was confined almost exclusively to men for the Congregational ministry. Moreover, theological liberalism had deeply affected Congregationalism. As a result, GWK discovered that he was the only student in college who held to a 'conservative' view of scripture. Once again, however, it was an interdenominational, evangelical group (this time the Cambridge Inter-Collegiate Christian Union [CICCU]) which, like Crusaders before it, provided – through its prayer meetings, fellowship, weekly 'Bible Readings' and Sunday evening services – the spiritual strength and support that he needed over the next five years of theological study and preparation for ordination.

Such was the influence of CICCU on GWK that, although in training ostensibly for the Congregational ministry, most of his Sundays were spent at the evangelical Anglican church of St Paul's. Here, along with the vicar, Jack Ainley, was to be found Basil Atkinson, a lay reader and an under-librarian at the university library. Atkinson exercised considerable influence as a 'father figure' on successive generations of CICCU students.[8]

In 1937, at the end of his fourth year at Cambridge, GWK attended his first Keswick Convention under the auspices of the Inter-Varsity Fellowship [IVF], to which CICCU was affiliated. 'We slept under canvas in the IVF camp,' he tells us, 'and it seemed to rain every day. In fact,' he adds with characteristic humour, 'that was the last time I went camping.'[9]

Interdenominational Sunday schools, Crusaders, CICCU and IVF, camps and house parties in vacations, attendance at Anglican services whilst training for the Congregational ministry and exposure to a galaxy of leading evangelical preachers of the day[10] – all were seed-beds of an interdenominational evangelicalism for which GWK is well-known. On the one hand, such influences cocooned him from much of the liberal theology of those days, and he saw himself as a 'defender of the faith', even in the lectures of such luminaries as Professor C H Dodd. On the other hand, the evangelicalism of the time was essentially pietistic and had little to say about the social and political issues of the day, though the threat of war in Europe hung heavily in the air.

One further legacy from the Keswick of 1937 must be mentioned: 'Up to 1937 . . . I had not been involved too seriously with the opposite sex, but at Keswick I did meet twin sisters, Joan and Jean McGaw, and Joan and I were attracted to each other'.[11]

Marriage and ministry

In his final year at Cambridge GWK received a unanimous call to Halstead Congregational Church, Essex. He was ordained and inducted on 7 June 1938 and married Joan the following month. The couple then occupied the manse with its seven bedrooms and three large reception rooms, GWK enjoying the 'princely' stipend of a mere £205 per annum! Poignantly he states:

> When I settled at Halstead to begin my ministry I could look back on five years' training at the University. I had an honours degree in theology. I was fully accredited by my denomination but as far as my experience of real life was concerned I was a greenhorn. Sadly my case was not unique. In those days all too many young men entered the ministry with a background all too similar to my own.[12]

Though GWK was painfully aware of being a 'greenhorn', the small congregation began to flourish in Halstead which was basically a small industrial town. There were, however, one or two incidents where his inexperience was exposed. Almost as soon as he arrived at the church, he was asked to take the part of William Tyndale in a local churches' pageant to celebrate the 400th anniversary of the English Bible being placed in every parish church. He was not sure what he had let himself in for. He quips, 'I quite enjoyed the experience even though it entailed being burnt at the stake.'[13] On another occasion, he called at the home of a deceased person to arrange the funeral. He did not know it was customary to keep the body in the house so that friends and neighbours could pay their last respects. 'I expect you would like to see her' were the words that greeted him on his arrival. Never lost for words and quick repartee, GWK replied, 'If you don't mind, I would prefer to think of her as I knew her.' This worked admirably for six months until he had to conduct the funeral of someone he had never seen![14]

The more serious side of pastoral ministry was, of course, encountered. At the local cottage hospital a child from the Sunday school lay dying with meningitis. There seemed to be no hope, and the kindly matron, herself a Christian, asked GWK to help the child's mother in particular to come to terms with the situation. When he called at the child's home, the Lord himself seemed to take over and GWK found himself praying for the child's full recovery. More than thirty years later, on a return visit to Halstead, GWK was greeted by a married woman, herself now a mother, who said, 'I was the little girl you prayed for all those years ago.'[15]

The comparative peace of Halstead was immediately shattered when war was declared on 3 September 1939. That very afternoon, bus-loads of bewildered youngsters began to arrive, to be billeted in local homes. The church was occupied by a school evacuated from Wood Green, London, and GWK was appointed a chaplain to 'other denominations'. This involved him in visiting gun sites and conducting padre's hours. A YMCA canteen was opened in the church's basement and many fruitful contacts were made with the troops – 70,000 sandwiches and 120,000 cups of tea being served up in one particular year!

Although the war inevitably cast its shadow over the work at Halstead, good local evangelical links were forged, and an annual convention was started in 1940. This was particularly significant since the church had not hitherto been exposed to an evangelical Bible-based ministry, especially from well-known Anglican and Baptist ministers. Once again the seeds of 'pan-evangelicalism' were being sown.

A darker, more personal shadow was yet to be cast over this time in Halstead. In a memorable poem Oswald Sanders reminds us:

When God wants to drill a man
And thrill a man
And skill a man . . .
Watch His methods, watch His ways!
How He ruthlessly perfects
Whom He royally elects!
How He hammers him and hurts him
And with mighty blows converts him . . .
How He bends but never breaks
When his good He undertakes . . .
By every act induces him
To try His splendour out –
God knows what He's about![16]

The joy of GWK and Joan at the birth of Gillian in July 1939 was to be matched nearly four years later by the arrival of their second child, David, born in February 1943. Although Joan made a good postnatal recovery, her condition then deteriorated and she was moved to Addlestone, Surrey, to be with her twin, Jean, who was a qualified nurse. Admission to hospital soon followed, and Joan was diagnosed as having meningitis and a cerebral abscess. GWK was conducting services at Coggeshall Congregational Church on 11 July 1943 when, before the service, a policeman arrived, informing GWK that his wife was dangerously ill. He rushed to be with his wife, only to be greeted with the news that she had passed away some time before his arrival.

One phrase from GWK's autobiography seems to cover the personal angst, pain and loneliness of that time: 'In my distress I cried unto the Lord' (Psalm 120:1). Though family, friends and others came to the rescue, 'It was God's grace alone that enabled me. Strangely, the thing I found hardest to bear was the sense that when I walked down the High Street people would be looking at me and feeling sorry for me'.[17] The Lord's help (and 'helper', Genesis 2:18) was near to hand.

Connie

In nineteenth-century Essex a revivalist group, founded in London in 1838, flourished. Noted for their evangelistic fervour, warm fellowship and belief in divine healing, 'The Peculiar People' (now known as the Union of Evangelical Churches) were presided over by a 'Supreme Bishop', a William Heddle, from 1901 to 1942.[18] He married twice, his first wife producing three daughters, his second wife ten further children. One of them, Oscar Heddle, was very involved in local Christian activities, and his daughter, Connie, had been posted to Halstead to work with the Women's Land Army and attended GWK's church. She was a keen Christian, good-looking, with an attractive personality and a good singing voice, rendering solos on various occasions at Halstead. GWK was smitten. But there were obstacles. Would it be fair to ask a girl so young (she was twenty at the time) to take on the responsibility of a husband, a busy manse and two young children, all against the background of an ongoing war in Europe?

His proposal of marriage met with approval and delight from Joan's mother, Connie's family and the church at Halstead. They married on 2 August 1944. Almost immediately she was coping with a new husband, family, leadership of the women's meeting and numerous people to entertain at the manse, including the local MP, the Right Honourable R A Butler, who was Minister of Education at the time! The following year would witness GWK and Connie single-handedly running a beach mission under the auspices of the Children's Special Services Mission (CSSM) at Frinton-on-Sea. Each day Connie played the harmonium and GWK gave the talk. 'It was an adventure we would not want to repeat,' GWK pithily comments![19]

Personal bereavement, the experience of six years of war and a growing acquaintance, through Halstead's annual convention, with a number of Christian leaders had brought a great measure of maturity to this 'greenhorn'. Though he was always learning, it was time to discard the 'L' plates as the 'open road' of future service beckoned.

Ashford and an evangelical 'Who's Who?'

In 1945 GWK was invited to become the minister of Ashford Congregational Church, Middlesex. Outwardly it was not an attractive proposition – a non-existent manse, a church hall that was no more than a tin hut, a ministerial predecessor who was liberal in his theology and strongly pacifist in his convictions, and a diaconate who were theologically clueless but willing to be led!

Evangelical witness, especially amongst the free churches, was not strong in the Thames Valley area. However, there were evangelical ministerial allies in the Congregational church at Staines, the Anglican church at Laleham-on-Thames and the Baptist cause at Duke Street, Richmond, which, under the dynamic leadership of Alan Redpath, drew folk from miles around. GWK and Alan soon became firm friends.

When Ashford Congregational Church celebrated its Diamond Jubilee in 1950 a whole series of events was arranged. Distinguished guests and speakers came to the church: Lieutenant-General Sir William Dobbie, one-time governor of Malta; Sir John Laing, the building contractor; Sir Eric Richardson, later director of education at the Polytechnic of Central London; Lieutenant-General Sir Arthur Smith, chairman of EA; and Lindsay Glegg who led an outreach, Life with a Purpose, in the October of that year.

Such links would prove to be highly significant in subsequent years for GWK's ministry at EA, LBC and the great Filey Convention (which started as a 'follow-up' to Billy Graham's UK crusades). The latter drew thousands of Christians together for a week each year over a near thirty-year period. From its inception in the mid-1950s, Lindsay Glegg played a major part, and GWK was a regular contributor. Two other hugely significant names appear during GWK's period at Ashford (1945–1956): Dr D Martyn Lloyd-Jones, minister of Westminster Chapel, London, and Dr Billy Graham, the now world-renowned evangelist.

Shortly after GWK's arrival in the London area, he was invited to join Dr Lloyd-Jones's Westminster Fellowship. In those early days the Fellowship consisted of only a dozen or so ministers, including Alan Stibbs of the Anglican theological college, Oak Hill, George Beasley-Murray who became principal of the Baptist college, Spurgeon's, Ernest Kevan, principal of the interdenominational LBC, and Morgan Derham who served for many years with Scripture Union. Even in those far off days the 'ministry of women' was frequently on the agenda! More pressing and serious, however, was the growing 'threat' from ecumenism, and the Fellowship subsequently grew beyond all recognition, seeking to address this and related issues.[20]

Later, Lloyd-Jones would be less than pleased with GWK when, in 1957, the latter became EA's general secretary. Nevertheless, he preached at GWK's induction when, in the same year, he became honorary pastor of Turners Hill Free Church. 'Over the years', GWK tells us, 'I kept in close touch with "the Doctor" and deeply appreciated his wise counsel.'[21]

Undoubtedly the highlight of this period at Ashford was the visit of Dr Billy Graham and his team to conduct the 1954 Harringay crusade. The church at Ashford, along with many others, organized early morning prayer meetings and coach parties to the stadium, and some very real conversions and additions to the church were witnessed. In Dr Graham's words, 'I ... have a great debt of gratitude to the Evangelical Alliance because they took a "pig in a poke" and sponsored a relatively unknown evangelist from America in 1954 at Harringay Arena'.[22] Dr Graham generously pays tribute to GWK's involvement both in 1954 and subsequently: 'It seems that everything I was involved in – he was part of. We spent many hours talking together and praying together, especially about evangelism and the possibility of revival in the UK.'[23]

Undoubtedly these years at Ashford were amongst the most formative and fruitful in GWK's ministry. His contacts across the evangelical spectrum continued to expand, close links being formed with Tom Rees who, from 1945 onward, organized evangelistic meetings for a decade at Westminster Central Hall and the Royal Albert Hall, drawing huge crowds. When, in 1945, Rees acquired and opened Hildenborough Hall in Kent as an evangelistic and conference centre, GWK soon found himself a regular speaker alongside the stalwart, veteran Brethren evangelist and Bible teacher, Montague Goodman. Such conferences and summer house parties have continued to play a huge part in the lives of GWK and Connie; hardly a summer in the last fifty years has passed without their involvement somewhere. Other outside commitments would be no less strategic.

As early as 1945 GWK had joined the consultative faculty of the recently inaugurated LBC, lecturing to the first batch of full-time students.[24] He taught 'Matriculation English' to enable them to proceed to a university degree course. Subsequently he taught homiletics. In addition, he lectured regularly at other Bible colleges, such as Redcliffe, Ridgelands and All Nations, usually on church history or modern cults.[25] Opportunities to serve on a variety of councils and mission boards continued to present themselves. With so many outside responsibilities devolving upon GWK, in addition to the thriving work at Ashford where a new manse and church hall had been built, the church wisely appointed a pastor's assistant, Evelyn Gulliver, who did a splendid job both at Ashford and its mission church at Stanwell. By 1956, however, new responsibilities were beckoning GWK.

Consolidation and controversy: 1956–1966

For a decade GWK had been involved with EA, being responsible with Hugh Gough, Bishop of Barking, for the appointment of Roy Cattell in 1946 as general secretary of EA in succession to Martyn Gooch who had served EA for some forty-four years. By 1956 a new general secretary was being sought. It was Hugh Gough who persuaded GWK that he was the ideal man! His initial reluctance to lay aside preaching for an office job had a 'simple' solution – he was to do both! As a result of this decision, upon leaving Ashford where Ruth, their daughter, had been born in 1950, GWK and Connie removed to Turners Hill Free Church in Sussex. Here

GWK would serve as honorary pastor. The hidden cost of this was a 6.30 start from home each morning to catch the commuter train to EA's office which was situated at that time in Bedford Place in Central London.

GWK knew he would need to lean heavily on his staff, having no office experience. Within an hour of his arrival the girl who looked after EA's finances announced she was leaving, though she assured GWK that it had nothing to do with his appointment! Still, he had inherited a good, efficient secretary – who decided to become a nurse shortly after he commenced his duties! On the positive side, there was a very talented line-up of staff. The editorial secretary was Timothy Dudley-Smith, the now well-known hymn-writer and subsequently Bishop of Thetford; Maurice Rowlandson, who subsequently joined the Billy Graham Evangelistic Association, was extension secretary; the chairman of the executive council was Lieutenant-General Sir Arthur Smith who had had an outstanding army career. When Dudley-Smith left his editorial position in 1959, he was succeeded by a relatively unknown young schoolmaster, David Winter, who one day would become head of religious broadcasting at the BBC. Men of the calibre of Lieutenant-General Sir William Dobbie (of Malta fame); Ernest Kevan of LBC; Maurice Wood, later Bishop of Norwich; the well-known Methodist, Dr W E Sangster; and John Stott, rector of All Souls, Langham Place – to mention but a few – served the council during this period. In his ten years in office at EA, GWK was able to visit most of the countries of Western Europe, the USA and India.

There are a number of developments and one major set-back to record from this period of GWK's general secretaryship. The scope of EA was widened during his tenure of office by welcoming not only individual members but also local churches. As a result, two of the largest pentecostal denominations, Elim and Assemblies of God, were welcomed as members, a ground-breaking event; some of EA's sister alliances in Europe had been less willing to allow pentecostalists to join their ranks.

In 1958, when EA's Overseas Committee amalgamated with the Committee of the Fellowship of Interdenominational Missionary Societies, the union gave birth to the Evangelical Missionary Alliance (EMA). Today EMA serves the interests of practically every evangelical missionary society in Britain.

As early as 1960 a fund had been set up to help refugees, some £500 being contributed through EA. By 1968 the Evangelical Alliance Relief Fund (TEAR Fund) had evolved. Today it is one of the largest distinctively Christian relief agencies, with a budget of some £21 million pa. GWK rightly counted it a privilege when, in 1982, he 'was invited to join Cliff Richard as one of the two vice-presidents of TEAR Fund'.[26] At one period, in addition to his numerous responsibilities to councils and committees, and his duties as pastor of Turners Hill Free Church,[27] he was simultaneously general secretary of EA, secretary of EMA and international secretary of WEF. His later colleague and a successor as principal of LBC, Peter Cotterell, has pithily summarized GWK: 'Of course there isn't a lazy bone in his body'.[28] With a new baby boy, Peter John ('PJ'), born just over a year after their arrival in Turners Hill, one wonders if GWK ever slept at all! However, with typical modesty – and with, no doubt, a great deal of truth – GWK acknowledges his debt to Connie, to his 'right-hand man' at Turners Hill, the previous honorary pastor, Quinton DeAth, and to Nancy Cater for her magnificent support as his secretary.

Although GWK himself has expressed the view that his 'greatest disappointment was to witness the gradual run-down of the Universal Week of Prayer',[29] traditionally promoted by EA in the first full week of January each year, the major set-back of his tenure of office – admittedly right at its very end – was the schism of 1966. In 1965 a National Assembly of Evangelicals had been held with some one thousand delegates attending, and an encouraging time had been experienced. A further assembly was planned and held at the Westminster Central Hall under the chairmanship of the Anglican, John Stott. The issue of evangelicals and ecumenism was high on the agenda. A commission on unity, under EA's auspices, had been set up and a report was issued to the delegates. The first evening's speaker was D Martyn Lloyd-Jones who had previously expressed his views to the commission. He was thus invited to state his misgivings publicly. Their substance was that the time had arrived to leave doctrinally 'mixed' denominations and seek realignment in a visible association of evangelical churches, free from such doctrinal admixture. When Lloyd-Jones had finished, Stott openly disassociated himself, on the basis of history and scripture, from Lloyd-Jones' call for secession from the historic denominations.[30]

By this date it was public knowledge that GWK was to succeed Ernest Kevan, LBC's first principal, who had died the previous year.[31]

The LBC era

Ernest Kevan had been a personal friend of the Kirbys and had conducted their elder daughter's wedding in 1964 at Turners Hill. GWK had the responsibility and privilege of now officiating at Kevan's funeral. Meanwhile, the board at LBC, which GWK had joined in 1958, set about the task of appointing a successor. Present faculty names were considered, soundings were taken and various approaches were made, all to no avail. It was a fellow governor, Tony Dannatt, who at a prayer meeting of the board suggested GWK's name. Eventually, the board 'officially' approached him, despite his protestations that he was not an academic 'high flyer' and had limited teaching experience. He accepted the challenge.

His final months at EA were extremely busy. Billy Graham was returning to Britain to conduct his 1966 Earls Court Crusade in which EA was fully involved. Moreover, a great deal of preparation was in hand for the second National Assembly referred to above, which was due to be held in the autumn of that same year. The long haul from Turners Hill every

morning would continue until LBC eventually relocated from 19 Maryle-
bone Road in Central London to the leafy suburbs of Northwood, Middlesex, in 1970.

Dr Kevan had been a brilliant organizer, with the result that the college
was very departmentalized. The LBC of 1966 had an air of formality,
almost a forbidding formality: gowns were worn by the students to all
lectures and private tutorials; ties must be worn by the men; slacks, save
on Saturday mornings, were not to be worn by the women; 'high table' for
the faculty was observed; and students and faculty alike were addressed as
'Mr' or 'Miss' as appropriate. Initially, though he had no pretensions to
his level of scholarship, GWK sought to ape his predecessor's 'decently
and in order in all things' mentality. Soon, however, he realized the
importance of being himself. On the one hand, Christians too easily
become flexible on the inflexible, resulting in theological liberalism; on the
other, they can become inflexible on the flexible and end up in a cultural
time-warp. The genius of GWK has been his ability to discern the difference and to be a catalyst for change in respect of matters that are merely
evangelical traditions. One example must suffice.

In the early Seventies, when 'high table' was still in fashion at LBC, a
discussion at faculty level was inconclusive and potentially divisive. 'I can
see it's not right to force the issue now,' announced GWK at the conclusion
of a faculty meeting. 'All I can say is that from next week onwards you
won't find me sitting at High Table any longer.' Derek Tidball, a faculty
member at the time and now principal of LBC, comments, 'From memory,
High Table lasted just a few days after Gilbert's coup.'[32] Such changes,
however, undoubtedly 'contributed towards a closer and more relaxed
relationship between staff and students. In making changes I was grateful
for the wholehearted backing I received from the board of Governors.'[33]

The LBC board had some greatly gifted, generous and wise members
over the years. P S Henman, according to GWK, was a superb chairman
who never wasted a word. Along with Sir John Laing, the famous builder,
whose gifts to the college and other Christian work were legendary, P S
Henman himself was also a most generous benefactor. Derek Warren, a
city solicitor, was a 'sheer delight' to work with, according to GWK, and
later became chairman of the board, always encouraging GWK to be
forward looking. One name, however, merits special attention because of
the ground-breaking implications of his vision. Sir Eric Richardson, who
succeeded P S Henman as chairman of the board, was an academic with a
distinguished career in various polytechnics, serving latterly as Director of
Education at the Polytechnic of Central London. He was also very
involved in the Council for National Academic Awards (CNAA) and
encouraged LBC to apply for recognition for a degree in theology. Hitherto CNAA had not dealt with comparatively small (some two hundred
students) private institutions like LBC. Further, to validate a theological
degree, CNAA needed to set up an entirely new board to handle the
application. I had the privilege to be amongst the first batch of degree

students to graduate with a BA (CNAA) in theology in 1975. Within a decade of that date LBC would be regularly offering higher degrees through the CNAA channel, and continued to do so until 1992 when CNAA was wound up and LBC became a recognized college of Brunel University.

However, LBC is not primarily about faculty, board members or degrees. GWK summarizes the 'real' LBC he enjoyed for fourteen years:[34]

> The greatest thrill of all at LBC was getting to know hundreds of men and women who were setting out on the Lord's service and who in the course of a few years would be scattered world-wide. I discovered that in almost every part of the world there were to be found former LBC students.[35]

GWK's ability to 'network' has a long track record. Whilst at Ashford Congregational Church, as early as 1947 he had helped to initiate a Congregational Evangelical Revival Fellowship (CERF). Networking had been essential in his position at EA. When he arrived at LBC, GWK had the distinct impression that LBC seemed to hold itself aloof from similar evangelical colleges. He set about rectifying the situation, inviting fellow principals for a conference at LBC. The result? There now exists an Association of Bible College Principals which meets annually. In addition, for four colleges in close geographical proximity to each other, GWK also initiated ALSO – a link between All Nations Christian College, London Bible College, Spurgeon's College and Oak Hill College.

GWK's wide network of contacts ensured that LBC was regularly visited by evangelical luminaries from across the nation and indeed the world. Dr Billy Graham came to the college at least twice during GWK's principalship. The Argentinian evangelist, Dr Luis Palau, who likewise visited the college, believes that GWK 'inspired two generations of young evangelical leaders', acting as 'the bridge between' the older evangelical leaders and the new.[36] Bishops, Members of Parliament, Cliff Richard, Malcolm Muggeridge and the then commissioner of the Metropolitan Police, Sir David McNee, were all welcomed, alongside a whole variety of 'lesser lights' drawn from right across the denominational divide. GWK's ability to hold together some of the disparate elements of evangelicalism – on the Reformed/Arminian, Charismatic/non-Charismatic, Separatist/Inclusivist divides, for instance – is misunderstood by some as mere 'fence-sitting'. In a time, however, when the 'twelve tribes of evangelicalism' threaten to become the '144,000', 'peacemakers' are even more necessary.

In spite of his onerous commitments at LBC, he continued as pastor at Turners Hill until 1970 when the college relocated to Northwood and an on-site principal's house became available. But GWK was determined not to lose contact with the 'outside world', as he saw it. He remained on EA's and EMA's councils, kept other irons in the fire and, in 1979, became chairman of the Movement for Worldwide Evangelization (MWE) which organized the Filey holiday weeks. Moreover a steady stream of books proceeded from his pen during his principalship, revealing both the breadth of his knowledge and some of the scope of his concerns and convictions.[37] Despite his numerous commitments during his LBC period, he remained, first and foremost, a pastor-preacher. Enter Roxeth Green Free Church, Harrow.

Pastures new

Roxeth Green is a council housing estate that is not quite as salubrious as its Harrow address might suggest. The church itself, staunchly evangelical without denominational links, was in 1970 without a pastor, though hopeful of a settlement. Tentatively GWK volunteered his services 'in the meantime', commencing as honorary pastor in May 1971. Twelve years later . . .

For the first three years the arrangement worked well: GWK preached two Sundays a month and conducted a mid-week meeting. An LBC student would serve as a pastor's assistant as part of his training. By 1974, however, more help was necessary. In September of that year Frank Gamble, who had just graduated from LBC, arrived. Some LBC-ers wondered if this was a 'suicide pact'! In the providence of God it was a 'nuclear explosion'. Frank quickly 'loosened things up' at Roxeth, and an informal, charismatic style of worship, replete with tongues and prophecies, was introduced. GWK had never viewed the part of the service prior to the sermon as the 'preliminaries'. An earnest Christian who suggested that it was such provided the 'one occasion which brought out GWK's anger. "Don't ever let me hear you call worship a formality." More remarkable, perhaps,' adds Andy Curtis, 'as he said this in the early 1950s' while serving at Ashford Congregational Church.[38]

With typical candour GWK records that, of course, mistakes were made at Roxeth. Sometimes the preaching of the word – of paramount importance to GWK – and the worship element lacked balance.[39] Nevertheless, Roxeth became a wonderfully caring community where people were regularly converted. Offerings rocketed and £85,000 was raised by direct giving, primarily from the church itself, for an extension. Frank moved in April 1981 to start a new work in nearby Stanmore. GWK, by now retired from LBC, 'soldiered on for a further two years before we moved back to Northwood, theoretically to begin our retirement'.[40]

Business as usual

GWK has never found the round of preaching in different churches every week particularly satisfying. Returning to live in Northwood near LBC in 1983 left him feeling somewhat bereft. However, a phone call from nearby Bushey Baptist Church, which had recently lost its pastor, provided a moderatorship until a successor could be found. When a new pastor arrived, in September 1985, a new spiritual home, within reasonable distance of where they lived, became a real need for GWK and Connie. Their new neighbours next door provided the answer! They belonged to Northwood Hills Evangelical Church, originally of Open Brethren persuasion but now replete with a pastor, staff and new building. Here GWK continues to exercise a regular ministry. He is often asked what he now does with himself 'in retirement'. He says:

> The answer is 'business as usual'. I have been given a strong constitution and see no reason to slacken off. Obviously the pressures of being in a full-time occupation are no longer there but there is plenty of work still to be done. I have noticed people nowadays do not find it easy to know how to introduce me. In their charity they refrain from too frequent use of the prefix 'ex'. In point of fact I still have a good many irons in the fire . . . I still find time to do some lecturing and fulfil numerous speaking engagements. Personally I like it that way and I am particularly happy that my wife Connie is now able to share fully in these activities.[41]

'Business as usual' seems to sum up GWK, so long as it is 'the King's business'. Hearing he was suffering from a bout of shingles, I dropped in to see him on a June day in 1994. He was obviously nowhere near 100 per cent fit. However, he casually remarked that, in spite of the shingles, he had preached twice the previous Sunday; then, after the evening service, he and Connie entertained a houseful of youngsters; and various folk had been round already that week, royally entertained as usual by them both. It is recorded of John Wesley that, at the age of eighty-six, he lamented, 'Laziness is slowly creeping in. There is a tendency to stay in bed after 5:30 in the morning.' He and GWK appear to be kindred spirits!

And finally . . .

A number of summary words spring to mind as I close this profile and tribute to my former principal and ongoing friend.

Humanity

Bishop Michael Baughen recalls that, as a student, he had a vacation job at the Charing Cross Hotel. One of his fellow-workers, from Cyprus, complained about the British weather, contrasting it with his own country where 'when the sun came up in the morning it was going to be up all day'. Michael continues, 'That really sums up what I would want to say about Gilbert Kirby. The sun always seems to be up in his life, face, personality and ministry.'[42] GWK is the most approachable of men, 'a minister with a warm pastoral heart and a rare gift of getting along with people right across the Christian board,' adds David Bubbers, vicar of Emmanuel Church, Northwood, during GWK's time at LBC.[43]

Humility

One never gleans the impression that certain duties are beneath GWK's dignity. Students at LBC in the Seventies regularly saw him in his gardening gear, ably assisting Connie, or humping boxes from the college van after a visit to the wholesalers to re-stock the college tuck shop which he and Connie ran for the students' benefit. GWK's long-serving colleague, Dr H D McDonald ('Derrie Mc'), vice principal of LBC in GWK's time, adds this moving tribute:

> I was to come to know Gilbert for the thoughtful, congenial and informed leader that he revealed himself to be. His Principalship of the LBC was quite outstanding. But it was not Gilbert's style to put on airs. He did not exercise his position of authority in remote isolation. Rather did he present himself to the members of the Faculty and other members of the staff as one among co-equals in the work of the Lord. He did not expect from them or demand of them action and service which he would not himself share. Indeed, he would be found betimes moving furniture, carrying packages and like menial tasks for the help of students and others. He was thus not only among us as a respected Principal, he was also in our midst as one that served.[44]

Similarly, Richard Bewes, rector of All Souls, Langham Place, recalls GWK and Connie's presence at Eurofest, a huge European youth event held in Brussels in 1975. GWK was there as a 'heavy-weight anchor man'. Yet, regularly, he and Connie babysat the Bewes' three children in a hotel room, to give Richard's wife a break.[45]

Honesty

Some who only know GWK from a distance have, unjustly in my opinion, thought of him as an 'appeaser'. Maurice Rowlandson, a colleague from the EA days and latterly of the Billy Graham Evangelistic Association, acknowledges him as a bridge-builder and 'great mediator'. However, in 1948, when Maurice was contemplating ministry in the Congregational Union, GWK dissuaded him. 'His discouragement to me, advising me not to follow such a course, proved to be good advice as the years went by'.[46] Indeed, 'faithful are the wounds of a friend' (Proverbs 27:6, AV). And who but GWK would confess to feelings of inadequacy and 'a good deal of trepidation' as he contemplated speaking at his first Keswick Convention in 1976?[47] Such honesty is so refreshing from a man who has held his own at conferences and conventions all over Europe and beyond, and who has been a regular at Filey and, latterly, the multi-sited, enormously popular Spring Harvest where, delightfully, he is known as 'Clive's father-in-law'!

Humour

GWK positively sparkles with a ready wit. His interviews of dignitaries visiting LBC were memorable. After one distinguished visitor had had his say, GWK 'brought the college chapel down' by reminding both faculty and students that three words mean the same in every language: Amen! Hallelujah! Coca-Cola! On another occasion he visited Oak Hill College. There had been some inter-college rivalry: LBC had 'stolen' Spurgeon's cutlery, and Oak Hill had 'swiped' LBC's lectern from the chapel. 'Gilbert was their guest speaker that week and arrived in their college chapel to find his own LBC lectern in place. Never at a loss for words he instantly said, "You really shouldn't have gone to so much trouble to make me feel so at home!" '[48]

Hopefulness

One of the distinguishing marks of Christian 'charity' (love) is that it 'hopes all things' (1 Corinthians 13:7). This has been a major GWK characteristic. Gordon Landreth, EA general secretary from 1969 to 1981, says that GWK was the type of person who is 'looking for the positive in people and situations, and organizations, and the English tendency to criticize and find fault troubled him deeply, especially in Christian circles'.[49] GWK's own son-in-law, Clive Calver, director general of EA, delights to recall GWK's personal faith in him. In his time at LBC (1968–1971), Clive had the reputation of being a rebel. When he and the principal's daughter, Ruth, a fellow student (1969–1971), became increasingly friendly, a student delegation was duly despatched to see the principal. The relationship was 'inappropriate'; it needed 'stopping'; it required the principal's 'intervention'. So what did the principal do? He replied, 'Well, I believe she's old enough to know what she wants. And after all God still works miracles today!' Clive seems unable to tell that story of GWK's confidence in God (and Clive!) without a lump in his throat!

Home

One does not need to be in their presence very long to appreciate how 'proud' GWK and Connie are of their four children. In addition, they dote on their twelve grandchildren, six boys and six girls. If a Christian home ought to be a microcosm of the gospel in terms of peace, joy, openness, hospitality and sheer fun, the Kirbys' respective homes in Halstead, Ashford, Turners Hill, Northwood (twice), Harrow and now Pinner have most certainly been such. The countless multitudes who have passed their way, through the door and into their hearts, and who have blessed God for the experience, are legion. Tim Buckley, a long-time friend and colleague at LBC, says, 'Wetherby, their home, was a place of gracious hospitality and fun. Christmas parties for staff and students . . . occasional evenings of zany games, singing . . . and an epilogue, with "good nights" at midnight, are lovely memories'.[50] No one should underestimate the incalculable contribution of Connie. The dedication in the fly-leaf of one of GWK's books in 1984 expresses his appreciation admirably:

To Connie my devoted companion and counsellor
for over forty years, who is 'worth more
than rubies'.[51]

'GWK . . . has certainly been one of the *great* Christians I have known in my ministry': many would add their 'Amens' to that sentiment of Billy Graham.[52] A life that has spanned much of the twentieth century including two world wars, and which has, with reference to the evangelical scene, both 'seen it and done it', is one the authors of these essays seek to honour. In the words of Mordecai to Esther, which form the title of this book, many of GWK's ex-colleagues, students, church members and friends believe he has come to the twentieth-century evangelical kingdom 'for such a time as this' (Esther 4:14). Appropriately, however, GWK ought to have a (nearly!) final say. Expressing his appreciation to the Lord for his leading over many years, and his gratitude for God's enabling him to share with others some of the lessons he has learned, nevertheless he sagely keeps in mind the prayer of a seventeenth-century nun:

> Lord, Thou knowest better than I know myself that I am growing older and will some day be old. Keep me from the fatal habit of thinking I must say something on every subject and on every occasion. Release me from craving to straighten out everybody's affairs. With my vast store of wisdom, it seems a pity not to use it all, but Thou knowest, Lord, that I want a few friends at the end . . . [53]

That GWK has many friends as he approaches the end is testimony to the grace of God in his life. Those friends now honour you, Gilbert, and pray that the 'friend who sticketh closer than a brother' (Proverbs 18:24) will continue to bless and guide you and Connie to his eternal kingdom. There the unity of the church, especially in its evangelical expression, for which you have prayed so hard and fought so valiantly these many years, is wonderfully and eternally experienced. To God be the glory.

Endnotes

1 Billy Graham, personal correspondence with the author, 17 October 1994.
2 Personal letter to Clive and Ruth Calver, 6 August 1992.
3 Clive Calver, personal correspondence with the author, 3 March 1993.
4 The Oscar-winning film, *Chariots of Fire*, tells the story of Eric Liddell's career. See also Sally Magnusson, *The Flying Scotsman* (London, 1981).
5 GWK has written an unpublished autobiography (hereafter referred to as 'Autobiography') to which I have had access. I gratefully

acknowledge my indebtedness to this work at many points, and this profile would have been immeasurably poorer without it.

6 Autobiography.

7 See G W Kirby, *The Elect Lady* (Rushden, 1972).

8 For a history of CICCU, see especially O R Barclay, *Whatever Happened to the Jesus Lane Lot?* (Leicester, 1977). For a more generalized history of the evangelical movement in universities and colleges, see D Johnson, *Contending for the Faith* (Leicester, 1979); G Fielder, *Lord of the Years* (Leicester, 1988).

9 Autobiography, ch 2.

10 CICCU regularly had visits from H Earnshaw Smith, rector of All Souls, Langham Place; Colin Kerr, St Paul's, Portman Square; Dr Howard Guinness, author of *Sacrifice* (London, 1936); and Norman Grubb, author of *C T Studd, Cricketer and Pioneer* (London, 1933). Additionally, G Campbell Morgan, W H Aldis, Bishop Taylor Smith and others were heard at Keswick.

11 Autobiography, ch 2.

12 Autobiography, ch 2.

13 Autobiography, ch 3.

14 Autobiography, ch 3.

15 Autobiography, ch 3.

16 J Oswald Sanders, *Spiritual Leadership* (London, 1967), p 141.

17 Autobiography, ch 3.

18 William Heddle died in Southend in 1948, a month short of his 102nd birthday.

19 Autobiography, ch 3.

20 See I H Murray, *D Martyn Lloyd-Jones: The Fight of Faith, 1939–1981* (Edinburgh, 1990), pp 86–89 *et passim*.

21 Autobiography, ch 4.

22 Billy Graham, personal correspondence with the author, 30 August 1994.

23 Billy Graham, personal correspondence with the author, 17 October 1994.

24 See H H Rowdon, *London Bible College: The First Twenty-Five Years* (London, 1968).

25 Out of a series of articles in *Crusade* magazine, doubtlessly based on his lectures, appeared the following: G W Kirby, *The Protestant Churches of Britain* (London, 1963). This was extensively revised and re-issued as *Why All These Denominations?* (Eastbourne, 1988). His 'cult' booklets include *Jehovah's Witnesses* (London, 1957), *Seventh Day Adventists* (London, 1958) and *The Mormons* (London, 1959).

26 Autobiography, ch 5.

27 His duties at Turners Hill should not be underestimated. During his pastorate there was an influx of disillusioned ex-Exclusive Brethren to be cared for and taught. In addition, the church was part of the

Countess of Huntingdon's Connexion; through Quinton DeAth, his ministerial predecessor, GWK was appointed a trustee of the Connexion and subsequently wrote a brief history of the Countess and her Connexion (see above, note 7). GWK has continued to serve the Connexion. See his *Revival – Then and Now, 1781–1981*, published by the Connexion in 1981.

28   P Cotterell, personal correspondence with the author, 31 August 1994.

29   Autobiography, ch 5.

30   See Murray, *D Martyn Lloyd-Jones*, pp 513–532. Also, in this present volume, see chapters sixteen and seventeen – I Randall, 'Schism and Unity: 1905–1966', and P Lewis, 'Renewal, Recovery and Growth: 1966 onwards'. On the eve of this second National Assembly, under the auspices of EA, GWK contributed a booklet, *The Quest for Unity* (London, 1966), emphasizing that 'Unity does matter', p 9. See also his earlier, *In All Things Charity* (London, 1964). His eirenic spirit is demonstrated on the controversial topic of the Second Coming by his editing a symposium entitled *Remember, I am coming soon!* (London, 1964). John Stott remarks that GWK's 'great concern has been the unity of the church, or rather the unity of evangelical people' (personal correspondence with the author, 11 August 1994).

31   See G W Kirby, *Ernest Kevan: Pastor and Principal* (Eastbourne, 1968) for a brief and moving tribute.

32   D J Tidball, personal correspondence with the author, 1 September 1994.

33   Autobiography, ch 7.

34   GWK should have retired in 1979 upon reaching his sixty-fifth birthday. His successor, Michael Griffiths, who was working at the time with Overseas Missionary Fellowship, was not available until the autumn of 1980. Typically, GWK did an extra year!

35   Autobiography, ch 7.

36   L Palau, personal correspondence with the author, 18 October 1994.

37   See for example LBC's annual public lecture, which GWK delivered, published as *The Nature of the Christian Ministry and the Meaning of Ordination* (London, 1968); he edited *Evangelism Alert* (London, 1972), *Understanding Christian Ethics*, also issued as *The Way We Care* (London, 1973); *Understanding Bible Teaching: Leadership* (London, 1975); *Too Hot to Handle* (London, 1978); *Christian Living* (Eastbourne, 1979).

38   A Curtis, personal correspondence with the author, 4 October 1994.

39   Autobiography, ch 8.

40   Autobiography, ch 8.

41   Autobiography, ch 8.

42   M Baughen, personal correspondence with the author, 25 August 1994.

43 D Bubbers, personal correspondence with the author, 31 August 1994.

44 H D McDonald, personal correspondence with the author, 18 August 1994. Similarly, Leslie Allen, the Hebrew lecturer in GWK's time at LBC and now Professor of Old Testament at Fuller Theological Seminary, California, narrates a 'day out' with GWK in Watford to purchase 'new easy chairs' for the 'senior common room' – a task the principal felt they should jointly undertake (personal correspondence with the author, 26 September 1994).

45 R Bewes, personal correspondence with the author, August 1994.

46 M Rowlandson, personal correspondence with the author, 14 September 1994.

47 Autobiography, ch 9.

48 D J Tidball, personal correspondence with the author, 1 September 1994.

49 G Landreth, personal correspondence with the author, 18 August 1994.

50 T Buckley, personal correspondence with the author, 15 October 1994.

51 G W Kirby, *All One in Christ?* (Eastbourne, 1984), p 5.

52 Billy Graham, personal correspondence with the author, 17 October 1994.

53 Autobiography, ch 8.

Part 1
WHO WE ARE AND WHAT WE DO

Chapter 2

UNITY AT GRASS-ROOTS LEVEL

Steve King

We had gone to offer the hand of friendship. We had felt prompted by God to look for ways in which we could get alongside and encourage a small evangelical church in Northern France. We had so much our side of the Channel, and they appeared to have so little. We now found ourselves being interrogated!

As we scanned our English-French dictionaries for ecclesiastical words that appeared not to have been deemed necessary for inclusion in a soft-back tourist edition but which now seemed crucial for the survival of our goodwill mission, we almost felt guilty for making this initial contact with Hermann. In rather ponderous English and almost non-existent French, two fellow elders and I, with our wives, were far deeper into doctrine than we had been for years!

We had been cautiously received by this dedicated German missionary and, as we sat with our backs to the wall in this tiny shop-cum-'Centre Evangelique' in the middle of Normandy, it was clear that we were being regarded with more than a little suspicion. Why were we wanting to cross denominational boundaries? What kind of church were we? What happened in our services? Why were we not as interested in their state-ment of faith as he was in ours?

Having spent an exhausting couple of hours doing our best not to buckle under the weight of seeming rebuff from a very principled Herm-ann, we carried away a veritable wad of statements, codes of practice, tracts and an assortment of other pertinent documents with the promise that we would carefully consider them and then post over to Normandy our equivalents.

On our return to Bournemouth we did consider them. We continued to pray and could only sense a growing conviction that God would have us bless this small work in France, a work much harder and more demanding than that which lay around us on the south coast of England. The one doubt that remained was whether or not we would be allowed to give of ourselves.

It would be important for our church family to meet Hermann and to catch something of our growing burden as leaders for Normandy. It would probably be a prudent next step, out of consideration for Hermann's misgivings, to invite him to visit us as a church and spend a few days with us as our guest. In early 1992 Hermann and a colleague made the journey.

From the moment we met them from the ferry it was clear that they had come to enjoy the occasion. Graciousness abounded and Hermann's guard was lowered. As we chatted over meals together, we were helped to see something more of the evangelical scene in France and Germany, and learned that, sadly, suspicion, hostility and division were far more of an everyday experience than in Britain. We warmed to Hermann and Norbert, and began to respect greatly their commitment and dedication to Christ and their immense love for the French people who were difficult to reach.

Hermann has a wonderful smile and compelling passion for his Lord and Saviour. With the help of a translator he preached at our evening service. The anointing of God was so clearly upon that hour or two. We listened, we laughed, we were touched by God's word. These pastors, who had left their preconceptions on the ferry, found a place in every heart. We were rather humbled at the realization that we were likely, and in fact already had begun, to receive more than we could ever hope to give. Gifts and handshakes were exchanged, and we wished our new friends '*au revoir*'.

Was it bad stewardship of our time and energy to pursue such a 'oneness' with evangelicals of quite another flavour? Surely it made more sense to seek out the like-minded somewhere else in France for a less demanding kind of unity. Although we were now friends, it was hard to view any further meaningful exchange of resources with pastor Hermann's small church as anything but precarious. Yet it was manifestly obvious that the name of Jesus was being honoured in this fledgling relationship. We were not forcing something unnatural. We were not attempting to create a oneness by our own efforts. Through the cross of Jesus we were already one. Our task and Christ's prayer as recorded in the seventeenth chapter of John was that the world might see it! This would not come easily; it might not come quickly. Even so, if Christians from rather different traditions on both sides of the English Channel could commit themselves to the pursuit of common ground, it was a goal worthy of our efforts.

We continued to correspond and to explore gently together the way ahead. It was thrilling to hear how Hermann had been profoundly affected by his time with us, how warm a welcome he had sensed, and how very different we were as a church from all that he had been taught our brand of evangelicalism to be like! Perhaps, after all, we had given to, as well as received from, this godly man.

Each year, throughout the month of July, Hermann plays host and team leader to an encouragingly large number of young people from France, Germany and elsewhere, who give some of their summer vacation to do evangelism in Normandy. By early 1993 the mission headquarters in Germany had finally agreed, and a team of fifteen from our church brushed up on their French, sat through a briefing on working in partnership with 'conservatives' and, clutching their Bibles and passports, threw themselves into a hugely rewarding and memorable week's outreach to the French.

I was personally combining team evangelism with further exploration of the spiritual needs in France. I had arranged to travel to the Belgian border to spend a few hours with an English missionary. It proved to be a very long day, necessitating a 5 am start. I sneaked out quietly, not wishing to disturb the weary troops, into a cool, hazy and typically beautiful Normandy dawn. I made my way to the station, parked my car and waited for the first train of the day to Paris. Glancing around me, wishing to take in every moment of this exquisite French morning, I was surprised and baffled to see Hermann smiling widely and advancing towards me. Having quite forgivably misunderstood my embarrassingly poor French of the previous evening, he thought I was not returning. Before I could explain, he threw his arms around me in the most convincing charismatic hug I have ever experienced and thanked me for everything! The demanding pursuit of common evangelical ground can prove to be very special indeed.

There are times when a pastor's mind cannot quite believe what his ears have just heard. It is, of course, best not to appear too shocked but rather to give the impression that, to an experienced church leader, revelations of such a nature are not new! Well, as I clasped a mug of coffee and reclined in one of his office chairs nestled comfortably in amongst piles of Christian magazines, rows of theological tomes, a large, attractive but cluttered desk and a stack of freshly folded church bulletins awaiting the coming weekend, I really could not believe what the local vicar had just told me!

I had asked to spend half an hour or so with Ian to explain a little about our fellowship's 'church-planting' vision and, more specifically, to ask rather boldly whether we might make his church hall the venue for our new congregation! St Saviour's has two church halls, the one in question being a third of a mile from the parish church. I was treading as gently and as tactfully as I knew how.

The decision to establish our fourth church-plant was almost definite. Even so, we had learnt over the years that our small collection of believers only represented a part of the Body of Christ as expressed in our locality. To leave other members of that Body out of the decision-making was a nonsense, an approach that would leave us all impoverished. Over the years I had telephoned, written to and drunk coffee with a healthy number of local ministers as we pressed ahead with our planting programme.

We were praying for a breakthrough. Past consultation had been beneficial, other local churches understood us and had never opposed our plans, just as we would be very unlikely to stand against any gospel advance they might suggest. However, a more active, integrated 'oneness' was our heart's desire, a sacrificial, selfless quality of unity that would glorify God and command his blessing. I was now experiencing the desire of our heart!

Having recently enjoyed the hospitality and ambience of more than a handful of vicarages, I am convinced that Ian's study is typical of every Anglican priest – strewn, very 'lived in' and in need of a good dust! Ian himself, however, is untypical of many men I have met. For once I was struggling for words as I searched for a suitable response to his reply to my carefully presented request.

Yes, of course we could use their church hall if the Parochial Church Council agreed, and they were very likely to. It seemed to him a very obvious arrangement. A main road split what was now an increasingly large parish, and anything we could do to communicate the love of Christ in the parish of St Saviour's was warmly encouraged. In fact – and it was this that I had never heard the like of before – Ian would personally suggest to twenty-five or more of his regular attenders who lived 'our side' of the main road that they might like to join our new congregation! Wow! What a gesture! What could I say?

I am reminded of a very memorable sentiment expressed by John Wesley. It is a well-known historic fact that the two great evangelists John Wesley and George Whitefield disagreed on doctrinal issues. Both of them were very successful, preaching to thousands of people and witnessing huge numbers come to faith. It is reported that somebody asked Wesley if he expected to see Whitefield in heaven, and the great man replied, 'No, I do not!'

'Then you do not think Whitefield is a converted man?'

'Of course he is a converted man!' Wesley said. 'But I do not expect to see him in heaven – because he will be so close to the throne of God and I so far away that I will not be able to see him!'

It is this high estimation of each other that so thrills the heart of God. It was Ian's preferring of us and our small church that birthed something selfless and invigoratingly new. As a church we were, by St Saviour's gracious attitude, spurred on to redouble the sincerity of our most regular prayer:

> Lord, we are doing our best to follow your plan for our church. Greatly anoint your work amongst us. Oh that we would see your blessing! But Lord Jesus, we bring to you the whole of your Body. We pray especially for our neighbouring churches. Grow them more quickly than you grow us. Bless them and prosper them more abundantly than you bless and prosper us.

Just the other week I was overjoyed to hear a new Christian of only a few months' standing pray in her own words the aforementioned prayer. It was quite possibly the first time she had prayed 'out loud'. Lord, may you hear that prayer for Ian and St Saviour's.

There is a mixture of excitement and trepidation in the soul of any young pastor as he leaves the secure surroundings of Bible college and launches out into the enormous challenge of full-time ministry. Every day throws up something new and horrifyingly unfamiliar! It is comforting, if perhaps a little sadistic, to know that just around the corner a good friend is facing precisely the same situation!

Tony and I had become quite close during our three years together at Bible college. We had graduated on the same day in 1987 and had both been invited by our respective placement churches to take on the role of assistant pastor. We lived about a mile apart. It seemed very natural to meet regularly for mutual encouragement and prayer. We began to meet together every month at Tony's home for breakfast.

The hour or two we would spend over cereal, toast and coffee quickly became very precious. This frequent interaction with a leader from another local church, delving deeper than the average, rather business-like ministers' fraternal, stimulated me greatly. I could really feel with Tony for the people under his pastoral care. The Holy Spirit began to impress upon me powerfully that the family of which Christ was head was far larger that the expression of it that I was serving as a less than competent assistant pastor. Tony and I began to see the bigger picture.

As the months passed we began to invite other church leaders to join us for breakfast. Friendship and trust grew. A very obvious question arose: why was it that the wider Body of Christ, which our churches collectively represented, did almost nothing together? We started to rectify that lamentable state of affairs. A programme was prayerfully drawn up that would enable our members to see the scope of the family they belonged to and the way the gospel could be advanced when our oneness was brought out and polished. Our individual distinctives were not threatened, but the reunited brothers and sisters revelled in the enlarged family they had never fully appreciated they had. We jointly evangelized in the open air, we worshipped together quarterly, we 'marched for Jesus'. We even barn-danced and swam together!

'Where do we go from here, Tony?' I asked. 'Is God asking us to take another step?' God spoke very clearly to Tony : 'It's time!'

'IT'S TIME' – in conjunction with Moorlands College, forty local evangelical churches and a lot of endeavour – became an innovative evangelistic campaign that was used by God in 1992. The emphasis was well away from the big name, big-budget rut; rather it was focused upon the mobilization of local churches to reach out into their own community in a way that they as a church felt comfortable with and by a method that was ultimately sustainable well beyond the end of the year. All this was oiled by the growing respect, love and oneness evidenced amongst church leaders.

'How does God want us to kick all this off, Steve? Surely it ought to underline our increasing oneness of heart.' To me the answer was blindingly obvious – we must worship together. Furthermore, it had to be prime time, not a Saturday evening, though Saturday evening would be an obvious choice to most ministers who would, at little cost to their own programmes, promote a combined service of commendation at a time that conflicted with nothing in particular (as long as things were all wrapped up in time to get home for 'Match of the Day')! We opted for a Sunday evening.

Proverbs 11:14 is a verse that has often halted me in the nick of time. It propagates the wisdom of listening to the advice of many if success is to follow. I solicited the opinion of many and I listened to the echoes of past cries: 'It cannot be done!' 'The churches of this town will never worship together in any significant fashion – it has always failed!' I turned to the 'IT'S TIME' steering committee. Although a little cautious, they agreed that perhaps the tide had turned; maybe now it could be done. The new leisure centre was booked, invitations were extended and big bills settled faith-shakingly early!

The Sunday evening in question arrived, the scene was set and final dress-rehearsals were being concluded. There was nothing for me to do but worry and pray! The intentions of a number of key churches had been disconcertingly vague. That aside, would the hundreds of Christians from the churches who had agreed to close their services actually make the effort to travel further, to unfamiliar ground, breaking the habit of years?

'Please, Lord,' I cried, 'it has got to work. This is the acid test of our oneness.'

Finally the doors opened and, to my amazement, bodies flooded in. Our army of stewards, mustered as a faith-statement, sprang into action but were rapidly overwhelmed as the twelve hundred seats the fire officer had rather stringently allowed were quickly filled. Still they came. Announcements were made asking people to move to the centre of the row. Still they came, happy to stand, sit or perch anywhere they could. The crowd seemed thrilled just to have made it in. By now the manager had exercised all the grace he could and shut the door with eighteen hundred inside and two hundred still outside, manifestly baffled by my earlier gloomy predictions. Spontaneously, the eager worshippers began to sing to the background music provided by the worship group. Quite unplanned, the service was in full swing ten minutes early!

As the evening began to unfold I caught Tony's eye. What a wonderful thing that so many were now seeing the bigger picture! As David du Plessis once said, 'I will have no fewer brothers and sisters than God has sons and daughters.'

There are few greater obstacles to evangelical unity than proudly parading our own achievements in a way that belittles the contributions of others. Hackles rise, friendships cool, self-defence sets in. Jesus, after all, was described by Paul as having made himself nothing and taken the very nature of a servant. How careful we must be when we appraise ourselves and our own church or denomination! Is our part played with the humility modelled by Jesus himself?

I had good reason to check my own excess in this respect at a worship conference in Holland in 1990. I was particularly pleased by the growth and development of our most recent congregation. In fact, I reasoned that as a church we had grounds to be well satisfied with recent progress. Around the conference meal table I had found myself drawn on the issue and had painted a rather rosy picture of what God was doing through our church.

I was now reflecting on my tea-time conversation as I waited for the evening celebration to commence. I felt strangely uncomfortable, almost as if I had lied to my fellow delegate. Perhaps I had exaggerated a little, certainly I had spoken with pride. The evening programme got under way.

After an opening song or two we were asked to introduce ourselves to the person sitting next to us and to pray together. There was quite a buzz around the auditorium as five hundred people greeted each other in a wonderful variety of European languages. As I turned to the lady next to me, I saw, sitting in the row behind, an amiable-looking middle-aged man in shirt-sleeves. I recognized him immediately as the keynote speaker. It was his involvement in the conference that had clinched my booking, and I was looking forward very much to his Bible readings each morning.

This international conference speaker and author listened inquiringly to his nearest neighbour who clearly did not know who he was. After a few moments he was in turn asked about himself. His response was simple: 'I'm Terry and I'm a church leader from Brighton, England.' I felt thoroughly admonished!

Chapter 3

UNITY IN THE LOCAL CHURCH

Chris Seaton

How good and pleasant it is
　when brothers live together in unity!
It is like precious oil poured on the head,
　running down on the beard,
running down on Aaron's beard,
　down upon the collar of his robes.
It is as if the dew of Hermon
　were falling on Mount Zion.
For there the Lord bestows his blessing,
　even life for evermore.

Many of us will have heard David's Psalm 133 read in the context of a united service or other as a kind of vague exhortation 'to be together'. The problem is that, as has been said of the Week of Prayer for Christian Unity, these occasions usually serve only to show how disunited we are for the other fifty-one weeks of the year!

Yet I have noticed that over recent years, even months, very many local situations appear to be undergoing a transformation in the level of commitment to 'living together' in unity. Clearly there is a world of difference between keeping channels of communication open between churches – like contacts between Washington and Moscow during the years of the Cold War – and living together. As Derek Kidner has noted, the idea of 'living together' in this psalm is parallel to Deuteronomy 25:5, that of brothers living in close proximity to each other as extended family.[1]

However, I would suggest that most of the time it is the former experience which has been most typical of the local church scene over recent years. Yet not only is the latter experience a 'good and pleasant' one but it does release power from heaven. The oil pouring down upon Aaron is clearly the oil of anointing for priesthood. Exodus 29:7 tells us that this oil is intended for the head, but here we see that it flows right down the body, its fragrance filling the air. Surely, God's anointing power will bring healing and reconciliation between God and humanity and to every level of human society.

The psalmist also wished to emphasize the miraculous nature of this unity. It is as if the dew of Mount Hermon in the north of Israel could fall on Mount Zion down in the south. Quite impossible to achieve through our own efforts, true unity is a gift from God and is tasted as such. Finally, we see that the result of this unity is a blessing which the Lord commands (according to the older translations). Surely, this is the place we want to be – where God is commanding his blessing towards us.

But it is one thing to be convinced of the value of unity, quite another to see it come to our own localities. In practice, it seems that unity comes through prayer, humble relationship-building and a divine touch of grace. A brief study of historical revivals shows that when the Holy Spirit begins to move, a desire to be together is one fruit. This was certainly true of the Welsh Revival of 1859:

> At one time it was thought a great matter if union and co-operation in the simple but holy work of circulating the Bible . . . could be secured; and when ministers and people of different creeds met in one place and spoke on the same platform, on a subject about which there is hardly room for doubt, it was regarded as a great virtue, and a considerable stretch of Christian liberality! Now, however, in the light and warmth of the revival fire, we look back upon that only as the first step in the path of Christian union – a very small instalment of that love which we owe to our common Saviour, and to His people, as brethren and sisters belonging to the same spiritual family.[2]

Remarkably, it appears that in many of these historical instances unity was not sought, but like the dew and the oil of the psalm, it came downwards as a gift from heaven.

It has been observed by others that the great tragedy of the ecumenical movement – the main vehicle for institutional unity in the church – is that its focus became diverted from world mission. The movement's birthplace is usually seen as the great missionary conference which met at Edinburgh in 1910 in the first attempt to co-ordinate the efforts of different missionary initiatives. The conflict and traumas of the First World War no doubt helped to shift the emphasis of this enterprise away from what was seen to be the confrontational issue of evangelism. Instead, priority was given to internal issues of doctrine, polity and practice when the Faith and Order movement first met in Geneva in 1920 to plan a world conference that was held at Lausanne in 1927. The ecumenicals never placed the topics of evangelism and world mission at the top of their agenda. This naturally caused a deep antipathy to develop between the ecumenical movement and the evangelicals.

Since this time evangelicals have tended to view ecumenism with suspicion. Particularly in our generation, with the steeple's shadow receding in a secularized culture, concerns about harmonizing doctrine and practice appear to be as relevant as moving the piano on the Titanic. Unity and evangelism have often been polarized, and the 50% decrease in membership of the United Reformed Church in the first twenty years since the Congregationalists and Presbyterians combined is one oft-cited example of the problem.

But this does not mean that evangelicals always resist the idea of unity. One of the truths which has been restored to the church in recent years is that relationships and friendships are at the very heart of the local church. We have come to see that our church life does not consist in meetings, buildings or programmes. Rather, it is the people who are the church and not merely the outward manifestations of 'church life'. To become the 'living stones' (1 Peter 2:5) of God's house we need truly to be bonded together.

In our local situation, as soon as we planted our congregation in 1986, we realized that we were coming to a town where disunity was a controlling spiritual force. We realized that entering Bognor Regis in the opposite spirit to disunity was absolutely vital. Over the years, our strategies have become increasingly defined, and we have sought to pursue the goal of unity in three different spheres:

1 within the local congregation itself,
2 between the evangelical congregations in our town,
3 between the evangelical and non-evangelical congregations.

If I tell the story of my experiences over the past ten or so years, it is not to highlight achievements but rather to look at the issues which present themselves to any church leader seeking local unity.

Internal unity

As a zealous 22 year-old, young in my faith, I moved to Chichester with my job and joined the church fellowship known as 'Revelation' very near its genesis. I am personally grateful to Roger Ellis that he soon realized his need for a spiritual father. He began to build a friendship with Gerald Coates, which developed in time into an apostolic relationship. Thus my spiritual foundations were laid firmly on a bedrock of relationships within the local church.

As a priority was placed on friendship, we learned that believing the best, saying sorry, representing a friend in their absence, eating and drinking together, and building encouragement into one another were critical if we were to be united in reality. We also built a church where we allowed one another to sin. This does not mean that sin is condoned or encouraged, but neither is it denied. Realizing that sin operates in the dark but we are called to walk in the light became very releasing. Things were never perfect, and, for me, learning to say the hard things whilst holding on in love was one of the toughest lessons, but it was worth it to be able to experience a measure of the living together of the psalm.

The other critical element in the equation of internal church unity is vision. We all know what happens to the people who do not have a vision

– they perish, or 'cast off restraint' (Proverbs 29:18). Often that restraint relates to the quality of trust and relationship. Without a vision, it is only too easy for criticism, gossip, mistrust and resistance to the Holy Spirit to become endemic. 'Revelation' has never been an easy church in which to remain on the fringes. We have always had a strong vision for growth, influence, evangelism, justice and care. Encouraging every member to own and to find their part in this vision has been a cohesive factor in our unity.

Evangelical/non-evangelical unity

When I was released to work in a full-time capacity in our new Bognor church-plant, one of my greatest desires was to express these principles of love and friendship with brothers and sisters beyond 'Revelation'. To my surprise, it seemed easier to make friends with the non-evangelical than with the evangelical ministers. The latter were often more suspicious of a brash new young congregation, listened to rumours of 'sheep-stealing' or were too busy or too private to build relationships. Ecumenism was seen as pointless, with little perceived value in meeting with 'unsaved vicars'.

On the other hand, the non-evangelicals had more experience and sympathy with a desire for unity through the values of the ecumenical movement to which most of them subscribed. The lowest common denominator of our beliefs was often in danger of disappearing way beneath the crypt, but at least the local ministers' fraternal and council of churches provided a context within which to start bridging the gaps. Having taken part in fraternal meetings for a couple of years, we were eventually invited to join the local council of churches. In time, I became involved in working on the constitution of a new 'Churches Together in Bognor Regis and District' (CTB), which sought to place more accountability with local churches rather than simply with ecumenically-enthusiastic individual Christians.

However, in reality the agenda of our CTB was very limited. We soon came face to face with the inflexibility and lack of vision which grips so many historic denominational churches. Some church leaders often appeared to see CTB as a necessary inconvenience rather than something right at the heart of the gospel. The crunch came for me when we proposed a joint evangelistic mission and a more meaningful united service on a Sunday morning. These suggestions met a wall of indifference and opposition respectively. By the time I had completed a two-year period of office as CTB chair I wondered where we could go to next.

With hindsight, I am convinced that all these efforts were laudable but not Holy Spirit-inspired. Before explaining that statement, let me qualify it by saying that we are still very much involved with CTB and value its 'official' expression of unity to the wider community. What is more, there are encouraging signs that things are changing, and the brother from our leadership team who currently serves as our CTB representative has faith that God will touch many of these churches in a new way. It is simply that

– as I have had to learn many times – although I was right, I was also wrong. Unity is a gift from God coming down upon his people, and it is important to discern the relationships which he is preparing.

Local evangelical unity

However, true Christian unity is the 'unity of the Spirit' (Ephesians 4:3).

After years of working and praying for greater unity in the local Body of Christ, it seems that God took the initiative. Three leaders moved into Bognor in 1992 and 1993 who transformed the local scene. The first was John, a Yorkshireman (and a Leeds United supporter), who had been leading a local fellowship with congregations in Chichester and Bognor for a number of years. It was a combination of practical reasons and the prompting of God that caused John to move from Chichester to Bognor. The second was Gordon, another Yorkshireman (and a Sheffield Wednesday supporter!) who moved back to the UK from Australia to pastor the Baptist church.

I met each of these brothers individually to share vision and fellowship together. One of us suggested that all three should get together for prayer and friendship, which we did. At this time the third leader moved into Bognor. This was Hadge, an Anglican vicar (and a Manchester United supporter!) who had resigned from that ministry and relocated from Manchester to assist Gordon. At about the same time one of our younger leaders, James (another Leeds United supporter!), took on the leadership of our Bognor congregation under my oversight. With no agenda or bureaucratic title to give ourselves, we simply diarized our times together as 'Famous Five'.

We found that we all got on naturally together, sharing humour, fashion tips (as thirty-something men do!) and joking about one another's football teams (especially as I'm a Leicester City supporter!). We shared an earthy and realistic spirituality, along with a passionate desire to see Bognor saved and a deep antipathy towards hypocrisy, mediocrity and religion. We would discuss our local situations frankly, touching upon the things that encouraged us as well as our struggles. Then we would pray and prophesy into one another's lives and churches. The ethos of our times together was very much 'friends first'.

It was only on this foundation of friendship that we began to ask God what we should do with our relationships. Personally, I already benefited from our apostolic connection as part of 'Revelation' through being on the oversight team with James. Further, as part of Pioneer South, we had other links with churches in neighbouring towns and villages. However, whilst we had a vision that was broader than Bognor, we knew that our town-wide unity would have implications for strengthening what we could achieve in our 'Jerusalem' (using Acts 1:8 as an analogy).

After we had asked this question, the first thing we did was to look at broadening the scope of unity within the leadership. We began to hold regular elders' breakfasts, usually early on Saturday morning. The pain of the early start was mollified by the excellent Baptist catering! These times were useful for prayer, networking and an opportunity to carry our leadership teams with us in pursuing the relationships.

Then, in early 1994, came the step of meeting together on a Sunday morning. We felt that this was a critical step as it involved a genuine commitment from the churches to vote for unity with their feet. This was particularly true of the Baptists who had to leave their building so that we could all meet in a local school hall. As it turned out, we had a wonderful morning, with over 700 adults and 300 children present. Roger Mitchell, of Ichthus Christian Fellowship, spoke powerfully to us about his experiences of seeing local unity as a key element in the revival in Argentina. He exhorted us to work for one another's spiritual inheritances as Moses had exhorted the Reubenites and Gadites to fight for their brothers' (see Numbers 32). The reaction of most of the people to whom I spoke was, 'Why didn't we do this before?'! Taking this encouragement, we have repeated these meetings every six months or so.

We have found other means of co-operating. Administratively, we have shared the burden of organizing March for Jesus events, and our worship leaders have met for input and prayer. Further, a joint youth event, Tribal Sheep Dip, has emerged from the coming together of youth leaders from the three churches.

Perhaps the zenith of what God has done through our unity came in September 1994 after the current move of the Holy Spirit, popularly known as the 'Toronto Blessing', began to impact our churches. We had already begun to experience some mild 'times of refreshing' in 'Revelation'. However, in July Gordon, Hadge and John visited the Airport Vineyard in Toronto. As the momentum of the move of the Spirit increased, Hadge felt that God was calling us to meet together for an extended period. We set aside seven consecutive evenings and met for worship, teaching, prayer and personal ministry. Each of these meetings was remarkable in its own right and became a blessing to some other churches in the area whose leaders came and received a touch of the Holy Spirit. It became true that it was impossible to 'see the join' between the three churches.

In all this, we have been conscious that we are pioneering beyond any previous experience. Each of us is currently flowing with our own vision and is part of different national church denominations or streams. Likewise, each of us knows that we belong together. Whatever the implications structurally, we are praying for that one fruit for which all church leaders pray – a harvest of the lost.

Conclusion

Unity is not an optional extra in the Body of Christ. Part of the symbolism of the Lord's Supper, the breaking of the loaf, underlines this. The integrity of Jesus' body was broken on the cross, but 'we being many, are the one bread'. As individual grains, we find our true expression only when mixed together with others and the yeast of the kingdom.

In a local situation, the quality of relationships must be placed high on the agenda if we are to see healthy congregations. Likewise, whilst inter-church unity is a gift from God, it must be sought and prayed for and nurtured lovingly when it is found. Only thus might we be one, as Jesus prayed to the Father, 'just as you are in me and I am in you. May they also be in us so that the world may believe that you have sent me' (John 17:21).

Endnotes

1   D Kidner, *Psalms 73–150* (London, 1975), p 452.
2   T Phillips, *The Welsh Revival – Its Origin and Development* (Edinburgh, 1989).

Chapter 4

TOWARDS AN EVANGELICAL IDENTITY

David W Bebbington

In 1850 John Sirgood, a bootmaker originally from Gloucestershire, moved from South London to the village of Loxwood on the northern edge of Sussex and set up a religious community called the Dependent Brethren, or Cokelers. In London Sirgood had learned from William Bridges, the founder of the Plumstead Peculiars, the doctrine of the new birth. Sirgood proceeded to spread it in the rural area around Loxwood until, at his death in 1885, his followers numbered about two thousand. Their hymns were unaccompanied and, before each verse was sung, it was read out in the traditional manner designed for the illiterate. Spontaneous testimonies peppered their worship services. Like other holiness groups, the Cokelers believed that the power of God could preserve them from committing sins. They were teetotallers, pacifists and favoured traditional clothing. The men wore historic Sussex smocks long into the twentieth century. They strongly believed in mutual assistance, taking this principle to the length of running the village stores on a co-operative basis. One of their hymns ran:

> Christ's combination stores for me
> Where I can be so well supplied
> Where I can one with brethren be
> Where competition is defied.

For a while their commercial activities brought them a modest measure of prosperity. Another distinctive belief, however, undermined their very existence. Although Sirgood himself was married, the movement officially encouraged celibacy. In the light of 1 Corinthians chapter 7 it was thought better to avoid marriage if at all possible. Despite Sirgood's enthusiastic evangelism, the numbers in the community soon went into rapid decline, reaching a mere 200 by 1940. It retains only two congregations in the 1990s. The Cokelers have formed an unusual and highly localized body.[1]

In January 1883, by contrast, there assembled the Islington Meeting of evangelicals in the Church of England. The meeting had been an annual event ever since 1827, when Daniel Wilson, soon to be Bishop of Calcutta, had invited a few like-minded clergymen to consultations in his parish vestry at Islington. Numbers had grown, papers had been formalized and the occasion had turned into the best gauge of evangelical opinion in the established church. Attendees, proud to call themselves 'Evangelical Churchmen', were conscious of debating issues of public importance. How far, they asked in 1883, was it advisable to invoke the Public Worship Regulation Act of 1874 against ritualist clergy who imitated Roman Catholic practices? Such advanced high churchmen were breaking with the principles of the Reformation that many evangelicals saw as the bedrock of the Church of England. It was right, argued the more bellicose Protestants at Islington, to press the bishops to prosecute the ritualists and so harry them out of the national church. Canon Lefroy, one of the leaders of the militants, offered prayer that the eyes of one of the bishops should be opened to the evils he was permitting in his diocese. His petition, however, shocked those present who, under the spreading influence of the Oxford Movement, had themselves been swayed in a high church direction. One of this group, P F Eliot, vicar of Holy Trinity, Bournemouth, and later Dean of Windsor, contended that evangelicals must be more sparing in their criticism, more positive in their teaching and more insistent on the value of the sacraments. They must certainly not play down the authority of the Church of England for the sake of joint action with other evangelicals outside its bounds. 'I would not move one single inch from church principles,' declared Eliot, 'for the sake of conciliating or co-operating with Dissent.' Here was a robust assertion of loyalty to the established church as the divinely commissioned instructor of the whole English people.[2]

There is clearly a marked difference between the Cokelers of Sussex and the Evangelical Churchmen in conference at Islington. What was there in common between allegiance to 'Christ's combination stores' and to 'church principles'? On the one hand, there were humble folk, chiefly agricultural labourers and their families, who looked to their patriarchal leader for guidance on details of everyday behaviour. On the other, there were cultivated men, rising to the top of their profession, who were willing to disagree with each other over issues of policy in church and state. One body consisted of Dissenters; a speaker at the other expressed profound distaste for all Dissent. An intensely sectarian ideal contrasted with a vision of catholicity. Yet the two groups shared far more than simply being contemporaries in Victorian England. Islington Anglicans, like Sussex Cokelers, were Christians committed to proclaiming the gospel. Members of each party wished to turn their lukewarm neighbours, whether gentry or yokels, into zealous servants of Jesus Christ. They believed in evangelism. It seems plausible to call both groups evangelicals. The attendees of the Islington meetings were explicitly so: they represented the self-conscious Evangelical Party in the Church of England. The nineteenth-century Cokelers might not have avowed the label, but their remaining descendants in the faith were in the later twentieth century to form a bond with the Union of Evangelical Christians, an Essex grouping also established by a former follower of William Bridges and previously known as the Peculiar People.[3] Cokeler celibates as much as Islington sacramentarians were part of the diverse evangelical family.

The question arises whether the diversity has been so great as to render the description 'evangelical' meaningless. Donald Dayton has argued, in an American context, that the use of the word obscures reality. Apart from identifying different groups to different people, he suggests, the term is applied to bodies of such bewildering heterogeneity as to make the category useless. Dayton despairs of discovering any set of characteristics that separate off all evangelicals on the one hand from all non-evangelicals on the other. Since there is no cluster of qualities to constitute a 'family resemblance', the word should be dropped in favour of more useful terms of analysis.[4] It might be thought that the problem would be greater, not less, in a British setting. Gilbert Kirby, when becoming international secretary of the World Evangelical Fellowship in 1962, gathered (as he told readers in the United States) 'that the line between the evangelical and the non-evangelical is much more clearly drawn there than here'.[5] If the demarcation of evangelical boundaries in Britain has indeed been less sharp, then the task of defining the essential elements of evangelicalism becomes even harder. The theologian, concerned to specify what religion ought to be in principle, might be able to isolate the desirable features of evangelical faith, but the historian, content to analyse what religion has been in practice, might be excused for abandoning the effort to establish the common features of the evangelical movement. In that case Cokelers and Islingtonians would be assigned to different departments of the religious world. Evangelical identity would be dissolved.

Two considerations make that conclusion premature. One is that evangelicalism forms, on any account, one of three leading tendencies in modern British religion. In the period since the eighteenth century, evangelicalism together with liberalism and catholicism may have ebbed as well as flowed but has always been present in the ecclesiastical scene. Liberals (the Anglicans among them often being called broad churchmen) such as Thomas Arnold in the early nineteenth century have wanted to bring Christianity into line with modern knowledge. Catholics (both Anglican and Roman) such as John Henry Newman have insisted on the authority of the church, its ministry and sacraments. Alongside them evangelicals such as Charles Simeon have wanted to propagate the gospel. It is true that the streams have sometimes flowed together. There have been evangelicals with high-church tendencies, such as P F Eliot; between the 1920s and the 1950s there was a powerful liberal evangelical movement. Yet the evangelical tradition has not been broken, ever contributing its dynamic to the churches and beyond them to society at large. It must surely be possible to establish what characteristics, apart from transient incidentals, were transmitted from generation to generation. Together the characteristics would constitute evangelical identity.

The second consideration, pointing in the same direction, is that a significant proportion of the Christian world has been willing, over the same period, to accept the designation 'evangelical'. In the eighteenth century, admittedly, the word was rarely used in a party sense, yet that is a period in which it is fairly easy to identify who gave their allegiance to the revival movement led by John Wesley, George Whitefield and their contemporaries. From the beginning of the nineteenth century the description was gladly adopted by an increasing number inside and outside the established churches. It was common, especially in the twentieth century, to refuse the honour to others who claimed it. Thus those of a more conservative theological inclination often denied that liberal evangelicals were properly evangelicals at all. Yet the name retained its appeal as a self-description. At the 1989 English Church Census, when nation-wide churchmanship was investigated for the first time, 28% of all worshippers attended a congregation reported by its leader to be evangelical. More ticks were given to the category 'evangelical' than to any other label.[6] Christians have been ready, even eager, to avow their evangelical faith. They must have meant something, and it must surely be possible to give an account of what they meant. It seems reasonable to explore whether self-proclaimed evangelicals have displayed common characteristics over time.

It is sometimes suggested that 'evangelical' should be equated with 'low church'. In 1888, for instance, W H B Proby published *Annals of the Low Church Party in England* as a study of the evangelical movement. He was suggesting that, by contrast with his own high church position, evangelicals had consistently neglected catholic doctrines and dignified worship. It is true that evangelicals have commonly criticized Roman Catholicism and its admirers among Anglo-Catholics. Thus in 1850 Hugh Miller, the editor of the newspaper belonging to the Free Church of Scotland, denounced popery as 'Christianity's counterfeit', and as late as 1959 evangelicals petitioned that the use of vestments should cease in the Church of England because of their association with the Roman mass.[7] Anti-Catholicism has been a potent factor in modern British history, and evangelicalism has been a driving force behind it.[8] Yet an unreflecting hostility to Rome has not been a constant feature of evangelical history. Thomas Chalmers, later the founder of the Free Church of Scotland, was one of many evangelicals who supported Roman Catholic emancipation from legal restrictions in 1829; and several of those who signed the 1959 petition subsequently welcomed the creation of an organization of Evangelical Catholics loyal to the Roman communion but subscribing to the statement of evangelical beliefs in the Lausanne Covenant.[9] There have been many symptoms of Catholic taste and principle among evangelicals. Congregational chanting in the Church of England, for example, which has usually been attributed to the Oxford Movement, was in fact an innovation introduced by the evangelicals in York.[10] During its first decade in 1838 the Baptist Union of Great Britain and Ireland proclaimed its constituents a part of 'the Catholic [sic] Church'.[11] The truth is that, although wariness of Rome has often driven evangelicals towards a low church stance, it has not been an essential element of evangelicalism. More of the returns to the English Church Census of 1989 from low church congregations declined the title 'evangelical' than claimed it.[12] Evangelicalism cannot be identified with low churchmanship.

Again, the idea has been put forward that evangelicals are Christians with elaborate prophetic views. It is supposed that evangelicals are bound to the vista of world history known as dispensationalism. Under this scheme, it is held that the Almighty has dealings with humanity on different terms in each age or 'dispensation'. The age of the church is nearly over; the second coming of Jesus Christ may be expected at any moment; true believers will be 'raptured' to join him in the skies before a great period of tribulation; then he will return again to inaugurate a millennium of peace and plenty on the earth. Although this view is admittedly widespread in the United States, it has been shown that even there it does not unify evangelicals.[13] Dispensationalism has been much less prevalent in Britain. It was sufficiently strong during the Second World War for Ernest Kevan, Gilbert Kirby's predecessor as principal of London Bible College, to seek assurances before he assumed office that he could state his own rejection of the notion of a millennium when the need arose.[14] That juncture, however, probably represented the peak of dispensationalism's influence and, along with other schemes of prophetic interpretation, it has subsequently gone into decline. In the mid-nineteenth century, by contrast, it was the entirely different postmillennialism, according to which the second coming of Christ was to be expected after the millennium, that held the ascendancy among evangelicals. There has been no unanimity on this subject.[15] Beliefs contributing to evangelical identity have to be sought elsewhere.

Are evangelicals, then, to be equated with fundamentalists? It is often assumed that they are. During 1986–87 a vigorous correspondence in *Life and Work*, the magazine of the Church of Scotland, began with a denunciation by a former moderator of the General Assembly of 'fundamentalists'. Replies protested that conservative evangelicals were being misrepresented by the label.[16] In Britain, again by contrast with America, self-professed fundamentalism, though emerging in the 1920s, never developed into a major force.[17] Fundamentalism commonly has three prominent connotations: belief in biblical inerrancy, a pugnacious manner and a repudiation of the intellect. Although the idea of inerrancy has circulated among evangelicals, it was widely accepted by their nineteenth-century teachers that the Bible contains mistakes about inessentials. The belief that the scriptures must necessarily be immune to error was rare even during the first half of the twentieth century.[18] The vitriolic denunciations of opponents, so common in the United States during the 1920s, were paralleled in Britain but only on a small scale. Temperate Christian leaders such as F B Meyer deliberately set their faces against militancy.[19] And British evangelicalism has embraced many different attitudes to the mind. It is true that early General Baptist preachers in the East Midlands could be described by their own historian as 'generally very illiterate',[20] but the counter-example of John Wesley, an Oxford scholar who was constantly reading, writing and educating, is sufficient to disprove the suggestion that evangelicalism has been intrinsically anti-intellectual. In truth, the evangelicals, though including people with fundamentalist traits in their ranks, have never been uniformly marked by fundamentalist attitudes. The two terms are far from synonymous.

If evangelicals have not been consistently low-church, dispensationalist or fundamentalist, what features has their tradition consistently displayed? Although the principle of biblical inerrancy has not been uniform, love and respect for the scriptures have been deeply ingrained in the movement. In every room of the home of T B Smithies, a Victorian Wesleyan who was prolific in issuing Christian periodicals, it was said that the visitor could see that the place of honour was given to the Bible.[21] Likewise, Samuel Pollard, a minister in the Bible Christian denomination of the same period, was devoted to the scriptures. 'How he loved the Word of God his Bibles with their annotations plainly reveal. No duty, however important, was allowed to keep him long from his daily practice of reading the Word, which he usually did on his knees.'[22] The Bible was at the heart of the devotional life. Some Primitive Methodists of a remote village stuck pins in the family Bible to mark the promises of God until there were two or three thousand pins in the volume.[23] Ordinary people were passionately eager to grasp the message of the scriptures. A millhand at Middleton in Lancashire, who belonged to the Wesleyan Methodist Association, scraped together the enormous sum of £16 to purchase Adam Clarke's commentary so that he could understand his Bible better.[24] The curriculum of evangelical theological colleges was built around the Bible. The one aim of James Acworth, president of Rawdon Baptist College between 1835 and 1863, was that his pupils should read and understand what he loved to call 'the Words of God'.[25] Of a self-taught Welsh Baptist minister it was said that, though he did not know the meaning of verbal inspiration, he believed in practice that the scriptures were infallible. 'His Bible', commented his son, 'was everything to him.'[26] Delight in the scriptures has been a thread running through the whole evangelical movement from John Wesley, who called himself a man of one book, to John Stott, who has specialized in close exposition of the biblical text. Evangelicalism has been nothing if not biblicist.

Equally pronounced has been a preoccupation with the cross of Christ. In 'the system of evangelical truth', according to Dan Taylor, the leader of the eighteenth-century New Connexion of General Baptists, the atonement made for us by the sufferings of Christ as our surety was the remedy for the ruined condition of sinful humanity. 'By reading the New Testament,' he went on, 'you will easily see that it is not only the very fundamental doctrine of Christianity, and the only ground of hope of a sinner, but it is the chief stimulus to every part of holiness.'[27] Evangelicalism has been centrally concerned with the good news of salvation, and it was the cross that was the means of salvation. Pardon and purity 'through the blood of Jesus' was the burden of the Bible Christian Samuel Pollard's preaching.[28] Ministers, exhorted the Baptist Union in 1837, should 'keep the cross of Christ ever in view'.[29] 'Preach the doctrines of the cross,' echoed John Rattenbury in his 1872 ordination charge to new Wesleyan ministers.[30] It was normal, in theological reflection on the atonement, to stress the way in which Christ acted as a substitute for guilty human beings in suffering the penalty of their sin.[31] Liberal views diverging from evangelical orthodoxy were commonly detected primarily by their down-grading of the sacrifice of Christ on the cross. Thus the theology of the American Congregationalist Horace Bushnell was condemned by a reviewer in *The Baptist Magazine* of 1866 for making the death of Christ merely incidental to his incarnation. 'But in the sacred scriptures', the reviewer pointed out, 'the death or blood of Christ is everywhere promi-nent.'[32] The cross became the kernel of popular piety. When a Primitive Methodist class leader, seized with inflammation of the bowels, was told in 1849 that the doctor could do no more, his reply was to quote to his wife a Charles Wesley hymn recounting that 'Jesus died for me'. ' "Yes," said she, "the atonement." He then fixed his eyes upon her, responding emphatically, "Yes, he died, he died for me." '[33] For Christopher Chavasse, later a bishop, the evangelical message was still in the 1930s what it had been in the eighteenth century – the cross.[34] The theology of the movement constantly emphasized the work of Christ on Calvary.

Another distinguishing characteristic of evangelicalism has been con-version. People were not automatically Christians, preachers insisted, either by nature or by virtue of their baptism. A decisive reorientation was needed before a person could properly be called a Christian. The process could often make deep emotional demands. 'His experience prior to the spiritual change effected in his life', it was said of a Devon Bible Christian converted in 1859, 'is not unlike that of many others who "know their sins forgiven". Conviction, contrition, wrestling in prayer, and mighty struggling – these were the prelude to the happy day when the peace of God first became his blest possession.'[35] For this man the transaction culminated in an event that could be fixed at a point in time, but for others it was so gradual as to prevent any precise dating. A 1992 report showed that in evangelical churches only 37% of people had undergone a sudden conversion. Although this proportion was much higher than the figure of 20% for congregations of all churchmanships, it represents a definite minority.[36] The lack of a dateable experience often seemed a spiritual disadvantage. Thus a Manchester Methodist of the early nineteenth century who, though active in church work, could not fix the time or place of his conversion, was sometimes plagued with doubts about its reality.[37] Whether sudden or gradual, however, conversion was usually considered, as stated by an evangelical clergyman speaking at the Islington Meeting in 1860, a virtual synonym for regeneration.[38] Jesus himself had said that to be born again, to enjoy the new birth by the power of the Holy Spirit, was essential. Thus it created a great stir when George Whitefield denied that John Tillotson, an earlier Archbishop of Canterbury, had ever gone through the new birth.[39] The experience was what revivalists such as Whitefield aimed to multiply. Over five weeks during 1859 it was reported that two hundred souls had professed conversion at special services in Bethesda Chapel, Gateshead, run by William Booth, later the founder of the Salvation Army.[40] The post-war crusades of Billy Graham, which did so much to bring evangelicals together, stood in the same tradition. The movement has been conversionist throughout its history.

Consequently, it has also been activist. The quest for souls has constantly driven its adherents into fresh evangelistic initiatives. 'Activity for God', declared the visiting American revivalist, James Caughey, in the mid-nineteenth century, 'is a consequence of a healthy soul, as green to a healthy leaf.'[41] The urgent need to spread the gospel was likewise a theme of the great Baptist preacher, C H Spurgeon. 'Brethren,' he told his students, 'do something; do something; do something. While committees waste their time over resolutions, do something.'[42] He was echoed in the twentieth century by Ernest Kevan: 'Man was made for work,' he used to say. 'He is never happier than when he is doing it.'[43] The sheer energy of prominent evangelicals can be amazing. The Wesleyan John Rattenbury, for example, used to preach between 400 and 500 sermons a year.[44] Their dynamism spilled out in many directions – into the overseas missionary movement, into organized philanthropy, into social reform. Victorian Britain teemed with evangelical activity. Thomas Penrose, a Primitive Methodist minister, may be taken as representative:

> Penrose was above everything else a man of action, whose hands were ever willing, and whose feet were ever ready, to do the great Master's bidding . . . He was filled with a burning zeal for the glory of his Saviour and weal of his fellow-men, which was manifested in his indomitable perseverance in building chapels and schools, collecting large sums of money for this work; in promoting the cause of education; in sympathy and help for the poor, obtaining suitable situations for promising young men and women, and relief for suffering tradesmen; in his able advocacy of the temperance cause; and in the active interest he took in all local movements for the welfare of those amongst whom he lived.[45]

To be busy, to be useful, always ranked higher in the evangelical scale of things than more passive virtues such as the cultivation of the contemplative life. Evangelicals down the centuries have typically thrown themselves into work for God.

Devotion to the Bible, proclamation of the cross, zeal for conversions and unbounded activism have been the regular hallmarks of the evangelical movement. They have created a shared ethos that has transcended

44

denominational boundaries. That is not to deny the fierce rivalries that have sometimes existed. Debates within evangelicalism – between Calvinist and Arminian, between Baptist and paedobaptist – often formed the stuff of village life in nineteenth-century Wales.[46] Methodists could be dismissive of what they took to be Baptist formalism, as in the obituary of a Hull New Connexion woman. 'Her parents', ran the narrative, 'attended the Baptist chapel, but, like too many, they rested in outward ceremonies; for while honesty and integrity were in their moral character, there was no evidence of scriptural and saving piety.'[47] Baptists were entirely capable of responding with similarly critical sentiments. Yet from the eighteenth to the twentieth centuries there was often an overriding awareness of common ground among evangelicals. It was particularly strong around the beginning of the nineteenth century in the era that gave birth to the interdenominational London Missionary Society, Religious Tract Society and British and Foreign Bible Society.[48] Even the barrier between the established Church of England and Dissent was broken down. In 1799, for instance, Union Chapel, Islington, was set up as a joint Anglican-Congregational cause with a Prayer Book service in the morning and extemporary prayer in the evening.[49] Although the high degree of co-operation, especially between Church and Dissent, subsequently diminished, it became permanently embodied in the Evangelical Alliance from 1846 and continued to find expression in a multitude of local ventures such as the Mildmay conference for Christian workers and its associated institutions.[50] Mildmay's founder, the clergyman William Pennefather, voiced the spirit of evangelical unity in 1865. 'If the standard of the Cross be uplifted in Africa,' he wrote, 'and its banner unfurled in Asia, God is in each case glorified; though Episcopalians may have raised it in Sierra Leone, and Baptists have displayed its glories in Serampore.'[51] The Church Missionary Society and the Baptist Missionary Society were not so much competitive as complementary. Because evangelicals shared a common allegiance to the cross, they could rejoice in each other's missionary triumphs.

Evangelicals such as Pennefather, who have recognized the substantial unity of the movement, have existed in every generation. Prominent among them in the later twentieth century has been Gilbert Kirby. But even when there has been negligible desire for joint action and little awareness of common ground, there have been certain attributes that have given the movement a distinct character. It would have been inconceivable in the late nineteenth century for P F Eliot, the vicar of Bournemouth, to co-operate with John Sirgood, the leader of the Cokelers. Yet, for all their differences, the establishmentarian and the sectarian were united in the gospel emphases of the Bible, cross, conversion and activism. Although the balance between the elements in this quadrilateral has changed over time, each has always been prominent in the evangelical tradition. Wherever all four were stressed – whether or not contemporaries were aware of their affinities – evangelicalism existed. The boundaries of the movement could be sharp, as they were between Sirgood's body and the rest of the Christian world, or blurred, as they were between Eliot's brand of high church evangelicalism and full-blown Anglo-Catholicism. Yet the four criteria provide a way of defining what sections of the Christian world fell within the evangelical community at any particular time. In the 1990s this community embraces, alongside members of the established churches and historic branches of Nonconformity, a range of twentieth-century denominations – the Pentecostalists, the Afro-Caribbean churches and many varieties of independents, charismatic and non-charismatic. The evangelicals across these denominations are all united in the bonds of the gospel. As many of them discover, through joint expressions of their activism such as Spring Harvest or local evangelical councils, they all try to be obedient to the Bible and therefore faithful to the cross, and eager for conversions. They become aware of their common evangelical identity.

Endnotes

1   R Homan, 'The Society of Dependents: A case study in the rise and fall of rural Peculiars', *Sussex Archaeological Collections*, 119 (1981), pp 195–204.
2   *The Record*, 19 January 1883, p 56.
3   M Sorrell, *The Peculiar People* (Exeter, 1979), p 112. The foreword to this book is written by Gilbert Kirby whose wife originally belonged to the Peculiar People.
4   D W Dayton, 'Some doubts about the usefulness of the category "Evangelical" ', in D W Dayton and R K Johnston (eds), *The Variety of American Evangelicalism* (Knoxville, Tenn, 1991), pp 245–251.
5   G W Kirby, 'A Britisher writes a letter to Americans', *United Evangelical Action*, September 1962, pp 12–13, quoted by D M Howard, *The Dream that would not Die: The Birth and Growth of the World Evangelical Fellowship, 1846–1986* (Exeter, 1986), p 61.
6   P Brierley (ed), *Prospects for the Nineties: All England* (London, 1991), pp 50, 13.
7   *The Witness*, 9 January 1850, p 3. 'A memorial addressed to leaders of the Church of England in a time of crisis and opportunity', November 1959; Gilbert Kirby was among the signatories of the petition.
8   J R Wolffe, *The Protestant Crusade in Great Britain 1828–1860* (Oxford, 1991).
9   W Hanna, *Memoirs of the Life and Writings of Thomas Chalmers, DD, LL D*, 3 (4 vols) (Edinburgh, 1851–52), p 259n; *What is an Evangelical Catholic?* (Dublin, 1992).
10 N Temperley, *Jonathan Gray and Church Music in York* (York, 1977).
11 *The Baptist Magazine*, June 1838, p 256.
12 Brierley, *Prospects for the Nineties*, p 13.

13 Dayton, 'Some doubts', in Dayton and Johnston (eds), *The Variety of American Evangelicalism*, pp 249–250.

14 G W Kirby, *Ernest Kevan: Pastor and Principal* (London, 1968), pp 29, 55.

15 D W Bebbington, 'The advent hope in British Evangelicalism since 1800', *The Scottish Journal of Religious Studies*, 9 (1988), pp 103–114.

16 Especially N M de S Cameron to editor, *Life and Work*, January 1987, p 38.

17 D W Bebbington, 'Martyrs for the truth: Fundamentalists in Britain', in D Wood (ed), *Martyrs and Martyrologies*, Studies in Church History, 30 (Oxford, 1993), pp 417–451.

18 D F Wright, 'Soundings in the doctrine of Scripture in British Evangelicalism in the first half of the twentieth century', *Tyndale Bulletin*, 31 (1980), pp 87–106.

19 I Randall, 'A Christian cosmopolitan: F B Meyer in Britain and America', in G A Rawlyk and M A Noll (eds), *Amazing Grace: Evangelicalism in Australia, Britain, Canada and the United States* (Montreal, 1994), pp 180–181.

20 A Taylor, *The History of the English General Baptists*, 2 (2 vols) (London, 1818), p 56.

21 G Rowe, *T B Smithies (Editor of 'The British Workman'): A Memoir* (London, 1884), p 72.

22 W J Mitchell, *Brief Biographical Sketches of Bible Christian Ministers and Laymen*, 1 (2 vols) (Jersey, 1906), p 43.

23 J Stephenson, *The Man of Faith and Fire: Or the Life and Work of the Rev G Warner* (London, 1902), p 184.

24 *The Wesleyan Methodist Association Magazine*, October 1853, p 487.

25 W Medley, *Rawdon Baptist College: Centenary Memorial* (London, 1904), p 26.

26 E Davies and R Davies, *The Life of the Late Rev David Davies* (Maesyrhelem, Brecon, 1914), pp 174, 85.

27 *Minutes of an Association of General Baptists . . . 1789* (London, 1789), p 5.

28 Mitchell, *Brief Biographical Sketches*, 1, p 42.

29 *Account of the Twenty-fifth Annual Session of the Baptist Union* (London, 1837), p 30.

30 H O Rattenbury (ed), *The Rev John Rattenbury: Memorials* (London, 1884), p 109.

31 E G C Williams in *The Baptist Magazine*, March 1862, pp 161–164.

32 *The Baptist Magazine*, June 1866, p 365.

33 *The Primitive Methodist Magazine*, January 1850, p 61.

34 *The Record*, 13 April 1933, p 208.

35 Mitchell, *Brief Biographical Sketches*, 1, p 79 (Edmund Mountjoy).

36 J Finney, *Finding Faith Today: How does it Happen?* (Swindon, 1992), p 24.
37 *The Wesleyan Methodist Association Magazine*, February 1854, p 85 (James Mabbott).
38 *The Record*, 13 April 1933, p 208.
39 H S Stout, *The Divine Dramatist: George Whitefield and the Rise of Modern Evangelicalism* (Grand Rapids, Mich, 1991), p 101.
40 *The Methodist New Connexion Magazine*, April 1859, p 224.
41 *Earnest Christianity Illustrated: Or Selections from the Journal of the Rev James Caughey* (London, 1857), p 103.
42 C H Spurgeon, *Lectures to my Students* (London, 1954), p 217.
43 Kirby, *Ernest Kevan*, p 42.
44 Rattenbury (ed), *The Rev John Rattenbury*, p 50.
45 W J Browson et al, *Heroic Men: The Death Roll of the Primitive Methodist Ministry* (London, 1889), p 305.
46 D Davies, *Reminiscences of my Country and People* (London, 1925), pp 19–20.
47 *The Methodist New Connexion Magazine*, December 1850, p 614 (Sarah Carlton).
48 R H Martin, *Evangelicals United: Ecumenical Stirrings in Pre-Victorian Britain, 1795–1830* (Metuchen, NJ, 1983).
49 W H Harwood, *Henry Allon, DD: Pastor and Teacher* (London, 1894), pp 16–18.
50 H J Cooke, *Mildmay: Or the Story of the First Deaconess Institution* (London, 1893).
51 W Pennefather, *The Church of the First-Born: A Few Thoughts on Christian Unity* (London, 1865), p 10.

Chapter 5

THE EVANGELICAL ALLIANCE: A NATIONAL PHENOMENON

Joel Edwards

Evangelicalism in the UK has distinctive features which cannot be readily paralleled elsewhere in the world. For example, British evangelicalism, unlike its counterpart in the USA, is not synonymous with fundamentalism. Nor does it necessarily preclude pentecostal or charismatic Christians as it does in some European countries. It is not determined by political or denominational considerations. There is increasing acceptance of the view that the term 'evangelical' is most properly used as a noun. Hence someone may be a Baptist evangelical, an Anglican evangelical or a Pentecostal evangelical. Recently, there has been the growth of what some term 'evangelical Catholics'. Scripture itself and a commitment to its authority provide the essential criteria for evangelicalism. As John Stott expresses it, 'The supremacy of Scripture has always been and always will be the first hallmark of an evangelical.'[1]

The emerging profile of EA over the last twenty years and, more specifically, the last decade has both expressed and contributed to this phenomenon. EA's distinguished history since its inception in 1846 has marked it out as one of the oldest expressions of ecumenical church life. Inevitably, EA's position has reflected developments within evangelicalism. For instance, the high-point of evangelical co-operation reached in the Sixties was followed by a period of decline, in some measure precipitated by the Stott/Lloyd-Jones disagreement in 1966 and the realignment of evangelicals in the Church of England following the Keele Conference in 1967.

The subsequent renewal of British evangelicalism has been clearly linked with the growth of EA. EA in Britain has provided a container in which the kaleidoscopic nature of British evangelicalism has been sustained and stimulated. The phenomenon has also been described as a table-top on which all the pieces of the jigsaw are assembled, an umbrella that covers evangelical diversity, a platform for united action and, more latterly, a pan-evangelical movement.[2]

A number of factors combined to make the phenomenon possible. In the first place, it may be said that its time had come. As Victor Hugo once pointed out, there is nothing stronger than an idea whose time has arrived.

Someone once remarked that if EA did not exist, it would have to be invented!

Second, EA has undoubtedly benefited from the wave of optimism that has accompanied the renewal and charismatic movements of the last thirty years. Figures from the 1989 Church Census indicate that church growth has been most significant amongst charismatic and pentecostal evangelicals. It is estimated that these represent some 47% of evangelicals in the UK. Linked with this growth there has been an increase in interaction between the various streams. To some extent, this has been the legacy of some interdenominational Bible colleges such as London Bible College, and the interdenominational 'flavour' of theological colleges such as Spurgeon's and Trinity, Bristol. As a result, communications between evangelicals have developed, and long-term relationships have been forged.

This climate of co-operation over the past decade has helped to resolve some of the misunderstanding and even hostility between the various varieties of evangelicalism in the UK. The plethora of Christian publications which has developed, with all the potential for competitive overlap, has nevertheless provided a powerful facility for education and mutual awareness. Similarly, high profile worship and training events such as Spring Harvest, Word Alive, Greenbelt and Keswick – to name but a few – have added to an 'open house' culture that has developed amongst evangelicals. This has, in turn, provided frameworks within which evangelical unity in diversity has become possible.

Third, evangelicals are children of their age. It is not surprising therefore that, in a climate of tolerance which has a vested interest in the demise of the 'crusade' mentality and religious bigotry, evangelicals have imbibed the prevailing attitude. This is something we cannot ignore even if it threatens our comfort zone. Mutual tolerance on matters of secondary importance is one thing; compromise for the sake of unity is another. As Kenneth Myers expresses it:

> It is one thing to put aside theological differences about sacraments, spiritual gifts, church order, or the nature of sanctification for the purpose of a joint evangelistic campaign. That is how modern evangelicalism has grown. Evangelical Christians have wrongly concluded that what one believes about sacraments, charismata and other controversial issues does not matter (at all), that it is really more Christian not to have any opinion on such things.[3]

The success of the UK phenomenon has been its ability, on the whole, to avoid this particular danger whilst recognizing the potential for greater unity which exists within the increasing diversity of its growing membership.

Fourth, evangelicals have become increasingly aware of the global dimensions of evangelicalism. With over 53% of the international evangelical family located in the developing world, a new attitude of humility is being instilled which is gradually encouraging a general attitude of humility.

Finally, the development of EA is inseparable from the timely and visionary work of the current director general, Clive Calver. Upon his appointment as general secretary in 1983 he introduced the concept of 'metamorphosis'. Subsequently, the movement has grown at an average of 25% each year, the number of individual members soaring from 1,000 to over 53,000 and representing over one million evangelicals in thirty denominational churches and groups throughout the UK. His passion for the history of the evangelical movement has led to EA's rediscovery of its twin commitments to social action and biblical reflection. The new impetus has resulted in the growth of EA's staff from three in 1981 to its 1995 level of sixty, spread across the United Kingdom and striving to reflect the cultural, denominational and theological diversity of Britain's evangelicalism.

Derek Tidball has helpfully identified the fact that evangelicalism has always been based on unity in essentials, relationships, reality,[4] and a recognition of the necessity for change.[5] In his words, EA has emerged as 'a movement to be reckoned with'.[6] It owes its existence to the richness of its evangelical streams, and seeks to maintain its distinctive contribution to the international evangelical community by serving and reflecting the concerns of the whole range of its diverse membership.

Recovering the ground

In a national conference on church planting, Clive Calver pointed to the fact that evangelicals were no longer out of the world, but back in it and enjoying increasing unity and growth.[7] Evangelicals, he said, were taking ground but should not claim too much.

Post-war secularization left the legacy of a twilight zone of moral uncertainty, liberal theology and the caricature of a nervously irrelevant Christian church. Not surprisingly, church attendance slumped to an all-time low, and the voice of evangelical Christians became marginalized. Dr Billy Graham's 1958 visit to Earls Court at the request of EA was an important indication of the Alliance's commitment to impact the spiritual climate of the UK church and nation. Subsequently, the Alliance's commitment to affect the spiritual life of the church has been demonstrated over the years by its involvement in initiatives such as the annual Evangelists' Conference, prayer triplets and the development of a Church Life Team, serving its members in prayer, evangelism, mission and pastoral care.

Not all evangelicals have been persuaded of the relevance of social involvement in society. So much is owed to the excellent work of evangelical organizations such as Müller's Homes and the Shaftesbury Society who have maintained their historic roots, as well as new organizations such as CARE, Tear Fund, and Christian Impact (formerly known as the

London Institute for Contemporary Christianity) who have sustained this tradition.

EA has firmly identified itself with this position and developed a range of ministries with a specific focus on social and community issues. Much of this work has been done through a number of EA coalitions that have pooled the expertise of specialists in a number of fields including sexuality, addiction, youth and children, education, and support for South Africa. In 1989 the Alliance facilitated a nation-wide consultation that brought evangelicals together to discuss matters related to family life, work and welfare, pluralism, and the local church and its community. Called 'Salt and Light', it did not live up to everyone's expectations but certainly marked a determination to encourage the evangelical church to become more relevant. Against a background of two million unemployed people, the Evangelical Enterprise was launched in 1989 as a joint initiative between the West Indian Evangelical Alliance, EA and the Department of Trade and Industry. The Evangelical Enterprise later became the Community Initiatives Unit, with a specific responsibility to offer advice and consultation for churches wishing to make a contribution to the social needs of their community, and to draw together church groups of different cultural and denominational backgrounds.

The challenge to contemporary Christianity has been significantly enhanced within the Alliance by the development of the Home and Public Affairs Department. This has provided a watching brief on parliamentary matters for both EA staff and members, and has played an important role in national debates on such issues as Sunday trading and pornographic videos. An important element has therefore been EA's combination of social realities and gospel proclamation in holistic action. Over the years the Alliance has also acted either as a partnership or an encourager of specialist groups such as Evangelical Christians for Racial Justice, the Evangelical Coalition on Urban Mission, and indeed Tear Fund which was launched in 1968 and was itself a product of the Alliance's work.

Going for growth

EA's recent growth has been directly related to its ability to serve the evangelical church and reflect its values to the wider community. This service includes national, regional, and local initiatives, along with the provision of practical resources for its members. These have ranged from popular magazines dealing with specific concerns about new spirituality, addiction and evangelical identity, to parliamentary briefings and practical help to stimulate mission and prayer. *Idea*, EA's quarterly membership magazine, enjoys one of the widest circulations of a Christian publication in Britain, with over 50,000 copies.

Over the past ten years the growth of the movement has been a clear indication of the growing strength of evangelicalism in Britain. Between January and November 1986 individual membership increased by 105%, groups and societies by 90% and churches by 30%. In December 1989 EA had a total of 19,731 individual members, 453 groups/societies and 1,422 churches. By January 1995 its individual membership had risen to 49,764 with 688 groups/societies and 2,690 churches. Such growth has made it possible for EA to speak from a position of relative strength, with the consciousness that it reflects the perspectives of over one million evangelicals represented through their denominational and church affiliations.

The enhanced profile of the Alliance, together with the diversity of the 'tribes of evangelicalism', presents challenges to the unity of the movement. Some of these have been entirely practical, for instance the numerical growth of EA's staff and the purchase and refurbishment in 1992 of its Whitefield House headquarters as an evangelical centre. The commitment to develop an Alliance which reflects the range of evangelicals on its council and executive has been a corollary to its recent growth. Between 1980 and 1995 the council has grown from twenty to seventy five.

One voice, many accents

Ian Coffey, formerly field director of EA, once said that evangelicals needed a 'theology of diversity'. This insightful statement is a far more important notion than the acceptance of the principle 'unity in diversity'. It is a recognition that Christians have an obligation to reflect the rich tapestry of our cultural, historical and theological diversity within an authentic, biblically defined unity.

In 1983, it became evident that the culture of the Alliance was significantly that of South-east England. Despite the growing number of black and Asian churches within multicultural Britain, EA's membership failed to reflect this diversity. Consequently, requests came from the African-Caribbean Christians to close the gap between black and white evangelicals and for the Alliance to recognize the reality of the black Christian presence in Britain. Two leading black evangelicals, Philip Mohabir and Melvin Powell, forged links with senior staff at EA following the birth of the West Indian Evangelical Alliance in April 1984. This led to the appointment of its first general secretary in 1988.

In 1986 the first steps towards an EA in Northern Ireland were made by Arthur Williamson, Roy Gamble and Ken McBride. The Northern Ireland office was officially launched in June 1986 with Clive Calver, Ken Prior and Gilbert Kirby representing EA's council. Its first general secretary, George Sproule, was appointed in April 1988. In the same month the executive committee discussed plans for a Scottish EA (following earlier discussions with Douglas Flett), as well as an EA in Wales. This was a response to a recently established Welsh steering group, chaired by Philip Hill, which had been set up to explore the possibility of a full-time regional co-ordinator. In 1989 the Welsh EA was established with the appointment of its first general secretary, Arfon Jones. The Scottish office was formally opened in 1992, and its first general secretary, David Anderson, was inducted in November 1994.

The transition to a truly United Kingdom Alliance has been an involved process of detailed constitutional restructuring over a five year period. The procedure has not been without its difficulties and is necessarily under constant review. The current constitutional framework allows for a dynamism that is dependent on elements of trust and relationship as much as structural clarity! However, EA's council (made up of senior evangelical leaders) reflects the diversity of evangelical Christianity throughout the UK.

Similarly, councils and executives are responsible for the vision and direction of autonomous EA's in Scotland, Wales and Northern Ireland, and ACEA (African Caribbean EA). To preserve unity-in-diversity, each of these has a representative on the executive and council of EA (UK).

Perhaps a little more should be added about EA's council and executive. Drawn from the spectrum of its membership, the council includes senior church leaders from all sections of EA's UK constituency. Because each Alliance in Scotland, Wales and Northern Ireland and the ACEA has its own council and executive, EA's constitution stipulates that each national chair is also a member of the UK council. Members of the Asian Alliance of Christians are also represented on council through their general secretary. In addition, each national executive also has a member on the UK executive of fifteen, thereby guaranteeing a direct contribution at the decision-making level. Each of these representatives is automatically a member of the UK council. The UK executive, which meets ten times a year, monitors the work of the senior staff who initiate EA's policies before they are processed through council.

In this way the UK council's expressed desire 'to give proper recognition to the recently formed ACEA, EA Wales, EA Northern Ireland and the emerging EA Scotland' was fulfilled. At the same time there remained 'one United Kingdom EA with each body taking special responsibility for representing and serving those members who come within their ethnic or geographic boundaries'.[8]

Despite imperfections, EA has succeeded in giving expression to multicultural, evangelical ecumenism. In a period when issues of national, cultural and ethnic fragmentation have been described as one of the greatest challenges for the twentieth century, the spectacle of a multicultural Evangelical Alliance presents a worthy model for the international evangelical community and for pockets of evangelical Christianity throughout Europe who may not readily appreciate the urgency of the issue. Within this cross-cultural context the Welsh EA conducted its symposium on 'Language, Nationalism and Culture' in Aberystwyth in 1994, and the Northern Ireland evangelicals invited the entire UK Council to discuss the Northern Ireland 'situation' at its meeting in February 1995.

Of course, this matter of evangelical unity is not only concerned with respecting ethnic and national diversity in Britain. Since its earliest beginnings the Alliance has been a forum in which the breadth of evangelical theological perspectives could be expressed. As stated previously, EA has worked hard to promote the use of 'evangelical' as a noun. Evangelicals are learning increasingly that we may agree sufficiently on the fundamental truths of scripture to deal with our distinctives. In spite of the growing debates on biblical interpretation, evangelicals are unlikely to weaken their commitment to the person of Christ and the authority of scripture. The tension between primary issues of evangelical orthodoxy and secondary issues which produce legitimate diversity will always be with us. EA's commitment to evangelical unity consistently takes it into the heart of the debate. Women's ministry, charismatic Christianity and the use of spiritual gifts, ecumenism or the discussions of what has become known as the 'Toronto Blessing' are integral to the same essential issue – what is an evangelical?

There is a huge gulf between creative tension and compromise, although the two can seem identical in bad light! Spurious unity based on theological indifference is one thing, but a unity based on essential truths, with the freedom to differ on non-essentials, is actually a vital part of evangelical identity. Unity is not conformity. Providing a forum for mutuality has been a privileged role which EA has fulfilled on numerous occasions. Within that context it has become very evident that unity is often sustained not only by doctrinal convictions, but also by devotional lifestyles which respect other people and demonstrate that it is possible to disagree without being disagreeable. Increasingly, it is in the corridors and behind closed doors where personal encounters are taking place, that strong convictions are being retained whilst personal respect is being fostered. It has been encouraging for evangelical unity to see the growing links between individuals and organizations through special private meetings between members of the evangelical community or organizations who have seen the potential for greater partnership. The decision of Westminster Chapel to join the Alliance in 1990 was a significant step forward for evangelical unity.

A credible voice

Perhaps one of the most ambitious tasks the Alliance undertakes is 'to speak for' evangelicals in the UK. In recent years unprecedented opportunities have opened up to credible Christian spokespersons. Evangelicals, though still a minority group, have been 'discovered' by the secular press. It is no longer so easy for journalists or public figures to harbour comic stereotypes of evangelicals, although there still appears to be a vested interest in doing so. Having discovered that British evangelicalism is not politically determined, and that intelligent and relevant thinking exists amongst evangelicals, there has been a steady and growing interest in what evangelicals have to say on a wide range of given issues. The odd enquiry from the press has long since been a thing of the past, and a constant flow of enquiries from both the Christian and secular press has been the norm over the last four or five years. A random check with EA press office (20 June 1994) showed that there were unsolicited enquiries from *The Observer, The Times*, BBC TV and HTV West on that single day.

The EA's membership increasingly looks to its senior staff for 'guidelines' on a number of subjects. Over two hundred calls come to the London office each day, mainly from its members. As a key centre of evangelicalism in the UK, the Alliance acts as a clearing house for its members and the wider community.

True to its historic role, modern evangelicalism has maintained a watching brief on the international agenda, both through its renewed and growing relationship with the Evangelical Missionary Alliance (founded in 1958) and its traditional focus on mission, through its annual World Prayer Week and its missions secretary.

Although evangelicals are not popularly associated with religious liberty, EA has a long history of involvement in this field, with notable party-piece examples from the nineteenth century. In 1990 the World Evangelical Fellowship invited EA to facilitate its newly formed 'Religious Liberty Commission' under the auspices of its international secretary. Focusing on world events and strategies in order to encourage its members to respond to the suffering church has therefore been an integral part of the Alliance's work, with particular reference to European and Middle Eastern countries. In addition, the attention of evangelicals has been drawn again and again to 'hot spots' in our world, where human suffering has demanded a response from the UK church.

Since 1995 EA's Peace, Justice and Reconciliation Study Unit has drawn attention to Green issues through its Creation Care programme and has developed clear thinking on our stewardship of the environment.

To speak 'for' and 'on behalf' of a growing membership remains an acute challenge for an increasingly multifaceted movement. EA's ability to do this depends in part on the relationship between an energetic leadership which strives to remain contemporary in its vision, and a membership which retains the right to call the movement to account either for its actions or for public statements made on its behalf. This has been a function of EA's council and executive committee.

In order to develop a credible voice, evangelicals have been obliged to approach resourcing and information in a more purposeful way. This has involved growth in EA's press and information departments. It has also meant that its work has expanded to include popular apologetics covering subjects such as pluralism and a biblical assessment of addiction. When Martin Scorsese's film, *The Last Temptation Of Christ*, was released in 1988, evangelicals in the USA and UK were justifiably disturbed by the distorted portrayal of a Christ with a confused identity and a weakened deity. EA's response was the production of *Jesus of Nazareth*, an attempt to provide a popular apologetic for the humanity and divinity of Christ. EA has gained credibility both within its membership and beyond by its growing ministry to its membership and its readiness to respond to needs as they arise.

A pan-evangelical vision

In 1994 EA's council made a clear decision to define itself as a pan-evangelical movement. The council was clear that, given its growing links with the denominational bodies and para-church agencies within its membership, it was neither an alternative para-church nor a society of evangelical groups. Equally, there was clear agreement that it was not to be regarded as an anti-ecumenical movement, in spite of its earlier decision to remain outside the emerging ecumenical structures. Historically, EA had been a rallying point for individual evangelicals and, from 1957, for churches. Its ability to embrace individuals, churches and para-church societies around a basis of faith has been the critical factor on which its unity has relied. Invariably, this unity has been expressed in joint incarnational activity. The genius of EA is its ability to hold the diversity of evangelical nuances and cultural distinctives in an environment of growing trust and fellowship.

This unity-in-diversity raises the question, what do we mean by evangelical? As already stated this is one of the most pressing questions facing modern evangelicalism. British evangelicals have attempted to emphasize that 'evangelical' defines the nature of our Christian faith, whereas denominational affiliation determines the context in which we worship and serve the Body of Christ. The problem of definition is bound to be with us for some time to come, as the clarification exercise continues to establish distinctives, influenced by political, cultural and theological criteria.

EA is able to reflect the varying shades of evangelicalism within the tapestry of its membership without compromising its commitment to historic evangelicalism. The spectrum of its membership in 1995 indicates EA's diversity throughout the UK. Inevitably, denominational and group membership provides an element of flexibility in which churches can develop varying degrees of partnership with other bodies who may not themselves be associated with EA. Many Baptist, Methodist, Anglican or New churches will, for example, have links with ecumenical groups either through individual choice or denominational involvement. Admittedly, this is sometimes an area of difficulty between those who would identify with EA and other evangelicals, such as some in the Evangelical Movement of Wales and the British Evangelical Council, who would have considerable difficulty with this issue of secondary separation.

A pan-evangelical movement attempts to embrace the variety of evangelical groups without controlling them. For this concept to suceed, individuals, churches and groups must own that vision together.

Pan-evangelicalism fails if it is merely committed to evangelical activity, for it would then be susceptible to becoming a Christian pressure group driven by specific issues with political motivation. EA's pan-evangelicalism depends upon a consensus that all members own the cardinal tenets of the basis of faith and conduct their relationships in accordance with its practical resolutions.

Evangelical unity cannot afford to ignore belief. Biblical reflection is not an optional extra. In itself this has implications for EA's basis of faith. A commitment to a pan-evangelical movement does not insulate evangelicals from the traumas of current debates on such theological issues as eternal punishment, ecumenism or spiritual gifts. The task of theological reflection has become a major element in evangelical unity in general and EA in particular. The thinking process within the UK is being stimulated by EA's Commission on Unity and Truth among Evangelicals (ACUTE) which in recent years has tackled a range of issues affecting evangelical unity. It has done so by drawing on a range of evangelical theologians and church leaders who reflect the theological and cultural range of British evangelicalism, and by its attempt to tease out primary matters of evangelical doctrines from the secondary elements of denominational distinctives or private convictions.

Truth is never complete without grace. Sadly, evangelical commitment to 'evangelical purity' sometimes becomes a premise for theological intolerance and personal animosities. In the absence of grace, the 'crusader mentality' can produce religious bigotry at its worst. An evangelical leader once confessed that in his area people sharpened their doctrines to stab others! Bishop Baughen's call for 'grace and truth' at the Anglican Leaders' Conference in January 1995 has a wider appeal for the international evangelical community.

The pan-evangelicalism that characterizes the phenomenon of EA has been held together by a deliberate dynamic of constitutional restructuring and international, cross-cultural relationships. The size and diversity of EA's council reflects this. With its breadth of representation and the level of accountability, the council is ideally suited to act as an 'evangelical parliament'. It constitutes an excellent forum in which to discuss significant issues affecting evangelicals and to pass resolutions that speak to the wider church and society on behalf of EA's members.

Looking ahead

Its engagement with society has been a historic strength of evangelicalism. With the partial exception of the early part of the twentieth century, the evangelical has always considered the 'world as my parish'. Contemporary evangelicalism is anxious to speak again with prophetic relevance to those who live beyond its immediate boundaries.

In 1985 EA recognized the importance of speaking to the 'social, moral and spiritual issues that affect the nation'. It strengthened its resolve to develop this role with and on behalf of its members. As a result EA's senior staff in London and throughout Britain have identified the responsibility to speak to the nations of the UK as an integral part of the evangelical mandate.

The phenomenon of EA has come a long way in building a platform of evangelical unity on which British evangelicals can stand together, with servant hearts, in order to speak with increasing confidence to the church and the society they have been called to serve.

Endnotes

1   C Calver, I Coffey and P Meadows (eds), *Who do Evangelicals think they are?* (London, date unknown), p 4.
2   C Calver, a paper presented to EA council, February 1994.
3   K Myers, *A Better Way: Proclamation Instead of Protest* (Chicago, 1992), p 49.
4   D J Tidball, *Who are the Evangelicals?* (Basingstoke, 1994), pp 221–222.
5   Tidball, *Who are the Evangelicals?*, p 225.
6   Tidball, *Who are the Evangelicals?*, p 8.
7   Challenge 2000, held on 8 March 1995 at Nottingham.
8   EA Executive Minutes, 13 June 1991.

Chapter 6

THE WORLD EVANGELICAL FELLOWSHIP: FACING THE FUTURE

Jun Vencer

Steven Spielberg's *Back to the Future* can serve as a paradigm in understanding the nature of the World Evangelical Fellowship (WEF) and its proactivism into the future. The film's plot tells of the adventure of two men who go back into the past via a time machine and then back into the future – to their own time. We can appreciate WEF in the same way: we can go back into the past and learn of its history, and then back into the future – to our own time. One difference is that, in our adventure, we are really aligning our past and present with that which is really future, when our Lord will reign in justice and righteousness. For that which is both now and not yet, which is here and is still coming – the kingdom of God – will provide the ethics by which God's people ought to live out their witness in our world.

The dream that would not die

The WEF traces its beginning to August 1846 as the World Evangelical Alliance in England. In that year 915 delegates from 11 countries met to form an international organization that would represent evangelical unity and co-operation. Although the conference failed to bring such an organization into being, the dream of that conference did not die. In November of that year, a few months after the adjournment, the Evangelical Alliance (British Organization) was formed. This was incorporated as the World Evangelical Alliance in 1912. Other European alliances started to develop without a formal link to the Alliance. The same spirit was blowing in some countries in the developing world: India, Japan, Cyprus, Turkey. In North America the Evangelical Alliance (American Branch) was also organized, although only on paper until 1944. The organization that embraced the spirit of 1846 was the National Association of Evangelicals which was formed in May 1943.

In the light of these developments, another international conference was planned to make a fresh attempt to form a definitive organization to represent global evangelical unity and co-operation. The leaders thought that the time was ripe to organize a World Alliance. Elwin Wright and Paul Rees made their historic twenty-six-nation whirlwind visit to investigate the possibility. This resulted in the convening of an international consultation in August 1951 at Woudschoten in the Netherlands. In this historic meeting WEF was formed. The delegates committed themselves to unity in diversity in a world evangelical fellowship and to world evangelization. Dr David Howard – former WEF international director who was greatly instrumental in the revitalization of the fellowship – gave his brief historical sketch of the organization the title *The Dream That Would Not Die*. What had started in 1846 became much broader in international scope after 1951. In May 1953 the British evangelicals changed the name of their alliance from the World Evangelical Alliance to Evangelical Alliance United Kingdom in order to avoid confusion. WEF became the umbrella body for evangelicals through the growing number of national fellowships or alliances.

WEF is representative of the evangelical global family, giving concrete expression to our Lord's prayer, 'That they all may be one . . . that the world may believe' (John 17:21). The psalmist sings of Christian unity in terms of pleasantness, life and blessing (Psalm 133). WEF's aim is not to create unity, since this is a gift from God in Christ made real in our midst by the Holy Spirit. Evangelical Christians, regardless of denominational labels, are already spiritually one. They have one Lord, one faith, one baptism, one calling, one Spirit, one God (Ephesians 4:4–7). Paul referred to this unity by exhorting the Ephesians to 'preserve the unity of the Spirit in the bond of peace' (Ephesians 4:3). This exhortation assumes that something exists to be preserved, for one cannot preserve something that does not exist. Moreover, this unity, although a spiritual reality, also calls for human effort.

WEF is a credal organization. Membership demands an unqualified affirmation to its statement of faith. The Reformers advocated the 'communion of the saints' on the basis of faith only – *sola fide*. This communion, however, allowed for diversity. Hugh T Kerr, in *A Compendium of Calvin's Theology*, cites John Calvin's view that 'diversity of opinion, respecting . . . non-essential points ought not to be a cause of discord among Christians'. WEF seeks to demonstrate authentic unity in union with Christ. Waldron Scott captured this spirit of balance by citing, 'In essentials, unity; in non-essentials, liberty; in all things, charity.' This visible manifestation of the invisible reality is also a condition for world belief in Christ (John 17:21).

Understanding an evangelical

Who is an evangelical? Of course, the foundational qualification is that he or she professes personal faith in Christ Jesus as Saviour and Lord. But this is not enough. The affirmation of WEF's statement of faith is too abstract or theological for many to grasp. Let me suggest four ways to appreciate the term 'evangelical'.

First, the Greek NT word *euangelion* means 'good news', the NT gospel, the heart of the Christian message. To be an evangelical is to be saved through the gospel and to be a 'gospeller'. It must be remembered that the Reformers or 'Protestants' were also referred to as the 'evangelicals'. The latter term came into prominence when Luther reasserted Paul's teaching on *euangelion* (from which term we derive 'evangel', 'evangelicalism') as the indispensable message of salvation (Romans 1:16; Galatians 1:8). The heart-rending cry of Paul sums up this passion for souls: 'Woe is me, if I do not preach the gospel' (1 Corinthians 9:16). Evangelism and mission have always been essential to evangelicalism.

Second, in the sixteenth century it was believed that the church had slipped away from the genuine gospel. The Reformation became a mighty revolution to make the fundamentals of the faith the standard of orthodoxy. *Sola Scriptura, sola gratia, sola fide, solo Christo, soli Deo gloria.* To be an evangelical means to hold to the fundamentals of the faith. As John Stott has pointed out, 'the evangelical faith is not some eccentric deviation from historic Christianity. On the contrary, in our conviction, it is Christianity in its purest and most primitive form'. In the words of Lancelot Andrewes (1555–1626), 'Our business is renovation – not innovation.' Dr David Howard has said that the Reformation 'in time produced the evangelical movement'.

Third, following the liberal-fundamentalist controversy of the early twentieth century which split Protestantism, there followed another within fundamentalism itself. The fundamentalists' doctrine of separation and their great reversal on social concern led to the fundamentalist-evangelical controversy. Many fundamentalists did not subscribe to militant separatism and indifference to social issues. These non-conforming fundamentalists, such as Carl Henry and Harold Ockenga, called themselves and became known as the 'New Evangelicals' or simply the 'evangelicals'. Evangelicalism became a distinct movement in Protestantism and, to borrow a phrase, the dialectical synthesis of the commitment of liberals to social action and the passion of fundamentalists for evangelism. Evangelism, as epitomized by Billy Graham, remains as its central activity, while at the same time allowing room for radical social applications as demonstrated by the works of organizations like World Relief and Tear Fund. historically, however, the evangelicals simply recovered what they had abdicated for a while in social involvement. Evangelical social concern pre-dated that of liberalism. A holistic faith and life had always been normative for them.

Fourth is the centrality of the local church in Christian life and witness. To WEF, ecclesiology is essential. We not only affirm the oneness of the Body, we believe in its centrality in God's redemptive agenda for our world. Christ died for the church (Ephesians 2:1–10) and lives as its Head (Ephesians 1:22). Christ continues to build his church (Matthew 16:18) unto perfection (Colossians 1:24). One day soon, Christ the groom will meet his bride the church, for her completion and perfection (Ephesians 5:27; Revelation 7:9–10). Patrick Johnstone says it well: 'The whole of

God's plan of redemption centres round the Church of his beloved Son.' The church is not only central to reaching the world for Jesus Christ, it is also the one church of Jesus Christ. Its division is a sinful deviation from its oneness in Christ. Evangelical division, then, is logically and theologically absurd. If, in union with Christ, Christians are spiritually one, then why the division? We have failed to live up to our covenant as members of God's community of grace. This fact of evangelical disunity is the greatest scandal in the church of our Lord Jesus and a stumbling block to a watching world. For one thing, the enormity of the task is so great that no one denomination or organization is big enough to get the job done. For another, the Great Commission was given not to any one denomination or organization but to the whole church. It is interdenominational and multi-ethnic. We recognize diversity since the Body of Christ has many integral parts. For this reason, every National Evangelical Fellowship must work towards a 'critical mass' in order to represent the widest cross-section, if not all, of the evangelicals in that country. The church must provide a model of community as an antidote to the tribalization that is resulting in genocide, even among professing Christians, in Rwanda and Manipur. The urgent cry is 'Evangelicals of the world, unite!'

In short, an evangelical is defined not by his membership of an organization or church but by his basic belief in and stand for the truth and the gospel, the church and justice. Understandably, WEF's purposes and activities need to be clearly anchored in its past, consistent with its nature, and always committed to reaching the world for Jesus Christ. The commissions formed in 1951 were reflective of this holistic ministry.

The purposes of WEF

Even though the plans for a World Evangelical Alliance were aborted in 1846, the conference formulated a statement of faith that was adopted, word for word, by the international conference in 1951 which formed WEF. In Woudschoten the purposes were further clarified, using Paul's letter to the Philippians:

1 The furtherance of the gospel (1:12)
2 The defence and confirmation of the gospel (1:7)
3 Fellowship in the gospel (1:5)

These purposes, in turn, are expressed in WEF's mission statement:

> To establish and strengthen regional and national evangelical fellowships to empower and mobilize churches and Christian organizations to disciple the nations for Jesus Christ.

WEF's *vision* is clear: the world discipled for Jesus Christ. The *mission* is specific: the total mobilization of churches and Christian organizations in every nation to disciple the nations for Christ. The *strategy* is unique: the establishment of viable, visible and vital national evangelical fellowships. The world for Jesus, country by country! The *standard* is comprehensive: a world where there is a vital Christian witness in every society, justice for all, diminishing poverty among the people and the sharing of resources to meet human needs. Stated another way, a church is planted in every village, a Bible is made available to every family, the gospel is heard by every person.

From its historical onset WEF has been more than just a fellowship, though it is one. It was designed to be proactive, the whole church acting out the gospel to the world in word and works. It is spiritual unity in action. Called by God, men and women give their best to WEF. And as we move ahead, this commitment to a vision will, eventually, enable WEF to remove any ambiguity about its purpose, to develop programmes to achieve its purpose, to release itself from economic constraints and to be free effectively to fulfil its calling.

Our entrepreneurial and consumerist culture makes us individualistic and therefore prone to inertia with regard to any movement towards unity. The growth of denominations and super-churches have generally fostered more autonomous operations. Fear of the 'one church' or 'one government' grips many, unless, of course, one is that one 'church' or 'government'! It is worth noting that whenever the churches are 'underground' or under severe persecution, they tend to unite and co-operate. Where there is religious freedom Christians become more denominational or individualistic, thereby dividing the Body. Whenever I ask our evangelical leaders why the churches and evangelicals are divided in their country, the answers would include lack of a national vision, absence of a national crisis and denominationalism.

Facing the future

A leading German theologian, Wolfhart Pannenberg, was cited by Alister McGrath, a respected evangelical scholar, as having predicted that the next century will have room for only three major Christian groups – Roman Catholicism, Eastern Orthodoxy and evangelicalism. Rev Kovisto, in his book *One Lord, One Faith*, observes, 'Perhaps the most consistent effort toward international co-operation among those of evangelical faith has been the World Evangelical Fellowship.' These are bold claims. But if this is right, and the future of Protestantism lies with evangelicalism, then evangelicals will have to accept increasing responsibility to reach the world for Jesus Christ.

For this reason WEF exists to unite evangelicals to fulfil this vision of discipling the nations for Christ. This requires a co-operative effort on the part of the whole Body of Jesus. Our Lord reminds us that the world will believe that Christ is the sent One if all believers are one. Such a fellowship must be multi-level, multi-ethnic, multi-lingual. One expression is the National Evangelical Fellowship or Alliance (NEF).

Imagine a situation where, in every nation in the world, there is a viable, visible and vital NEF – a national evangelical structure that represents the 'critical mass' of evangelicals. Such a structure would be responsive to the crucial needs that confront both the churches and society. It would relate the unchanging Word of God to the changing world of people. It would stand in solidarity with all evangelicals in the world to defend the content of and right to proclaim the gospel. Imagine a condition where there is, in every nation, a national strategy to plant a church in every village, a national association for cross-cultural missions, an effective arm to do relief and development, a proactive public advocacy network promoting justice for all, a strong leadership training programme for leaders, and where the whole church – men, women, youth – are involved in biblical witness. WEF is dedicated to the task of bringing this into existence. Presently, there are 110 such NEFs with 127 more to go! The vision is to disciple the nations one country at a time. If I may be so bold, I believe that WEF is the structure of the future. Many others share this dream which is well worth living for. Gilbert Kirby, at one time concurrent international secretary of WEF and general secretary of the EA, pledged himself to 'give all of [his] strength, under God, to promoting the interests of WEF'.

Chapter 7

THE CHURCH 'IN' THE WORLD

Ken Gnanakan

The church has been challenged right through its history to be a body that is relevant to the world within which it is seeking to be a witness. Jesus exhorted his disciples to let their light shine before men (Matthew 5:16); Paul described believers as those that 'shine like stars in the universe' (Philippians 2:15); while Peter, in a different vein, encouraged submission to 'every authority instituted among men' (1 Peter 2:13). The question today is, how far has the church been faithful to these commands? Is it related and relevant to the world within which it is called to witness? There is an urgent need for us to become God's people in God's world.

Sadly, we find ourselves distanced from the world and even eager to draw upon scripture to justify an other-worldliness that has weakened our witness. Jesus told his disciples to be a body 'in the world' yet not 'of the world'. The distinction is clear. While we certainly must stay away from a total identification with the godless or anti-God thinking of this world, we are still very much a body that has an identity within the world. A super-ficial glance at the history of the evangelical movement reveals various ways in which separationist attitudes have been espoused and, as a result, the church has found itself an irrelevant group of people more concerned with their own salvation than with the need to proclaim the message to others.

Just a brief look at history shows that our problems go right back to the earliest days of the church. Various heresies had to be dealt with in relation to the attitudes of the church, and the disciples attempted to correct one-sided emphases that were misleading younger believers. The impact of Gnosticism, definitely the single largest influence advocating an emphasis on the other-worldly attitudes, was immense. Matter was seen as totally corrupt, hence the farther one remained from it the better. Early Christian writings seem to carry many such teachings. Books like *The Acts of Thomas, The Acts of Paul* and *The Banquet of the Ten Virgins* clearly showed the preference for some in the early church for other-worldliness, separation from possessions and celibacy.

Although other factors were involved in the rise of monasticism, there was a similar emphasis on separation from the world. A life of poverty and isolation was seen as the virtuous alternative to life in the world and an imperative for spirituality. While one cannot fault the desires of such saints to live sacrificial lives, the arrogance shown by some of them to everything outside of their little world is questionable. The church must be in touch with the world outside, or else it is not what its Lord wants it to be.

The intent of this essay is missiological, and that is why we pursue the theme of the church in the world in order for it to be a more effective witness to the world. To clarify, I am not advocating that we lean heavily on our non-Christian context for such relevance. What we need to do is to get back to firm biblical roots in order to recover our lost touch with the world.

The church comes of age

Messages have come to us from different parts of the world, and traditional attitudes have been challenged. A fresh approach is being demanded of us, but we have not responded as positively as we should, or in the way that Jesus Christ requires of us. Evangelicals are generally on the defensive! What is needed is a far bolder approach to our mission within the world in which God has placed us.

When Dietrich Bonhoeffer wrote about the end of the 'religious' era he was writing with a deep concern for the church to be aware of its context. What others spoke about as 'secularization' he was identifying as 'adulthood' or 'coming of age'. He was concerned that our nineteen hundred years of Christian preaching rested on a religious world-view. He saw that the time was coming when this would be outdated. He was concerned with the consequences of such development for the church and Christian faith. He therefore pleaded for a Christianity more appropriate to a 'world come of age'.

Bonhoeffer opposed any division of life into 'two spheres'. Life should not be divided up between Christian and non-Christian worlds, whether on the basis of the medieval differentiation between nature and grace, the Lutheran doctrine of the two kingdoms, or the common distinction between the sacred and the secular. The urgency of Bonhoeffer's message derived from the fact that he was convinced that the world's 'adulthood' or its 'coming of age' had arrived. Bonhoeffer's views have some far-reaching implications for the church and its witness. We have to wrestle with the question of our identity within the world. We may not agree with Bonhoeffer's premises and conclusions, but they are enough to make us think about the nature and mission of the people of God. We need to take an honest look at ourselves and listen carefully to what the world is saying. Mere attempts to reassert 'other-worldly' theologies will only make us more ineffective in our mission within the world today.

The 'post-Christian' era in which we live calls for a far more positive evaluation of the world around. We have grown used to accepting the dichotomy of the sacred and secular, the Christian and non-Christian, and have sought to understand the world in terms of such distinctions. A more holistic view is needed. The 'missionary era' forcefully propagated these distinctions, for instance by setting up Christian villages for its converts. Sadly, such attitudes still prevail both in life and doctrine in the so-called 'mission field' so that the church's witness is stifled. In some cases, there is little concern for witness and these so-called 'Christian' areas may prove to be a breeding ground for crime. As long as the church is located within the world it will need to give serious consideration to its identity.

Belonging to the world

Some may have reservations about speaking in terms of a Christianity that could accommodate itself to the world. But the biblical use of the term 'world' is not always negative. We have often used the term 'worldliness' to mean anything contrary to Jesus Christ's desires. This view needs to be corrected. We need to emphasize the concrete concern of God for his world. In this sense, there is a kind of 'worldliness' that we need to recover where the church in mission recognizes its 'belongingness' in the world, thereby demonstrating the reality of the incarnational mission of God to the world.

Some of us may shudder to think that we are really part of this world and that there are things that we share in common with others in it. This arises from our common creation in the image of God. God's concern for all to be saved is because of this commonality of his created beings. So our mission to the world must first and foremost be grounded in this fact. The criticism of many non-Christians is that we have approached them with a superior, alien attitude, sometimes, regrettably, identified as the 'missionary mentality'. In contrast, the biblical model is one of identification and incarnation: 'He came to that which was his own . . . The Word became flesh' (John 1: 11,14).

We need to take a fresh look at what Jesus said to his disciples. Jesus certainly said that his disciples, like himself, were not 'of the world' (John 17:16). So there is a sense in which we do not belong to the world. This is not to say that we live in some illusory 'world' remote from the 'real world'. Rather, Jesus is referring to following the attitudes of this world, and conforming to its standards, which undoubtedly are antagonistic to God's demands. Hence John's advice: 'Do not love the world or anything in the world' (1 John 2:15). He is concerned with the love and attachment to things of this world that are contrary to the demands of God on our lives.

On the other hand, the Bible does not imply a totally negative attitude to the world. Jesus immediately counteracts such a misunderstanding by stating: 'As you [the Father] sent me into the world, I have sent them into the world' (John 17:18). John's Gospel contains a graphic representation of Jesus' coming into the world, the incarnational reality, 'the Word become flesh'. Jesus' life was not some phantom-like existence without reference to the context into which he came. Being fully human, he identified with the world, enjoying his sojourn in human history. Even more, he submitted himself to all the world's demands, as long as they did not conflict with God's demands, and experienced the pressures we face.

Social involvement

The kind of attitude to the world handed down to us has made us wrongly shun any social involvement. This kind of attitude despises any activity of the church apart from preaching the gospel. Socio-political activities have been seen as 'liberal'. But if Jesus' incarnation is the model for us, 'Christlikeness' must be demonstrated not only in individual spirituality but also in a social context. This gives more tangible demonstration of our Christlike concern for the world. Jesus did not hesitate to get involved in more than merely preaching to his hearers. His was a very practical demonstration of divine love. One must not give the impression that the church has never been concerned for such witness. Writing from within India, I am constantly reminded of the positive contributions of Christian missionaries. Some of the most influential educational and medical institutions in India owe their existence to the zeal and commitment of Christians. It is surprising that, despite this, we shy away from any thought of the social, political or ecological activity that is urgently required today. However small our contribution, it could make a significant impact to the glory of God and the good of others.

Much has been written about the church's social involvement over the past two decades, and little more needs to be said. What is required is to see the need for a social involvement because of our belonging to the world. As part of the community of people created in God's image, we need to respond in Christlike compassion to the needs around us. It is heartening that many evangelical Christians have been moved positively into socio-economic and political activities and are experiencing a renewed sense of Christ's presence and power through their involvement.

Environmental concern

While we appear to be getting to grips with the importance of our societal involvement, there are now cries for the church to become aware of its environmental responsibility. The church has been blamed for the ecological devastation we have witnessed over the past few decades. There have been scathing attacks on the biblical doctrine of creation as necessarily exploitive, thus contributing to the ecological disaster. Nevertheless, many Christians have refused to get involved, offering arguments based on a dispensational theology or naive thinking that involvement would diminish zeal for preaching the gospel. The need to continue preaching is universally accepted. But to ignore environmental concerns is tantamount to handing over God's world to those who neither know him nor acknowledge him as Creator of the environment that is being desecrated.

A renewed interest in a 'creation theology' is required, a theology witnessed to in both Testaments. Although there is not as much reference to creation in the New Testament (NT) as there is in the Old (OT), we are not to conclude that it is an unimportant doctrine for the Christian. Some may argue that, because of 'sin', concern for the present creation is superseded by anticipation of the new heaven and new earth. But scanty reference to the doctrine of creation in the NT may be explained by the fact that the early church was predominately Jewish, for whom such a fundamental fact was accepted without question. As Paul declares, 'everything God created is good' (1 Timothy 4:4).

The NT writers were more concerned with the spelling out of the ministry of redemption and reconciliation that was anticipated in the OT. Their Creator-God was now made available in the Redeemer-Christ. Salvation is no mere redeeming of the soul, or even of a few individuals, but is something with implications for the whole of God's creation. Christ's all-inclusive reconciling ministry brings everything under God's control and thus to its original purpose: 'God was pleased to have all his fullness dwell in him [Jesus Christ], and through him to reconcile to himself all things, whether things on earth or things in heaven, by making peace through his blood, shed on the cross' (Colossians 1:19–20).

We have yet to recognize the full significance of such passages which ascribe so much more to Jesus Christ's Lordship than we have been willing to do. If God has plans for the whole of creation, his people must be involved fully in God's world. To say that we should distance ourselves from social, political or environmental activities is the easiest way to deny Jesus the total scope of his Lordship. A sound understanding of the church's relationship to creation will lead to a more effective mission of his people to the whole world.

Looking for OT images and building our theology from there could be helpful. But since some question an overemphasis on the OT for the church today, the alternative is to build such a theology in terms of Jesus Christ and his relationship to creation. In fact, any biblical theology of ecology for the church today will have to be Christological. If Jesus Christ is the Lord of history and the one through whom all things are to be made new and thereby actualized in the new heaven and the new earth, he must undoubtedly have a crucial part to play in creation even now. It is by him that all things 'hold together' (Colossians 1:17), and it is through him that 'all things in heaven and on earth' will be united (Ephesians 1:9–10). He is the one who 'upholds the universe' (Hebrews 1:3).

Such a Christological foundation to creation is essential, since this helps us recognize our part in the mission of Jesus Christ. Our environmental involvement opens up opportunities to point the world to its true Lord and Creator. Even more, if we decide to opt out, we could be abandoning the world more and more to satanic influences. The way for the world to recognize its Redeemer is for it to accept first its Creator. A full biblical theology starting from creation and culminating in Jesus Christ needs to be developed. Such a theology should urge us into environmental action with a concern to make known his Lordship.

There have been criticisms that most of our theology, with its Augustinian roots, leans too heavily on sin, the Fall and redemption rather than on creation. Subsequent 'creation theologies' have developed which are questionable. But this should not lead us to abandon any emphasis on creation. If such a theology is well-founded on Christological concerns, we will have the kind of theology that would powerfully demonstrate our belonging to the world. We must note that in the NT the strong Christological emphasis underlies the theme of creation. The whole sweep of history is under the sovereign purpose of God as revealed in Jesus Christ. Our witness within the world is primarily a demonstration of this fact.

A deeper understanding of Jesus' relationship to the world he created would help us to recapture a clearer understanding of our relationship to this same world. Then our mission to this world would be more concrete. Theologies that negate the need for a positive involvement are far from biblical. The church must get involved in making known this Lord to a world that has been abandoned to the people who do not believe in him or who are even controlled by Satan who opposes Christ's Lordship. We proclaim redemption through Jesus Christ, a redemption for which all creation is 'groaning' (Romans 8:22).

Conclusion

In conclusion, let us make two further comments on Jesus' prayer in John 17 in order to clarify any misunderstanding. Praying this prayer just prior to his going away from the world, Jesus states that his disciples are 'still in the world' (John 17:11). The disciples would love to have accompanied their master, but Jesus locates them in the world. This tension needs to be worked out. On the one hand, we do not belong to the world: we are to conform to Jesus' standards. Yet, on the other hand, we are 'in the world', working out our witness in practical terms. Our social or environmental involvement, in fact our 'worldliness', is therefore to be defined in terms of living out Jesus' standards within a world where, in one sense, we exist as strangers.

Jesus says that he has 'sent' us into the world. There is a sense in which we do not belong; we are only sent. We are ambassadors, messengers, representatives or agents, sent on behalf of the Lord Jesus Christ. This is the essence of our position as witnesses. We live in God's world, grateful for the fact that he has placed us within our earthly context. There is much to discourage us as we observe current trends, but there is even more to encourage us. We know our Lord is Lord of this world, and we will seek to live out our lives to demonstrate this Lordship.

The question will continue to be asked, how can we communicate the gospel of the kingdom to a world with people who are growing more and more alien to God's purposes? For the answer we look at Jesus himself, recognizing the fact that he actualized the kingdom in his life and ministry. Speaking with the authority of God, he reminded his hearers, 'The kingdom is near you'. If we realize this means nothing less than the fact that Jesus himself is the kingdom, then his nearness signifies the nearness of the kingdom. Hence the mission of the kingdom is the mission of Jesus himself. When the church faithfully seeks to follow its Lord closely in this kingdom-mission, its mission to the world becomes more effective. The message is truly actualized and the church is true to its call. This is the concrete way in which the church becomes relevant to the world.

We need to actualize the gospel within the world in which we live through concrete expressions of God's kingdom. The actualization of the gospel is a true expression of the relevance of the kingdom message inside and outside the church. This needs to be seen in the way in which Christians are socially, politically and environmentally relevant to their world. Only when the message is actualized is the church able effectively to communicate the good news to the world. The church needs to be surrendered to Jesus Christ within the world, living as a church available for God to express his kingdom concern.

We offer our world what we have. When the people of God are charged with the power of Jesus Christ, their words and their deeds demonstrate the kingdom. True witness, therefore, is not something external to the believers of Jesus Christ, for they are living out what they have already experienced and doing so within a context to which they belong. Relevance to the world is therefore no longer a question. It is a natural response to the demands laid on us by Jesus Christ as we seek to live in obedience to him in the world where we have been placed as his ambassadors.

The message made flesh in the life of the church gives it the solid platform from which to witness to the gospel of the kingdom. This platform is within the world and not somewhere in the other-world. The church needs to recognize its own identity as well as its belonging within the world, in order to discover the full potential of the gospel. Such an actualization helps to restore to the church its true missionary character and thereby to demonstrate its relevance in the world today.

Part 2
HERE WE STAND

Chapter 8

THE BIBLICAL GOSPEL

Donald A Carson

The question of what the biblical gospel is must be especially important to 'evangelicals', whose very label includes the word 'evangel', the English transliteration of the Greek word for 'gospel' (*euangelion*). Historically, evangelicals have been concerned to preserve and promulgate the gospel. But precisely what is this gospel? All sides recognize that it is 'good news' in some sense. But what is the content of this good news?

Although it is worth saying something about the 'gospel' words in the NT, the issue cannot be answered by mere word studies. Some NT books, eg John's Gospel, never use the word 'gospel', even though from a thematic perspective they obviously have as much 'good news' to tell as books that abound in the 'gospel' word-group. In the pages that follow, therefore, after some observations on the relevant words, I outline some of the broader considerations that must be taken on board if we are to grasp what the biblical gospel is. And, finally, I outline the primacy of the gospel in all Christian thought and mission over against competitors and would-be usurpers.

Gospel words

In non-biblical sources before the NT period, *euangelion* customarily referred to the reward given a messenger who brought good news – of military victory, perhaps, or of escape from danger. By an obvious transfer, it came to refer to the good news itself. Modern discussions of 'gospel' commonly cite the enthronement inscription, dated 9 BC, from Priene in Asia Minor. In this inscription the birthday of the emperor Augustus is hailed as 'the beginning of the joyful news (*euangelia*) for the world'. The noun occurs once in the LXX with the meaning 'reward' (2 Samuel 4:10), and five times referring to military 'good news' (2 Samuel 18:20, 22,25,27; 2 Kings 7:9).[1] On the other hand, the cognate verb, *euangelizomai* ('I announce or proclaim good news', sometimes parallel to *kēryssō*, 'I preach', 'I proclaim') is found more frequently. But clearly it is the NT that repeatedly invests *euangelion* with the meaning 'good news', just as it is the NT that must establish what that good news is.

The use of 'gospel' to refer to a particular kind of book, as in the phrase 'the Four Gospels', would not have been understood in the apostolic period nor for another century. In the NT period Christians spoke of only one gospel. The first four books of the NT, nowadays called 'gospels', were thought of as records of or witnesses to that one gospel which Paul calls 'the gospel of God . . . regarding his Son' (Romans 1:1,3). Thus the first book in our NT canon was thought of as '*the* gospel *according to* Matthew', the second '*the* gospel *according to* Mark', and so on. So far as the evidence goes, the first source to refer to the books themselves as 'gospels' is Justin Martyr (mid-second century) who writes that the 'memoirs of the apostles' were called 'gospels' (note the plural form) and were read out to the congregation (*Apology* i.66).

The distribution of both the noun *euangelion* and the verb *euangelizomai* in the NT is extraordinarily uneven. Mark deploys the noun 8 times, and not the verb; at 1:14, it is 'the gospel of God'. Matthew uses the verb once (11:5), and adds 'of the kingdom' to 'gospel' (4:23; 9:35); Luke-Acts attests the noun only in Acts 15:7 and 20:24, but uses the verb 25 times. The gospel and letters of John use neither. Paul is the NT author most given to 'gospel' words: in the 13 canonical epistles, the noun is found 60 times and the verb 21 times. The scattering of occurrences in the rest of the NT books I shall mention below.

The content of the gospel is briefly given in Mark 1:15: 'The time has come. The kingdom of God is near.' So also is the conclusion to be drawn: 'Repent and believe the gospel.' Thus the gospel is not, in the first instance, the call to repentance and faith; rather, the gospel is the joyous news that grounds the call to repentance and faith. This good news is that the long-awaited kingdom, the kingdom of God, is dawning.

Such a formulation, had we space, would bring us into extended reflection on the nature of the kingdom in the NT. Although 'kingdom' can refer to the unlimited sovereignty of God, or to the realm of a particular king, in the NT the word more commonly refers to that invasive aspect of God's sovereignty under which there is eternal life. Everyone is under the kingdom in the first sense, ie under God's sovereignty, whether they like it or not; only those who have passed from the kingdom of darkness into the kingdom of God's dear Son (Colossians 1:13), those who have been born from above (John 3:3,5), are under or in the kingdom in the dominant NT sense.[2]

This kingdom has two peculiar features to it. First, the king of this kingdom is commonly said to be God (not least in the common expression 'the kingdom of God') but can also be said to be Christ: 'My kingdom is not of this world,' Jesus said (John 18:36). The point is that all of God's sovereignty is mediated through the resurrected and exalted Jesus (1 Corinthians 15). Before the Sanhedrin, Jesus himself insisted, in the terms of the vision of Daniel chapter 7, that as the Son of Man he would be seen sitting at the right hand of the Mighty One and coming on the clouds of heaven (Matthew 26:64; Mark 14:62; Luke 22:69). Once resurrected, he insists that all authority in heaven and on earth is his (Matthew

28:18–20). It is vital to recognize that these themes are repeatedly under-scored in the NT even when 'kingdom' language is not used. For example, in the vision of Revelation chapters 4–5, God is disclosed as utterly tran-scendent, the one who receives ceaseless worship from the highest order of angels, the one whose throne is above all other thrones. Nevertheless, Jesus Christ, disclosed as the Lion of Judah, the Lamb of God, the Root of David, *emerges from the throne* to take the book in God's right hand and open the seals. Thereafter there is a recurring designation of Deity: 'the One who sits on the throne and the Lamb'. In short, this kingdom is God's, and it is no less Christ's. There is no sense of anomaly. The glory of the Lamb's triumph has roots in OT history, OT scripture, even as it is grounded in the person and work of the historical Jesus, and anticipates the unshielded radiance of the new heaven and the new earth.

The second peculiar feature to this kingdom is that King Jesus 'reigns from the cross', as early patristic writers put it. John subtly develops this theme in his passion narrative (John chapters 18–19). Pilate cannot quite grasp what kind of king Jesus is (18:36–37). Is he the kind of king who threatens Caesar (chapter 19)? If he is the king of the Jews, why do these manipulated crowds of Jews reject him as king? 'Shall I crucify your king?' Pilate asks them (19:15). And, of course, he does crucify him, for King Jesus establishes the peculiar nature of his kingdom by dying on behalf of his rebellious people. Pilate may not grasp the theology, but he likes the irony and posts a notice above the cross: 'Jesus of Nazareth, the King of the Jews' (19:19).

If the gospel is the gospel of the kingdom, it is no less, as we have seen, the gospel of God regarding his Son (Romans chapter 1). There is no conflict between these two designations, and both drive us to focus on Jesus Christ, the Son of God, the King, whose utterly extraordinary mis-sion was to die the odious death of an accursed wretch, in fulfilment of OT patterns and pictures and prophecies of sacrifice. The good news that focuses on Jesus and his cross-work was anticipated, according to Paul, two millennia earlier in the promises given to Abraham (Galatians 3:8), and repeatedly promised in the scriptures (Romans 1:2).

The message that Paul preached was 'Jesus Christ and him crucified' (1 Corinthians 1:18–2:5). 'Remember Jesus Christ, raised from the dead, descended from David. This is my gospel' (2 Timothy 2:8). The gospel is this 'word of truth' (Ephesians 1:13). However hidden this gospel might be to unbelievers (2 Corinthians 4:3,4) and to those who try to domesti-cate it by demands for supernatural proofs and oratorical demonstrations (1 Corinthians 1:21–23), Paul knew that the secret of this gospel's power lay in the message of the cross, mediated by the Spirit. His aim was to preach in such a way that people were not swayed by his eloquence and rhetoric; he wanted to preach 'with a demonstration of the Spirit's power' so that his hearers' faith 'might not rest on men's wisdom, but on God's power' (2:4–5). Paul knew that God himself had chosen the Thessalonian converts because his gospel came to them not simply with words but also with power, with the Holy Spirit and with deep conviction (1 Thessalonians 1:5). So much is power an accompaniment of this gospel that Paul can insist the gospel *is* 'the power of God for the salvation of everyone who believes' (Romans 1:16). This gospel discloses a righteousness from God that is appropriated by faith (1:17), a righteousness inextricably tied to Christ's sacrifice, by which God demonstrated his justice while justifying the ungodly (3:21–26).

Paul's grasp of the gospel, with all of its intricate connections with antecedent revelation and all of its comprehensive framework, came to him by revelation (Galatians 1:11–12). Paul knew himself to be entrusted with the gospel (1 Thessalonians 2:4; 1 Timothy 1:11, 'the glorious gospel of the blessed God, which he entrusted to me'). The message he preached was not merely the word of human beings but the word of God (1 Thessalonians 2:13). In Paul's proclamation of the gospel, God himself was making his appeal through the apostle (2 Corinthians 5:20). This does not mean that Paul was a disengaged mannequin: far from it, for he writes to some of his converts, 'We loved you so much that we were delighted to share with you not only the gospel of God but our lives as well, because you had become so dear to us' (1 Thessalonians 2:8). He feels under divine compulsion to proclaim this gospel (1 Corinthians 9:16), and therefore asks fellow believers for prayer that he may discharge this obligation with boldness (Ephesians 6:19), whatever the opposition (1 Thessalonians 2:2) and suffering which he wants younger preachers to experience: 'But join with me in suffering for the gospel, by the power of God, who has saved us and called us to a holy life – not because of anything we have done but because of his own purpose and grace' (2 Timothy 1:8–9).

Paul sees his own apostleship peculiarly bound up with the declaration of this gospel, especially to the Gentiles. He had been chosen to herald this good news, this 'mystery' of God's plan for Jews and Gentiles alike (Ephesians 3:2–7; Colossians 1:24–29). Not surprisingly, he could think of it in personal terms: 'my gospel' (Romans 2:16; 16:25), 'our gospel' (2 Corinthians 4:3). Yet this was not some simple alignment between message and ego, as if whatever Paul might conceivably have said could properly be called good news simply because Paul said it. On the contrary, the gospel is objectively true, non-negotiable, exclusive: for Paul, a 'different gospel' is no gospel at all (Galatians 1:6–7). Therefore, if Paul himself, or even an angel of heaven, should tamper with this gospel or announce something other than the eternal gospel, 'let him be anathema' (1:8–9). He could happily tolerate other preachers with doubtful motives, provided their content was the veritable gospel (Philippians 1:12–18). On the other hand, preachers whose aim was to make money by 'peddling' the word of God he despised (2 Corinthians 2:17); while preachers whose content was 'a different gospel' or 'a Jesus other than the Jesus we preached', instead of 'the gospel of God' (2 Corinthians 11:4,7), he exposed as 'false apostles' (11:13; *cf* 1 Timothy 4; 2 Timothy 2:17).

Elsewhere in the NT, the 'gospel' word-group is rather rare. The verb is used twice in Hebrews (4:2,6), in a fashion reminiscent of Galatians 3:8: the 'good news' that God would act to redeem his people was already announced millennia earlier. 1 Peter 1:12 insists this was only an anticipatory announcement; with the coming of Christ the salvation announced by the prophets (1:10) was actually coming: 'It was revealed to them that they were not serving themselves but you, when they spoke of the things that have *now* been told you by those *who have preached the gospel* to you by the Holy Spirit sent from heaven' (my italics).

Two passages are slightly anomalous.

(a) In 1 Peter 4:6 the apostle provides a tantalizing mention of the gospel being preached to the dead, quite possibly meaning (as the NIV Bible has it) 'to those who are now dead' (but who were alive when they heard it).

(b) One or two have understood 'the eternal gospel' in Revelation 14:6 to refer to an announcement of judgement on the final day;[3] many more detect a kind of general disclosure of benevolence in nature or in other religions. It is far more likely that *euangelion* is by this time such a standard term that its content is fixed: we are to understand that in Revelation chapter 14 it is the gospel itself, as outlined above, that is proclaimed 'to every nation, tribe, language and people'.[4]

Broader considerations

Although this survey has not cited every passage in which the 'gospel' word-group appears, the main lines of its usage are pretty clear. One could add various refinements. For instance, one might ponder what distinctive emphases are underlined by the peculiar choices made by the individual evangelists. Luke's marked preference for the verb and his entire neglect of the noun (save two occurrences in Acts) might reasonably suggest that he emphasizes 'preaching the gospel' rather more than 'gospel' – in much the same way that John repeatedly deploys the verb 'to believe' but avoids the noun 'faith'. But such a conclusion is somewhat offset by the fact that Mark, who uses only the noun and not the verb, is nevertheless certainly interested in the preaching or heraldic ministry of Jesus (proportionately he uses the verb *kēryssō*, 'I preach', much more than either Matthew or Luke). And certainly the *content* of what Jesus preaches in the gospel according to Mark is nothing other than what all the synoptic evangelists would call the gospel, however many different words they use to refer to it or to describe the activity of heralding it. For similar reasons I am unpersuaded by other proposals that some have advanced to explain the unusual distribution of noun and verb among the synoptics.[5]

More important for our purposes is the fact that any responsible biblical theology of 'gospel' must extend far beyond an examination of the *euangelion/euangelizomai* word-group. For reasons that are quite uncertain, the fourth gospel does not use the word-group at all, but the early church quite rightly referred to the book as 'the *gospel* according to John'.

So an integrative theological summary of what the 'good news' is would have to consider John's emphases and themes. Further, the NT writers who use the 'gospel' word-group often deploy synonyms: eg 'word' or 'word of God' or 'word of the cross'. Thus the 'word of the cross' (NIV, 'message of the cross') in 1 Corinthians 1:18 is clearly shown by the context to be nothing other than the gospel (*cf* 1:17) – and that means one would have to engage in a thorough exegesis of all the cross and atonement passages in Paul, in order to grasp what Paul understands the message of the cross to be. We have already seen that the 'gospel' word-group is linked with kingdom language and with other words for preaching. It is also sometimes parallel with *kērygma*, the content of the message preached.

By the time these and related themes had been properly explored, we would have gained a very comprehensive view of 'gospel' indeed. Shadings and nuance there may be in specific contexts, but from a comprehensive theological perspective the gospel is the good news of the coming of Jesus – who he is, his mission, above all his death and resurrection, the inauguration of the final eschatological kingdom even now, and all that this means for how we live as individuals and as the church, the eschatological people of God, in fulfilment of all the promises God made in the scriptures that led up to Jesus. In content, the gospel is virtually indistinguishable from the *kerygma*; if anything, it is even more comprehensive. But in connotation, 'gospel' insists that this is good news, joyful news, the best news any sentient being in the universe could imagine.

Thus the gospel is integrally tied to the Bible's story-line. Indeed, it is incomprehensible without understanding that story-line. God is the sovereign, transcendent and personal God who has made the universe, including us, his image-bearers. Our misery lies in our rebellion, our alienation from God, which, despite his forbearance, attracts his implacable wrath. But God, precisely because love is of the very essence of his character, takes the initiative and prepares for the coming of his own Son by raising up a people who, by covenantal stipulations, temple worship, systems of sacrifice and of priesthood, by kings and by prophets, are taught something of what God is planning and what he expects. In the fullness of time his Son comes and takes on human nature. He comes not, in the first instance, to judge but to save: he dies the death of his people, rises from the grave and, in returning to his heavenly Father, bequeaths the Holy Spirit as the down payment and guarantee of the ultimate gift he has secured for them – an eternity of bliss in the presence of God himself, in a new heaven and a new earth, the home of righteousness. The only alternative is to be shut out from the presence of this God forever, in the torments of hell.[6] What men and women must do, before it is too late, is repent and trust Christ; the alternative is to disobey the gospel (Romans 10:16; 2 Thessalonians 1:8; 1 Peter 4:17).

This story-line, and its connection with the gospel, could be fleshed out in a number of ways. But the point is simply this: the good news of salvation through Jesus Christ *makes sense in the context of this story-line and in no other*. If, instead of this world-view, this story-line,[7] some other is adopted, the good news of Jesus Christ no longer makes sense or is so badly distorted it is no longer the same thing. For instance, if one adopts a pantheistic world-view, then 'sin' takes on an entirely different configuration and there is no transcendent God to whom to be reconciled. In that case, the 'good news' cannot be the announcement of God's reconciling act in the death and resurrection of his Son, by which he bore his people's penalty. If one adopts some naturalistic world-view, something similar could be said. If one holds that history is going nowhere or in circles determined by impersonal fate, then the notion of final judgement and ultimate division between bliss and the abyss is incoherent – and so too is the good news that Christ reconciles rebels to their Maker, prepares them for glory, enabling them even now to enjoy foretastes of the kingdom still to be consummated.

It would be easy to document what happens when what may still be called 'the gospel' is detached from this story-line, including this analysis of the core human need. Contrast, for example, the definition of gospel in Erickson, an evangelical theologian, and in Ernst Troeltsch. The former writes:

> To summarize: Paul viewed the gospel as centering upon Jesus Christ and what God has done through him. The essential points of the gospel are Jesus Christ's status as the Son of God, his genuine humanity, his death for our sins, his burial, resurrection, subsequent appearances, and future coming in judgment . . . that one is justified by faith in the gracious work of Jesus Christ in his death and resurrection. . . . [It is not] merely a recital of theological truths and historical events. Rather, it relates these truths and events to the situation of every individual believer.[8]

By contrast, Troeltsch writes, 'The gospel proceeds on the tranquil and childlike conviction that the intentions of the human soul must be realized in terms of the complete lordship of God.'[9] Redemption is *'the development of the God-filled personality'*.[10] Doubtless one could, by ripping the words out of their context, understand these latter quotations in a fashion that could be squared with the historic biblical gospel. But they do not drive us in that direction and, in their context, take us elsewhere.

This is not to say that devout and knowledgeable Christians have never disagreed on the exact formulation of the gospel. So far I have tried to avoid forms of expression of the gospel from which believers desirous of remaining faithful to the Bible would want to dissent. But it would be disingenuous to restrict myself to a 'lowest-common-denominator' form of evangelical confession that fails to recognize genuine differences of opinion.

One of the most persistent differences among believers during the past three centuries, so far as the understanding of the gospel is concerned, is tied to the differences between Christians of Reformed conviction and those with Arminian or Wesleyan conviction.[11] The former will think of the gospel as the good news of God taking action to save men and women by the death and resurrection of his Son; the latter will think of the gospel as the good news of God taking action to provide the possibility of salvation for men and women by the death and resurrection of his Son. Both sides will insist that repentance and faith are necessary; both will insist that repentance is human repentance, faith is human faith. But the Reformed believer will want to add that repentance and faith are brought about by God's elective grace, mediated by the Spirit, in those who believe; while the Wesleyan believer will want to add that, although prevenient grace is necessary for an individual to repent and believe, all human beings enjoy such prevenient grace, so that the ultimate distinction between believers and unbelievers cannot be assigned to God but only to the individuals themselves.

The distinction between these two ways or articulating what the gospel is turns out to be not a small one. What appears to be a small difference in wording turns out to have substantial ramifications in practice. Moreover, candour demands that I acknowledge that my own convictions lie unequivocally with the former. Inevitably, there are assorted complications in the heritage of both of these positions. Extrapolated to various extremes, a wide array of disturbing anomalies can be introduced. But it must be said, in the strongest terms, that in their best forms these two streams of understanding have far, far more in common than is sometimes thought. Each of the two thinks the other has distorted the gospel somewhat; neither habitually insists the other side has divested itself of the gospel.

One final distinction deserves mention. For complex reasons many in the Western church came to speak of 'the simple gospel', by which they at one time meant the gospel summarized in convenient and simple form, usually for evangelistic purposes. The result is that for many today 'the gospel' or 'gospel preaching' refers not to the glorious, comprehensive good news disclosed in scripture but to a very simple (some would say simplistic) reduction of it. Some churches distinguished between 'worship services' and 'gospel services': one wonders which term, 'worship' or 'gospel', has been more seriously abused.[12] Doubtless the motives behind these developments were often excellent. But the fact remains that a variety of serious problems were thereby introduced. For many, evangelistic preaching became identified with simplistic preaching. Worse, 'the gospel' came to be associated in their minds exclusively with the initial steps of faith rather than with God's comprehensive good news that not only initiates salvation but orders all our life in this world and the next.

The primacy of the gospel

Here I want to make only two points:

First, pundits have often noted that many in the Western world have become single-issue people. The church is not immune from such influences. The result is that many Christians *assume* the gospel (often, regrettably, some form of the 'simple gospel') but are passionate about something on the relative periphery: abortion, poverty, forms of worship, cultural decay, ecology, overpopulation, pornography, family breakdown, and much more. By labelling these complex subjects 'relatively peripheral' I open myself to attack from as many quarters as there are subjects on the list. For example, some of those whose every thought is shaded green will not be convinced that the ecological problems we face are peripheral to human survival. But I remain quite unrepentant. From a biblical-theological perspective, these challenges, as serious as they are, are reflections of the still deeper problem – our odious alienation from God. If we tackle these problems without tackling what is central, we are merely playing around with symptoms. This is no excuse for Christians not to get involved in these and many other issues. But it is to insist that where we get involved in such issues, many of which are explicitly laid upon us in scripture, we do so from the centre out, ie beginning with full-orbed gospel proclamation and witness and passion, and then, while acknowledging that no one can do everything, doing our 'significant something' to address the wretched entailments of sin in our world. The good news of Jesus Christ will never allow us to be smug and other-worldly in the face of suffering and evil. But what does it profit us to save the world from smog and damn our own souls? There are lots of ways of getting rid of pornography. For instance, one does not find much smut in Saudi Arabia. But one doesn't find much of the gospel there, either.

The point is that in all our efforts to address painful and complex societal problems, we must do so from the centre, out of a profound passion for the gospel. This is for us both a credal necessity and a strategic choice. It is a credal necessity because this gospel alone prepares men and women for eternity, for meeting our Maker – and all problems are relativized in the contemplation of the cross, the final judgement, and eternity. It is a strategic choice because we are persuaded that the gospel, comprehensively preached in the power of the Spirit, will do more to transform men and women, not least their attitudes, than anything else in the world.

Boice puts it nicely:

> [T]he true *nature of the gospel* also emerges in this understanding of the death of Jesus. The gospel is not just a new possibility for achieving joy and fullness in this life, as some seem to suggest. It is not just a solution to what were previously troublesome and frustrating problems. It is rather something much deeper that has been done,

something relating to God, on the basis of which and only on the basis of which these other blessings of salvation follow. Packer says, 'The gospel does bring us solutions to these problems, but it does so by first solving . . . the deepest of all human problems, the problem of man's relation with his Maker; and unless we make it plain that the solution of these former problems depends on the settling of this latter one, we are misrepresenting the message and becoming false witnesses of God.'[13]

A second category of phenomena is in danger of displacing the primacy of the gospel. A litany of devices designed to make us more spiritual or mature or productive or emotionally whole threatens to relegate the gospel to irrelevance, or at least to the realm of the boring and the primitive. The gospel may introduce you to the church, as it were, but from that point on assorted counselling techniques and therapy sessions will change your life and make you happy and fruitful. The gospel may help you make some sort of decision for God, but 'rebirthing' techniques – in which in silent meditation you imagine Jesus catching you as you are born from your mother's womb, imagine him hugging you and holding you – will generate a wonderful cathartic experience that will make you feel whole again, especially if you have been abused in the past. The gospel may enable you to be right with God, but if you really want to pursue spirituality you must find a spiritual director, or practise asceticism, or discipline yourself with journalling, or spend two weeks in silence in a Trappist monastery.

These are not all of a piece. What they have in common, however, is the diminishing of the gospel in order to magnify the current device that is guaranteed to bring you toward wholeness. By contrast, the NT passionately insists that everything we need for life and godliness and a walk in the Spirit is secured for us in the gospel. It follows that if someone chooses to adopt some ascetic practice in order the better to focus on the Jesus of the Bible, the attention is still on Jesus. But if someone so ties asceticism to altered moods or to experiences of 'spirituality' that the gospel itself is virtually ignored or is implicitly dismissed as a sort of initial stage now to be improved by ascetic practice, the name of the game is idolatry. Again, if someone has experienced cathartic relief and emotional integration after an imaginative 'rebirthing' session, I am glad that the emotional integration has taken place. But we must insist that a better emotional integration could have been achieved by meditating on, say, the passion narratives, or on Ephesians 3:14–21. For then the emotional catharsis would have been tied to what God himself insists is the clearest and most complete demonstration of his love for us in Christ Jesus. In other words, the emotional integration would have been tied to the gospel instead of to something as ephemeral and diverting as manipulated imagination.

This is a time for Christians to return to the basics, the comprehensive basics, and quietly reaffirm with Paul, 'I am not ashamed of the gospel, because it is the power of God for the salvation of everyone who believes: first for the Jew, then for the Gentile. For in the gospel a righteousness from God is revealed, a righteousness that is by faith from first to last, just as it is written: "The righteous will live by faith" ' (Romans 1:16–17).

Endnotes

1   Why a substantial number of writers say that the noun is not found in the LXX, or found only once, is quite unclear.

2   This sort of understanding of the 'kingdom' in the NT is not necessarily at loggerheads with more recent discussion that affirms the word is a 'tensive symbol' – ie 'the kingdom of God' does not refer to a single entity, but evokes a complex range of notions rooted in the understanding that God is king. See N Perrin, *Jesus and the Language of the Kingdom* (Philadelphia, 1976), pp 29–34; and especially R T France, 'The church and the kingdom of God: some hermeneutical issues' in *Biblical Interpretation and the Church: Text and Context*, D A Carson (ed) (Exeter, 1984), pp 30–44.

3   Eg J Jeremias, *Jesus' Promise to the Nations* (London, 1958), p 69.

4   In this case, of course, the burden of 14:7 is not to provide the content of the gospel, but an eschatological threat if it is ignored. See G Friedrich, '*euangelion*', *TDNT II*, p 735; G B Caird, *The Revelation of St John the Divine* (New York, 1966), p 182.

5   For a typical list of the often-cited redaction-critical distinctions that may be found, see R P Martin, 'Gospel', *ISBE II*, p 531.

6   I am well aware that a small but growing number of evangelicals have recently subscribed to annihilationism. In my view the evidence is stoutly against them. I have dealt with this difficult subject at greater length in chapter 13 of *The Gagging of God: Christianity Confronts Pluralism* (Grand Rapids, forthcoming). The language I have used above is simpler and less shocking than Revelation 14:10–11.

7   What experts in epistemology would nowadays call a meta-narrative.

8   M J Erickson, *Christian Theology* (Grand Rapids, 1983–85), p 1063.

9   E Troeltsch, *The Christian Faith* (Philadelphia, 1991 [orig. 1925]), p 131.

10 Troeltsch, *The Christian Faith*, p 304 (emphasis his).

11 Perhaps I should add that the issues at stake surface again and again in the history of the church. There are significant differences in the definition of the issues and in the surrounding politics, but one can easily detect similar polarities of opinion between Augustine and Pelagius, or between the Jansenists and the Molinists in pre-revolutionary France.

12 On the nature of worship, the best recent theological treatment is now that of D Peterson, *Engaging with God* (Leicester, 1992).

13 J M Boice, *Foundations of the Christian Faith: A Comprehensive and Readable Theology* (Downers Grove, 1986), p 319.

Chapter 9

PREACHING AND THE PREACHER

John Stott

I am very grateful to have been included in the team of contributors to this volume, and I gladly pay my tribute to Gilbert Kirby. He has given long and distinguished service to the world-wide evangelical cause and, in particular, to evangelical unity. I specially enjoyed working with him when he was general secretary of the Evangelical Alliance.

I am grateful, too, to have been invited to write about preaching. For it is my firm conviction that nothing is more necessary for the balance, health and growth of the church today than a recovery of biblical preaching. If it is true, as Jesus said, quoting Deuteronomy, that human beings live not by bread only but by God's word, it is equally true of churches. Churches live, mature and flourish by the word of God; they languish, wither and die without it. This is the verdict of history. Martyn Lloyd-Jones wrote of 'the decadent periods when preaching has declined'.[1] He was surely right in his assessment.

In our generation, however, there are signs of the trivialization of preaching. This past summer a new magazine appeared in Britain entitled *The Pulpit and Good Sermon Guide*. 'We are not so shy about recommending good restaurants or public houses,' wrote the editor, 'so why not a Good Sermon Guide?' A *Times* leader wondered whether one can 'rate the rhetoric of the godly . . . as thought it were a simple consumer product like beer or washing machines', but was generally favourable to the idea. Why? Because it would reintroduce 'competitive consumerism to an activity where it is needed'. Soon afterwards it was announced that an annual prize was to be awarded to Britain's Best Preacher. Thus the solemn declaration of God's word is cheapened into a prize-winning competition.

Although preaching, a Christian form of communication, is still practised in virtually every church and denomination, there are distinctives in the evangelical understanding of preaching, whose main constituent elements are the preacher, the word, the hearers and the Spirit.

First, there is the preacher. This states the obvious, since of course there can be no preaching without a preacher. But it also encourages us to clarify what place the preacher occupies in the delivery of a sermon.

One of the best-known definitions of preaching was given by Bishop

Phillips Brooks in his 1877 *Yale Lectures on Preaching.* 'Preaching . . . has in it two essential elements,' he said, 'truth and personality . . . Preaching is the bringing of truth through personality . . . The truth is in itself a fixed and stable element; the personality is a varying and growing element.'[2] This should be an acceptable definition as far as it goes, since in authentic preaching divine truth is being conveyed through a human personality.

Yet 'personality' is an ambiguous word. Often it is merely a synonym for a person together with his or her distinctive characteristics. At other times, however, a 'personality' is a celebrity who excels in the field of stage, screen or sport. So how far should preachers express themselves? Our first answer is that preachers are not required to suppress their personality. Our doctrine of creation should protect us from pretending to be someone other than we are. So when Paul declared that he did not visit Corinth 'with eloquence or superior wisdom' (1 Corinthians 2:1), what he had renounced was a self-conscious parade of professional Greek rhetoric, not the expression of his personality or the careful choice of words and arguments.

At the same time, some lecturers in homiletics encourage their students to listen to themselves on tape and look at themselves on video. It is not difficult to understand the reason, but the dangers exceed the advantages. A better way to cure oneself of mannerisms of speech and gesture is to ask a friend or relative to assume the role of constructive critic. Deliberately to hear or watch oneself preaching is bound to generate an unhealthy self-consciousness. However, the pulpit is not a stage, nor are preachers actors. So, in place of an artificial self-awareness, preachers need to develop a natural self-forgetfulness.

Second, there is the word, by which I mean of course the word of God. A high view of scripture as being unlike any other book, as possessing a unique inspiration from God and a unique authority over us, is indispensable to faithful and effective preaching. Nothing undermines preaching like scepticism about the Bible, and nothing inflames it like the confidence that this is the word of God. It would be difficult to arouse much enthusiasm for speculative messages of our own; at best we would have to be very tentative about them. But when preachers are persuaded that in the pulpit they are handling the very word of the living God, a dramatic change of scene and atmosphere takes place. It is then that the heart begins to beat and the blood to flow with the excitement of being stewards and expositors of God's self-revelation.

Because we evangelical people have the highest doctrine of scripture in the church, we ought also to be the most conscientious students of it. For what would be the point of holding and defending an orthodox view of biblical infallibility and inerrancy if in practice we deny it by our careless neglect? It is something of a scandal that our actual evangelical treatment of the Bible does not always correspond to our professed belief about it. With what painstaking diligence should we give ourselves to the study of this uniquely inspired text!

Moreover, our study of the text should conform to our view of it in hermeneutics as well as in personal discipline. The principles by which we interpret the Bible should arise naturally from the kind of text it is. For example, it is because God chose to speak in precise and particular settings (whether of the Ancient Near East, Palestinian Judaism or the Graeco-Roman world) that we are under obligation to reconstruct them. No word of God was spoken in a cultural vacuum; every word of God was spoken in a cultural context. Consequently, it would be impossible to grasp the meaning of God's word in isolation from its context. So we have to give ourselves the labour, even the pain, of thinking ourselves back into the history, geography, culture and language of the biblical authors, to and through whom God was pleased to speak. To decline to do this, or to undertake it in a half-hearted or slovenly way, is to insult the God of revelation and to presume to wish he had chosen some other, culture-free way in which to make himself known. This attitude is as unproductive as it is unbecoming. The worst blunder we can commit is to isolate a text from its context, to impose a meaning on it arbitrarily, and then to claim the patronage of the biblical authors (even of God himself) for our opinions.

No, the right way is to sit humbly under the authority of the biblical authors, to allow them to say what they do say and not to force them to say what we might wish them to say. No hermeneutical principle is more important than this. Yet the conviction that the meaning of the text lies within the text, and must be yielded up by the text, runs counter to the prejudices of post-modernism. Deconstructionists insist on divorcing meaning from text and even deny that a text has any objective, discoverable or universal meaning. So, they say, a text is infinitely interpretable, and what seems a true meaning to you may be meaningless to me.

We may perhaps be forgiven if, in preference to this pure subjectivism, we follow the wisdom of Professor E D Hirsch who rightly affirmed that 'a text means what its author meant'.[3] That is to say, every text does have a meaning; its meaning is to be found within its words and does not float free of them; and its meaning is established by its original author, not by its subsequent readers.

In thus emphasizing the necessity of grammatico-historical exegesis, I am not wishing to suggest that preaching and exegeting are identical activities. Rather careful exegesis, whose goal is to discover the meaning of the text, is the indispensable foundation of biblical preaching. Preaching is more than exegesis, but it presupposes it.

Yet it is here that many of us fail. Exegesis is demanding. It takes time. It requires concentration and perseverance. But we are busy, yes and busy with many admirable pursuits. So we are tempted to take short cuts and to neglect the discipline of exegesis. Besides, we are good at bluffing. People do not notice at first. But in the end they will as our preaching lacks substance, our interpretations become questionable and our manner becomes ever less genuinely confident. Skimping our homework is a recipe for disaster.

Third, there are the hearers. Exposition is more than exegesis. It includes application. We have no liberty to preach the word in such a way as to be indifferent to whether anybody is listening, or to whether our audience consists of wooden pews instead of living, breathing persons. If we are to preach from the word, we must preach it to people also, indeed out of the word into their situations.

This is still denied by some. They maintain, as indeed I did long ago, that our business is simply to open up the text, while it is the Holy Spirit's task to apply it. And, of course, the Spirit of God does drive his word home to different people in different ways. Yet our evangelical doctrines of incarnation and inspiration should protect us from denying the need for application. For both the incarnation of the Son and the inspiration of the word were highly particularized events. Did the Son enter our world in order to reach us, and shall we not enter other people's worlds in order to reach them? Did God speak to his people in precise cultural contexts, and shall we neglect to contextualize our message? Did God condescend to reveal himself within the cultures and the languages of the people he was addressing, and shall we not bother to do the same?

Moreover, I guess that there is only one way to learn to contextualize, and that is to listen. We have to listen to what people are saying before we may presume to talk to them. Their voices express the whole range of human experience – the sighs and cries of the oppressed, the groans of the suffering, the complaints of the bitter, along with people's questions, criticisms, longings, doubts and fears. Our listening will often be tuned to their speaking to us directly, *viva voce*. At other times we may listen with our eyes rather than our ears, as we read books and magazines or view films or television. As people speak in different ways, so we have to listen in different ways. We preachers are usually so busy teaching that it does not come easy to us to confess our ignorance and our need to learn. Yet we have to engage in an honest struggle to understand who, what and where people are before we are in any position to dare to address them.

This is not (to use familiar phraseology) to 'allow the world to set the agenda for the church', to let people's 'felt needs' dictate what we say to them, let alone to 'worship at the shrine of modernity'. No. Our prior commitment remains to the word of God. Our primary agenda is what God has revealed to be his agenda, namely the fullness of life which is available through his Christ who died and was raised to secure it for us. Yet we still have to ask precisely how the gospel speaks to our alienated contemporaries. 'Double listening' is an exercise in basic Christian humility, as we listen first to what God has said in Christ and in scripture, and next to what our contemporaries in the world around us are saying and asking. Of course we do not listen to the voices of our fellow human beings with the same deference with which we listen to the voice of God.

But unless we listen to both, we cannot relate his word to their world without either compromise or irrelevance.

H E Luccock expressed this concern well when, a few years ago, he wrote that 'there are really four trinities for a preacher to keep in mind'. First and foremost, of course, there is that of the Father, the Son and the Holy Spirit, whose self-revelation we are concerned to guard and to proclaim. But then there are two other biblical trinities. In the Old Testament there were Abraham, Isaac and Jacob, and in the New Testament Peter, James and John. Both represent a variety of human beings with a variety of human experiences. But fourth, there are 'Tom, Dick and Harry, a never-to-be-forgotten trinity standing for the varied people among whom the preacher lives and to whom he speaks. A man may be a formidably orthodox Trinitarian in his theology and preaching, and still be curiously ineffective if he forgets or denies that other trinity of Tom, Dick and Harry (or, we might add, Joan, Jane and Jean) around him and in front of him.'[4]

Fourth, there is the Spirit, who gives life and power to the word, and without whom the word remains a dead letter, bones without breath.

All evangelical people are convinced that to preach the word without the anointing of the Spirit is a fruitless endeavour. As the Lausanne Covenant put it: 'We believe in the power of the Holy Spirit. The Father sent his Spirit to bear witness to his Son; without his witness ours is futile' (1974, para 14). One of the main reasons for this conviction of ours is that we know the gravity of the human condition. Human beings without Christ are spiritually dead, deaf and blind, and it is not given to us by ourselves to give life to the dead, hearing to the deaf or sight to the blind. So every stage of God's unfolding purpose in human beings is a work of the Spirit. Here is a comprehensive statement of this in the Manila Manifesto (1989, para B5):

> The Scriptures declare that God himself is the chief evangelist. For the Spirit of God is the Spirit of truth, love, holiness and power, and evangelism is impossible without him. It is he who anoints the messenger, confirms the word, prepares the hearer, convicts the sinful, enlightens the blind, gives life to the dead, enables us to repent and believe, unites us to the Body of Christ, assures us that we are God's children, leads us into Christ-like character and service, and sends us out in our turn to be Christ's witnesses. In all this the Holy Spirit's main preoccupation is to glorify Jesus Christ by showing him to us and forming him in us.

In every generation of church history, and not in times of revival only, believers have confessed their need for preaching and evangelism to be undertaken in the power of the Spirit. In the preface to Jonathan Edwards' famous essay, 'The distinguishing marks of a work of the Spirit of God' (1741), a certain Mr Howe is quoted as having longed for 'a plentiful effusion of the Holy Spirit'. Without this, he bemoaned, 'we know not how to speak living sense unto souls; how to get within you; our words die in our mouths, or drop and die between you and us'.[5]

Neither Christ nor his apostles imagined that they could preach the word without the Spirit. Jesus himself in the Nazareth synagogue applied Isaiah 61:1 to himself, saying; 'The Spirit of the Lord is on me, because he has anointed me to preach good news to the poor' (Luke 4:18). Then Peter wrote of all the apostles that they 'preached the gospel . . . by the Holy Spirit sent from heaven' (1 Peter 1:12). And the apostle Paul made the same claim: '[O]ur gospel came to you', he wrote to the Thessalonians, 'not simply with words, but also with power, with the Holy Spirit and with deep conviction' (1 Thessalonians 1:5). Similarly, he insisted to the Corinthians that his message and preaching 'were not with wise and persuasive words, but with a demonstration of the Spirit's power' (1 Corinthians 2:4). Only he can take our words, spoken in human frailty, and carry them home with divine power to the minds, hearts, wills and consciences of the hearers.

In emphasizing that the word is weak without the Spirit, we must, however, avoid the opposite extreme of declaring the Spirit to be sufficient without the word. Yet it is often in those churches which are most concerned to honour the Spirit that this mistake occurs, as room is made for the ministry of the Spirit at the expense of the ministry of the word. It would not be possible to justify this imbalance from scripture, however, since we are specifically told that the word of God is the Spirit's sword (Ephesians 6:17). So then, if the word does not operate without the Spirit, the Spirit does not operate without the word. If the word needs the power of the Spirit, the Spirit needs the sword of the word.

We have considered four essential ingredients of the process we call preaching, namely the preacher, the word, the hearers and the Spirit. It is a remarkable combination, not least because the preacher and the hearers are feeble, vulnerable human beings while the word and the Spirit are from God. Yet all four ingredients blend. Indeed, if there is one main lesson, which I have been concerned to emphasize in this chapter, it is that in preaching several diverse elements cohere, especially the human and the divine, the text and the context, exegesis and application, the word and the Spirit. We must not separate what God has joined.

Endnotes

1   D M Lloyd-Jones, *Preaching and Preachers* (London, 1971), p 24.
2   Phillips Brooks, *Lectures on Preaching* (New Haven, 1877), pp 5, 28.
3   E D Hirsch, *Validity in Interpretation* (New Haven, 1967), p 1.
4   H E Luccock, *The Minister's Workshop* (Grand Rapids, 1977), p 79.
5   Jonathan Edwards, *On Revival* (London, 1965), pp 77–78.

Chapter 10

PAUL'S IDEA OF COMMUNITY

I Howard Marshall

From one point of view this essay should be unnecessary: there already exists a book with the very same title by Robert Banks, an Australian scholar, who has been one of the pioneers in exploring the NT understanding of the church and its implications for the people of God in the twentieth century.[1] From another point of view, this essay is necessary in that the topic deals with an essential aspect of the biblical basis for evangelical unity which is the theme of this book. It is also eminently appropriate in a symposium which expresses our appreciation of Gilbert Kirby and his work, and our thanks to God for his unique contribution to the development of Christian education and scholarship at LBC, and to the promotion of Christian co-operation in the work of the gospel through EA.

I do not know why the editors of the book limited the scope of this essay to *Paul's* idea of community and chose to ignore the rest of the NT, unless it was to avoid an even more superficial survey of a large field. For the fact is that the notion of community is integral to NT Christianity. Students of the historical Jesus have rightly emphasized that his mission was concerned with the establishment of a new Israel, and that he came to reconstitute Israel as the people of God under his rule.[2] Numerous lines of thought in the gospels demonstrate that Jesus can be regarded as the founder of the church, even though the actual word *ekklesia* is scarcely found and the developed life of the Christian community is not reflected to any significant extent.[3] In a classic treatment of the theme,[4] R N Flew identified five 'notes' which sound in the gospels and in the early church, and used these to show that the idea of a community, centred round the Messiah, based on the 'message', committed to mission, standing in continuity with Israel and sharing a common ethic, forms the unifying link between the work of Jesus and the development of the church. Despite later criticisms[5] the argument appears to me to be sound. It follows, then, that the idea of a community is basic to the mission of Jesus; he did not come simply to 'win individuals', still less merely to save 'souls' for the next life, but to create or re-establish a 'flock' (Luke 12:32) which would be conscious of being the community associated with the kingdom of God.

Similarly, in the book of Acts the early church is inevitably a community of people joined together in relationships. In the early days some kind of communal living, with important implications for the ownership and sharing of property, was practised in Jerusalem (Acts 2:42–47; 4:32–37), although it was manifestly temporary and nothing similar is heard of elsewhere.[6] It may well be that the growth of the church rendered it impractical. But it has also to be remembered that we know extraordinarily little about the history of the church in Jerusalem anyhow.

Equally, there is important material on the Christian church as community in the other areas of the New Testament. For example, C F D Moule commented that John's Gospel is generally thought of as one of the chief documents of Christian unity and organic life. One's thoughts immediately fly to the temple of Christ's body, to the Shepherd and the one flock, to the vine and the branches, to the *'ut omnes unum sint'*.[7] And the importance of the community and its meetings in the letter to the Hebrews is manifest: if only the believers would come together and support one another, they would not fall into the danger of apostasy, implies the writer (Hebrews 10:24–27).

But enough of these brief direction indicators about the rest of the NT. What about Paul? In what follows we shall find that the idea of community was embedded in his self-understanding as an apostle and the way in which he corresponded with his converts. It found expression in the imagery that he used for the congregations. He was active to overcome social barriers that prevented its development. We shall explore the ways in which community existed in the work of mission and between the missionaries and the churches. Finally, we shall observe the nature of community within the life of the congregations, and note very briefly the existence of limits to fellowship.

Apostleship and community

The central factor in Paul's self-understanding is that he is an apostle. For him an apostle is a person who establishes groups of believers for which he has some responsibility (1 Corinthians 9:1–12). It is true that he speaks more in terms of proclaiming the gospel and preaching Christ so that people may be individually converted (1 Corinthians 1:17; 9:16; Galatians 1:16; Ephesians 3:7–9; Philippians 1:18). Nevertheless, he comes close to describing himself as a church-planter (1 Corinthians 3:5–9),[8] and he certainly thinks of himself as a church-builder (1 Corinthians 3:10–15). His role was to found communities of believers.

Paul understands his role as an apostle to include not just bringing people to the point of conversion; he sees himself as a father to his converts (1 Corinthians 4:14–17), as the person who has powers of discipline and oversight over the believers (1 Corinthians 4:21). In other words, the apostolic role involved the creation of a community that included the apostle (and his associates) and placed him in a significant continuing relationship to the new believers.

There is a sense in which this leadership of Paul was a 'given' factor;

apostleship, with all the authority that this conveyed as a steward of the mysteries of God (1 Corinthians 4:1), was his by divine appointment, so that he was ultimately responsible to God alone and not to the churches (1 Corinthians 4:3–5).[9] There are important questions raised by this self-understanding of Paul as an authority figure, which must not be ignored in an era when some people would do away with leadership or insist that everything must be done democratically by elected representatives, although they lie rather beyond our scope in this essay.

Epistles to congregations

All the extant writings of Paul are letters addressed directly or indirectly to Christian congregations.[10] Most are to individual congregations (Rome, Corinth, Philippi, Colosse, Thessalonica). At least one is sent to a group of congregations (in Galatia; the letter that we know as 'to the Ephesians' appears originally to have had no stated address and is thought to be intended for a church or churches unknown).[11] One is addressed to an individual (Philemon) but is clearly also intended for the house church to which he belonged (Philemon 2). Even in the case of the three that are addressed to colleagues of Paul, who are responsible for the oversight of churches, the indications are that they were meant for the churches as well as for the named recipients, Timothy and Titus.[12] Thus in every case the extant letters are to churches, or to individuals and the churches associated with them.

In one case the local church leaders are explicitly named in the salutation (Philippians; see 1:1) but, with the exception of Philemon and the Pastoral Epistles, all the letters are written to the congregations as a whole.[13] This indicates that, on the basis of the available evidence, Paul's normal means of communication with his converts was by means of letters addressed to the whole congregations; he did not write to the local leaders rather than to the congregations as a whole, and when he wrote to Philemon it was about a matter that concerned his household personally rather than Philemon's relationship with the church. As for Timothy and Titus, these were Paul's colleagues in mission and not local leaders of churches. Paul thus treats his converts as groups or congregations and not as individuals, and generally speaking he did not differentiate between the body of the congregation and the leaders. While he recognized the responsibility of the local leaders (Acts 20:28; see, outside the Pauline corpus, Hebrews 13:17), he laid the responsibility for the life of the church on the congregation as a whole (1 Corinthians 5:4). (However, is it not the case that the leaders of modern denominations communicate with local leaders rather than the actual congregations?)

The use of the language of community

The language which Paul uses indicates that he saw his converts in terms of communities and not just as individuals. This is evident from the most basic term which he uses, 'church' (Gk *ekklesia*). The history of this word shows that it was used in the secular world for an assembly (usually of the citizens of a town), and in Greek-speaking Judaism it was used (admittedly rarely) to refer to the 'people of God', the 'congregation' of Israel in OT times (eg Numbers 27:16–17; 31:16); basically it refers to people gathered together in some kind of meeting, and hence it can refer to the group of people who would come together in this kind of way. We may compare how a group like a general synod or general assembly actually exists only when it is meeting (although it has a list of members).[14]

The church is understood in this way as the people of God, and other terms, borrowed or taken over from the OT, are used in this connection. The most important of these is 'saints' or 'holy ones' (eg 2 Corinthians 1:1), referring to the people who are set apart from the rest of humanity as God's own people and characterized by their way of life. It has often been remarked that this term is always used by Paul in the plural ('saints', 'every saint'), as if to say that people cannot be saints on their own but only in company with other people. This conclusion is probably due to the accident that Paul is always addressing people as groups because he is writing to them as groups, but it is nevertheless the case that basically 'saints' is a term for a group, 'the people of God', to which individual saints belong.[15]

Again, the church is compared, in a well-known metaphor, to a body, an organism composed of different parts which work together; each part is indispensable, and each helps the others and is helped by them. This is the picture in Paul's earlier letters (Romans 12; 1 Corinthians 12). Here it is interesting that the parts of the body function for the good of one another and the body as a whole rather than to create an organism which interacts with its environment; the 'body' metaphor is not used in connection with the church's mission to the world.[16] In the later letters (Ephesians; Colossians) the metaphor is developed further in that special significance is assigned to the head of the body, which becomes a symbol for Christ as the source of strength and direction for the rest of the body. In this later use, the idea of bodily growth is explored but apparently in terms of spiritual development rather than the addition of new members.

A concept that is significant in the Pastoral Epistles is 'house' (1 Timothy 3:15).[17] The Greek word, like the English one, can be used to refer to the dwelling occupied by a family and also to the people who live together in a 'household'. The latter sense is important in various ways. Ancient society was organized in terms of households that included not only the members of the family but also their servants and slaves and other people who were 'clients', bound by various obligations to the householder who acted as their 'patron' and provided them with various benefits. The household could be a fairly extended kind of family. Such groups were the basis for the house churches, although much remains obscure about how exactly the churches were organized and how far each family constituted an individual house church.

But the term 'house' could also refer to the dwelling of a god, ie a temple, and this term is also applied to Christian congregations (1 Corinthians 3:16–17; 2 Corinthians 6:16; Ephesians 2:21). They constitute the temple of God in whose midst God is present. Here, the metaphor of the 'house' as a building is being applied to the members of the congregation, and is expressed most vividly not by Paul but by Peter in his description of believers as 'living stones' (1 Peter 2:5; 4:17).

Without going into further detail, we can see that Paul's favourite expressions for the people to whom he writes bring out the communal character of their life.[18] We also note that this community extends in two directions. It is a community that extends horizontally across all the present members of the group, but it also extends vertically through time so that the present people of God form part of a people with an existence that goes back through the centuries to the call of Abraham. This particular point is important when Paul considers the situation of Gentile believers and insists that they are a part of the Israel of God, grafted on the vine constituted by believing Jews (Romans 11:17–24). It is fundamental for Paul that there is one people of God constituted by faith from Abraham onwards.

Overcoming the barriers to community

It follows from what has just been said that a major task in Paul's mission was the creation of a church composed of both believing Jews and believing Gentiles, as well as encompassing both male and female, both slave and free, both Greeks and barbarians, in a genuine unity. He emphasizes that these several groups are 'all one' in Christ Jesus (1 Corinthians 12:13; Galatians 3:28; Colossians 3:11). These various categories were of course polarized in various ways. Basically, one group claimed superiority over another on such grounds as race, religion, sex and education. Boundaries were erected such as religious rituals and customs regarding food. No doubt Christian groups could have developed for each category, which would have been separate from one another (a Jewish church, a Gentile church), or there could have been groups within which the social and other divisions were strictly maintained (masters and slaves, the subordination of women). It was the genius of Paul to recognize that, ideally, this could not be the case and that the churches must unite separate groups and do away with inequalities. This was far from easy in a society where the religious, social and national customs were closely tied together. How can a Jewish believer remain a Jew while abandoning some of the fundamentals of Judaism (like circumcision or festivals) or regarding them as a matter of indifference? How does a master relate to his slaves in the household and in the house church? What difference does it make to relationships if the people are 'one', and the social relationships are as if they did not exist? We have not yet solved the problems today, and it is not surprising that the early churches progressed at different speeds and in different ways so that the NT presents us with a varied picture of diverse developments. But for our present purpose the vital point is that Paul saw that faith in Christ must lead to a new set of social relationships. As a practising Jew, he was prepared to eat with Gentiles, to insist that all believers have freedom to live in different ways from one another but that they must tolerate one another and do nothing that constitutes a stumbling block to other believers. Living in community is demanding!

The significance of Paul's missionary methods

Paul himself presents an example of community in respect of his missionary methods. It has been noted that his missionary work was accomplished at all points by some kind of 'team ministry'. This is obvious from Acts where his companion is first Barnabas and then Silas, both of whom are regarded as apostles. Other people, such as John Mark, also share in the mission, and then Timothy is brought in as a junior partner. This picture is strikingly confirmed in the letters from which it emerges that a considerable number of people shared in the itinerant mission with Paul.[19] It seems that evangelism, in the sense of preaching the gospel in new areas and founding new congregations, was the responsibility not of the local churches but of this group whom Paul sometimes calls 'the workers' (eg Romans 16:2,9,21) and sometimes 'the brothers' (1 Corinthians 16:11–12; 2 Corinthians 1:1; 2:13; 9:3), and we also hear of other groups, presumably similar in organization, who were rivalling the Pauline mission and attempting to break into the field with variant understandings of the gospel. Mission, then, was done by a group working together, with Paul as the dominant partner *de facto*, although he appears to have regarded the apostles as 'equals' *de jure*; other colleagues are sent to and fro at his bidding. The significance of this fact is that the various helpers were to some extent drawn from the new churches and represented them in the 'team'. The responsibility for evangelism therefore was not taken from the churches, but they were expected to contribute to the task of the apostolic mission.

The apparent separation between the work of the local churches and the apostolic mission produces a challenge and a puzzle for the contemporary church. On the one hand, the apostolic mission is emulated by the various missionary societies, whether denominational or non-denominational, which send out workers into new areas to establish churches; these churches then ideally become independent of the parent body. We should perhaps be prepared to draw the alarming conclusion that a church cannot properly claim to be a church if it is not discharging its missionary function by sending out co-workers to share in the common task of all the churches, the proclamation of the gospel. On the other hand, the task of evangelism in areas where churches already exist is generally considered to be the work of these churches themselves through the witness of the members (and especially of the leaders or paid workers). It is this second element which it is curiously hard to document from the New Testament.[20] Here is a point for further investigation.

Relationships between missionaries and churches

The element of community in mission is further evident in the responsibility that Paul lays upon the churches to pray for him and his companions in his work, for the success of the mission and for protection against the various opponents of the work (Romans 15:30–32; Ephesians 6:19; Philippians 1:19; Colossians 4:3–4; 1 Thessalonians 5:25; 2 Thessalonians 3:1–2). The congregations are deeply involved in the ongoing task not only through sending individuals to help Paul but also through their prayers for him and his companions. This would also have included prayers for the other churches (Ephesians 6:18). Here Paul himself is probably the best example, with his expressions of deep concern for the congregations. Most of his letters begin with a 'prayer-report' in which he relates how he prays for them and is quite specific about the matters for which he gives thanks and for which he intercedes to God (eg Romans 1:9–10; 1 Corinthians 1:4; Philippians 1:3–11). The prayer is the expression of a deep personal bond between the people involved (*cf* the moving language in Galatians 4:12–20), and it develops a reciprocal relationship in which Paul prays for them and they for him.[21]

We should also note at this point the development of bonds between churches and missionaries in the provision of financial support for one another. Christian love, patterned on the example of Christ who became poor in order to enrich other people, must express itself concretely in those who are rich at any time helping those who are poor. The example *par excellence* of this – interesting because it is a case of spontaneous action by some congregations, which Paul can cite in order to encourage others to a like generosity – is that of the churches in Macedonia. It is also highly significant in that their action led to the writing of 2 Corinthians chapters 8–9 which is quite a lengthy section of the epistle (39 verses) and demonstrates the central place that mutual generosity had in the mind of Paul.[22] Alongside this example of generosity intended to alleviate material poverty, which we might regard as the Christian Aid or Tear Fund of the early church, we must also note the giving by the churches to Paul and his colleagues in their evangelistic work (2 Corinthians 11:9; Philippians 4:10–20), which we would consider to be the equivalent of support for a missionary society today. It can be taken for granted that generosity was also practised within the congregations; we have evidence for support of those who served the church at the cost of not earning a normal wage (Galatians 6:6; 1 Timothy 5:17–18) and for the development of an organized system of support for widows (1 Timothy 5:3–16).

The communal character of ministry in the local congregation

We now turn back to the life of the churches themselves. I have drawn attention elsewhere to a generally neglected feature of church life in the NT, but it is a point that does not appear to have been generally grasped and therefore it needs repetition.[23] There is a surprising lack of vocabulary that relates to worship in the descriptions of church meetings and the allusions to what went on in them. The language of worship is well-known in the New Testament in other contexts, including what pagans did in their temples, but it is virtually absent from the material relating to Christian congregations. When we look at the fullest discussion of Christian meetings in 1 Corinthians, we find that Paul is concerned above all else that what happens should 'edify' the people present (1 Corinthians 14:3–5,12,17,26). By this term he refers to a process which aids their spiritual development. The items that were questionable in Paul's opinion included, in particular, the gift of speaking in tongues which could not be understood by other members of the congregation so that they could not share in what was being said. The gift of tongues was used to give praise and thanksgiving to God, but other people could not share in the praise unless they understood it. Paul's discussion of this matter shows that the church meeting was an occasion for praising and thanking God and praying to him. It was, therefore, certainly an occasion for what we call 'worship' in the proper sense, of rendering thanks to God in prayer; even petitionary and intercessory prayer can be included under the heading of 'worship' since they are an expression of dependence upon God and, in effect, an acknowledgement of his status. But the point which Paul is making is that, whatever the functions of the different actions in the church meeting, each and every one of them must be helpful to the other people present. This is a different thing from saying that the main or even the only purpose of the church meeting is to edify the members present. However, Paul does argue that the various events – the hymn, the word of instruction, the revelation, the tongue, the interpretation – must all be done 'for the strengthening of the church' (1 Corinthians 14:26) and, it is implied, if they do not have this effect, they must not be practised in the church. A person who prays in a tongue can do so silently in church, speaking to himself and to God (1 Corinthians 14:28).

The discussion of prophecy and other forms of instruction in the church meeting shows that the members were to be strengthened not just by being able to be drawn into prayers of thanksgiving and praise to God, but also by receiving words from God which would help to develop them spiritually. In this way, the gifts of the Spirit are used for the benefit of the body as a whole.

Within the life of the church these gifts of the Spirit were intended for the mutual edification of the believers. Whatever gift was given to any individual was intended to be used to help the church as a whole. Moreover, the Pauline picture in 1 Corinthians strongly suggests that the believers in general would each have some gift to use for the common good of the church. It is generally said that Paul thinks each and every believer will have a gift of the Spirit.[24] I suspect that this may be a misreading of the statement 'to each one the manifestation of the Spirit is given for the common good' (1 Corinthians 12:7); it is not saying that each person has a manifestation of the Spirit, but that in each case where there is a manifestation of the Spirit it is intended to be used for the common good.[25] Nevertheless, when Paul comes to compare the believers to parts of a body, each of which is integral to the body and has a role to play in it, he may well imply that all believers have some manifestation of the Spirit to utilize for the good of the congregation.

What may need to be emphasized, however, is that in this situation all of the congregation should expect to be edified by the gifts of others among them and therefore should attend the church meeting in a humble, receptive mode. Paul's description can be misunderstood as simply turning the church into a set of activists in which we feel that we are falling short if we are not sharing our gift with other believers, whereas it is his intention that we should all of us be thankful recipients of the ministry of others.

Paul's teaching is in further danger of not being heard today because we have perpetuated an identification of the recipients of the gifts of the Spirit with the leaders of the church. It is crucial to recognize that there is a difference! An important contribution here, out of all proportion to its slender size, is a booklet by Kevin Dyer[26] written in the context of the Christian Brethren. His thesis is that churches have failed to make the Pauline distinction between eldership and leadership, the former being an 'office' based on character (but involving gifts of the Spirit), concerned mostly with pastoral relations with the other believers, whereas the latter is a function based on the particular gift of the Spirit (Romans 12:8; 1 Corinthians 12:28), which is concerned with the administration and management of the church. Dyer's point is that, through not observing this distinction, churches have expected elders to take on leadership roles for which they were not equipped. This insight needs to be developed further: we need to recognize that ministry in the sense of manifesting the gifts of the Spirit for the good of the congregation is not the preserve of the elders or (in Dyer's sense) of the leaders, but is the task of all the believers who are equipped by the Spirit for their varied functions. To share in ministry does not necessarily imply that a person is also called and equipped to be a leader or an elder. Once this point is grasped, the way is open for a recovery of the Pauline understanding of the gifts of ministry in the congregation, and the task of ministry will again become a communal activity rather than a one-person (or usually a one-man) performance.

The limits of community

A comprehensive discussion of Paul's attitude to community should not ignore the fact that there were occasions when he found community to be impossible. There were sinful people who were to be excluded from fellowship in the hope that they would repent and put aside their sin (1 Corinthians 5:1–5,11–13). There were others whose understanding of the gospel was regarded by Paul as so harmful that he denounced them in the strongest terms, using language which would be frowned upon today as inappropriate (2 Corinthians 11:13–15; Galatians 1:6–9; Philippians 3:2,18–19). The sheer vehemence of Galatians chapter 1, Philippians chapter 3 and 2 Corinthians chapters 10–13, which may have been acceptable in the first century, causes problems for modern readers, but it underlines the basic fact that Paul was quite simply intolerant of those whom he regarded as undoing his work. His attitudes and practice in these areas are largely foreign to the modern Western church, but they must surely also be taken into account in developing a pattern of church life based on the New Testament.

Conclusion

Throughout this essay I have tried to indicate some of the points where Paul's teaching challenges and raises questions for the contemporary church. Whatever we make of the particular applications of it that were appropriate in the first century with its different social patterns (eg the ancient household), the essential principles stand out clearly, and it should not be too hard a task to apply them today. The difficulty may lie more in our unwillingness to face the risks and the unknown roads to which the Spirit may be calling us.

Endnotes

1 R Banks, *Paul's Idea of Community* (Exeter, 1980).
2 See especially B F Meyer, *The Aims of Jesus* (London, 1979).
3 No doubt the gospels were written by people who were fully aware of the needs of the churches in their own day, and recorded the life and teaching of Jesus in such a way as to be relevant to them; even so, it is remarkable how little there is on many of the concerns of the church. The word *ekklesia* occurs only in Matthew 16:18 and 18:17.
4 R N Flew, *Jesus and his Church* (London, 1938, 1943), p 2.
5 E Schweizer, *Church Order in the New Testament* (London, 1961).
6 See especially B J Capper, 'The interpretation of Acts 5:4', *Journal for the Study of the New Testament*, 19 (1983), pp 117–131.
7 The quotation comes from an essay in which the author attempted to redress the balance by drawing attention to 'The individualism of the Fourth Gospel', *Essays in New Testament Interpretation* (Cambridge, 1982), pp 91–109, quoted from p 92.

8   The emphasis is perhaps more on bringing individuals to faith, but the communal element is certainly present.

9   The topic is highly significant for questions of leadership and authority in the church today. See J H Schutz, *Paul and the Anatomy of Apostolic Authority* (Cambridge, 1975); B Holmberg, *Paul and Power: The Structure of Authority in the Primitive Church as Reflected in the Pauline Epistles* (Philadelphia, 1983).

10 In what follows I discuss the letters in the Pauline corpus as being ostensibly from Paul himself to various churches and individuals, without entering into questions of their authenticity which would not seriously affect the course of the argument.

11 The words 'in Ephesus' are omitted by the most ancient and reliable manuscripts, but the resulting wording is so difficult that it is unlikely to represent the original text of the letter.

12 In each case the final greeting is addressed to 'you' [plural].

13 The view that one of the letters to Thessalonica was sent to the church leaders and the other to the church as a whole has failed to establish itself. See E E Ellis, *Prophecy and Hermeneutic* (Tubingen/Grand Rapids, 1978), pp 19–21, and the discussion in I H Marshall, *1 and 2 Thessalonians* (London, 1983), p 27.

14 *Paul's Idea of Community*, see above. Banks is in some danger of carrying this point too far and not stressing sufficiently the universal and permanent character of the church as a divine institution.

15 Paul, however, does not use the word 'people' for the church, except in 2 Corinthians 6:16; Titus 2:14. Contrast Romans 15:10 which shows that he tends to reserve this word for the Jews.

16 *Cf* Banks, *Paul's Idea of Community*, p 70.

17 D Verner, *The Household of God: The Social World of the Pastoral Epistles* (Chicago, 1983).

18 We should not overlook the fact that Paul uses other terms which do not bring out the communal aspect of the Christian life, such as 'believers'.

19 *Cf* Ellis, *Prophecy and Hermeneutic*, pp 3–22. The major study, however, is W H Ollrog, *Paulus und seine Mitarbeiter: Untersuchungen zu Theorie und Praxis der Paulinischen Mission* (Neukirchen, 1979). Ollrog's most interesting conclusion is that Paul's colleagues were drawn mostly from the churches that he had founded, and functioned as representatives of these churches (1 Corinthians 16: 17b; Philippians 2:30b; Colossians 1:7b; Philemon 13). These fellow-workers were attached to the mission rather than to Paul, in order to involve newly-founded churches in mission as the task of the whole church.

20 See W P Bowers, 'Church and mission in Paul', *Journal for the Study of the New Testament*, 44 (1991), pp 89–111; also Bowers, 'Mission' in G F Hawthorne (*et al*), *Dictionary of Paul and his Letters* (Downers Grove, 1993), pp 608–619. On the other side, see P T

O'Brien, *Consumed by Passion: Paul and the Dynamic of the Gospel* (Holmbush West, NSW, 1993), who argues that the concept of the gospel contains implications that include evangelism by local congregations.

21   G P Wiles, *Paul's Intercessory Prayers: The Significance of the Intercessory Prayer Passages in the Letters of Paul* (Cambridge, 1974); P T O'Brien, *Introductory Thanksgivings in the Letters of Paul* (Leiden, 1977).

22   Something more than simple generosity to those in need lay behind the collection which Paul took among the Gentile churches for the poverty-stricken believers in Jerusalem; attempting to strengthen the bonds of fellowship between Gentile and Jewish Christians was certainly a factor. See S McKnight, 'Collection for the saints' in Hawthorne *(et al)*, *Dictionary of Paul and his Letters*, pp 143–147, for a brief overview.

23   I H Marshall, 'How far did the early Christians *worship* God?', *Churchman*, 99:3 (1985), pp 216–229. The purpose of the article was to show that the one-sided view of Christian meetings as primarily God-ward directed activity by us which results from the use of the terms 'worship' and 'service' to designate them needs to be corrected by the recognition that what God does for his people (in speaking to them) and what they do for one another in fellowship are equally important factors. Theologically speaking, grace precedes faith.

24   'Each member of the church, then, receives some spiritual gift which is a manifestation of the Spirit', F F Bruce, *1 and 2 Corinthians* (London, 1971), p 118.

25   '[Paul] does not intend by this to stress that every last person in the community has his or her own gift', G D Fee, *The First Epistle to the Corinthians* (Grand Rapids, 1987), p 589.

26   Kevin Dyer, *Must Brethren Churches Die?* (Exeter, 1991), pp 35–47.

Chapter 11

JUSTICE FOR ALL? BIBLICAL ETHICS

Fran Beckett

An incident is recorded of a woman in need who encountered a well-meaning Christian leader whose reactions reflected his priorities. As a result of that encounter she wrote this poem and handed it to an employee of Shelter:

> I was hungry,
>   and you formed a humanities group to discuss my hunger.
> I was imprisoned,
>   and you crept off quietly to your chapel and prayed for my release.
> I was naked,
>   and in your mind you debated the morality of my appearance.
> I was sick,
>   and you knelt and thanked God for your health.
> I was homeless,
>   and you preached to me of the spiritual shelter of the love of God.
> I was lonely,
>   and you left me alone to pray for me.
> You seem so holy, so close to God,
>   but I am still very hungry – and lonely – and cold.[1]

This poignant heart-cry for something more radical and far reaching than platitudes or quick-fix answers, this plea for involvement in the pain of human existence, strikes right to the core of who God is and who he calls us to be. It also epitomizes the divide that many Christians either consciously or unconsciously hold between personal spirituality and practical social ethics.

An inadequate view of God's heart for people in society, coupled with a feeling of helplessness when faced with the sheer immensity of the task of pursuing justice, can reinforce for some Christians a preoccupation with personal faith and the word of God, to the exclusion of putting that word in all its fullness into practice. For some, issues of personal morality crowd out any consideration of the wider need for justice in the world around us. Thus important issues, such as homosexual practice within the church, take precedence over other important issues of poverty and homelessness in society. Within the Bible, there is no such polarization between concern about sexual behaviour and social justice. For example, the prophet Amos was passionate about social justice and immeasurably distressed by the religious hypocrisy and sexual sins of his day (Amos 2:4,6,7,12; 4:1; 6:4–6).

Yet others within the church pursue radical agendas of combating racism and sexual inequality, confronting unjust structures and institutions in society, and generally speaking out for those who are oppressed. In the past, with a few notable exceptions, they have been uneasy companions with those Christians who are preoccupied with spiritual warfare and wanting more of the Holy Spirit's anointing of power on their personal and church lives.

However, as we draw to the end of the twentieth century, one of the heart-warming trends that we see within the evangelical world is a greater willingness than ever before to listen to and to learn from each other's emphases and insights and, where possible, to work together, so that the 'whole church can take the whole gospel to the whole world'.[2]

It is at the heart of the debate concerning what constitutes the 'whole gospel' and the 'whole world' that the consideration of biblical justice lies. Justice as a concept is with us from a very early age, with exclamations of 'It's not fair!' being part of the normal vocabulary of young children. Justice has a strong political dimension but views on the source of justice vary, and that is where the Bible has something distinctive to say that should influence the behaviour of all Christians everywhere.

A commonly held view is that people must create justice with their own reason, which is then upheld by social consensus. The problem with this approach is that it is very difficult for human-centred justice to be impartial, and a bias towards maintaining sectional interests is difficult to avoid. A graphic, large-scale example of this can be seen within the former apartheid regime of South Africa.

A biblical view of justice brings a framework within which we are all accountable to God. 'It is God's radical judgment on our lives. God is no respecter of persons; He is not partial and as our Creator He relativises all the advantages and disadvantages that we put so much weight on, and sees us as we are.'[3]

It is out of this that there flows an understanding of justice that is rooted in a fear and love of God, a commitment to impartiality and a need to maintain consistent statements of what are right and wrong public actions. Justice is about who God is, and God is about the business of bringing justice into being.

Doing justice because of who God is

Why should we be concerned about justice for all people everywhere? And how do we flesh out all the reasons for that concern in such a way that an impact is made on the world? It is in grasping, with ever-increasing depth in our hearts and minds, the fact that God is passionate about justice. It lies at the very core of his being and is demonstrated time and again in the Bible and in human history. Our God is not lukewarm in responding to the world. Just as he loves his creation with a burning ardour, so he hates injustice and oppression, wherever it is and whatever shape it takes. This side of God's character is sometimes easy to forget. It is something that can make us feel uncomfortable, so we keep it at the margin of our minds. The radical nature of his zeal for justice can too easily impinge upon our lives, causing disruption and forcing a troubling re-examination of priorities.

The Bible presents a God of justice and righteousness who is concerned about violation of human rights and who has not abandoned the world that he has created. Yet that is not all. God's justice gives more than ordinary human justice provides, because he is also a God of grace, giving people what is undeserved. It is the fact of his love that 'takes justice beyond common sense'.[4] He desires people not merely to talk about but to practise justice and righteousness (Amos 5:24) and experience peace (Isaiah 54:10,13,15; 55:12). It is not enough for human rights to be met but, beyond this, for the deepest, personal human needs to be satisfied.

The OT authors consistently emphasize that social justice reflects the very character of God (Psalms 33:5; 37:28; 99:4; Proverbs 21:3,15). His passion for justice shows itself throughout redemptive history, as a prime condition of covenant with Israel (Deuteronomy 16:20). God intended Israel's witness to the world to be a witness of justice and righteousness, with their defence of oppressed people making them shine as a light to the nations (Isaiah 58:5–10). They were to work with God in bringing justice (Isaiah 1:16–17), to have a vision for change (Isaiah 16:4,5) and to embrace the truth that the blessing of justice was for other nations as well (Isaiah 51:4,5). All this was to come from a place of relationship, of intimacy with God, which was to be outworked in whole-life discipleship that encompassed the pursuit of social justice (Isaiah 58:1–14). 'Those who oppress the poor show contempt for their Maker, but whoever is kind to the needy honours God' (Proverbs 14:31). From this, it can be seen that 'salvation in the Old Testament has a strong social and this-worldly flavour, in contrast to the predominantly individualistic and other-worldly understanding'[5] that many have held.

The words spoken by prophets like Amos and Nahum are frightening in the white-hot intensity of God's anger against evil. And, throughout, he demonstrates a particular concern for those who are poor and oppressed, weak or vulnerable, urging his people to defend their cause. Economic and sexual exploitation are roundly condemned. Corruption of the judicial system is not to be tolerated. Idolatry, slavery and barbaric cruelty in war all qualify for his wrath. This is 'no weak, insipid God but one who burns with a zeal for holiness and justice, acting powerfully on behalf of oppressed people'.[6]

The OT calls for justice are rooted in the practicalities and stuff of everyday life. Impartiality is continually commanded, with no favouritism to be shown to the rich and powerful (Exodus 23:2–3; Isaiah 3:9). There is to be justice for the small and great alike (Deuteronomy 1:16,17; 10:17; 16:18,19). Special care is to be given to those who cannot help themselves. The needs of widows, orphans, refugees, those who are materially poor, people in debt or oppressed in other ways are to be dealt with fairly and compassionately. The prophets called for justice on a common human scale, with particular emphasis upon those who were least likely to have their rights considered by others. The prophets never demanded less than justice, but they promised more. Their passion for justice for the poor was notable for a zeal that went beyond just an emotional plea for charity. Theirs was a commitment to doing justice. The OT laws were based on God's character as a liberating God, concerned for freedom from oppression. They were given to prevent exploitation (Leviticus 19:13; Exodus 22:25–27) and to set new standards for life in community, to include a special place for outsiders and those in need (Deuteronomy 10:17–19). The Year of Jubilee (see Leviticus 25:8–55) envisaged a society of 'equal opportunity'. The right to individual ownership was recognized, but the sabbatical and Jubilee laws prevented permanent creation of great differences of wealth. The vulnerability of those in debt was not to be exploited, and possessions were to be held lightly.

Maybe it would be easier to consign this God full of passion for poor people and zeal for justice to the pages of the OT, and thus question his relevance for today. But we cannot do so because he refuses to be confined – he is here, now. Jesus demonstrated the same holy anger against religious hypocrisy and injustice when he threw the money-changers out of the temple courtyard (John 2:14–16). In his relationships, his teaching, his identification of the gospel with oppressed people, he demonstrated that the kingdom of God has wider implications than merely personal ones. His manner of coming into the world makes it impossible to claim that the gospel is not about the very stuff of human existence:

> A gospel that attempts to speak only to the heart, and is silent when faced with the physical, social and relational chaos of someone's life is no gospel and bears little resemblance to the gospel of Jesus – the Word made flesh who dwelt among us full of grace and truth.[7]

Through his lifestyle, we see Jesus making radical statements about the inestimable worth of human beings. He treated all persons with respect, regardless of race, sex, age, physical condition or economic status (Luke 15:1–32). He taught and treated everyone as responsible human beings, whether educated or uneducated. He called to account the powerful for, amongst other things, neglecting justice (Matthew 23:23).

He taught that his kingdom applies to all of life, transforming human existence and relationships, bringing them to a place of wholeness, justice and peace (Luke 1:51–53). Jesus embodied justice, coming to bring good

news (Isaiah 61:1–2; Luke 4:16–21) into a society dominated by discrimination and oppression. Women, children, refugees, the poor, people with
disabilities or disfiguring diseases were devalued and degraded by a society
that cared more for outward show than human dignity. Jesus was different
because he expressed the heart of the God of whom we read in the OT. Yet
he was utterly realistic about human nature, teaching that the root causes
of oppression are within people themselves (Mark 7:20–23). From this it
can be seen that social injustice springs from a variety of factors, including
lust for power, greed, hatred and insecurity.

As for the early church, although we do not find them taking political
action, the presence of Jesus had obviously profoundly affected them.
Early on, they had to decide their racial policy, and they did so in a way
that transcended narrow, nationalistic aspirations, and made a positive
statement about the equality of all human beings (Acts 6:1–4; 10:9–48;
15:1–29). They had grasped something of the transforming effect of
Christ's death and resurrection upon relationships based formerly on
domination and exploitation (Galatians 3:26–29; Colossians 3:9–11). A
new attitude of selflessness and concern for the needs of others was to
characterize their relationships (Philippians 2:4), underlining the fundamental truth of people's equal value. Relationships were to be shaped by
the fact that God has no favourites, and this was to make a tangible
difference in the workplace (Ephesians 6:9; Colossians 3:23) and in the
treatment of people from different social classes (James 2:1–9). They
found themselves with an inner motivation that moved them to be concerned for the rights of others. The primary character trait in the biblical
model of the new person in Christ was that of a passion for righteousness,
(Ephesians 4:22–24; 1 Timothy 6:11). The destiny that the early church
anticipated, and called others to participate in, was one of justice and
righteousness within the new heaven and new earth (2 Peter 3:13).

Doing justice because of who we are

The church is called to a deep commitment to social justice that makes a
tangible difference for good in the lives of individuals, communities and
nations. This commitment is to be an expression of the character and heart
of the living God, our God. It is out of our understanding of the doctrine
of God, and out of lives that are gripped by the tenderness and passion of
the love of God, that we will be able to make a difference. It is because
of who human beings are and what they are intended to be that we can
know how and where justice should be done.

Described as the pinnacle of creation, human beings were made in the
image of God and as such have been accorded a unique dignity. Everyone,
irrespective of race, intellect, ability, appearance, social or economic
status, or attractiveness of personality has been created by God's will in
his image. Inherent within that are rational, moral and spiritual qualities.
To a greater or lesser degree, we can think, reason and make choices,

exercising responsibility and initiative. We are able to feel deeply, express a wide range of emotions and enter into relationships that can bring healing and fulfilment. Creativity and the ability to appreciate the rich variety of the world around us through the senses also single out humans as being special. C S Lewis has said, 'There are no ordinary people. You have never talked to a mere mortal . . . it is immortals whom we joke with, work with, marry, snub and exploit – immortal horrors or everlasting splendours.'

The origin of human rights is creation which brings with it the right to be fully human, enjoying the dignity of being created in God's image. It is the biblical affirmation of the worth and value of the individual human being that must set the standard by which we evaluate whether or not acts are discriminatory. In denying certain people their human rights in comparison to other people, we are saying that, for some reason, they as people are worth-less. In contrast, in the parable of The Good Samaritan (Luke 10:25–37) the basis for care is clearly not some externally pre-scribed discriminatory practice but basic human need. This means that we should not prejudge or stereotype individuals, but instead work for a society where individuality is not crushed. Human liberty is of fundamen-tal importance, but this does have to be held in creative tension with the need not to exploit others. One person's individuality and freedom can mean another person's pain. On a cautionary note, a concern for human freedom in isolation can easily breed competition that militates against co-operation for the common good. However, freedom of worship, con-science and speech should be worked for and protected if we are to live in a world where the uniqueness of human beings is a truth to be celebrated. The breathtaking truth that we, as human beings, have inestimable value (Psalm 8:3–5) has considerable implications for the value on life that our individual and corporate actions communicate. For, whilst as individuals we have innate dignity, the Bible teaches that individuals were not created to be in isolation, but instead to be in a network of meaningful and affirming social relationships. Human life is meant to be genuinely per-sonal and relational. The doctrine of the Trinity points us to a positive and integrated community experience of relationships. God created human beings in society (Genesis 1:27,28; 2:18) and throughout the Bible we read of his word being given in the context of community life. For example, he spoke to a family in Abraham, a nation in Israel and to individuals representing the human 'family' (Ephesians 3:15).

Personal, family, work and social relationships are all part of God's creative purposes for people and, as such, everyone has a right to partici-pate in them. As social beings, created in the image of God, people have a right to receive respect and be treated with dignity. God is concerned that our community life is characterized by justice (Psalm 146:7–9) and, whilst he expects this to be particularly true of his people, he extends this to all people. The prophets condemned social evil within Judah and Israel (Amos 2:4–8) but also pronounced judgement on the surrounding nations

(Amos 1:3–2:3) for their injustice and sin against humanity and community. God hates injustice and oppression, and desires justice to be the hallmark of every community and nation (Nahum 3:1).

The implications of this are that God requires us to embrace his concerns for relational justice and so actively to oppose every evil that divides and separates people. Anything that makes for an impersonal, dehumanized society and robs people of their worth should be vigorously combated. The church should both speak out and act, demonstrating that knowing relationally a God of justice transforms us into a people of justice. Our tolerance of racism both inside and outside the church presents some large questions about our understanding of our common humanity before God. Our failure to speak out against marital rape and domestic violence (and indeed all acts that dehumanize women and men) and to provide safe places for refuge, healing and reconciliation, are an indictment against us. Our stigmatism and fear of those who are 'different' because of mental illness, or disability, or sheer inability to cope with the pressure of modern living is a travesty of the gospel which has at its heart the breaking down of barriers. Our unwillingness to raise our voices, both in protest and in offering solutions, within a world increasingly polarized between those who have and those who have not appears light years away from the priorities of the OT prophets. Even the humour that some of us entertain, that belittles individuals and groups, can be far removed from laughter that is characterized by bubbling freedom and celebration of our common humanity.

However, there is yet more to this doctrine of creation. Not only were we created in the image of God and so have dignity. Not only were we created to belong to the one human family. We were also created to have a relationship to the earth, one of stewardship and dominion. Consequently, all people have a right to share in the earth and its riches. Although capacities and interests may vary, no one has inherently a greater or lesser right to take responsibility for and share in the resources made available to human beings. Therefore, justice demands that we speak out and do something to address the major imbalance between the rich and poor nations of this world, including addressing those structures and institutions that, as a matter of policy, actively perpetuate those imbalances.

The scale and scope of the implications for justice in our relationship to the earth can seem at best daunting and at worst totally overwhelming. However, it is this biblical truth that holds within it a key to a way forward in doing justice in the arenas of work and rest, housing and homelessness, and freedom from poverty, hunger and disease. How we build our villages, towns and cities should be influenced by this and by the fact that people were created with a right to dignity and access to meaningful social relationships.

Last, but certainly not least, people were created for relationship with their Creator. The focus of our being is intended to be that of loving God with all we have and loving others too (Matthew 22:37–40). The very costliness of our redemption underlines our worth as individuals. Consequently, both Jesus and the prophets thundered their indignation at those who prevented others through their actions and attitudes from gaining access to a life-giving relationship with God. Therefore, implicitly, justice has to have something to do with religious freedom and a willingness to stand with those who are being unjustly treated because of their faith. How far that extends to people of other faiths is a hotly debated issue, but anything that degrades or dehumanizes another person, whatever their beliefs, is to be resisted.

Reality demands that we face the facts of our situation. We live in a world where all is not as it should be and yet still has the capacity to make us catch our breath in awe as we glimpse the glory of what it is meant to be. Ours is a fallen world, and no aspect of human life and no institution in society is free of the effects. As Christians, we share in the tension of living in a world which is both wonderfully created but which tragically has sin and evil woven into its very fabric (Romans 8:19–22). Self-interest lies at the root of much individual and group behaviour, and biblical realism demands that we face this.

The structures and institutions of human life have been provided by God for our good (Romans 13:1–7). However, a doctrine of sin that focuses on individual wrongdoing, and fails to come to terms with the corruption that has crept into the power structures and cultural norms of different societies, lacks an important dimension of that biblical realism. Structures that undermine social relationships, tear families apart and weaken responsibility towards others must be challenged. Admittedly, whilst compassionate action can be costly, it is sometimes easier than facing up to the demands of justice when confronted with complex, impersonal and corrupt 'systems' that are bigger than we are.

As the twentieth century draws to a close, Christians live in a world with a burgeoning and secretive arms trade, multinational corporations that exploit the needs of the poor for the sake of profits, and national policies that help create an ever growing 'underclass'. The God of justice who spoke all those centuries ago through the prophets, with a voice like the sound of a deafening trumpet (Isaiah 58:1) and a roaring lion (Amos 1:2; 3:8), is still speaking today, and whilst the context is different, the message is the same. He is calling us to embrace justice in what we do, recognizing who we are, and helping others to do likewise.

Doing justice

If we are to share in God's pursuit of justice, then we need to seek to 'understand the times' (1 Chronicles 12:32) more adequately. Society is full of words and the clamour of conflicting voices which, too often, we attempt to drown out by speaking even more loudly and without first listening carefully. Our awareness of the issues of injustice has to start with our being open to things we may not have considered before, even if they make us feel uncomfortable. We have to be prepared to have our eyes opened to unpleasant facts, distressing accounts of the results of injustice and, in some instances, to our own culpability. We need to create space for God to speak with us about his concerns through his word, by his Spirit and out of the cries of the world around us.

In order to do this, we should ask God to help us read the Bible through the eyes of people who are poor or oppressed. We need to pray for opportunities to listen to those who are victims within society, and for the grace and wisdom to know what to do with what we hear. Everyday practical things like reading a newspaper, listening to or watching news broadcasts and documentaries can be transformed as we ask God to give us insight into what we see and hear. Keeping informed through the work of campaigning and charitable organizations will help, although we will need to make sure they are not just Christian ones. We have much to learn from the many people around the world who may not own the name of Christ but who are touched by common grace and passionate about human rights.

Doing justice starts with rigorous self-assessment under the scrutiny of God's word illumined by his Spirit. It means facing up to our attitudes and prejudices, acknowledging those blind spots that we have and being ruthless about sin in our own lives. Racial and sexual prejudice; pride regarding social status; fear or disgust concerning those with disabilities, Aids or mental illness; exploitation within our relationships that is overt, or more subtly disguised with emotional manipulation; using people to get what we want, no matter what the cost; grasping after and hanging on to power and so disempowering others: all of these must be faced up to and, with God's help, dealt with in our lives. We need each other in this, too, as we grow and change. Facing our own frailty, brokenness and selfishness is not an easy thing, and yet it must happen if, with any integrity, we are to speak out and act against injustice on a wider platform.

It is in our family relationships, our workplaces and our handling of finance and material possessions that these challenges have to be faced. We need to examine our lifestyles (James 5:1–6). The decisions we make and the attitudes we adopt can influence social change and the lives of other people. We need to be honest about what can go on in our churches as well. As Christians it is the fact of our oneness in Christ (John 17:11,21–23) that is important, not our positions. Hence, we should strive for a unity that is not just words but reality. This means dealing with anything in our churches that devalues or fails to treat with dignity all those who come within their orbit. In John Stott's words, 'The church should be the one community in the world in which human dignity and equality are invariably recognized and human responsibility for each other accepted.'[8] Again, this is not easy, and working these things out in practice is costly and complicated. But consider the power of the message to the surrounding world, sometimes even without words, of communities of believers who, for all their frailties, are committed to justice and reconciliation in a way that counts in their everyday lives together. A wonderful demonstration of the person, the God, who is at the heart of it all!

Like a stone thrown into a pond, the challenge of doing justice ripples ever outwards beyond our immediate personal lives. There will be justice issues in our locality, in our village, town or city: people with disabilities denied access to essential services and leisure activities because of the physical layout of buildings; young adults leaving school with no hope of obtaining meaningful work; homeless people likely to stay that way because many need much more than just a roof over their heads; whole housing estates where more than 80% of the potential workforce are unemployed because it is expedient to wind down local industry in order to gain larger profits elsewhere. The list is endless.

Within this, we need to consider the structural implications implicit in a concern for justice. This includes analysing the possible structural reasons for some people being poor and others not, the breakdown of community life, and how experiencing oppression is a way of life in some communities. Social institutions, whether great or small, can provide a framework within which people are helped in the relationships for which they were made, and it is for us to invest our energies into sustaining these. This is about maintaining justice in a fallen world. The question has been graphically raised: 'In working for the kingdom, is our sole task to run the ambulance service at the bottom of the cliff, treating the victims of injustice and violence, or do we also have a responsibility to challenge the forces that push the innocent off the cliff?'[9] Do we perhaps separate our lives into compartments by generously contributing to overseas aid agencies, whilst closing our eyes to a system of trade which makes the poor poorer at the price of satisfying our desire for luxuries? Our very actions meant for good may be short-sighted in that our Christian caring can become the maintenance of an unjust order and so prevent necessary change. This can be countered by becoming more informed and getting involved with organizations, many of which have local groups, whose lifeblood is issues such as these. It is from this position of growing insight that we can pursue this central part of the church's mission of representing a just God.

> The proclamation of God's kingdom necessarily demands the prophetic denunciation of all that is incompatible with it ... In our concern for the poor we are distressed by the burden of debt in the Two-Thirds World. We are also outraged by the inhuman conditions in which millions live, who bear God's image as we do.[10]

This statement reminds us of the sheer scale of the issues and the many formidable obstacles to the pursuit of a more just world, not least the complexities of human society and conflicting interests. However, there are parameters around this, in that human rights should be limited to what is compatible with being the people God made us and meant us to be. We might be tempted to reduce our involvement to the attainable and be content with that. It is understandable that we might retreat into pursuing our personal lives because our individual spheres of influence seem so limited. But, together, we can make a difference. More than that, especially with our God, the God of justice, we *will* make a difference. George Bernard Shaw is quoted as saying 'You see things as they are and ask "Why?" But I dream things that never were and ask "Why not?" '

Justice and righteousness are mentioned over eight hundred times in the Bible. However, one verse perhaps sums up the demands of biblical ethics for individuals, grounded as they are in the belief that justice is for all: 'He has showed you, O man [and woman], what is good. And what does the Lord require of you? To act justly, and to love mercy and to walk humbly with your God' (Micah 6:8).

Finally, and most importantly, it is out of deepening relationship with the God of justice that we will be envisioned and equipped to look at the world with new insight, and to go out and do justice, not of an angular, condemning-of-people type, but justice that is tempered with mercy and flows out of intimacy with God, reflecting his character and concerns. May God give us the grace and courage that we need for the task!

Endnotes

1   Quoted in J R W Stott, *Issues Facing Christians Today* (Basingstoke, 1984).
2   Subtitle of the Lausanne II International Congress on World Evangelization Report, *Proclaim Christ Until He Comes* (Minneapolis, 1990).
3   A Storkey, *A Christian Social Perspective* (Leicester, 1979), p 302.
4   L Smedes, *Mere Morality* (Tring, 1983), p 37.
5   W Scott, *Bring Forth Justice* (London, 1982).
6   F Beckett, *Called to Action* (London, 1989), p 74.
7   A Kirk, *Theology Encounters Revolution* (Leicester, 1980), p 105.
8   Stott, *Issues Facing Christians Today*, p 151.
9   V Samuel, C Sugden (eds), *The Church in Response to Human Need* (Grand Rapids, 1987), p 15.
10 *Proclaim Christ Until He Comes*, p 30.

Chapter 12

NEW TESTAMENT EVANGELISM

Tom Houston

'New Testament Evangelism' sounds like a good definitive title. Yet even to use these words raises problems.

I discovered this when I travelled in many countries and tried to convey that World Vision, the organization for which I worked, was 'evangelical'. I discovered that the word 'evangelical' means something different in almost every country. It tends to have bad connotations in many languages, so much so that I was not sure I wanted to be known as an 'evangelical' in some. Equally, to say in some places that we wanted to be engaged in 'evangelism' had entirely the wrong connotations.

That set me thinking. I began to realize that the history of the terms that have the root 'evangel-' in them has not been straightforward. The problem is that they are all transliterations and not translations of words in the New Testament (NT). Like 'amen', 'hallelujah' and 'baptize', the letters of the original Hebrew or Greek word have been taken and made a new word in the receptor language.

The trouble with transliterations is that they leave the meaning of the word to be supplied by the person who uses or hears it. This is the situation with 'evangelism'. Whenever co-operative efforts in evangelism are contemplated, sooner or later someone will say, 'What do you mean by evangelism?' and differences begin to emerge. Evangelism then becomes a source of division where unity is most needed.

The purpose of this article is to try and bring out the issues where ideas of evangelism divide people, and then to see if by exploring the meaning of *euangelion* and its cognate words in the NT we can resolve some of the tensions.

Differences of view about evangelism

Continuity or discontinuity?
Historic churches which practise infant baptism believe that baptized persons become Christians, at least potentially, when they are baptized. Everything after that is a continuous process by which the potential is realized through Christian nurture. Evangelism tends to be an internal church activity.

The main example of this is in the Roman Catholic Church, and it is not surprising that they have named the process as 'evangelization' especially after Vatican II. This underlies the two very helpful documents, *Evangelii Nuntiandi* and *Redemptoris Missio* that have come out from the Vatican in the last twenty years.

The same view is held by many of the other main line churches and cannot be forgotten when we begin to talk of evangelizing together. Others are much more aware of the sinfulness of humankind and the need for a conscious 180-degree conversion. The repentance and faith that accompany regeneration mark the discontinuity from the old life to the new life in Christ. For those churches who take this view, evangelism is both an internal and an external activity.

Evangelism or proselytism?

Evangelism is saying, 'Come to Jesus Christ!' Proselytism is saying, 'Join our group!' The person who is proselytized often becomes a clone to the group rather than a disciple of Christ. It is not an easy distinction, because a Christian has to be part of the fellowship of a church and what more natural than the church of those who do the evangelizing? Those who are accused of proselytizing often point to the fact that those whom they 'win' have been only nominally Christian and they are being brought into a vital experience of Jesus Christ. Those who lose such people emphasize that, if this experience is real, then it is a welcome stage in their nurture for which they would like to continue to be responsible.

Evangelism by ritual or reality?

Charles Finney is credited with the origin of the 'invitation' by which people were asked to demonstrate by some act that they were responding positively to a presentation of the gospel. It has taken myriad forms since his time. The two best known are probably the methods used by the Billy Graham Evangelistic Association and Campus Crusade for Christ. At Billy Graham meetings, a 'decision' for Christ is recorded after a person has come forward, been counselled in a prescribed fashion and has been encouraged to pray according to a suggested formula. There are many statistical studies to show that only a small proportion of those who make such a 'decision' are found in the life of a local church, if they were not there already. The charge against this kind of ritual is that, sometimes, it descends to crowd manipulation.

The Four Spiritual Laws tend to be used more in personal witnessing. The 'laws' are presented in a little booklet with diagrams that aim to enable a person to grasp the essential facts of the gospel and 'pray the sinner's prayer'. Again the proportion of those thus 'led to Christ' who continue as practising Christians is thought to be small. The charge against this is that it sometimes uses pressurized sales techniques.

The other view is that a person needs to have a basic minimum of understanding of the truths of the gospel before they are likely to make a commitment of their lives that will last. This understanding is what those who evangelize must aim to create over time, until the person is ready intelligently to believe and obey the gospel. This is often called friendship evangelism and is seen as a long-term task in which local churches encourage their members to engage.

Evangelism by head-hunting or heart-change
The magic method of raising funds for evangelism is to be able to say that so many people have given their lives to Christ. This may drive some mass evangelists into methods of eliciting and measuring response to the gospel that leave much to be desired in terms of honest reporting. The most recent examples of this have been in the old Soviet Union where evangelists from the West have come and held their meetings in stadia and culture halls. They have seen thousands of people respond to their appeals, some of whom are not to be found in the local churches and often end up in the communes of the false sects. The church-planting movement represents a reaction to this statistics-driven approach. Local Christians are encouraged to take an incarnational approach. They live and meet people in the locality and, over time, witness to their neighbours until they show an interest in what makes Christians different.

Evangelism defined by evangelists
Elmer Gantry is the Hollywood model of the undesirable evangelist who is loose in his morals and motivated by money. Every generation has its examples. We have to take account of the fact that, both within and outside the church, our talk of evangelism is affected by the caricature of evangelism represented by its worst examples. The televangelist is the current image with which we have to contend.

Evangelism and finishing the task
Evangelization became a 'watchword' at the end of the nineteenth century. The slogan was 'The evangelization of the world in our generation'. It was felt that the church had the people and the means to complete the task described by Jesus: 'This good news of the kingdom will be proclaimed through the world as a testimony to all the nations; and then the end shall come'. The story of how this target was missed is told by Todd M Johnson in *Countdown to 1900*.

In the last quarter of the twentieth century, the same vision has been resurrected, and thousands of plans have been drawn up to try and complete the evangelization of the world. The debate that this has engendered hangs on the definition of evangelization, what is meant by a 'nation' and when we may say that evangelization has been completed.

This is an important debate because it affects where we decide to put our efforts in evangelism. Do we continue to work where the gospel is already accessible or do we, like Paul, proclaim the good news where Christ is not yet named?

The semantics of evangelism

'Evangelism', 'evangelization' and 'evangelical' are not English Bible words. After an initial attempt by Wycliffe in the fourteenth century, almost all the earlier English translations of the Bible avoided the transliteration and used a phrase like 'preach the gospel' for *euangelizomai* and 'gospel' for *euangelion*. The only exception to this has been the consistent use of 'evangelist' in the three uses of *euangelistes* in the NT.[1]

It adds to our difficulty that *euangelion* is translated as 'gospel', an old English word whose origin is forgotten and is now only used in a metaphorical sense to indicate a particular body of belief, eg 'the gospel of temperance'. The use of 'evangelism', etc, in Great Britain is really a phenomenon of the last 150 years. None of these expressions are to be found in the writings of John Wesley or George Whitefield, or in William Carey's famous *Enquiry*. They are used in the period during which the Evangelical Alliance has functioned and which this book celebrates. Sometimes the words have had a positive and sometimes a pejorative meaning in the mind of the public.[2]

Generally, 'evangelism' has referred to the methods employed; 'evangelization' has referred either to the process or the result; and 'evangelical' has referred to the beliefs held to be essential.

How the New Testament talks about the communication of the Christian message

We shall now examine the uses of the words *euangelion* and *euangelizomai* in the Greek NT, to see if there are any clues as to how we might get out of the dilemmas that are represented in the first section above. There are inherent limitations to this word-study approach. Language is very imprecise and there is a great range of synonyms in the NT that refer to the communication of the Christian message. We should, however, be able to grasp something of how Luke and Paul approached the subject.

If we were really to translate *euangelizomai*, we would say 'good-news-ize' or 'tell good news'. Some of our more recent translations take this approach, but they still leave the content and process of spreading the good news to be defined. So what do we find?

Evangelism is not the only way of talking about Christian communication

Not all the writers of the NT use the concept of *euangelion* or the verb *euangelizomai*. They are not to be found at all in John's gospel or letters. In fact, their use is scarce except in the writing of Luke (27 times) and Paul (81 times). Next to these, comes Mark with 8 references. John mostly used the concept of 'witness' and 'testimony', and also the familiar term 'born again'.

This reminds us that the early Christians had different ways of talking about the message that meant more to them than anything else in the world. They did not damn each other because they did not use the same vocabulary. In fact they used the language that suited their readers.

The pre-Christian uses of euangelion and euangelizomai

In the Septuagint Greek translation of the OT, *euangelion* is used in the royal psalms that *heralded* God's universal victory over the world and his subsequent kingly rule (Psalms 40:9; 68:11; 96:2–3). It is also found in Isaiah, to 'proclaim' the return of God to Zion and the beginning of a new era with his enthronement there (Isaiah 52:7; 40:9). This heralded the hoped-for return of the great days of King David. The Greek understanding of *euangelion* came from the cult of emperor worship. It is the word used to announce and celebrate the birth or accession or new decree of an emperor.[3] In both cases, it referred to the 'proclamation' of a new era in which things would be different and better than anything that had gone before.

Euangelion is not a lightweight concept. It has a declaratory feel to it, like a prime minister announcing the inauguration of a National Health Service in which everyone can participate. It is not surprising that it was translated by the somewhat formal word 'preach' and sometimes by the word of the herald, 'proclaim'.

The author and content of the Good News

The weight of the concept is borne out by the nature of its author and its content. It is the gospel 'of God' (7 times). It is the word of the Lord (Acts 15:35; 1 Thessalonians 2:2). God is its author. It is the gospel 'of the kingdom of God' (7 times: Luke 4:43; 8:1; 16:16; Acts 8:12), the inauguration of a new era when, for its hearers, things can be different if they enter this kingdom and submit to its king. It is the gospel 'of Jesus Christ' (17 times). This Jesus, who is the content of the gospel, is described most frequently as the Christ or Messiah (Mark 1:1; Acts 5:42). He is also the one crucified for sin (1 Corinthians 15:3); the resurrected one (1 Corinthians 15:4; Acts 17:18); the Lord (Acts 11:20) and the Son of God (Mark 1:1; Romans 1:3).

The gospel has its roots in the OT. It is the promise made to the fathers (Acts 13:32). It is about peace (Acts 10:36; Ephesians 2:17; 6:15), the grace of God (Acts 20:24), truth (Galatians 2:5,14; Colossians 1:5), salvation (Ephesians 1:13), hope (Colossians 1:23), 'the unsearchable riches of Christ' (Ephesians 3:8), the glory of Christ (2 Corinthians 4:4; 1 Timothy 1:11). In short, its content is huge. It is almost everything. It is not surprising that, for instance, the Roman Catholic documents define evangelization so comprehensively.

This is probably the place to mention the use of *euangelion* to describe a written gospel. Although this use of the word occurs only from the second century onwards, it traces its origin back to Mark 1:1, 'The beginning of the gospel about Jesus Christ, the Son of God'. This seems like a title and it appears to have created a precedent that Christian writers began to follow in talking about the Four Gospels. Historically, it appears that after the initial surge forward of the church in the first thirty years of its life, there arose a need to codify and limit what essentially constituted the 'gospel'. No doubt this was primarily for the purpose of teaching those who had responded to the preaching, but was also used evangelistically. It was the minimum content that a person needed to understand about Jesus in order to have a commitment to him that would last.

The bearers of the Good News

In the Gospels, the angel Gabriel, John the Baptist, and Jesus and the twelve apostles all proclaim the good news (Luke 1:19; 2:10; 3:18; 4:18,43; 9:6). When we turn to the Acts, the communicators are the apostles, those scattered from Jerusalem who were not apostles, Philip the evangelist, and various pairs like Peter and John, Paul and Barnabas, and so on (Acts 5:42; 8:4,12,25,35; 14:15). It seems to be a task for which some people have a particular gifting but may be assisted also by rank-and-file Christians.

The recipients of the Good News

Both people and places are said to be evangelized. People are described as the poor, the Ethiopian eunuch, Greeks, Gentiles, people in synagogues and in Macedonia, or simply people. The places are villages, towns and cities (Luke 4:18; 7:22; 3:8; Acts 8:25,34–35,40; 11:20; 13:6–7,13–32; 14:6–7,21; 16:10).

Of the 16 places/audiences in Acts, no response to the message is reported in 9 of them. This seems to indicate that evangelizing may consist of communicating the message irrespective of any response or result. In the other seven cases a response is mentioned. Sometimes the success is complete, as is the case when the Ethiopian eunuch believes and is baptized (Acts 8:38). More usually, there is a modest response in a number of immediate converts, although these are usually a minority of the hearers or of the local population (Acts 14:21). At other times there is a mixed response, as with Paul on Mars Hill: some people mocked; some kept an open mind; others believed (Acts 17:32,34).

Yet in all of these cases people are spoken of as having been evangelized. Peter and John evangelized many villages of Samaria. Philip evangelized the Ethiopian eunuch. He then went on to evangelize every town from Ashdod to Caesarea, which is most of the Mediterranean coast of Palestine, a distance of sixty miles. In this case no converts are reported, although the language is that they were evangelized.

We get some help with the dilemma of evangelism without converts from two other incidents in Acts. In Derbe, Paul and Barnabas evangelized and made disciples (Acts 14:21). This seems to imply that to evangelize and to make disciples are connected but not exactly synonymous. In Antioch, these same two men taught and evangelized (Acts 15:35). Teaching is closely related to evangelizing but, again, is not quite the same thing.

Perhaps this is the place to introduce the parable of The Sower (Matthew 13:1–9). There is no reference to the term 'gospel' in this teaching, but the seed that was sown is described as 'the word of the kingdom', which is close. This parable adds the dimension that evangelism may appear at first to be successful but later prove to have been abortive because the message was not properly understood.

The process of evangelizing

Evangelizing is a co-operative process, linked to local churches. The various pairs and teams in the Acts show this. When Paul is describing his Christian friends, one of the highest commendations he can give them is that they were partners in the gospel (Philippians 1:4–5,11; 4:3). The picture is of a great company geared to making the good news of Jesus and the kingdom known wherever, whenever and to whomsoever they could. The picture is not one of 'lone ranger' evangelists operating apart from the fellowships of believers.

Evangelizing was not a uniform process. There was a gospel for the uncircumcised that was entrusted to Paul, and a gospel for the circumcised entrusted to Peter. These were not regarded as different gospels although they had very different applications. Even Paul switched roles, depending on what audience he was addressing (1 Corinthians 9:19–23; Galatians 2:7). The Four Gospels and the different vocabularies of the letters of the NT all point to the variety of expression that was used to convey the one essential message.

It was, however, a controversial process. There were other gospels which could not be tolerated (2 Corinthians 11:4; Galatians 1:6). There were occasions when they had to defend the gospel, and this meant strife (Philippians 1:7,16,27). This would seem to refer to the content of the gospel. It would be a study in itself to see how Paul and others defined what needed to be defended and defended against. There is another interesting word. Paul asks for prayer that he might make known the 'mystery' of the gospel. In context, a 'mystery' tended to be something that could be known only from the inside. This is why Jesus emphasized that the Spirit was upon him so that he would 'preach good news to the poor'. Peter also says that the apostles evangelized by the Holy Spirit (Luke 4:18; 1 Peter 1:12). While the gospel must be understood to be effective, it takes the work of the Holy Spirit in the hearer to achieve this.

God also works through circumstances to 'further the gospel' (Philippians 1:12). In the case in point, it was Paul's arrest and imprisonment that enabled him to bear witness among the praetorian guard in the capital, Rome.

Inferences from the use of *euangelion* and *euangelizomai* in the New Testament

Allowing for the fact that there are a great many other ways by which the communication of the Christian message is described by the writers of the NT,[4] what can we say about evangelism based on the survey above?

Evangelism is a momentous activity

It offers people a totally new regime to live under, with incalculable benefits for those who genuinely enter God's kingdom ready to live under its king. It encompasses the whole range of the truths by which people are meant to live.

The use of *euangelion* and its cognates is the closest the NT comes to describe Christian communication as a formal activity of crucial importance. They underline the danger of corruption and degradation of the message. If public relations is the harmonizing of the expectations of the audience with the objectives of an organization, then there is a case for some quality control to be exercised in the way we 'evangelize'. Of course, any manufacturer wishes to have the unsolicited recommendations of the users of his product, but he makes sure that the message he wants to get across is clear and distinct. Similarly, there is a role for witness and testimony on the part of all Christians. Yet the essential message needs to be safeguarded from alternative versions.

The quality control needs to be both of the content of the message and of the character and preparedness of those who spread it. I heard recently of a city where more than a hundred churches agreed that in their statements outside the church, they would focus only on the absolutes of the gospel they held in common. They would avoid comparative language in referring to one another. It made a great difference to their advertisements and the notice boards outside their buildings. The city began to get one message from all the different churches and began to take notice.

Evangelism is a shared activity

It has to be a shared activity, because the people we are to evangelize are very different and it will take all of us together with our different emphases to reach them. The task will not be accomplished only by those who take the 'comprehensive continuity' approach. Not everyone is in church now as they tended to be when the parish system worked and church attendance was compulsory. There are still some who will be nurtured for a lifetime. Many more, however, need those who emphasize conversion and discontinuity.

Similarly, we need to relax and be realistic about what proselytism may be perceived as. If our primary commitment is that each person should have a first-hand experience of Jesus Christ, by whatever means God chooses to use, then we need to be glad and not jealous when it comes by someone other than ourselves. Equally, we need to recognize that God has different ways of reaching different people. To standardize the way God has blessed us and insist that others must have what we have or do as we do, or be disqualified, is to play God and insult his image in others.

Evangelism is a multi-phased activity

Evangelism may be said to have occurred whether there is a positive or negative or a non-committal response. We must not be discouraged when people do not listen, always provided that we have sensitively endeavoured to speak within the understanding of our hearers.

Evangelism takes place when it is started, but it is not finished when it is started. There is a lot of wonderful small print that will take a lifetime to get into, after the initial signing-up to God's offer of salvation. If there is not the opportunity to be taught more and encouraged to be disciples, evangelism is likely to prove abortive.

We can say when evangelism is started. We cannot say when it is finished, for it is never finished. There is more of the gospel that we all have to learn. Each generation has to be evangelized in turn. We do need to concentrate on both the task of starting where Christ is not named and continuing where the teaching and discipling have to be progressed.

This implies that it is vital to get the process started. I recall having a conversation with Bill Bright of Campus Crusade for Christ about our difference of outlook. For many years I have only been interested in fruit that will remain and have acted accordingly. Bill took the view that, although many who prayed the sinner's prayer after being taken through The Four Spiritual Laws did not go on to be practising Christians, the net result was that more did follow Christ than was the case in those who took a more cautious approach. I could not deny it. We must not allow our concern for the fullness of the gospel to deter us from activities that will make sure the process is started in the maximum number of people. Plato said, 'Well begun is half done!' But it is only half done. We are irresponsible if we deliberately start the process where there is no likelihood of its being followed through by teaching and discipling. Of course, we have to sow beside all waters, but the waters should be where we are able to cultivate and harvest that which may germinate and take root.

Evangelism is a contested activity

When the tares were discovered in the field, the Master said, 'An enemy has done this.' False or inadequate gospels are and will be in the field, and we need to move with care so that the enemy is resisted with the only means that can keep him from succeeding. This is by exercising the seven disciplines of spiritual warfare that Paul enunciates before he twice asks the Ephesians to pray that he might evangelize effectively. These have to do with truth, righteousness before God and justice before our fellows. They have to do with relationships of peace, a persistent faith, a grasp of salvation and a good use of scripture (Ephesians 6:14–19). Evangelism is relatively easily corrupted by the selfish expectations of those who hear the gospel and respond too quickly to its message. We ought to be cautious about the soil in which we sow the good seed of the word, and break up fallow ground and tackle thorns before we sow. For this the sovereign Spirit is given to make us wise as well as to give us power, to teach us truth as well as to stir our emotions, to make us holy as well as bold.

Evangelism is a divine activity

God is the author of the gospel. It was he who sent his Son to be the Saviour of the world. It is the risen Christ who sends us to preach the gospel to every creature. It is he who promises to be with us always, until the end of the age. It is he who gives gifts to his church, including the evangelists and the ancillary activities that many of the members of the Body need to exercise for the evangelist to be effective.

It is a task that will be completed, as Christ has foretold. When that will be depends on God's mercy and grace on the one hand and, on the other hand, our response to his call to evangelize. This is a limited call for each of us. Yet when all respond together it is the way the task will be finished.

Endnotes

1   D B Barrett, *Evangelize: A Historical Survey of the Concept* (Birmingham, Alabama, 1987), p 22.
2   Barrett, *Evangelize*, pp 24–26.
3   C Brown (ed), 'Gospel', *NIDNTT II*, pp 108–109.
4   Barrett, *Evangelize*, pp 15–19.

Chapter 13

OVERCOMING SOCIAL BARRIERS TO THE GOSPEL

Roy McCloughry

The end of the millennium finds the church searching for answers to questions about the presentation of the gospel in a society which appears to be indifferent to its claims. A number of experiments in worship have been started all over the country, and churches have been planted in pubs, nightclubs, supermarkets and other diverse venues in order to reach people who may not find it natural to come into a purpose-built church building. The evangelical church itself has fragmented, with conservative, charismatic, contemplative and radical strands each creating their own subcultures. Evangelicals are committed people. They have a message which they want to communicate effectively, hence the experimentation. The problem is that most evangelicals still live in the modern world, but the modern world is passing away. Outside the church things are changing fast. People are talking about the post-modern agenda which seems to change every time one comes across it. One thing that does seem to be fairly certain, however, is that meta-narratives are dead. This means that big stories which bring together all the different elements of culture in one explanation of their meaning are supposed to be a thing of the past. Christianity, like Marxism, is one of those stories which purported to explain all of life. Post-modernity cannot take people who try to convey meaning or who are trying to persuade others of their moral stance.[1] In the plural world of the post-modernist, Christianity is seen as arrogant and patronizing in its claims to have discovered objective truth.

In such a world, the church is at sea. It can reach those who still live in the modern world with its scientific certainty, its commitment to progress and its family morality. But the world portrayed in the cinemas, magazines, youth cultures and music needs different touchstones, methods and approaches. It is crucial that Christians are enabled to see the difference between that which is essentially Christian and that which is cultural and transient in our own beliefs. Otherwise, we will repeat the mistake which the parents of the Fifties made of the generation of the Sixties – to condemn their culture rather than to attempt to understand it.

In a fast-changing society, barriers to the gospel are not the same in every generation. The world changes, technology moves on, the family breaks down and ideologies disappear. It is true that the basic questions and problems of survival, purpose and belonging are the same in each generation. But the faster the culture moves on, the less one generation understands the answers or compromises that the previous generation has made. Rapid change puts up barriers between the generations so that the wisdom of an older generation is not seen as relevant to the information age. This can be frustrating to those who are convinced that such wisdom is what is required. It is here that creativity is needed if barriers are to be broken down. For, while the opportunity to moralize to the young has long gone, the opportunity to mentor them is only just beginning to be recognized. Training has now given way to 'coaching' and 'mentoring', and 'one to one' or 'relational' methods are challenging more didactic formal modes of learning. On the one hand, a barrier appears, but at the same time an opportunity is given. If something is true and necessary for human flourishing, then it will crop up again in another form. If society can get on without it and still survive, maybe it was transient. Such an exercise of discernment on the part of Christians between what is import-ant and what is trivial within Christianity is vital if we are not to give up on the world and wait for heaven with a resigned sense of self-righteousness.

This introduction is meant to prepare us for a difficult set of questions. The gospel is 'good news'. But while one in three people in the world professes to be Christian, and many churches in the developing world are booming, the church continues to struggle in Europe. We know that the world harbours all kinds of behaviour and beliefs which do not honour God and which Christians are committed to change. But the world looks at the church and asks what is so special about Christianity? The task of the church in mission is to make Christ visible to a world for whom he is invisible. We are the Body of Christ. If the visible institution of the church is in difficulties, then it may not be able to convey good news because its own life is not a convincing portrayal of it. Before anything else we have to look at the institutional church.

Overcoming barriers to faith

There are many different kinds of difficulties that the Christian church faces in trying to be an effective witness to the gospel. Some of these are cultural barriers to understanding the gospel which the church itself presents to people. These are not legitimate barriers, such as the cost of discipleship, which the prospective disciple has to evaluate. They may be to do with the behaviour patterns of the institutional church that actually distort or obscure the gospel itself. Many people do not understand the gospel in the terms in which it is presented to them. This may be because it is presented in religious language to a culture that no longer understands it. Understanding the word 'sin' is vital to an understanding of salvation, yet the word 'sin' is fraught with difficulties. Talking about the guilt that results from sin may not communicate easily to a generation which has relativized all moral codes. The idea that the contravention of an ancient Judaeo-Christian code of ethics might be the criterion by which access to eternal life is judged may seem a nonsense to many people for whom pluralism is an expression of tolerance rather than a threat to authority. People can see that, if one believes in Christianity, such a breaking of its code may be a problem. To state that it is a problem for those who do not believe the code is viewed not as wrong but as a denial of freedom of choice, an imposition by one person or group of their world-view upon another. The problem is not that Christians have to play down the concept of sin, since it is foundational to their understanding of the world. It is that they have to understand its place in a new culture.

Christian strategies may also pose a problem for people. Much has been written about methods of evangelism, such as the mass crusade, or 'door to door', which were useful strategies in a previous generation but which are not acceptable to many people today. But if the understanding of the self that lies behind the teaching of the church is out of step with people's understanding of themselves, then the effect can be to drive people away from faith. An emphasis on a message of judgement and hell-fire may not have a positive impact on those who already feel inadequate. They may have been attracted to church, sensing that awareness of God brings with it self-awareness and a sense of confidence which they lack. Being told that they have a 'monstrous ego' and are 'rebelling against God' may not easily resonate with their experience of life.[2] Instead of being encouraged and affirmed by the love of God, they are alienated by the judgement of God. Again, we need to be clear that Christians are being asked not to lay down their belief in judgement but to rediscover its place within the culture. It is simply lazy to protest that the gospel is 'truth unchanged, unchanging', as if that lets us off the hook of understanding people and the cultures they live in. To protest that God will work, whatever the words, is to reduce the work of the Holy Spirit to magic since, no doubt, he could work if one stood on one's head.

This raises an associated issue about the methods of presentation used to reach people with the gospel. Much of the communication of the gospel by the church assumes that the listener comes from an articulate book culture. Many of the talks given in churches assume that people are conceptual in their approach to the gospel and enjoy wrestling with the challenges of the doctrines of justification by faith or atonement. Often the assumption is also made that the listener is willing to listen to a long oration that follows a series of logical steps without much narrative content. When we compare such presentations to the methods of the media-society in which we live, we find that they are entirely different. People are captivated by stories and by soap operas which are essentially relational in content. This divergence between the two methods of presentation raises serious questions about the learning potential of many sermons. This does not mean that we can relax into the anti-intellectualism of so much of modern evangelicalism. Communicating the gospel in the way Jesus did took much study, reflection and wisdom. However, what it does mean is that we cannot assume that the methods enjoyed by some are enjoyed by all. While biblical exposition is a vital tool, too often over-looked or done badly, it is not the only way of conveying biblical truth to the hearer. The old teacher's proverb, 'It is not what you say that matters, it is what they hear', illustrates the way in which assumptions about communication can become a barrier to the gospel itself.

We turn to consider the values of the institutional church. We live in a society in which tradition is under threat and traditional institutions are no longer assumed to convey timeless truths from a previous generation. Instead of institutions, such as the church, being mediators of truth to each generation, they are now perceived to be part of the problem that people have to overcome if they are to believe the gospel. In a post-modern world the institutional church is a problem not a solution. Part of the difficulty lies with the rapid moral change that has happened since the Second World War, but which has its roots in the historical develop-ment of our culture since the Reformation. The advent of cultural plural-ism and the attendant rejection of authoritarianism has posed a problem for the church. Christians are on the defensive from a new expression of morality which has at its roots attitudes such as non-discrimination (of sexual lifestyles), tolerance (as a moral virtue) and a privatized individual-ism based on rights. In such a context, people look to Christianity only as a source of ill-defined 'virtues' such as 'love', but will not accept the authority of the church in speaking out against the evils of such a society. This places the church at odds with the prevailing ethos which sees plural-ism as an essential precursor of morality in terms of individual freedom rather than as undermining a culture of shared moral values based on divine revelation.

The task of overcoming this dilemma rests on achieving a balance between authority and relevance. One strategy which evangelicals have rejected has been adopted by liberal theologians. This strategy sees bar-riers to belief arising from the structure of Christian theology itself. It sees the world-view of the Bible as constrained by its social and intellectual context, and is willing to negotiate about what it is realistic to ask people to believe. In a modern society that is based on concepts of the rational individual and the scientific method, this view ends up by negotiating about the supernatural or moral content of the biblical narrative. It sees it as not believable since it is not consonant with scientific rationalism or the moral freedom of the individual. Negotiation with the world about what it is prepared to believe asserts relevance over authority. However, at the other extreme of a Christian response to a pluralistic and secularized world is fundamentalism. This reasserts the unquestioning acceptance of tradition as it refuses to enter into dialogue with contemporary culture and becomes dogmatic. In this response, authority (or rather authoritarianism) asserts itself over relevance. Fundamentalism is a defen-sive position taken by those who believe that all change is ultimately for the worse. It crushes the human spirit which longs to asks questions and state objections. It is suspicious of dialogue since it sees nothing to learn from 'the world' and, in promising 'the answer' to people, refuses to answer their questions honestly.

It was sociologist Peter Berger[3] who labelled these as strategies of accommodation and defence in a secularized world. They raise a question with which we now have to deal: 'How are Christians to deal with those problems in society which are an offence to God and are in themselves a barrier to people experiencing the goodness of God? The church is either a signpost to the existence of the kingdom of God or it is nothing. Under the reign of God there is no room for injustice, oppression or evil. Christians are not called only to proclaim the message of the gospel: they are called to live by faith as if the kingdom has come'. Many of the ills of our society such as racism, poverty, violence, abuse and sexual irresponsibility are an offence against God. If we reject the option of moralizing about the sins of others from the sidelines of society, what strategies should we adopt to overcome those persistent social evils which bar people from experiencing life as good news?

Overcoming barriers to love

In the time of Jesus the definition of the 'kingdom of God' by those who were part of the religious establishment excluded groups who were not 'acceptable' to the establishment. Interestingly, the same groups of people still struggle for recognition. The impression given from Jesus' own ministry is that he spent his time with people who were predominantly poor or who were in some kind of need. For them the gospel was 'good news' in a very immediate sense. The blind received their sight, the sick were healed and the poor were told that 'the first shall be last and the last shall be first'. Although we live in a society where the general standard of living is much higher than in the days of Jesus, the same groups of people still struggle to have a place in the community. The institutional church is perceived, perhaps unfairly, as mostly meeting the needs of the middle classes rather than those who are on the underside of society. This is despite the problems we face in our communities today. It is not as if there is no poverty, violence or abuse of people in our own world. We live with problems of racism, discrimination, anomie, unemployment and urban decay which all cry out for love and justice effectively to be demonstrated in the modern context.

Jesus modelled the task of overcoming social barriers to the gospel by being willing to risk misunderstanding and rejection through being with people who were the other side of religiously maintained barriers. Jesus was the one who ate with 'tax collectors and sinners' and who got a bad reputation for doing so. He lived and worked among prostitutes, con-men, the demon-possessed and the vilified, saying that it was the sick who needed a doctor. He told stories that appealed to poor people about patching ragged garments, having parties and searching for lost coins. He brought salvation to the people by being with them where they were. Not only this, he explicitly taught that loving those who love us in return is not an expression of the love of God. In one of the most famous passages in the New Testament, Jesus tells his disciples that they are to love and lend to those who can offer nothing in return.[4] 'Even sinners', Jesus says, 'love those who love them and lend to those who give them their money back' (Luke 6:32–36).

Against this background of the teaching and ministry of Jesus, evangelicals have returned to scrutinize the Bible for its message about justice. For, until recently, evangelicals thought of their task as engagement with the personal agendas of 'individuals' whose personal response to Christ was the only way in which the church could hope to influence society. As more people became Christians, so society would become more Christian. In this view there was a tendency to see anything which was not overtly religious as 'belonging to the world' and this, in turn, ensured that it was either disregarded or vilified. This atomistic view has declined in recent years, not because evangelicals have lessened their commitment to the transformation of the person through the work of Christ, but because they have seen that Christianity offers a far more radical and comprehensive view of salvation history than can be described by such means. Now, evangelicals frequently talk about engaging with contemporary culture, the partnership of evangelism with social action, the necessity to address political issues, and the concept of the Christian mind as part of an agenda that seeks not only to preserve evangelical unity and integrity but also to influence contemporary culture to favour Christian norms and behaviour.

Evangelical churches are now setting up all kinds of church projects to reach into the community in order to demonstrate that the gospel is good news about justice. But it is one thing for the local church to put on projects for the 'poor'; it is quite another to associate with the 'poor' oneself. It is this which remains on the agenda of the church. Arm's-length involvement is a compromise not proposed by the ministry of Jesus. When one suggests to people that they might make friendships with people whom they perceive as a threat, one comes face to face with the fear of the abnormal and its resultant stigmatizing and stereotyping. Yet it is the very foundation of the gospel that Christ died for us while we were still enemies.

The authenticity of Christianity in social terms depends on the community of the church having distinctives within it which witness to the power, love and justice of God. Yet one of the reasons why the church finds it so difficult to engage in mission is just such a lack of distinctiveness. The church is at its most remarkable when it is a unified community of former enemies in which people who are separated by all kinds of barriers in the world call each other brothers and sisters in the kingdom of God. The recovery of the social dimension of the gospel has brought many local churches into contact with people they would not otherwise have met. The challenge now is to draw those people into friendship and a new experience of the love of God. We now know that it is friendship which brings people into the Christian faith rather than pamphlets, books, videos or conferences. If those who are marginalized in our society are going to hear the gospel, then somebody, somewhere, must befriend them.

I am not talking here about a technique known as 'friendship evangelism' in which a Christian appears to offer someone who is not a Christian friendship in order to bring them to a mission or evangelistic meeting. I am talking about open, sincere and committed friendship in which Christians are willing to love others, foster intimacy and admit to vulnerability. Such a view of love seems to be at the heart of what Jesus is saying in Luke chapter 6. He seems to be saying, 'People who are not Christians give and receive love on a reciprocal basis, but you are called to love those who may not love you in return. That is the kind of love God loves you with.'

Christians who cross cultural barriers to love others, and to bring about justice for them, are respected by others. The history of the church is not only the history of inquisition and institutional power. It is also the history of courage and bravery on behalf of the gospel. The problem which faces us in this country, and in similar cultures, is that many of us have normalized our Christian commitments so that we remain within our comfort zones. The history of Christian mission shows that God becomes a reality when one steps outside the comfort zone. Taking a risk is another way of describing a step of faith.

With this kind of love in operation the task of mission begins to fall into place. It poses a challenge to which we can respond only if we are empowered by the Holy Spirit. In effect, it creates community where there was none, instead of servicing a community which already exists on a reciprocal basis. It ensures the diversity of the church while providing the basis of unity. It means that the world can look at the church and say, 'See how they love one another.' In a stratified society where rich and poor, employed and unemployed, black and white live in different subcultures, it witnesses to a view of justice that is not separate from love but actually based on it. John Stott has said, 'What love desires, justice demands.' By this I take him to mean that, if we are willing to form loving relationships with those who are in need, we will soon begin to care about justice with a passion fuelled by our love for them. If we do not know anybody in that situation, justice may well remain academic for us. It is essential to a Christian view of words such as love, mercy and justice that they are relational. We may use political means to create a better society or start community projects to create opportunities for people who have no hope, but if we put up barriers against people who need our friendship and support, then those who are not Christians may step in to help, as the story of the good Samaritan illustrates.

Overcoming barriers to hope

If the church reforms itself as an institution and learns to communicate clearly with the society in which it finds itself, and even if Christians engage in cross-cultural mission, drawing people into community and friendship, we still have to face a world which is deeply compromised. Christians are called to work for a world that is more pleasing to God. Yet we face a world in which the old confidence of modernity is ebbing away. The halcyon days of belief in the power of politics has given way to a cynicism about leadership. Faith in the inevitability of progress has turned into a concern about ecological crisis. Change is now presented as something that happens to us rather than something we initiate in order to transform our communities.

Against the background of post-modernity there is more anxiety about our global future than there has ever been. The pace of globalization links the world into a global market and a global media. We are aware of events happening around the world as they happen. We are barraged with information to which we have little hope of responding. We turn away from the events in Bosnia, sick at heart but feeling powerless. Globalization is defined as action at a distance, the ability to do deals in Asia while living in Europe or to buy fruit grown in the Cameroon in our local supermarket. We are becoming one world. There is much to celebrate about this, yet a pervasive sense of unease and instability abounds. We are the first generation to face up to the consequence of our past actions on the environment. Whereas previous generations lived with natural uncertainty about the timing of earthquakes or volcanic eruptions, we live with 'manufactured uncertainty'[5] about the impact of acid rain, global warming, desertification, population growth and urban blight, which are all the unintended consequences of human actions. We have no way of knowing how the world will respond to the way we have been treating it. We are learning hard lessons about the abdication of the theology of stewardship with its attendant ideas of responsibility, accountability and sustainability.[6]

People are more aware of the fragility of their future than they have been at any time since the Second World War. Our global future continues to alarm us; but people are also anxious about their personal future. In Europe, the growth of industrialization elsewhere in the world is putting us under pressure economically. We are living with high levels of unemployment, and the idea of the career has been replaced by the need to be as flexible as possible during one's working life. Unemployment is most tragic among young people, with unemployment rates for black young people (especially men) being unacceptably high. Yet those who are in work have 39% less leisure time than in 1979 and face high stress levels. The predominance of words like 'efficiency' as a goal of employers means in practice that those who are made redundant have their work distributed among people who are already carrying a full load. This means that those out of work face depression while those in work face stress.

I have chosen ecological crisis to illustrate global uncertainties, and problems in the world of work to illustrate personal uncertainty and anxiety, yet many other subjects illustrate the same trends whether it is the break-up of the family, the prevalence of child abuse, the fear of incoherent acts of terrorism or the advent of AIDS. In such a world, Christians can be a source of hope, believing as they do in the power of God to redeem the world and God's preparation of a new world in which we shall live and work in a community of justice and love. Christians can be a source of hope only if they themselves are hopeful about the future and if they experience a sense of hope as a motivation in their lives. As in the case of a love which crosses boundaries, it is the ability of Christians to offer hope where anxiety may seem more rational, or even more comforting, that witnesses to the gospel.

Overcoming barriers to the gospel

This essay has been about the need to focus on the foundations of the Christian faith in a changing and often unjust world. The heart of the gospel is best portrayed by the church when it exhibits faith, hope and love. In a post-modern world which has lost its sense of transcendence, faith is vital to Christian witness. If we displace the life of faith with membership and maintenance of the institutional church, our churches will empty and our message will be disregarded. Post-modernity is not a rejection of faith but a scepticism about institutions. Similarly, an unjust world needs Christians to love others with the love of Christ. Such relationships may lead to action for justice, political lobbying or community action; but at the heart of them is a commitment to a kind of love that is willing to cross cultural, economic and social barriers to demonstrate the nature of the kingdom of God. Finally, in a world which is anxious about its own future and in which people may be less certain about what life will bring them, Christians are called to exemplify hope. These three foundations of Christian living are at the heart of the calling of the church. New leadership and vision is unlikely to come from the power structures of our day, which are already associated with the failures of the status quo.[7] It is the courage of ordinary people, who are determined to overcome all obstacles in order to reach out to people and touch their lives, that will produce genuine change in our society.

Endnotes

1 N Mercer, 'Post-modernity and rationality: the final credits or just a commercial break?', A Billington, T Lane and M Turner (eds), *Mission and Meaning: Essays Presented to Peter Cotterell* (Carlisle, 1995).
2 C Lasch, *The Culture of Narcissism* (London, 1980).
3 P Berger, *Facing up to Modernity*, (Harmondsworth, 1979), p 221.

4 R McCloughry, *The Eye of the Needle* (Leicester, 1990) p 56.
5 A Giddens, *Beyond Left and Right: The Future of Radical Politics* (London, 1995).
6 T Wright, *New Tasks for a Renewed Church* (London, 1992), p 140.
7 J Wallis, *The Soul of Politics* (London, 1994), p 45.

Part 3
WHERE WE COME FROM

Chapter 14

ROOTS OF PAN-EVANGELICALISM: 1735–1835

Ken Hylson-Smith

The whole ethos of Protestantism – its theological basis, the behavioural patterns it inculcates, its attitudinal emphasis and its authority structure – make it inherently liable to schism and fragmentation. It has a built-in tendency to be centrifugal rather than centripetal. Whereas the other two major Christian traditions, Roman Catholicism and the Orthodox Churches, are essentially monolithic structures in which universal conservatism and universal conformism are the order of the day, Protestantism is the very reverse. By its very nature it encourages individuality, stresses personal faith and promotes distinctive individual or group expressions of faith and practice. Such characteristics ensure a large measure of personal and corporate creativity; but they also almost guarantee divisiveness, and a hard task faces anyone who strives to achieve any form of Protestant ecumenism. And what is true of Protestantism as a whole is especially so for those archetypal Protestants, the evangelicals.

Such characteristic Protestant tendencies are well illustrated by the history of Protestantism in England from its formal origins in the Acts of State of the 1530s to the beginning of our period in 1735. These two hundred years witnessed the division and re-division of an initially united church. From a quite early stage there were those who were dissatisfied with the extent of change that had been effected and who sought further reformation.[1] For some decades they were prepared to work from within the existing structure, but it was not long before the patience of the more radical of these 'Puritans' wore thin and, by the end of the reign of Elizabeth, the Church of England had spawned its first 'Separatists'.[2] By 1735 the situation had been transformed. The Church of England, which had once monopolized the Protestant interest in England, found itself in a pluralistic situation in which it was confronted by four fully-fledged denominations – the Presbyterians, the Congregationalists, the Baptists and the Quakers – as well as some sects such as the Muggletonians and the recently emergent, ominously energetic and influential Unitarians. The mid-seventeenth century had also brought forth a host of sects at the time of the Commonwealth, thus adding to the confusion and the complexity of the post-Reformation Protestant scene.

It was in the 1730s that the English-speaking world experienced what has been described as 'a more important development than any other, before or after, in the history of Protestant Christianity: the emergence of the movement that became Evangelicalism.'[3]

Some obstacles to pan-evangelicalism

Having provided this brief, broad framework, let us turn to our particular theme: pan-evangelicalism.[4]

It is well to note that there had been little attempt to achieve pan-Protestantism before 1735. The English Protestant story for 150 years had been dominated by division and non-co-operation. The Westminster Assembly was an attempt to unite differing Christians, but it foundered for a host of reasons including Anglican reluctance and Presbyterian intransigence. Faced with the onslaught of the Clarendon Code during the Restoration period the Dissenters might have closed ranks in a union of sympathy based on common suffering, but no such move was made. The Toleration Act of 1689 was followed by a federation of Presbyterians and Congregationalists known as the Happy Union, but the participants differed over their ideas of church polity and the drawing together was of short duration. Anglicans and Nonconformists united at the end of the seventeenth century in the Society for Reformation of Manners with the aim of combating vice and immorality in and about London. This co-operation was also short-lived as the society first fell into Anglican hands and then slowly dissolved. Mention should also be made of the visionary ecumenism of William Wake and his outstanding efforts to advance the ecumenical cause at home and abroad; but it ended in failure. It remained to be seen if evangelicals could achieve a unity which had either not been sought by or had eluded their Protestant forebears.

In its early phase the revival united into societies people from various religious traditions, or from outside any religious body, in a fraternity of like-minded converts. They found a common identity in their newly discovered and life-transforming experiences. Their fellowship was profound and disregarded previous denominational allegiance. But rifts soon appeared. As early as 1740 there was such a serious conflict between John Wesley and his followers and the Moravians with whom they met in society meetings at Fetter Lane in London, that Wesley established a separate society. The dissension was mainly over doctrinal issues, with Wesley questioning Philip Molther's quietism and possible antinomianism. Then there was the protracted strife between John Wesley and George Whitefield over predestination and related matters. This reached such a pitch of bitterness in the years between 1770 and 1780 that many evangelicals abandoned gospel religion in disgust.[5] At various times in the second half of the century there was strong resistance from many of the Church of England evangelicals to the doctrine of perfection, a belief which John Wesley held dear and which he expounded as central to the Methodist message, but which some other evangelicals considered unbiblical and unnecessarily divisive.

Nor was doctrine the only ground for evangelical discord and disunity. The Methodists soon found themselves at odds with some Anglican evangelical clergy over the question of church order. A number of the scattered 'gospel clergy', who were at one with the Methodists in their basic evangelical beliefs, could not tolerate itinerancy and field preaching, especially when such unacceptable practice was made even more reprehensible in the eyes of their critics by the use of laymen as preachers. Increasingly, evangelical parish clergy strictly interpreted their duty to give full canonical obedience to the established church. Some of the most influential clergy, and most notably Charles Simeon in the late eighteenth century and early nineteenth century, were strong churchmen who taught ordinands to keep to their parish boundaries and to value their membership of the Church of England. There was also the frequent fear among evangelical clergyman that they might painstakingly build up a fervent congregation only to see it desert to a local Dissenting group when they left the parish or died and were replaced by an 'unconverted' incumbent. Anglican evangelicals were further worried and frustrated when local parishioners of humble education and means were called under their preaching to enter the Anglican ministry, only to be refused ordination in the Church of England and to seek a ministry in an evangelical Nonconformist denomination. Perhaps, above all, there was Anglican evangelical resentment that field preaching provided Nonconformity with a host of converts. Why, thought Charles Simeon and others, should 'the clergyman beat the bush, and the Dissenters catch the game'?

Then there were wider ecclesiastical and political considerations. By the late 1780s a revived Dissent was pressing for the repeal of the Test Acts and began to whisper menacingly of disestablishment, and some Anglican evangelicals began to take fright. They were anxious that past irregularity might reap an unforeseen harvest.

As the scattered evangelical clergy increased in numbers and started to draw together in clerical associations and by correspondence, they were brought into a closer fraternity. This powerful sense of common faith, combined with a common religious tradition, tended to distance them from their fellow Methodist or Nonconformist evangelical brethren. As they increasingly became a power within the church and developed a special *esprit de corps*, they tended to disown some of the enthusiastic doctrines and practices that had been characteristic of much of the early revival, and they started to emphasize the mediation of grace by quiet and rational means. Instantaneous conversion was no longer regarded as the necessary pattern of Christian experience, nor was a strong feeling of assurance. There was a widespread stress upon the work of the Holy Spirit in the intellect and an accompanying reaction against emotionalism. Initiatives were also taken, most significantly and effectively by Charles Simeon, to buy proprietary chapels and the right to appoint clergy to help ensure evangelical ministerial continuity, and to prevent the drain to Dissent.

All of this was very understandable, but it did not encourage pan-evangelicalism, and the increased internal cohesion of Anglican evangelicals tended to isolate them, to some extent, from complete involvement with evangelicals outside the Anglican fold. Indeed, it made regular evangelical churchmen reluctant to participate in what was a definite surge of pan-evangelicalism in the last decade of the century. But before we turn to that high watermark of evangelical co-operation, it is well to realize that, despite the forces ranged against any form of pan-evangelicalism, efforts were made to achieve this before the more fruitful years around the turn of the century.

Pan-evangelical initiatives in the period 1735–1795

In 1742 Philip Doddridge introduced one of the earliest experiments in interdenominational co-operation among evangelicals when he established quarterly prayer meetings as a first step towards a foreign missionary movement. The Society for Promoting Religious Knowledge among the Poor, founded in 1750, was probably the first interdenominational evangelical society in England. This 'Book Society', which gave away Bibles and other books, numbered among its patrons in 1770 evangelicals such as Lady Huntingdon, Thomas Haweis, Martin Madan, John Newton, John Ryland, William Romaine, Henry Venn and George Whitefield.[6]

In 1757 Wesley made two attempts to promote pan-evangelicalism, of which one rapidly aborted and the other was partially successful but on a rather limited front. The more ambitious was the proposal for a union between the Methodists and the Church of England evangelicals.

Wesley had progressively come to believe that the secret of a revived church in England lay in securing the co-operation of the evangelical clergy. He dreamed of 'a national union of evangelical clergy who might keep in touch with each other by correspondence and occasional itinerancy, and who could both serve Methodism and be served by its ensuring a continuing evangelical witness within the Established Church.'[7] This possibility appears first to have been publicly adumbrated at the Methodist Conference in 1757, and Wesley subsequently raised the matter privately on a number of occasions, but he received little encouragement to proceed with his efforts. Seven years later he wrote a lengthy manifesto in an effort to rally sympathizers to his side. In this document he described the beginnings of 'a great work in England' but lamented that 'as labourers increased, disunion increased'. He suggested that any clergyman would be welcomed to join in a bond of unity who agreed 'in these essentials: I. Original sin. II. Justification by faith. III. Holiness of heart and life – provided their life be answerable to their doctrine'. He elaborated on the practicability of this somewhat nebulous scheme, addressing such contentious issues as the often fierce theological debates over 'imputed righteousness', and the degree to which 'irregularity' – that is, preaching outside one's own parish – was permissible; and he answered the questions he raised:

> 'But *what union* would you desire among these?' Not a union in *opinions*; they might agree or disagree touching absolute decrees on the one hand and perfection on the other. Not an union in *expressions*: these may still speak of the 'imputed righteousness' and those of 'the merits of Christ'. Not an union with regard to *outward order*; some may still remain *quite regular*, some quite *irregular*, and some *partly regular* and *partly irregular*.[8]

In 1765 he circulated his proposal for an expression of unity to forty or fifty clergy of like mind theologically. He received three replies: one from his former Kingswood colleague, Walter Sellon; one from his old friend, Vincent Perronet of Shoreham; and the third from the faithful Richard Hart of Bristol. By 1769 he had abandoned all hope of such a union. 'I give this up,' he wrote. 'I can do no more. They are a rope of sand: and such they will continue.'[9]

Perhaps this attempt at union was doomed to failure, and Wesley should not have been surprised at the attitude of many of the Church of England evangelicals. 'Had he not broken church rules whilst they (or, at least, the greater part of them) confined themselves to their parishes? Had he not employed lay-preachers – a step which most of them had shunned? Had he not preached "Perfection" whilst they maintained "Final Perseverance of the Saints"? Did they not hold to Election and Predestination (even if they did cautiously avoid mentioning Reprobation) instead of joining him in proclaiming Universal Redemption?'[10] All true and reasonable, but sad nevertheless.

The second, more successful if less significant, pan-evangelical initiative of Wesley in 1757 was the re-founding of the Society for Reformation of Manners. Like its predecessor in the late seventeenth century, the new society attempted to improve the manners of the lower classes by legal threats and literary encouragement, and sought to agitate for laws that would check the profaneness of the British Sunday. The society was undenominational, and in 1763 it included fifty Wesleyans, twenty followers of Whitefield, twenty Anglicans and seventy Dissenters.

Other Wesleyans and Anglicans also made moves in an interdenominational direction, and it was as a consequence of one such move that the Naval and Military Bible Society was founded in 1779 to provide British forces at home and abroad with Bibles and religious tracts.

Pan-evangelicalism from the 1780s to *c*1805

From 1735 until the 1780s it is not unfair to say that, with very distinguished exceptions, the Methodists, the Church of England evangelicals and the few Nonconformist evangelicals in sympathy with Methodism had all gone their own way, and the matters of disagreement and conflict among them had largely ensured that there was no widespread or significant co-operation between them. But by the 1780s there dawned a more eirenic spirit. The realization of shared fundamentals began to reassert itself, and a reaction began to set in against the acrimonies of the Calvinist controversy. Moderate Calvinism came to the fore and exercised a mediatory function. There was a perceptible softening of doctrinal rigidity regarding baptism and other issues, and with this came a greater awareness of a common interest among evangelicals which crossed denominational barriers. There was a diminution in the rigidity of many Baptists and the advent of a new breed of 'open communionists' who, in the tradition of Bunyan, welcomed evangelicals to their table and thereby demonstrated their recognition of them as fellow Christians. The hyper-Calvinism of the old Dissent, which had precluded any interest in evangelism, was seriously challenged in 1785 when a leading Baptist, Andrew Fuller, published *The Gospel Worthy of All Acceptation*. The founding in 1793 of the *Evangelical Magazine* was an expression of the growing consciousness that evangelicalism was a nation-wide movement and embraced Christians from various traditions. Although a high proportion of Methodists, evangelical Anglicans and Baptists resisted such moves, the new tenderness at least provided a basis for the impending pan-evangelical impulse.

The greatest organizational expression of these eirenic developments during the 1780s was the Sunday school movement. It took both denominational and undenominational forms, and evangelicals were actively involved in it at all levels.

The pressures of the 1790s with the impact of the dramatic and fast-changing events in France, the highly charged politico-religious debates and the proliferation of radicalism, tended to crystallize and polarize attitudes and reactions.[11] There was, on the one hand, a surge of undenominational and pan-evangelical activity, which we will consider in a moment, and, on the other hand, a hardening of denominational divisions. Among the Church of England evangelicals there were basically three types of reaction. The least common was that of 'irregulars' or, more accurately, 'half-regulars' such as Thomas Haweis and Rowland Hill, who refused to suspend their undenominational activities. At the other extreme, there were those, like Cornelius Bayley of Manchester, who were alarmed about the political principles of Dissenters and firmly convinced that the Establishment could best preserve order and subordination, and who dramatically severed their working ties with Dissent. The third type of reaction, which was the most common, was that of reluctant disengagement, perhaps, as in the case of John Newton with his Baptist friend William Bull of Newport Pagnell, only for a limited time.

It is also possible, as W R Ward has argued, that 'in the face of social divisiveness and the dispersion of authority consequent upon revolutionary influence, church leaders sought to consolidate their own position by asserting control over undenominational institutions such as Sunday schools and itinerant societies'.[12] There was undoubtedly a growth in denominational consciousness, and this was manifested in the foundation of denominational societies, the foremost examples being the Baptist Missionary Society of 1792 and the Society for Missions to Africa and the East, founded in 1799, which ripened into the Church Missionary Society.

The latter was a direct consequence of the rejection – by Simeon and fellow Church of England evangelical members of the Eclectic Society, such as John Venn and John Thornton – of the pan-evangelical concept, at least when applied to the mission field. But, object as they did, pan-evangelicalism had its decade of at least partial glory from 1795 to 1804. The founding of the London Missionary Society in 1795 may be reckoned as the first major attempt at pan-evangelicalism on a large scale in Britain. It was supported largely by Presbyterians, Independents and a few Anglicans. The meeting of directors of the new society stated its aims on 9 May 1796:

> It is declared to be a fundamental principle of the Missionary Society that our design is not to send Presbyterianism, Independency, Episcopacy or any other form of church order and government (about which there may be differences among serious persons) but the glorious gospel of the Blessed God to the heathen; and that it shall be left (as it ever ought to be left) to the minds of the persons whom God will cast into the fellowship of His Son from among them to assume for themselves such form of church government as to them shall appear most agreeable to the word of God.[13]

Three years later, the Religious Tract Society was established to distribute Christian literature for the edification of Christians, and in order to act as an evangelistic agency. It played an important part in the evangelical domestic mission in the early years of the new century. Many Church of England evangelicals gave it their support. Among those who agreed to have their tracts printed and circulated by the society were Charles Simeon, Thomas Biddulph, Leigh Richmond and Richard Cecil.

The first organization to achieve pan-evangelical co-operation on a grand scale was the British and Foreign Bible Society, which was started in 1804. It was unique in these pioneer years in that it won the patronage of most evangelicals in all Protestant denominations. Evangelicals were encouraged to participate in the Society because of its one, uncomplicated objective, to distribute the Bible; because it restricted the Bibles circulated to those established by public authority; and because it stipulated that the committee should consist of an equal number of churchmen and Dissenters. It was viewed as an essentially Christian business venture, with a single objective, which did not impinge upon denominational interests or autonomy.

> For in this campaign, as in that to abolish the slave trade and slavery, early nineteenth century evangelicals proved to be essentially pragmatic: they sought and acquired influential patronage, mobilised mass support by constructing a network of local auxiliaries, and co-operated with any who shared their aims regardless of belief.[14]

It is also worthy of note that, although there were denominational missionary societies all committed to working within the distinctive structures, beliefs and practices of their particular religious traditions, there was a general sense of unity in a great cause in the early nineteenth century, and from 1813 to 1855 *The Missionary Register* chronicled the work of all the societies.

Pan-evangelicalism from *c*1805 to 1835: confusion and discord

For the Anglican evangelicals in the last years of the period we are reviewing there was a decline from the halcyon days of the eighteenth century and the era of the Clapham Sect. There were major differences of opinion on theological issues, which had devastating effects upon their unity and their morale. There was a growing split between 'the respectable Clapham Sect and its followers on the one hand, and the pentecostal, pre-millenarian, adventist, and revivalist elements on the other'.[15] In the 1820s the *Record*, under the control of Alexander Haldane, provided a focus for such painful differences of opinion, with its somewhat puritanical, anti-clerical views combined with pessimism about the church. The breach between the 'Saints' and the 'Recordites' became severe.[16] The 'Saints' (the evangelical Members of Parliament associated with the Clapham Sect) regarded the 'Recordites' as fanatical. The 'Recordites' condemned the 'Saints' for their association with Dissenters and even with Socinians, and they censured them for an over-concentration on secular issues. The differences in ethos and theological perspective found another focus in the British and Foreign Bible Society. A revolt against the alleged doctrinal indiscipline of the Bible Society resulted in the establishment of the rival Trinitarian Bible Society. Also, to add to the confusion, those evangelicals who sought a strong and uncompromising defence of Protestantism founded the militantly anti-Catholic British Society for Promoting the Religious Principles of the Reformation (the Reformation Society). It was hardly a time when evangelicals were conspicuous for loving one another.

Meanwhile, the Methodists had to wrestle with severe internal conflicts after the death of John Wesley in 1791 – internecine struggles which sapped their strength to a large extent. Secessions proliferated. In 1797 the Kilhamites founded the Methodist New Connection; the revivalist activities of Hugh Bourne and William Clowes, and the contention over camp meetings, resulted in the formation in 1812 of the Society of Primitive Methodists; a similar agitation focused on William O'Bryan and led to the founding of the Bible Christian Society in 1815; and there was an extended, often fierce and even aggressive, debate over means of government and freedom of action between the more progressive Methodists and the conservatives, epitomized in the life, career and struggles of Jabez Bunting.[17]

Much of the energy of the other main denominations was taken up with internal troubles, with the widespread and intense eschatological debate that affected all denominations; with the problems of adjustment to a complex post-Napoleonic War situation and with the campaign for the repeal of the Test and Corporation Acts. These all distracted evangelicals from any serious involvement in pan-evangelicalism. The emergence of the so-called Plymouth Brethren and the Catholic Apostolic Church was symptomatic of a discontent and stirring within the ranks of the evangelicals. Following the repeal of the Test and Corporation Acts in 1828 there was a deterioration in relations between Anglican and Nonconformist evangelicals. The Nonconformists found new confidence and attacked the church establishment, and Anglican evangelicals openly expressed their indignation at such assaults, their vexation about the loss of converts to Nonconformity and their low estimate of Nonconformist spirituality. Then there was the fracturing of Anglican evangelicalism over Catholic Emancipation in 1829, with the more liberal 'old guard' supporting it and the newly started *Record* representing the political views of the majority of evangelicals in its strong opposition to the measure.

None of this augured well for pan-evangelicalism. Indeed, as we approach 1835, division among and within the existing pan-evangelical societies and organizations is more noticeable than the creation of further opportunities for co-operation. This is most poignantly demonstrated in the heated controversies within the ranks of the Bible Society, first over whether under any circumstances the Bible should be circulated without the Prayer Book, then over the issue of whether to accept the continental practice of circulating Bibles containing the Apocrypha, and, finally, over the desirability of applying a Trinitarian test at various levels of membership. 'Indeed, if the opening of the Exeter Hall in March 1831 symbolized evangelical achievement, the Bible Society meeting, held there for the first time only weeks later, exposed the depths of the movement's divisions.'[18]

With hindsight there were, however, two developments in the late Twenties and in the Thirties which helped to unite many evangelicals. The issue of urban evangelism made Church of England evangelicals question the wisdom of their unwillingness to co-operate with Dissent in a task that was in many ways hampered by parochial boundaries and the limitation of parochial resources.[19] The founding of the District Visiting Society in

1828 was therefore important for the future development of pan-evangelical evangelism, and the formation of the London City Mission was a great
boon to pan-evangelical evangelistic co-operation. Then there was the
remarkable galvanizing effect of anti-Catholicism. The Recordites conducted a strong anti-Catholic campaign which reached a peak in the
summer of 1835, remained at a high level until 1841, and was renewed
with the anti-Maynooth agitation of 1845. The centuries-old Protestant
fear of a resurgent Catholicism was found to be a potent force in persuad-
ing many evangelicals of the merits of united evangelical action. But this is
a development which we must leave to another chapter.

Endnotes

1 Key books on Elizabethan and early Stuart Puritanism include P
   Collinson, *The Elizabethan Puritan Movement* (1967), and *The
   Religion of Protestants* (Oxford, 1982); W Haller, *The Rise of Puri-
   tanism* (New York, 1957); M M Knappen, *Tudor Puritanism*
   (Gloucester, Mass, 1963); P McGrath, *Papists and Puritans under
   Elizabeth I* (London, 1967); and N Tyacke, *Anti-Calvinists* (Oxford,
   1987).

2 For the Separatists, see especially M Watts, *The Dissenters* (Oxford,
   1978). For separate denominational histories, see A C Underwood, *A
   History of the English Baptists* (1947); R Tudur Jones, *Congre-
   gationalism in England* (London, 1962); G C Bolam, J Goring, H L
   Short and R Thomas, *The English Presbyterians* (London, 1968); W
   C Braithwaite, *The Beginnings of Quakerism* (London, 1912), and
   The Second Period of Quakerism (London, 1919).

3 D W Bebbington, *Evangelicalism in Modern Britain: A History from
   the 1730s to the 1980s* (London, 1989), p 20.

4 The present comments owe much to R H Martin, 'The pan-evangelical impulse in Britain 1798–1830; with special reference to four
   London societies' (D Phil, University of Oxford, 1974).

5 Martin, 'The pan-evangelical impulse', p 25.

6 Mention should be made of the Prayer Call of the early 1740s in
   Scotland in which John Erskine of Edinburgh was much involved:
   this may have inspired one or two interdenominational societies such
   as the Society in Scotland for Propagating Christian Knowledge in
   the Highlands and Islands, founded in 1745.

7 F Baker, *John Wesley and the Church of England* (London, 1970),
   p 183.

8 Quoted in Baker, *John Wesley*, p 191.

9 Minutes I, pp 87–88, quoted in Baker, *John Wesley*, p 196.

10 A Brown-Lawson, *John Wesley and the Anglican Evangelicals of the
   Eighteenth Century* (Edinburgh, 1994).

11 The following comments are based on N Murray, 'The influence

of the French Revolution on the Church of England and its rivals 1789–1802' (D Phil, University of Oxford, 1975).

12   D Rosman, *Evangelicals and Culture* (London, 1984), p 20.

13   J M Turner, *Conflict and Reconciliation Studies in Methodism and Ecumenism in England 1740–1982* (London, 1985).

14   Rosman, *Evangelicals and Culture*, p 23.

15   B Hilton, *The Age of Atonement: The Influence of Evangelicalism on Social and Economic Thought 1785–1865* (Oxford, 1988).

16   See I C Bradley, 'The politics of godliness: evangelicals in Parliament, 1784–1832' (D Phil, University of Oxford, 1974); and I S Rennie, 'Evangelicals and English public life, 1823–1850' (Ph D, University of Toronto, 1962).

17   Important books covering these various schisms and divisions include R Davies, A R George and G Rupp (eds), *A History of the Methodist Church in Great Britain*, 2 (London, 1978); D A Gowland, *Methodist Secessions: The Origins of Free Methodism in Three Lancashire Towns* (Manchester, 1979); W R Ward (ed), *The Early Correspondence of Jabez Bunting 1820–1829* (London, 1972); W R Ward, *Religion and Society in England 1790–1850* (London, 1972); and J T Wilkinson, *Hugh Bourne, 1772–1852* (London, 1952).

18   Rosman, *Evangelicals and Culture*, p 31.

19   See especially P B Coombs, 'A history of the Church Pastoral Aid Society, 1836–1861' (MA, Bristol University, 1960); and D M Lewis, 'The evangelical mission to the British working classes: a study of the growth of Anglican support for a pan-evangelical approach to evangelism with special reference to London 1828–1860' (D Phil, University of Oxford, 1981).

Chapter 15

THE RISE AND FALL OF THE EVANGELICAL
ALLIANCE: 1835–1905

Clive Calver

The most surprising thing about the birth of the Evangelical Alliance (EA) in the first half of the nineteenth century is that it happened at all. The emergence of an alliance to unite Anglicans and Dissenters might have been anticipated in the more ecumenically-minded climate of opinion which distinguished the opening years of the twentieth century. What is startling is that EA arrived when it did!

EA originated as a largely unexpected intrusion into the internecine rivalry that prevailed between established churchmen and their Nonconformist counterparts. The restrictions faced by those outside the Anglican church acted as a continuing irritant and a major obstacle to mutual co-operation. These limitations included restrictions on university entrance, standing for Parliament and the licensing of places of worship. They extended to restrictions on the rites of passage – the registration of births, the performance of marriages and the conducting of funerals. The ultimate indignity was provided by the compulsory payment of a church rate to the very institution that marginalized and oppressed them.[1]

Popular Nonconformist opinion insisted that religion should always be supported by voluntary giving and never through state aid. Such sponsorship was seen as providing resources for unconverted clergy to assume high religious office in the established church. Independent churches considered that 'the true church ought to consist of those only who offer the evidence of a consistent Christian life'.[2]

It is not surprising that many Anglicans were equally offended by their Nonconformist rivals who could easily be dismissed as schismatics inimical to Protestant unity. The divisions between church and chapel were a matter of class, culture and politics as well as theology.[3] Anglican leadership largely came from the upper classes who were solidly Tory. Nonconformity was middle-class and decidedly non-Tory in its majority view. As Anglicans enjoyed a considerable numerical growth in the 1840s, so one Congregational leader reacted to its challenge for the allegiance of the middle classes by claiming that Anglicanism destroyed more souls than it saved.[4]

The Liberation Society emerged in the 1840s with a vigorous campaign for the disestablishment of the church. At that very time, some were being imprisoned for their failure, on conscience grounds, to pay the church rate. However, this was countered by the establishment in 1859 of the Church Defence Association. From the 1830s onwards the battle-lines were already being drawn in anticipation of coming conflict.

Those who began to swim against this tide of mutual hostility were not immune to its influence. Two of the key founders of EA could write of their deep suspicion across this divide. The minister of Carrs Lane Congregational Church in Birmingham, John Angell James, commented that 'it seems to be the present policy of the Church of England to build us down and to build us out'. The godly Anglican, Edward Bickersteth, rector of Watton, commented on an anti-church 'poison in the veins of dissent'.[5] What is therefore remarkable is that such people could come together at the time that they did. For the original idea of John Angell James for an alliance of 'Dissenters', or Nonconformists, developed into an alliance open to all evangelicals.

Despite its inherent weaknesses, one modern historian has affirmed that 'the Alliance, from the first, produced certain remarkable and far-reaching results'. She continued by affirming that it 'holds a unique place in the history of nineteenth century ecumenism'. Indeed, it marked 'the coming into being of a new thing in Church history'.[6]

Tracing the roots of the Alliance

The individuals who were instrumental in provoking the emergence of EA were approaching the close of their lives and ministries. They came from an earlier generation which had been hugely influenced by the Evangelical Awakening of the eighteenth century.

Prior to this period of revival the primary focus of the church was on preaching the word, celebrating the sacraments and maintaining church discipline. Afterwards, the church was defined in missionary terms as the 'attraction of souls'. Once 'evangelical' had simply meant 'Protestant': now it meant emphasis on the importance of individual conversion.[7]

Early in the nineteenth century the experience of co-operation across denominational divides was fostered in a variety of different evangelical enterprises and societies. Missionary endeavours like the London Missionary Society, literary initiatives such as the Bible Society and Religious Tract Society, or evangelistic projects including the London Society for the Propagation of the Gospel among the Jews, began to explore the potential for co-operation across denominational divides. These were to lead to the question whether it would be possible to act together simply for the sake of demonstrating their collective unity.

During the 1820s, J H Stewart of Liverpool summoned together church leaders from various denominations to engage in meetings for united prayer. Those present included the Wesleyan Jabez Bunting, the Anglican Edward Bickersteth and the Congregationalist Josiah Pratt, who were all to play a part in the inception of EA.[8] A decade later, a number of Scottish

Presbyterians, who were later to secede from the Church of Scotland, joined with John Angell James to produce *Essays on Christian Union*. A similar desire for co-operation between evangelicals was also stirring on the continent of Europe.

A series of popular meetings in England where Anglicans and Nonconformists joined together were followed by a request from Thomas Chalmers and other Scottish secessionists for a major conference. This took place in Liverpool in 1845, and a provisional committee was appointed to prepare the way for an international gathering in London during 1846.

Meanwhile a similar trend was emerging in the USA. Dr Samuel S Schmucker, the president of the Lutheran Theological Seminary at Gettysburg, presented a 'Fraternal Appeal' to encourage evangelicals from different denominations to concentrate on those major issues that united them, rather than the more peripheral matters that created their divisions. He urged that they investigate what co-operative efforts could then emerge from their mutual involvement.

His attempt to create a 'Society for the Promotion of Christian Union' foundered in 1838 in the face of Presbyterian disruption and internal conflicts. However, the idea would not die. One of his supporters, Dr William Potton, a Presbyterian minister in New York, wrote to John Angell James to urge for a 'General Protestant Convention' to be called by English and Scottish leaders.[9] Potton was to lead the party of seventy-one delegates who left the USA for the great 'London Conference' of 1846. Schmucker was among them and was acclaimed as 'the Father of the Evangelical Alliance'.[10]

Their finest hour?

EA was finally formed as a result of agreements concluded at a conference held at the Freemasons Hall in London between 19 August and 2 September 1846. Nine hundred and fifteen churchmen were involved. They brought with them the background and perspectives of more than fifty different denominations, including 215 Presbyterians, 187 Methodists, 181 Congregationalists, 172 Episcopalians and 80 Baptists. No Roman Catholics or Eastern Orthodox were present.[11] They were drawn from Europe, Asia, Africa and America. Nearly 84% came from Britain, 10% from America and 6% from continental Europe. It was the first major interdenominational ecumenical conference, though restricted to evangelicals, that the world had witnessed in modern times.

In one sense, this conference represented EA's greatest success. The mere fact that it took place, and brought together so many leaders from different denominations, constituted a major achievement. Its supporters believed that such a gathering was unprecedented since apostolic times. It was greeted with great optimism by some who hoped that it might even inaugurate a new period in the history of the Christian church![12]

The first week of the conference seemed to justify many of the expectations of those present. Agreement was reached on a basis of faith which defined the doctrines to be adhered to by all members of EA. It also witnessed the production of a series of practical resolutions outlining the manner in which evangelicals should conduct themselves in secondary areas where disagreement and separate distinctives were deemed to be permissible.

Then came a hammer-blow which produced the disintegration of all hopes for a world-wide alliance of evangelicals. John Angell James had enthusiastically called upon the conference to fulfil its destiny, urging them to 'go to one of the greatest achievements which God, through all the Christian era, has called his people to accomplish'.[13] By the end of the ninth day the dream was reduced from a level of confident anticipation to a memory of what might have been.

The problem revolved around a single issue – slavery. J Howard Hinton, general secretary of the Baptist Union, proposed that no slave-holder would be admitted to membership of the proposed alliance. As a British evangelical this was perfectly consistent with the stand that had been taken in the successful anti-slavery campaigns earlier in the century. But it presented an enormous problem to the American delegation. At least one of the American churches represented at the conference admitted slave-holders into its membership. It therefore became likely that American opposition to Hinton's motion would destroy the possibility of a world-wide ecumenical alliance. After extensive deliberations it became obvious that it was unacceptable to the Americans for the British to force on them a general measure of exclusion which ignored the involuntary situation in which some slave-holders found themselves. For the British it was intoler-able that some American evangelicals still attempted to justify slavery on biblical grounds.[14]

As a direct result of this significant schism in its unity the conference concluded by abandoning the idea of an ecumenical alliance. Instead, the British suggestion of loosely-linked independent national organizations, not accountable for each other's actions, was accepted.

Humanly speaking, the idea of a world alliance was gone. Officially, it was postponed until a further conference could be called. This has never taken place. In terms of its grandiose aspirations the London conference was therefore a failure.[15] What it did produce, however, was a loose network of independent branches in France, Canada, Sweden, Germany, India, the United States, Portugal, Turkey, Spain and Britain. The dream had died.

The early years

At Manchester, in November 1846, the British organization of EA was formally established. Already two pronouncements had indicated the diversity of opinion which existed about its founding conference. Edward Bickersteth had confidently affirmed, '[W]e feel assured that this Alliance will furnish a great help to kindle our love, heal our strifes, abate our jealousies, remove our offences and thus prepare the way for a gracious outpouring of the Spirit of God on us all.'[16] A more sober judgement was offered by Lord Shaftesbury when he commented:

> The Evangelical Alliance is, like the Anti-Corn Law League, a 'great fact'. It does not appear likely, however, to have practical results in the same proportion – its chief result, for the present, must be that such a meeting could have been collected and conducted on such principles and in such a manner.[17]

This latter verdict has been indicative of the general image of ineffectiveness and unfulfilled potential applied to the early years of EA. It has been affirmed that 'Ashley was right. The Alliance did not possess the vital influence to be expected from the nineteenth century Evangelical Revival's only ecumenical movement'.[18]

Thomas Chalmers was not alone in his fears that EA would prove to be a 'do-nothing society'.[19] EA had decided on a policy of 'specific and vigorous action' but sought to avoid the twin dangers of creating a 'political organization or duplicating the efforts of existing religious societies'. Consequently their 'action' was primarily defined in terms of active 'investigation'. This was concentrated on issues of rationalism, popery, sabbath observance and Christian education.[20]

Rather than operate as a self-contained unit, EA chose to channel its concerns through the medium of other evangelical organizations. It would assume the character of a body designed for consultation and the transmission of information. By promoting the activities of others, it would avoid the danger of duplication of effort. As its name implied, EA would become an 'umbrella body', providing support and linkage for diverse sectors of evangelical activity.

These aspirations were warmly commended yet, during the first decade of its existence, EA encountered three major obstacles to its growth. It suffered from the absence of official denominational support, strong leadership and a 'single-issue' agenda. EA was continuing, in the way it had begun, as a loose coalition of individuals linked together by mutual recognition of shared interests and principles. Designed to bring together individuals rather than denominations, it was open to the damage caused by a conflict of interest between denominational loyalty and its own requirements.

To compensate for this disadvantage EA required strong central leadership and organization in order to promote its cause and secure its objectives. Yet it possessed neither. Its founders owed their mutual allegiance to matters of principle not personality. Unlike many other contemporary evangelical organizations, EA lacked a recognizable leader. Those it had – Bunting, James, Bickersteth, Chalmers and their chairman, Sir Culling Eardley – all died before it really began to grow.

Apart from the separate national organizations, no centralizing structure existed. While 'spiritual and intellectual leaders in the Churches approved it and spoke on its platforms; strong men presided at its conference', no outstanding leader or coherent structure emerged.[21]

The one issue that would have provided a focus for the newly-formed EA was the contemporary struggle against Catholic encroachments and the emergence of an Anglo-Catholic emphasis in the Tractarian movement. These views had been popularized in a steady stream of 'Tracts for the Times'. They had aroused evangelical opposition by their espousal of the place of purgatory, the Real Presence of Christ in the sacrament, the significance and celibacy of the priesthood, the apostolic succession and the veneration of relics and images of the saints.[22]

It has been common to regard EA as purely an anti-Catholic movement.[23] While it is true that some of its early leaders can be readily identified with this emphasis – and EA shared the common anti-Catholic views of evangelicals at that time – such a judgement ignores its failure to launch a crusade on the one issue that would have clearly united its constituency. John Angell James had called for a union of evangelicals to combat, 'infidelity and Popery, Puseyism and Plymouth Brethrenism'. The Scottish churchman, Dr Candlish, had also seen the wisdom of promoting unity on the grounds of shared antipathy: 'The unity of the church is greatly promoted by a resistance to the common enemy'.[24] However, these views concentrated on a negative issue, which EA's founders accepted but wanted to keep in check by maintaining the positive merits and gains of their unity.

The Congregationalist James Hamilton declared, 'I should regret to say that this were even chiefly or principally an anti-papal movement.' He urged a positive base for union. Many others, including Candlish himself, were far more concerned for the conversion of individual Roman Catholics than the wholesale destruction of the Catholic system.[25] Consequently, a proposal by Thomas Chalmers for this union to be called the 'Protestant Alliance' was soundly defeated. Its chosen name, the Evangelical Alliance, was intended to declare its positive character. In respect to its anti-Catholic views it confined itself collectively to the limited measure of collecting relevant information. An essay competition on the Papacy, won by Dr J A Wylie in 1851, was its most notable contribution to the issue.[26]

One recent evaluation insists that EA was 'noticeably milder' than other societies. The same author has also suggested that the perceived non-militancy of EA was to result in the birth of a more stridently anti-Catholic evangelical society. 'Frustration with the Evangelical Alliance's inertia led to the formation of the Protestant Alliance in the autumn of 1851.'[27]

Shorn of its leadership, devoid of popular issues and deprived of its original vision, EA moved slowly forward – a vehicle for union, yet still searching for a cause that would unite evangelicals under its banner.

Religious liberty

It would be relatively easy to affirm that the greatest achievement of EA was to come into existence. Once this was achieved it would fall into relative obscurity through failing to capture popular interest, imagination and involvement. However, such a view ignores the single issue that was to dominate EA's activities over the next fifty years. Its most effective sphere of practical action was discovered in championing the religious liberties of persecuted minorities.[28]

This aspiration was among the four stated objects for which EA was created. Those who attended the London Conference had affirmed their commitment to give support and encouragement to all Christians who faced opposition and persecution. Dr Baird, an American Presbyterian, observed that the 'right to preach the Gospel everywhere ought to be recognized by a Christian government'.[29]

By this statement he indicated a dilemma that EA would continue to confront. Though abjuring 'political' activity, it would solicit the aid of government agencies and politicians to secure its objectives. In June 1848, at its annual conference in Bristol, the British organization applauded moves being made to oppose the legal restrictions enacted by the Council of State in the Canton de Vaud against the local Free Church denomination. At the same time the conference deprecated any political involvement.[30]

This inconsistency was further underlined after the Swiss Canton had published a decree forbidding religious assemblies outside the state church. Not content with holding protest meetings, EA's annual conference of 1850, held in Glasgow, issued a statement denouncing this intrusion into the religious liberties of the individual and despatched it to the Council of State of the Canton de Vaud.[31]

This issue of religious liberty became the single greatest continuing activity of EA. It 'sought to be a champion of those who suffer for Christ and conscience', maintaining that 'where spiritual freedom is denied and men and women are punished for seeking to exercise it, the Alliance counts it its duty, and privilege, to go to the succour of the persecuted'.[32]

Whether secular or spiritual authorities were involved, EA saw no contradiction in employing similar powers on behalf of the persecuted. Nor were their efforts limited to evangelical Christians. They also campaigned on behalf of Protestant, Roman Catholic and Orthodox minorities.[33]

Few areas of socio-political and ecclesiastical concern have commanded such a consensus of evangelical opinion as that of religious liberty. The continued re-emergence of this problem, in various parts of the world and among different groups, provided EA with the opportunity to act as the focal point for the evangelical response to such injustice. A not-uncritical commentator concluded:

[EA] had one distinctive, strong and continuous practical activity –

the defence of religious liberty. Again and again it successfully defended oppressed religious groups and persons, and secured government action in their favour, including, be it noted, non-Protestant groups – Roman Catholics, for instance, in Russia or in Sweden, or the Nestorian Church under Moslem rule in Turkey.[34]

It is intriguing to note that throughout the nineteenth century an alliance comprised of Anglican and dissenting evangelicals was prepared to campaign on behalf of any nonconforming minority restricted by a religious establishment.

However, its early efforts were confined to making representations to various governments on behalf of the persecuted in countries like Sweden and the various states in what later became Germany and Italy. Such efforts were commendable but not always adequate to achieve their objective. Until EA could establish its reputation and extend its influence, structures and organizations, it would remain totally dependent on the goodwill of those to whom it appealed.

Sometimes EA's efforts misfired, as in the case of Dr Achilli, a former priest, whom EA defended on the ground that charges against him had been manufactured by papal authorities. Its demands for his release were successful, but EA had acted on inaccurate information and Dr Achilli was subsequently exposed as a charlatan whose reprehensible moral conduct had justified the charges on which he had been initially convicted.[35]

The turning point for EA came in 1855 when, as a result of a memorial sent to the Sultan of Turkey, a declaration of religious freedom was made by the Sultan. Recognizing the importance of this issue, EA appointed a foreign secretary, Hermann Schmettou, during the 1860s. EA effectively co-ordinated its efforts for religious liberty by linking representations from various national alliances. Participation in petitions, direct access to government, meetings with foreign ambassadors and even the sending of deputations overseas, became recognized strategies.

EA was now beginning to assume the character, if not the stature, of a nineteenth-century version of Amnesty International. In May 1861 two Nestorian Christians began a walk from Armenia to Hamburg. Their intention was to reach England with the purpose of enlisting support for the 200,000 Nestorian Christians in Persia who had faced consistent Moslem persecution. It took them six months to reach Moscow. They then travelled through Poland to Germany, where friends sent them by ship to England. They managed to acquire a few words of English and, on their arrival in London, the first question they asked was, 'Where is the Evangelical Alliance?' An appeal to the Shah of Persia from EA resulted in the gift of land on which to rebuild churches that had been destroyed and the dismissal of the official who had spearheaded the persecution.

During 1871 EA took action on behalf of 'some 160,000 Letts and Estonians in Russia'. Christians in the Baltic provinces faced persecution if they proselytized from the state church. Their worship was forbidden and punishments for disobedience included fines, imprisonment, flogging, loss of civil rights and even banishment to Siberia.[36] A united delegation was formed after talks were held between James Davis (British EA's general secretary) and Philip Schaff (the corresponding secretary for the American Evangelical Alliance) in New York. This delegation united French, British, German, Swiss and American leaders of their respective alliances in a common attempt to gain clemency from the Tsar of Russia. They met with Prince Gartschokoff, the Russian chancellor, during a visit by the Tsar to Friedrichshafen. The result of this initiative was typical of many in which EA was engaged. No formal change in the law was obtained, but its application was less rigorously enforced. EA could rejoice in an amelioration of the situation in the Baltic provinces.[37]

Such gains would often prove to be short-lived. In Russia, Spain, and time and again in the Turkish Empire, EA had to bring issues of persecution to public attention and plead for government intervention on behalf of the victims. While its role was not unique, its motivation was clearly both humanitarian and apolitical.

EA focused on the defence of fellow-Christians because 'if any suffer tribulation for conscience's sake, the tribulation is no longer theirs exclusively – it is ours also'.[38] In 1872, missionaries in Japan had appealed to EA for help. Four thousand of their indigenous converts had been exiled, facing hardship. Crosses were trampled underfoot, and Christianity faced the prospect of severe restrictions. Strong representations were made to the British government on behalf of both Protestants and Roman Catholics.

Similarly, in previous months, the American branch had campaigned on behalf of Romanian Jews and Japanese Roman Catholics, requesting intervention from the US government. It gradually became clear that EA's major objective was:

> To obtain everywhere throughout the world the recognition of the right of liberty of conscience. In the pursuit of this last object it can use its influence on behalf of persecuted Jews and Roman Catholics (as it has lately done) as freely as on behalf of Evangelical Christians.[39]

Evangelical unity

In defining the vision and purpose of EA, Philip Schaff drew attention to its twin aims. He spoke of 'the promotion of Christian union and Christian liberty throughout the world'.[40] While the cause of religious liberty represented a straightforward objective for EA, its espousal of Christian union was a more difficult issue for which to devise a clear agenda.

EA's *raison d'être* was in the promotion of Christian union among those who 'hold and maintain what are usually understood to be evangelical views'.[41] However, EA emerged during the early part of a period of seventy years' progress towards religious equality in nineteenth-century England. This phase, inaugurated by the Repeal of the Corporation and Test Acts in 1828, was to witness the removal of the majority of the religious and political disabilities which confronted Dissenters at the beginning of the Victorian era. The result has been called the 'gradual disestablishment' of the Church of England.[42] It was not easily obtained. Some issues were settled to Nonconformist satisfaction only after thirty years of campaigning, while other matters remained unresolved.

Not surprisingly, mutual suspicion continued between Anglicans and Nonconformists. It was far easier for these to be submerged within a society devoted to Bible translation, tract distribution or the conversion of the heathen than in an alliance whose existence depended on mutual goodwill and co-operation based only on shared evangelical views. Various attempts were made to underpin this fragile sense of unity. Occasional excursions into issues of sabbath observance, anti-Catholicism or evangelism (especially in Ireland) were all attempted at appropriate times. But no clearly defined strategy or set of precise objectives was to emerge.

The continuation of EA was really secured by international rather than national issues. Alongside the shared concern for religious liberty came a mutual commitment to international dialogue and world-wide prayer between evangelicals. International conferences of EA were held at periodic intervals throughout the nineteenth century. In 1851, the year of the Great Exhibition, a general conference in London welcomed 180 delegates from France, Germany, Switzerland, Holland, Belgium, Sweden and the United States. Visitors also came from Russia, East and West Indies and China. In 1855 1,200 people from 15 nations gathered in Paris for a conference and to host a *salle evangelique* in order to reach nationals and visitors to that city with the gospel. It even proved possible to hold a shared communion service, with the words of institution pronounced in seven languages. At Berlin in 1857 the King and Queen of Prussia welcomed 900 guests to an EA conference. Further conferences took place in Geneva (1861), Amsterdam (1867), Basle (1879), Copenhagen (1884), Florence (1891) and London (1896). Perhaps the most outstanding of this series took place in the United States in 1873, when President Grant hosted a reception for the delegates in New York. The gatherings overflowed the largest available ecclesiastical buildings. Again, leaders from Episcopalian, Lutheran and Presbyterian churches joined in a united communion service with Nonconformists.

This same spirit of international co-operation was witnessed in the development of the Universal Week of Prayer. The first week of January each year was set apart for this purpose. Since 1847 it has called for national programmes, interdenominational meetings and private devotions to take place around a common theme. The shared material was translated into several languages, and tens of thousands of copies were printed each year.[43]

As the decades passed, and the disabilities that Nonconformists faced were progressively removed, so the impetus towards transdenominational fellowship grew. While church leaders might choose to devote time to their denominations, influential laymen and churchmen of more ecumenical inclination saw EA as a useful vehicle for partnership together.

In the 1870s EA could claim a council that included nine Peers, several Members of Parliament, two High Sheriffs, the Dean of Canterbury and the Lord Mayor of London. Its membership was expanding, as was the readership of the magazine, *Evangelical Christendom*. This was a substantial production containing copious information about evangelical life and progress around the world. Under the energetic leadership of its general secretary (1859–1878), James Davis, EA at last appeared to be approaching the stature hoped for by its founders. Yet its very nature made it a delicate child, at its most fragile in its structure and composition. For it lacked the opportunity to exercise any discipline or ensure cohesiveness among its members. One observer commented that 'it is not an official or semi-official representative body, but rather a union of individuals. It is not an attempt at a union of churches, but only at a union of Christians'.[44] Its greatest strength would also prove its greatest weakness, for it lacked the centralized authority necessary to control its own supporters.

Time and again controversies flared up to threaten its unity. One of the honorary secretaries, the Anglican T R Birks, was accused of holding annihilationist and universalist views. Charles Haddon Spurgeon felt excluded from EA because of his hostility towards 'modernist' approaches to scripture. Swedish Lutherans rejected the idea of a conference at Stockholm in 1884 because of the alleged 'disestablishmentarian' views contained within EA. On each occasion the EA retrieved a degree of unity through personal relationships. Spurgeon, for example, gave the opening address at a series of apologetics lectures hosted by EA, though he had been hurt and wounded by previous rejection.

Rooted only in the suspect soil of contacts and friendships united by an ideal, EA's position would always be precarious. At its half-centenary conference in London, serious questions about its identity and continuation began to be raised. For the denominations were beginning to consider the potential for some form of organizational Christian unity. Lord Polworth, EA's president, announced that many were hoping for, 'a vast re-organization of the outward visible churches of Christendom'. He hoped that such a union would be of a spiritual rather than an organizational character. Others affirmed the same view, J H Rigg pointing out that 'organic union gives the death blow to real unity'.[45] Emphasis was placed on individual commitment to Christ as the basis for unity. All that was necessary was for this unity to be recognized; proper behaviour towards each other and co-operative activities together received little mention. As J B A Kessler has observed, 'the Alliance had been founded for the specific purpose of manifesting Christian unity, but if recognition of that unity among the individual members were all that was needed then the Alliance had virtually no task to fulfil'.[46] EA was in danger of becoming a union without a function, its past work providing little impetus for the future.

From 1879 the general secretary had been A J Arnold. He had achieved much, and, in partnership with his opposite number in the United States, the social reformer Josiah Strong, a strong Anglo-American axis had been formed. The twin thrusts of religious liberty and Christian union had been enhanced in these years. But by 1896 Arnold was an old man, his energies diminished, and he died in 1898. Strong resigned his role the same year.

Clearly, fresh direction was urgently needed. EA appointed as Arnold's successor Percy Field, the son of General Sir John Field, who had worked with Arnold. Percy Field was a strong-willed man who fell out with his chairman, Lord Kinnaird. The council felt that they were no longer in control of the work, and Percy Field was dismissed in 1903. He then sued Lord Kinnaird and the council for wrongful dismissal, and the matter was only finally settled in the High Court in 1905.[47] Field's case was dismissed, but it was to prove to be a hollow victory for EA.

In 1904 H Martyn Gooch, the son of one of their council members, had been appointed to succeed Percy Field. He proved to be a 'safe' appointment, but one possessing little imagination or strategic insight. At the very time that the Edinburgh Conference of 1910 was lighting the fires of ecumenical enthusiasm EA was content to conserve its energies. Little went wrong but few gains were achieved. Gradually prestigious lay-leaders left EA, its council became dominated by clerics only, most of whom were men devoid of major influence in their denominations.

H Martyn Gooch was to remain in the post for forty-five years, only being finally deposed when two younger men, Gilbert Kirby and Bishop Hugh Gough, led a movement for change in 1946. These years under Gooch saw the decline and stagnation of EA. It was only after the Second World War that it would begin to recapture its past emphasis and discover a role for the future.

Endnotes

1   See A D Gilbert, *Religion and Society in Industrial England* (London, 1976), pp 162–168; D Read, *England 1868–1914* (London, 1979), pp 74–77; G Parsons, 'From dissenters to free churchmen: the transitions of Victorian nonconformity', G Parsons (ed), *Religion in Victorian Britain*, 1, *Traditions* (Manchester, 1988), pp 67–116.

2   E Steane (ed), *Evangelical Christendom*, June 1863, pp 257–258.

3   D A Harmer, *The Politics of Electoral Pressure* (London, 1977), ch 8; D Smith, 'Church and society in Britain: a mid-nineteenth century analysis by Edward Miall', *Evangelical Quarterly*, 61:2 (April 1989), pp 143–156.

4   *Congregational Magazine* (1833), p 818.

5   A Peel, *These Hundred Years, 1831–1931: A History of the Congre-*

gational Union of England and Wales (London, 1931), p 149; O Chadwick, *The Victorian Church*, 1 (London, 1966), p 441.

6 R Rouse, 'Voluntary movements and the changing ecumenical climate', R Rouse and S C Neill (eds), *A History of the Ecumenical Movement, 1517–1948* (London, 1954) pp 321–324.

7 P G A Griffin-Allwood, 'Contemporary evangelicalism: a question of continuity', *Faith Today*, February 1988.

8 D King, *Historical Sketch of the Evangelical Alliance* (London, 1846), p 4.

9 Quoted by J A James as an appendix to his essay, 'Christian Union views in relation to the religious parties of England', *Essays on Christian Union* (London, 1845), pp 224–225.

10 E B Sandford, 'A History of the Evangelical Alliance' (unpublished, undated), available in the Burke Library, New York.

11 See J W Massie, *The Evangelical Alliance, its Origin and Development, Containing Personal Notices of its Distinguished Friends in Europe and America* (London, 1847), p 286. Statistics calculated from 'Autographs of the Members of the Conference' (unpublished, 1846).

12 L Edwards, 'The Evangelical Union' (Traethodydd, London, 1846), pp 105–109; Massie, *The Evangelical Alliance*, p 112.

13 Evangelical Alliance, *Report of the Proceedings of the Conference held at Freemasons Hall, London, from August 19th to September 2nd inclusive, 1846* (London, 1847), p 10.

14 See J B A Kessler Jr, *A Study of the Evangelical Alliance in Great Britain* (Goes, Netherlands, 1968), pp 43–47.

15 E Steane (ed), *The Religious Condition of Christendom* (Paris, 1855, London, 1855), p 8.

16 E B Bickersteth, *A Brief Practical View of the Evangelical Alliance in regard to its Character, Principles, Objects, Organisation and Christian Spirit* (London, 1846), p 55.

17 Lord Shaftesbury's Diary, 16 September 1846.

18 C Binfield, *George Williams and the YMCA* (London, 1973), p 158.

19 R W Dale, *The Life and Letters of J A James* (London, 1861), p 418; Bickersteth, *A Brief Practical View*, pp 38–39; Massie, *The Evangelical Alliance*, pp 251–256.

20 King, *Historical Sketch*, pp 15–16; Massie, *The Evangelical Alliance*, p 176.

21 Rouse and Neil (eds), *A History of the Ecumenical Movement*, p 323.

22 See 'Unauthorised innovations ... at Oxford', *Christian Observer*, August 1846; E B Bickersteth, *Remarks on the Progress of Popery* (London, 1836); Chadwick, *The Victorian Church*, pp 168–216; B M G Reardon, *Religious Thought in the Victorian Age* (London, 1980), pp 93–121.

23 M Hennell, *Sons of Prophets* (London, 1979), p 82; E R Norman,

Anti-Catholicism in Victorian England (London, 1968), pp 50–51; G I T Machin, *Politics and the Churches in Great Britain, 1832–1868* (Oxford, 1977), pp 176, 254–255; D Thomson, *England in the Nineteenth Century* (Harmondsworth, 1950), p 108.

24 Dale, *The Life and Letters of J A James*, pp 397–398; Massie, *The Evangelical Alliance*, p 167.

25 Massie, *The Evangelical Alliance*, pp 119–121, 167.

26 T Chalmers, *On the Evangelical Alliance; its Design, its Difficulties, its Proceedings and its Prospects: with Practical Suggestions* (Edinburgh, 1846); J A Wylie, *The Papacy* (London, 1851); J R Wolffe, 'The Evangelical Alliance in the 1840s: an attempt to institutionalise Christian Unity', W J Sheils and D Wood (eds), *Voluntary Religion*, Studies in Church History, 23 (Oxford, 1986), pp 340–341.

27 Wolffe, 'The Evangelical Alliance in the 1840s', *Voluntary Religion*, pp 340–341, and 'Protestant societies and anti-Catholic agitation in Great Britain, 1829–1860' (D Phil, Oxford, 1984), p 281.

28 D F Durnbough, *The Believer's Church* (London, 1968), pp 293–294.

29 Evangelical Alliance, Report of the Proceedings, pp 231–240.

30 Evangelical Alliance, Minutes of Annual Conferences (Bristol, 1849).

31 Evangelical Alliance, Minutes of Annual Conferences (Glasgow, 1850).

32 J W Ewing, *Goodly Fellowship* (London, 1946), p 58. Ewing provides an uncritical outline of the Alliance's wide-ranging activities in this field, pp 58–79.

33 Durnbough, *The Believer's Church*, p 294.

34 Rouse and Neill (eds), *A History of the Ecumenical Movement*, p 322.

35 M Trevor, *The Pillar of the Cloud* (London, 1962), pp 547–602.

36 See Minutes of the Evangelical Alliance (British Organization), 25 May 1870. Also Minutes of the Evangelical Alliance (US branch), 17 May 1870; 15 July 1870.

37 Minutes of the Evangelical Alliance (British Organization), 3 January, 1872.

38 E Steane, *The Evangelical Alliance and Religious Liberty* (London, no date), p 5.

39 *Christian World*, 14 July 1870.

40 Minutes of the Evangelical Alliance (US branch), 23 September 1870.

41 *Conference on Christian Union held in Liverpool on Wednesday, 1 October 1845 and subsequent days* (Liverpool, 1845).

42 W H Mackintosh, *Disestablishment and Liberation: The Movement for the Separation of the Anglican Church from State Control* (London, 1972), p xvi.

43 Ewing, *Goodly Fellowship*, pp 36–37.

44 *Christian World*, 14 July 1870.

45 Evangelical Alliance, *The Jubilee of the Evangelical Alliance* (London, 1896), pp 18, 22.
46 Kessler, *A Study of the Evangelical Alliance*, p 80.
47 Minutes of the Evangelical Alliance, 1903–5, which contain the transcript of the High Court proceedings.

Chapter 16

SCHISM AND UNITY: 1905–1966

Ian Randall

The appointment on 8 September 1904 of Henry Martyn Gooch, then aged thirty, as general secretary of the Evangelical Alliance, was the signal for a reappraisal of the organization's work. At the beginning of 1905 F B Meyer, a Baptist minister and a prominent interdenominational figure, expressed the hope that there would be 'a drawing together on the Evangelical Alliance lines', with more frequent meetings at which every shade of political and ecclesiological opinion was represented.[1] It was this programme which Gooch adopted. His secretaryship was characterized by its remarkable length – forty-five years – and also by its breadth. From 1905 until the end of the Second World War the 'World's Evangelical Alliance (British Organization)', which was the rather cumbersome official title used between 1912 and 1953, operated rather like a broad Protestant alliance. The first part of this short study examines the way in which the Alliance attempted, up to the 1940s, to preserve evangelical unity, to campaign against those seen as enemies of the evangelical faith, and to work for evangelical renewal. The latter part has as its focus the period from the 1940s to 1966, a period when commitment to mission and tensions over ecumenical involvement came to the fore. The Alliance secretaries during this period were Roy Cattell (1949–1955) who had worked for the British evangelist, Tom Rees, and also for Inter-Varsity Fellowship, and Gilbert Kirby who moved from the pastorate of Ashford Congregational Church in 1956 to take on the secretaryship. In 1966 Kirby followed Ernest Kevan as principal of London Bible College.

A broad alliance

In order to achieve maximum evangelical co-operation, the Alliance adopted as part of its strategy an appeal to those who might have found it difficult to subscribe to its original eight-point basis of faith. At the annual meeting of the Alliance in 1912 a briefer trinitarian statement, which also included acknowledgement of the inspiration, authority and sufficiency of scripture, was proposed and accepted. J B A Kessler, in *A Study of the Evangelical Alliance in Great Britain*, argues that the change, which the Alliance's council saw as establishing 'comprehensiveness without compromise', represented a futile attempt to appeal to more liberal Protestants.[2] However, it does seem that the Alliance was able to achieve the objective of attracting wide support. J W Ewing – who was to become superintendent of the London Baptist area and who wrote a centenary history of the Alliance, *Goodly Fellowship* – had said at an Alliance meeting in 1906 that it was time to stand together on the basis of a common experience of grace, common enterprise for righteousness, common life in the Body of Christ and the individual indwelling of Christ in the heart.[3] This fairly open agenda could be taken up by those who wanted a broader evangelicalism. Amongst some evangelical Anglicans the idea of a position with the unexciting title 'Central Churchmanship' was being promulgated. Central churchmen made the Bible the ultimate authority, held the death of Christ to be pivotal and were committed to liberty of access to God through Christ. It was a stance which was commended in the Alliance's journal, *Evangelical Christendom*.[4] Being 'central' was particularly attractive to the Alliance in the 1920s when the unity of evangelicalism was strained to breaking point as liberal and conservative theological tendencies diverged.[5] The Alliance regretted that theologically right-wing bodies like the Fraternal Union for Bible Testimony 'instead of uniting at the centre, appear to be concerned to create divisions in the Evangelical ranks' and, by contrast, the Alliance defended its own open-minded and central position.[6]

At a time when fundamentalist spokesmen believed there was a need to engage in militant protest against what they saw as 'shilly-shallying . . . in the name of charity',[7] some major evangelical leaders took a determined stand against narrowing tendencies. *Evangelical Christendom* carried, in 1924, a clear statement from Graham Scroggie, minister of Charlotte Chapel in Edinburgh, that neither premillennialism nor subscription to a particular theory of inspiration was a true test of doctrinal orthodoxy. 'If you demand', Scroggie said, 'that I subscribe to your theory of inspiration, I shall decline, but I am not on that account a Modernist.'[8] During the 1930s Scroggie was the definitive teacher at the Keswick Convention, an interdenominational holiness gathering which attracted up to six thousand evangelicals each year. In 1929 Scroggie delivered a series of studies at Keswick on the Apostles' Creed and argued that, given the conflict between fundamentalism and modernism, it was preferable to have the Creed as a basis of faith than for small groups to construct their own bases and splinter from the wider church.[9] The theme of centrality was taken up two years later by Bryan Green, later rector of Birmingham, who confessed to being dissatisfied with what he termed old-fashioned evangelicalism with its 'narrow negations' and its 'hard austere worship'. Liberal evangelicalism, too, was unsatisfactory. Green wished to identify with the Alliance's 'clear basis, broad in its width and interpretation, on the great fundamental doctrine of the Gospel of Christ'.[10] By 1939 Hugh Gough, who was to become Bishop of Barking and then Archbishop of Sydney, was able to make an authoritative affirmation of the commitment of the

Alliance to a new evangelicalism that avoided the extremes of either the fundamentalist or liberal wings. For Gough the problem was that the term 'evangelical' covered 'a multitude of variegated and hyphenated Evangelicals' (the reference is primarily to liberal evangelicals), many of whom, he believed, should drop the label 'evangelical' and instead adopt the 'hyphen'. The task for those who believed in the 'atoning and substitutionary death of Christ' was to combine to proclaim the 'full gospel' of the cross.[11]

The Alliance also had to contend with historic denominational divisions. A list of about 250 churches where sermons were preached in connection with the Alliance's 1907 international conference suggests that perhaps one-third of the Alliance's constituency was Anglican and a quarter Baptist, with Congregational and Methodist the next largest groupings.[12] There were frequent laments by the Alliance that denominations were financially supported by their own members while the Alliance was left to struggle. Divisions between Anglicans and Nonconformists in the early twentieth century were exacerbated by the government's education policy which, as some Nonconformists saw it, discriminated in favour of Anglicanism by giving help from the rates to church schools. Meyer made such strong pronouncements on this subject that he had to apologize publicly at Keswick in 1906.[13] The Alliance, worried about a widening rift, publicized instances of harmonious relationships. At Blackheath, in London, for example, where there had been tensions, interdenominational meetings were in 1906 attracting 2,000 people.[14] Yet problems could not be swept completely under the carpet. In 1910 Guy Warman, a member of the Alliance's council (who became, in succession, Bishop of Truro, Chelmsford and Manchester), emphasized the need to face up to opposing views of episcopal ministry.[15] A year later, when Charles Brown, a leading Baptist minister, said that he had abandoned any hope of union with the Church of England, the Alliance's response was that there could be unity without church union, and it welcomed the comment by Hensley Henson, Bishop of Durham, that denominationalism was ending.[16]

Shock waves were caused, however, by the news in 1911 that local Free Church Councils were organizing their own prayer meetings at the same time as the traditional January Alliance Week of Prayer. Worse still, Meyer, a good friend of the Alliance, was behind the move. It was known that Meyer, as secretary of the National Free Church Council, was keen to stimulate local spiritual initiatives,[17] but Gooch, outraged, wrote to Meyer asking what would happen if the Alliance pitched a tent at Keswick for a separate conference during convention week.[18] The Free Churches, with their commitment to voluntary religion, were in fact natural allies of the Alliance. In 1915 Gooch – who was an Anglican lay reader – expressed his deep disagreement with the Church of England over its refusal to sanction inter-communion, and from this point on the Alliance seems to have adopted a more critical stance in relation to Anglican affairs.[19] The

Alliance was, of course, conscious that its vision of the unity of individual Christians tended to play down the role of the institutional church. A significant statement, presumably by Gooch, appeared in *Evangelical Christendom* in 1938 under the heading 'Church and State – Unholy Alliance'. It suggested that 'the entanglements of the Body of Christ, because of its organic relations with national life, form one of the chief barriers to its progress among men'.[20] The structures of 'Christendom' might themselves be barriers to an effective broad Christian alliance.

Knowing the enemies

Lord Polworth, who was president of the Alliance for forty-two years, said in 1907 that the Alliance had been founded to cultivate brotherly love and to protest against error. At first the error had been Romanism. Now, he believed, everything that was essential to the faith was being denied.[21] Rome, the old enemy, was still, in the eyes of the Alliance, a sinister menace. Although the populist anti-Catholicism of nineteenth-century Britain had faded to a considerable extent by the 1920s, the Alliance played a role in promoting a sense of Protestant identity within evangelicalism.[22] An Alliance meeting was convened in 1911 to protest against the Roman Catholic Church's decree that marriages between Catholics and Protestants, even if legal in civil terms, were not valid unless conducted in the presence of a Catholic priest and according to Catholic rites. Speaking to the audience of 3,000, John Clifford said that as president of the Baptist World Alliance he spoke for eight million Baptists who were 'in direct and explicit antithesis to Rome'.[23] The other main speaker, F S Webster, rector of All Souls, Langham Place, although he had claimed that as an Anglican he belonged to 'the most Scriptural Church in Christendom', used patriotic rather than specifically Anglican arguments.[24] Inevitably, the Irish dimension came into the picture. A crucial contribution made to Ulster by late Victorian evangelicalism was a vigorous anti-Catholicism.[25] The Alliance made great play of the case of a Protestant, Mrs McCann, whose Catholic husband had left her and taken away her two children, allegedly with the encouragement of the Catholic authorities who insisted that the marriage was invalid. 'Ulster stands aghast,' declared William Corkey of Townsend Street Presbyterian Church, Belfast, who was Mrs McCann's minister.[26] The Alliance claimed credit for having initiated the campaign against the Roman decree, and it attempted to keep the issue alive up to the time of the Second World War. 'Rome never relents – never loses one piece of ground it has won,' said *Evangelical Christendom* in 1939.[27] Protestant unity could be forged in resistance to a common enemy.

A second front was closer at hand. In 1907 R J Campbell, minister of the City Temple, published *The New Theology*. He argued that humanity and divinity were parts of one great consciousness and thus drastically revised the traditional concept of Christ.[28] Controversy raged. The Alliance informed its constituency in 1908 that it had carried out an effective campaign against The *New Theology* through meetings and pub-lications.[29] It reported that at the 1907 Free Church Council Congress an elderly delegate, John King, protested against a talk by Campbell and asked, to a background of cheers and cries of 'out of order', for 'When I survey the wondrous cross' to be sung. This was done.[30] A more scholarly Alliance contribution to the debate came from the Scottish theologian, James Orr.[31]

Liberal theology long remained a source of concern to the Alliance. In 1920 E W Barnes, later Bishop of Birmingham, addressed a meeting of the British Association for the Advancement of Science, and his defence of evolution and repudiation of the traditional doctrine of the Fall in this and subsequent 'monkey' or 'gorilla' sermons (as they were dubbed) provoked hostility.[32] Although Barnes and the Modern Churchmen's Union with which he was associated were criticized by the Alliance, it was admitted that Genesis seemed to suggest 'a possible evolutionary process in the creation of the lower animals'.[33] In Britain, by contrast with America, evolution did not create a fundamentalist fault-line.[34] The MCU achieved notoriety at its 1921 Girton Conference in Cambridge when theological views were promulgated which caused tremors throughout the Church of England.[35] Gooch's comment began, 'The antidote to Cambridge is Christ.'[36] A more trenchant critique of liberalism came in the late 1930s from Martyn Lloyd-Jones, minister of Westminster Chapel, who was to become a shaping force in British evangelicalism. He suggested in 1939 that the authority of 'men of knowledge' had been too readily accepted by the church. Jesus Christ, he asserted, never trimmed his gospel to fit the people.[37] New theologies must still be opposed.

Even more threatening than liberal theology was the power of Anglo-Catholicism. After the First World War huge Anglo-Catholic congresses were organized, beginning with one in 1920 which attracted 13,000 people.[38] Proposals to revise the Church of England's Prayer Book in a more Catholic direction were bitterly opposed – the adoration of the Reserved Sacrament was one of the most contentious issues – in a cam-paign led by the retired Bishop of Manchester, E A Knox. Over 300,000 signatures were obtained protesting against the changes. Hensley Henson ridiculed the campaigners as 'an army of illiterates generalled by octogen-arians'[39] but, for the Alliance, warfare against Catholic tendencies was serious business. At a meeting convened by the Alliance in the Royal Albert Hall in 1925, Sir William Joynson-Hicks, the Home Secretary, gave a stirring speech, punctuated by applause, in which he claimed – with dubious historical warrant – that Nonconformists as well as members of the Church of England claimed a heritage in the Book of Common Prayer.[40] At a similar Alliance meeting in 1926 even Bishop Barnes was applauded for his battle against Anglo-Catholicism in Birmingham. The Alliance's campaign, however, meant that it alienated a number of the bishops who wanted to see liturgical change. Nevertheless, the Alliance was delighted when the House of Commons rejected the proposals for revision. *Evangelical Christendom* summed it up: 'Evangelicals in the National and Free Churches were linked together and under God's guidance the House of Commons spoke frankly and soberly the mind of the Nation'.[41] Evangelical Protestantism had, for a brief period, been able to take centre-stage.

Common causes

Although the Alliance could readily generate support for negative campaigns, it also had a vision of a renewed church within a renewed society. Unity was important for the health of church and nation. Stuart Holden, vicar of St Paul's, Portman Square, who was the dominant Keswick figure in the 1920s, typically saw divisions between Christians as a major factor hindering revival.[42] United prayer was vital. Each January the Alliance's meetings for prayer were held at centres throughout Britain – for example, at sixty locations in 1911 – and across the world. International awareness was strong. Special prayer events, usually in London, were also organized. During the First World War monthly meetings for prayer, which attracted over 2,500 people, took place in the Queen's Hall. On occasions there was an overflow into All Souls Church next door. Gooch's strategy was to use prominent church leaders, not all of whom were evangelical, to further the cause of renewal. The notable feature of the prayer meetings tended to be the speakers. Thus Randall Davidson, Archbishop of Canterbury, spoke at Alliance meetings in the Royal Albert Hall designed to promote family prayers in the nation. A F Winnington-Ingram, Bishop of London, and Hensley Henson spoke at the Queen's Hall. More predictably, there were Free Church speakers like J Scott Lidgett, a leading Methodist, and J D Jones, an influential Congregational minister. There was a breadth of co-operation in prayer, but there were also clear limits beyond which evangelicals would not venture. The Second World War saw an unexpected attempt to broaden the base of Christian unity when the Roman Catholic Archbishop of Westminster, Cardinal Hinsley, shared public meetings in London with Protestant leaders. Gooch condemned George Bell, Bishop of Chichester, for his participation and branded the new movement, which was entitled the 'Sword of the Spirit', as the 'sword of hypocrisy and deceit'.[43]

The inter-war period saw some emphasis on political issues, but these were always seen within a spiritual context. In 1920 the Alliance held a large meeting to make a case for a spiritual dimension within the League of Nations. This showed a degree of support for a world institution that many evangelicals, influenced by a gloomy form of premillennialism, did not share.[44] Gooch's father, Fuller Gooch, was a noted advocate of premillennialism.[45] A number of readers of *Evangelical Christendom* probably warmed to the argument by D M Panton of Norwich that all world reform was based on denial of the Second Coming and was doomed.[46] But the Alliance determinedly carried on its efforts to achieve improvements in society. Its two long-standing concerns were for religious liberty through-out the world – instances of persecution were given considerable publicity – and for the preservation of the character of the British Sunday.[47] These two issues were not unrelated to the Alliance's anti-Catholic position, since Catholic countries, like Spain and Portugal, which restricted the freedom of Protestants, were regularly highlighted by the Alliance, and it was Catholics who were seen as being soft on the Sunday issue. In the 1930s there was a new threat to liberty – the rise of Hitler. Anti-semitism would, it was argued, develop into anti-Christianity.[48] *Evangelical Christendom* relied heavily for its German news items on statements by the German theologian, Karl Barth, who, it was said, was teaching a 'revived Calvinism'.[49] The Alliance accepted Barth's contention that the cause of the Confessing Church in Germany was 'the cause of all Evangeli-cal Christendom' and when Barth was in London in 1937 the Alliance sponsored a meeting to pay tribute to him.[50] The policy was to make common cause with those seeking to bring spiritual priorities to bear on society.

Ultimately, however, it was the biblical message of salvation which was foundational. A significant contribution to the maintenance of a robust, yet thoughtful doctrine of scripture was made by Henry Wace, Dean of Canterbury.[51] Speaking at an Alliance conference in 1908, Wace argued – in an address that produced enthusiastic applause – that the authority of scripture was guaranteed by the superintendence of the Spirit. Wace explained that textual variants remained in the Bible but 'the substance of the history and of the teaching' was 'divinely authenticated'.[52] The inter-war period saw large Alliance celebrations of the place of the Bible in Protestant history. It was this emphasis that led the Alliance to distance itself from three inter-war movements of spirituality. The first movement, Pentecostalism, did not find favour because, according to an Alliance apologist, Sir Robert Anderson, 'it subordinates the great facts and truths of the Christian revelation to the subjective experience of the Christian life'.[53] Campbell Morgan of Westminster Chapel agreed, suggesting that the age of miracles was over and that the 'tongues movement' was evil.[54] The second unsatisfactory movement was the Anglican Evangelical Group Movement.[55] The emergence of the AEGM in 1923 was related to the liberal-conservative storm a year before in the Church Missionary Society.[56] Gooch commented in 1922 that the time was not right to raise questions about theories of biblical inspiration.[57] But increasingly critical comment was to be heard from Gooch about the AEGM.[58] By 1934 liberal evangelicals were judged to have left their first love since they were advocating an international forum for peace that would involve the Pope. Such compromise, the Alliance maintained, had to be met by the 'definite presentation of the Gospel of Christ as it is revealed in the Holy Scrip-tures'.[59] The third movement to be tried and found wanting was the Oxford Group – led by an American Lutheran minister, Frank Buchman – which, in the early 1930s, created a huge impact through house parties attracting thousands of mainly young people through its claim to receive direct divine guidance and through the practice of confession of sin to a group.[60] A number of evangelicals gave a cautious welcome to a force that was clearly evangelistic. Buchman had been influenced by D L Moody and by Keswick. *Evangelical Christendom* asked in 1931, 'Can there by any more hopeful movement in our day than this?'[61] During 1932, however, queries were raised about the Group's lack of clarity on the atonement and the place of the Bible.[62] The final straw for the Alliance was a Group meeting in 1936 in the Albert Hall when there were many testimonies of changed lives but prayer and scripture were entirely absent.[63] The Alliance was determined to take its stand on the Bible.

Evangelicals and mission

There are continuities and discontinuities between the features to be found in the Alliance up to Second World War and in the post-war era. When Gooch eventually retired (probably after some encouragement to do so) in 1949 and Cattell, an evangelical entrepreneur, took over, it was stated that the Alliance would continue to promote unity, assist persecuted Christians, be involved in evangelical and evangelistic work, and emphasize prayer.[64] But discontinuities were apparent. Hugh Gough, who was a key figure in a time of transition, warned in 1947 against unthinking loyalty to the Protestant cause and to the 'old paths', saying that he had discovered during the war that evangelicals were not necessarily preachers of the evangel.[65] Gilbert Kirby was in agreement with Gough that a new way forward had to be found. At the annual meeting of the Alliance in 1948 Kirby made the statement that 'modernism is dead; it is no longer a thing to worry about'.[66] Even the special days of prayer were called into question. At an Alliance meeting in Westminster Chapel, Lloyd-Jones – who was, unusually, sharing a platform with Sir Stafford Cripps and W R Matthews, Dean of Westminster – suggested that days of prayer wrongly emphasized human needs. Worship should be paramount.[67] It is not surprising that Gough signalled at the Alliance's executive in 1948 that the time had come for a complete change in leadership and policy.[68] Gough and Kirby called for a special meeting of the executive and this was followed in September 1949 by a residential conference at which ten Alliance leaders hammered out a new direction. The new ideas were taken up enthusiastically by Cattell. It was decided to have a major evangelical exhibition and public meetings during the Festival of Britain which was being planned for 1951. An editorial in *Evangelical Christendom*, 'Evangelicalism in Action', captured the new note of confidence. Meetings that featured evangelistic preachers such as Tom Rees, Alan Redpath, Stephen Olford and W E Sangster were held during September 1951, and on two nights 7,500 people filled the Methodist Central Hall, Westminster Abbey and Westminster Chapel. Mission was to be at the heart of this new phase of the life of the Alliance.

Further steps were taken in 1952. Cattell had been involved in nego-
tiations with Billy Graham who had achieved fame in America as an
outstanding evangelist, and in March 1952 Graham addressed about 250
church leaders in Church House, Westminster, about the possibility of a
British crusade. The British Council of Churches wanted a pilot crusade to
be held outside London, but Graham was not interested in such a proposal. His goal, he told Bryan Green, was to mount 'the greatest evangelistic effort, humanly speaking, that the Church had ever committed itself
to'.[69] The responsibility for arranging what became the Greater London
Crusade at Harringay Arena from March to May 1954 fell, perhaps
inevitably, to the Alliance. In what was to be the last issue of *Evangelical
Christendom* (September 1954) it was suggested that Harringay marked a
turning point in the history of the EA.[70] For Cattell, who liked to operate
on a grand scale, it was a dream come true. Staff working at the EA rose
to seventy. The Alliance was at the hub of evangelical affairs. Even before
Harringay, Graham's visits to Britain had helped to raise the level of
confidence in British evangelicalism, to establish and strengthen networks,
and to deepen unity.[71] Harringay served to promote conservative evangelicalism in a way that would have been unthinkable earlier in the century.
Afterwards, numbers of evangelicals training for Anglican ministry
surged. The support Graham received from those outside the evangelical
camp encouraged him to pursue a policy of distancing himself from narrower American fundamentalists.[72] In 1955 John Stott, who was now
recognized as the leading evangelical Anglican figure of the future, put to
the London Crusade committee plans to launch *Crusade* – to be modelled
on *Punch* – as a monthly journal which would continue the spirit of the
London and Scottish (1955) Crusades.[73] There were plans to unite the EA
and the Movement for World Evangelization, but these came to nothing
and Cattell, who had been earmarked as secretary of the merged organization, left the EA to train for the Anglican ministry. By this time, however,
Cattell and his colleagues had drawn evangelicals together in a common
commitment to mission.

When Gilbert Kirby became general secretary of the EA in 1956, he
was already intimately acquainted with its strengths and weaknesses. He
consistently took the view that the strength of the Alliance was the role
which it could play in encouraging evangelicals to put evangelism and
revival at the top of their agendas.[74] Its weakness was that it was often
able to bring only limited influence to bear when evangelicals disagreed.
The challenges faced in the realm of evangelism were the need to recover
the social dimension of the gospel, the possibilities of interdenominational
co-operation and the questions raised by the Puritan revival, as it was
called, of the 1950s and 60s. From 1959 *Crusade* began to cover social
issues like the atom bomb, race relations and family planning. David
Winter, the editor, urged readers not to dismiss such matters with the
words 'social gospel', arguing that the gospel had collective and social
consequences.[75] On the question of co-operative evangelical activity,

Kirby could point to the examples of interdenominational missionary societies, Keswick, the Children's Special Service Mission, the Inter-Varsity Fellowship and the EA itself to show the effectiveness of unity in action.[76] In order to build confidence between evangelicals, Kirby wrote a series of articles on the denominations. The Brethren were given special praise for their evangelistic efforts. It was estimated that 28–30% of Billy Graham counsellors had been from Brethren assemblies.[77] Kirby also worked successfully at bringing the Pentecostals, previously rejected by the Alliance, into the mainstream of evangelicalism. Success was not forthcoming in the case of the Calvinist wing of evangelicalism as evidenced by the critique of Graham's methods produced in 1966 by Erroll Hulse, minister of Cuckfield Baptist Church.[78] Nevertheless, the period from the mid-1950s to the mid-1960s was one in which evangelical co-operation in mission was widespread. The Alliance slogan introduced by Kirby in 1962 – 'Spiritual Unity in Action' – seemed to be justified.[79]

Ecumenical tensions

All was not well, however, in the area of evangelical relationships with the ecumenical movement. Increasingly, pressure came from the separatist wing of evangelicalism to cut off all contact with the World Council of Churches. There had always been a part of the evangelical constituency that criticized the Alliance for its breadth. A C Dixon, minister of the Metropolitan Tabernacle, had accused the Alliance in 1917 of fraternizing with 'sacerdotalists' and 'liberals'.[80] In 1922, when attacked by the fundamentalist Wesley Bible Union, the Alliance had appealed to the Methodist leader, Dinsdale Young, for help.[81] Post-Second World War pressure came initially from the United States. The American branch of the Alliance had officially ceased to function in 1944, and a new evangelical body, the National Association of Evangelicals (NAE), had been formed.[82] In 1946 Lloyd-Jones called a meeting at Westminster Chapel at which Harold J Ockenga, President of the NAE, was the speaker – a move which provoked Alliance fears that the NAE might be about to create a new pan-evangelical organization in Europe. Gough went to see Lloyd-Jones who was noncommittal over the American moves.[83] Lloyd-Jones did, however, persuade the NAE to consult Alliance leaders. It was understood that the NAE would wish to proceed on narrower and more exclusive lines than the Alliance.[84] In 1948 a meeting was held in Clarens, Switzerland, and in preparation for that meeting Gough and Gooch met in London with Lloyd-Jones and E J Poole-Connor, the founder, in 1922, of the Fellowship of Independent Evangelical Churches. Differences over policies of evangelical co-operation became increasingly apparent in the summer of 1948.[85] By the end of the year the FIEC had made it plain that it could not condone the way in which the Alliance invited to its platform those whose views were largely at variance with the Alliance's doctrinal basis.[86] In 1951 NAE plans came to fruition when a World Evangelical Fellowship was formed that joined together evangelical bodies in eleven countries. Despite some worries in Britain about the WEF's use of the word 'infallible' in relation to scripture – a problem that initially kept a number of European Alliances out of the world body – the British Alliance joined.[87] Kirby subsequently became general secretary of the WEF. Separatist evangelicals in Britain were, however, dissatisfied and in 1953 the British Evangelical Council was formed to provide fellowship for those evangelicals who wished to be free from all links with ecumenical bodies. Unity had not been achieved.

Pressure also came from the WCC and the British Council of Churches (BCC). In 1946 the Alliance stated that it had nothing but goodwill for these great and representative bodies but that the Alliance was evangelical.[88] A request from the WCC in 1947 to merge WCC and Alliance weeks of prayer was rejected. Gough suggested in 1948 that the Alliance could provide spiritual inspiration for the WCC and should continue to adopt a middle, or bridge, position.[89] A T Houghton, the chairman of Keswick, believed that Keswick and the EA had pioneered an ecumenical path.[90] In 1949 EA policy towards the ecumenical movement was defined as 'benevolent neutrality'.[91] The aim was to work with evangelicals in the WCC and to offer constructive criticism. A harder line was taken in 1952 when the WCC was charged with having an inadequate doctrinal basis. Gough continued to try to maintain the bridge position, but Poole-Connor dismissed Gough's efforts as 'the vaguest platitudes'.[92] Tensions grew during the 1960s. Kirby, more acutely aware of the problems than anyone else, began, in 1962, planning for a national evangelical conference. By this stage Kirby had enabled churches as well as individuals to affiliate to the EA. Six thousand evangelical churches were invited to send delegates, and 1,155 registrations were received. Anglicans formed the biggest group, with Baptists not far behind, followed by members of FIEC churches. When the conference met in 1965, it was decided to set up a representative group to study evangelical attitudes to ecumenism, denominationalism and a future united evangelical church.[93] A report was to be prepared for a 1966 assembly. Kirby wanted a balanced picture. Undue deference must not, he suggested in July 1966, be given to the right wing or the left wing of evangelicalism.[94] Within a few months the two wings of evangelicalism had publicly gone their separate ways.

Conclusion

Over the period of sixty years that has been studied here, the Alliance attempted to occupy a central position in British evangelicalism. In the period up to the Second World War it acted as a meeting point for evangelicals from diverse traditions and with differing perspectives. A measure of united action was achieved through the focus of the Alliance on particular issues. These reflected the evangelical Protestantism of the Alliance at a time when there was fear of Catholic and Anglo-Catholic dominance and concerns about liberal theology. There was also, however, a more constructive agenda which had to do with religious liberty and the improvement of society. The international stage was important. After the Second World War, perspectives and issues changed. Leaders like Gough, Kirby and Stott reshaped the work of the Alliance. The organization's constituency was now clearly defined as conservative evangelicalism. Mission within Britain became paramount. Evangelicals in all the main denominations drew more closely together. The Alliance concentrated much more on co-ordination than on the high profile meetings of Gooch's era. Evangelical resurgence engendered new confidence. But the Alliance was unable to prevent division over evangelical reactions to the vision of church unity being pursued by the ecumenical movement. The search for unity led, in 1966, to schism.

Endnotes

1   *Evangelical Alliance Quarterly*, January 1905, p 58.
2   J B A Kessler, *A Study of the Evangelical Alliance in Great Britain* (Goes, Netherlands, 1968), pp 73–74.
3   *Evangelical Christendom* (hereafter *EC*), November-December 1906, pp 165–166.
4   *EC*, November-December 1911, p 196.
5   D W Bebbington, *Evangelicalism in Modern Britain: A History from the 1730s to the 1980s* (London, 1989), ch 6.
6   *EC*, May-June 1924, pp 77–78.
7   *The Bible League Quarterly*, October-December 1926, p 180, quoted by D W Bebbington, 'Martyrs for the truth: Fundamentalists in Britain', in D Wood (ed), *Martyrs and Martyrologies*, Studies in Church History, 30 (Oxford, 1993), p 425.
8   *EC*, November-December 1924, p 188.
9   *The Keswick Convention* (London, 1929), p 139. Each year Keswick addresses were published.
10 *The Record*, 5 June 1931, p 373.
11 *EC*, May-June 1939, p 112.
12 *EC*, May-June 1907, pp 68–70.
13 I M Randall, 'Spiritual renewal and social reform: attempts to develop social awareness in the early Keswick movement', *Vox Evangelica*, 23 (1993), p 75.
14 *EC*, May-June 1906, pp 8–9.
15 *EC*, September-October 1910, p 98.
16 *EC*, May-June 1911, p 107; July-August 1911, p 158.
17 D W Bebbington, *The Nonconformist Conscience: Chapel and Politics, 1870–1914* (London, 1982), pp 80–83.
18 Letter of 16 June 1911 in Executive Council Minute book.
19 Kessler, *A Study of the Evangelical Alliance*, pp 86–87.
20 *EC*, September-October 1938, pp 165–166.

21 *EC*, May-June 1907, p 80.
22 J Wolffe, *The Protestant Crusade in Great Britain, 1829–1860* (Oxford, 1991), p 307.
23 *EC*, November-December 1911, p 230.
24 *Evangelical Alliance Quarterly*, April 1905, p 71; *EC*, November-December 1911, pp 231–232.
25 D Hempton and M Hill, *Evangelical Protestantism in Ulster Society, 1740–1890* (London, 1992), pp 181–184.
26 *EC*, September-October 1912, p 155.
27 *EC*, March-April 1939, p 80.
28 K W Clements, *Lovers of Discord: Twentieth Century Theological Controversies in England* (London, 1988), p 39.
29 *EC*, March-April 1908, p 49.
30 *EC*, March-April 1907, p 58.
31 A P F Sell, *Defending and Declaring the Faith: Some Scottish Examples, 1860–1920* (Exeter, 1987), pp 137–171.
32 J Barnes, *Ahead of His Time* (London, 1979), pp 125–132.
33 *EC*, January-February 1921, p 5.
34 For America see G M Marsden, *Fundamentalism and American Culture: The Shaping of Twentieth-Century Evangelicalism, 1870–1925* (Oxford, 1980).
35 A M G Stephenson, *The Rise and Decline of English Modernism* (London, 1984), p 124.
36 *EC*, September-October 1921, p 107.
37 *EC*, March-April 1939, p 77.
38 K Hylson-Smith, *High Churchmanship in the Church of England* (Edinburgh, 1993), pp 256–257.
39 A Hastings, *A History of English Christianity, 1920–1990* (London, 1991), p 206.
40 *EC*, January-February 1925, p 45.
41 *EC*, January-February 1928, p 18.
42 *Evangelical Alliance Quarterly*, April 1905, p 71.
43 S Mews, 'The sword of the Spirit: a Catholic cultural crusade of 1940', in W J Sheils (ed), *Studies in Church History*, 20 (Oxford, 1983), p 425.
44 I M Randall, 'Cultural change and future hope: premillennialism in Britain following the First World War', *Christianity and History Newsletter*, 13 (1994,) pp 19–27.
45 For Fuller Gooch, see H M Gooch, *William Fuller Gooch* (London, 1929).
46 *EC*, November-December 1924, p 178.
47 J W Ewing, *Goodly Fellowship* (London, 1946), chs 8 and 9.
48 *EC*, November-December 1933, p 234.
49 *EC*, January-February 1930, p 35.
50 *EC*, January-February 1936, p 24; March-April 1937, p 44.
51 Bebbington, *Evangelicalism in Modern Britain*, pp 189–190.

52 *EC*, May-June 1908, p 62; July-August, p 93.
53 *EC*, March-April 1909, p 37.
54 *EC*, March-April 1909, p 37.
55 See E A Smith, *Another Anglican Angle* (Oxford, 1991).
56 K Hylson-Smith, *Evangelicals in the Church of England, 1734–1984* (Edinburgh, 1988), chapter 16.
57 Kessler, *A Study of the Evangelical Alliance*, pp 76–77. Kessler wonders why Gooch felt the time was not right in 1922. The background controversies give the answer.
58 Report in *The Life of Faith*, 20 January 1926, p 61.
59 *EC*, January-February 1934, p 30.
60 D W Bebbington, 'The Oxford Group Movement between the Wars', in W J Sheils and D Wood (eds), *Studies in Church History*, 23 (Oxford, 1986), pp 495–507.
61 *EC*, November-December 1931, p 241.
62 *EC*, January-February 1932, pp 40–41; July-August 1932, pp 145–146.
63 *EC*, July-August 1936, p 157.
64 *EC*, October-December 1949, p 85.
65 *EC*, January-March 1947, pp 1–2.
66 *EC*, April-June 1948, p 13.
67 *EC*, January-March 1948, p 13.
68 Executive Council Minutes (hereafter ECM), 28 October 1948.
69 Billy Graham to Bryan Green, 5 July 1952, in *Billy Graham Archives*, Wheaton College, USA.
70 *EC*, September 1954, p 65.
71 See forthcoming article by I M Randall, 'Conservative constructionist: the early influence of Billy Graham in Britain', in *The Evangelical Quarterly*.
72 G M Marsden, *Reforming Fundamentalism: Fuller Seminary and the New Evangelicalism* (Grand Rapids, 1987), pp 162–165.
73 Minutes of the Executive Committee of the Billy Graham 1955 London Crusade, 22 February 1955.
74 ECM, 29 January 1965.
75 *Crusade*, July 1959, p 5.
76 *Evangelical Broadsheet*, Winter 1959, p 1.
77 *Crusade*, July 1962, p 34.
78 E Hulse, *Billy Graham: The Pastor's Dilemma* (Hounslow, 1966).
79 *Evangelical Broadsheet*, Winter 1962/63.
80 *EC*, May-June 1917, p 81.
81 *EC*, January-February 1922, p 8.
82 D M Howard, *The Dream that would not Die* (Exeter, 1986), pp 26–27.
83 ECM, 25 April 1946; 25 July 1946.
84 ECM, 1 July 1948.
85 ECM, 22 July 1948; 23 September 1948.

86 ECM, 25 November 1948.
87 ECM, 24 July 1952.
88 *EC*, April-June 1946, p 50.
89 ECM, 17 November 1948.
90 *Crusade*, November 1964, p 4.
91 *EC*, October-December 1949, p 87.
92 I H Murray, *D Martyn Lloyd-Jones: The Fight of Faith, 1939–1981* (Edinburgh, 1990), p 306.
93 *Crusade*, December 1965, pp 18–19.
94 ECM, 27 July 1966.

Chapter 17

RENEWAL, RECOVERY AND GROWTH: 1966 ONWARDS

Peter Lewis

During this period the evangelical scene in Britain has seen more upheaval, growth, challenge and public impact than at any time in the twentieth century. This has not come about without pain and discomfort, and a heavy price has at times been exacted. Yet the gain of these years has unquestionably been great in terms of lives changed, issues faced, churches revitalized, and evangelicals brought together for worship in all its variety and mission in all its forms.

The period began with a major upheaval involving one of the most widely respected and influential evangelical leaders in Britain, Dr Martyn Lloyd-Jones of Westminster Chapel, arguably the greatest preacher of his day and a theologian of great ability. He had argued for some time for the need for a closer and more visible *evangelical* unity as distinct from the *ecumenical* unity that was being so strongly pushed in the church at large, and of which he had always been critical.

Iain Murray has summarized his position particularly well:

> He differed with ecumenism on its fundamental principle namely, that all dialogue should proceed on the understanding that it was between fellow *Christians*. He objected to this because it meant giving a breadth to the meaning of 'Christian' which was unknown in the New Testament ... Certainly he believed that a man might be a Christian who did not employ the name 'evangelical' ... But the fundamentals of evangelicalism are the fundamentals of the gospel and to concede the title 'Christian' to those who deny those fundamentals is to undermine Christianity itself.[1]

During the 1950s and 1960s various schemes were afoot for unity between a number of denominations, which increased the pressure on evangelicals in these groupings. Lloyd-Jones believed that this situation presented evangelicals with a great opportunity. 'Instead of simply adopting delaying tactics in their denominations, evangelicals should themselves take up the New Testament emphasis on unity and on the evil of schism' seeking a true biblical unity outside of the 'mixed' (evangelical/non-evangelical) denominations, a unity that would involve not simply individuals but churches. Lloyd-Jones saw no hope for evangelicalism in the ecumenical movement or in the mixed denominations, since he believed it would inevitably be compromised and watered down in its essential 'gospel' character.

Most evangelical leaders, however, were moving in the opposite direction, optimistic about the future and taking a principled stand within both their denominations and the ecumenical movement. Many believed that their denominations could be won back to their evangelical roots and that, meantime, non-evangelical Christians had the right to be treated as fellow Christians. Many liberals might be right in their heart and wrong in their thinking; many Catholics might believe in a saving core of gospel truth even while accepting teaching that was unbiblical and dangerous.

EA, with Gilbert Kirby as its general secretary, sought to take the middle ground, raising the level of visibility of evangelicalism in Britain by allowing local churches, in addition to private individuals, to become associate members. The sessions of the National Assembly conference would be 'reserved for those who come as representatives or delegates of local churches or of Christian societies'. However, as Iain Murray says, 'Instead of regarding this as a move in the right direction, ML-J [M Lloyd-Jones] believed that it would bypass the whole issue of whether a true unity of evangelicals could be maintained if it included those who simultaneously believed in the possibility of ecumenical unity.'[2]

The National Assembly of Evangelicals 1966

In 1966 the Evangelical Alliance organized the second National Assembly of Evangelicals to meet in Westminster Chapel, London, 18–21 October. The opening address was given by Dr Lloyd-Jones at the Westminster Central Hall on the subject of unity. The hope had been 'to clear the air', but in the event the air was ignited rather than cleared as the speaker argued passionately for a new historic step toward unity – an *evangelical* unity that involved *churches* (and not only individuals) in a visible *association* (not a 'denomination' or an 'Evangelical Church') free from the compromises inevitably associated with ecumenical involvement and previous denominational loyalties.

Many who listened were convinced by the logic and excited by the vision. Others, however, were not. John Stott, chairing the meeting, said in reply: 'I believe history is against what Dr Lloyd-Jones has said . . . Scripture is against him, the remnant was within the church not outside it. I hope no one will act precipitately . . . We are all concerned with the same ultimate issues and with the glory of God.' Many evangelical leaders agreed with Stott rather than Lloyd-Jones, as one major event the following year was to illustrate.

The effect of Lloyd-Jones' call on the membership of EA was minimal and only a few churches withdrew. However, EA's new general secretary, A Morgan Derham – who had in fact come into office only in September

1966 and had 'inherited' the explosive assembly agenda – left in January 1969 feeling he could no longer claim to be a representative of an evangelical constituency that was now so profoundly divided. Nevertheless, amongst the positive achievements of the National Assemblies were the setting up of such commissions as the Evangelical Alliance New Towns Study Group which published its report under the title *Evangelical Strategy in the New Towns*, and the Commission on World Mission which produced a report, *One World, One Task*.

The British Evangelical Council (BEC)

BEC had been launched in 1952 in order to represent churches and bodies that were unwilling to be connected with the ecumenical movement. Till 1966 it had been a fairly small organization, though it did include the Free Church of Scotland (250 churches) and the Fellowship of Independent Evangelical Churches (then about 350 churches).

After the watershed of the 1966 National Assembly of Evangelicals, BEC provided the umbrella under which many churches that had left their 'mixed' denominations, as well as bodies that had always been exclusively evangelical, united in a loose fellowship or association of churches. These included the Evangelical Fellowship of Congregational Churches (142 churches joining in 1969), the Apostolic Church (160 churches joining in 1977), the Grace Baptist churches (120 churches joining in 1969) and the Evangelical Movement of Wales (about 30 churches, but more pastors, joining in 1967).

Thus BEC developed quite suddenly into a large and notable body on the British evangelical scene. In 1995 it numbered 1,200 churches, most of these being in affiliation through their membership in the denominations and groupings mentioned above. Meanwhile, however, momentous changes were taking place within one of the 'mixed' denominations, and that the largest.

The National Evangelical Anglican Congress 1967 (NEAC)

NEAC was held at the University of Keele, 4–7 April 1967. It was the first time that British Anglican evangelicals had gathered on such a national scale. The historian, David Bebbington, has written that it was 'the chief landmark in a post war evangelical renaissance that was gathering momentum well before the charismatic movement reinforced the process'.[3]

It was addressed by such leading evangelicals as John Stott, Philip Edgcumbe Hughes, Jim Packer and Michael Green, and was attended by a thousand clergy and laity. It articulated clearly and enthusiastically the loyalty of those evangelicals it represented to the Church of England and their commitment to regaining the high ground in their denomination. Yet NEAC accepted the right of 'broad' and 'high churchmen' to co-exist with evangelicals in the Anglican church, and also expressed their desire to enter and take a full part in current ecumenical dialogue at local, national and international levels.

The other especially important decision of the congress was to support evangelical social involvement. Timothy Chester points to Keele '67 as 'the first public expression of a growing social concern among British Evangelicals.'[4] Michael Saward believes that the all-important factor at this stage was the note of repentance that was sounded in this regard. The report confessed that there had been a failure in the past among evangelicals at large to be truly involved in the world, and stated, 'We believe that our evangelical doctrines have important ethical implications' and 'evangelism and compassionate service belong together in the mission of God.'[5]

The discussions, position papers and resolutions of NEAC drew deeply upon Anglican evangelical resources at parish level, from its intellectual think-tank in Latimer House, Oxford, and from elsewhere. Alister McGrath writes:

> Under the erudite and wise guidance of its warden J I Packer, Latimer House became a focus of theological and liturgical working parties which brought together leading evangelical thinkers and representatives from across the nation ... Keele was thus no hasty response to the crisis of October 1966; it was a well prepared attempt to face the challenge of an unknown future, armed with the historic resources of the evangelical tradition fully deployed.[6]

The resulting Keele statement is widely regarded by evangelicals and non-evangelicals alike as 'one of the most important ecclesiastical documents not only of the sixties but of this century'.[7]

Meanwhile, EA under its general secretary, Morgan Derham, was pressing ahead with several projects that were to prove significant on the wider evangelical scene, including the Arts Centre Group, the Shaftesbury Project and, best known of all, what became known as TEAR Fund. The Arts Centre Group exists as a nation-wide support group for Christian professionals in all areas of the arts and now numbers some 700 members and 300 'friends'.

The emergence of TEAR Fund 1968

TEAR Fund, one of the largest relief and development organizations in Britain today, was spawned by EA. It is distinctively Christian and evangelical. It began in its present form in 1968 but developed from a fund which had existed since 1959 (World Refugee Year) to help meet the needs of refugees. However, Morgan Derham had decided that this fund should be broadened to include relief work in general, and the name was changed to 'The Evangelical Alliance Relief Fund (TEAR)'. Timothy Chester writes:

Derham was convinced that the Fund had potential. Evangelicals, he felt, were waking up to their social responsibilities. At the same time he was concerned to remove what he called 'the evangelical alibi' for non involvement in relief schemes, namely that there were no evangelical bodies through whom money could be given and care expressed.[8]

In 1968 the late George Hoffman (1933–1992) joined EA as part-time assistant to Morgan Derham. Hoffman had been profoundly influenced by Keele and eagerly took the project to heart. A new committee met on 29 May 1968, and the fund was publicly launched in November. Its income grew from £34,000 in its first year to £208,000 in 1971. By then it had become effectively independent of the EA and later changed its name from The Evangelical Alliance Relief Fund (TEAR Fund) to simply 'Tear Fund'. Today its budget is £21 million and it serves over 1,000 projects in over 90 countries in Latin America, Asia, Africa and the Middle East. It has a secure and central place in evangelical life and, while it is the twenty-fifth largest charity in the UK in terms of income, it is the fourth largest in terms of covenanted (ie committed) giving.

In 1969 Gordon Landreth became the general secretary of EA and fostered the early stages of TEAR Fund's life as well as helping to convene the Evangelists' Conference, a forum for fellowship and networking. It began with about 40 and now numbers around 500 meeting annually at Swanwick. He also took a particular interest in Christian broadcasting, serving as chairman of the Church's Advisory Committee on Local Broadcasting. In his thirteen years with EA (1969–82) Landreth was closely connected with the European Evangelical Alliance and the World Evangelical Fellowship and served as the minute secretary for the executive of the Lausanne Committee, having a great concern for international relations between evangelical bodies.

International Evangelicalism: Berlin 1966 and Lausanne 1974

So far I have spoken of British evangelicalism being influenced from within. However, one of the most noteworthy features of this whole period (1966–95) is that, just as the greatest growth and development of the world-wide church has been in the non-Western world, so Western churches have been increasingly influenced by pastors and theologians from Latin America, Africa and South East Asia.

A new era of world evangelization was also signalled during these years. On 25 October 1966 more than a thousand evangelical leaders, carefully chosen from over a hundred countries, gathered in Berlin for a congress under the title 'One Race, One Gospel, One Task'. Major Western figures, notably Carl Henry, Billy Graham and John Stott, figured largely. The Lutheran, Valdi Steverngel, has stated that 'Berlin was the first evangelical congress that was affected by its own internationality'. He declared that 'at Berlin the Third World began to speak out and to offer criticism of the West and the West began to listen'.[9] Berlin 1966 spawned a number of national and regional congresses in the years immediately following, most notably the Latin American Congress on Evangelism held in 1969 at Bogota. The address by Peruvian Samuel Escobar, insisting that political activity and evangelism, social responsibility and evangelism, go together 'brought delegates leaping to their feet in a standing ovation'.

The International Congress on World Evangelization, which met in July 1974 at Lausanne, Switzerland, was a notable milestone. *Time* magazine described it as 'possibly the widest ranging meeting of Christians ever held'.[10] It brought together 2,500 participants (over half under the age of forty-five years) and 1,000 observers from 150 countries, representing 135 denominations. While John Stott urged that *mission* includes both evangelism and social action and Carl Henry argued that political involvement had a biblical mandate, it was two younger 'Third World' theologians, Rene Padilla and Samuel Escobar, who, to use Chris Sugden's words, 'lit blue touch paper' for evangelical social responsibility by placing the issue of social action and its relationship to the gospel at the centre of congress discussion. 'The only true evangelism', argued Rene Padilla, 'is that which is orientated toward that final goal of "the restoration of all things" in Christ Jesus.'[11] Padilla warned against worldliness in the church existing as 'cultural Christianity' as well as 'secular Christianity'. Escobar publicly disagreed with Dr Billy Graham's contention that concentrating on social issues would lead to an abandonment of evangelicalism. Escobar declared, 'I would like to affirm that I do not believe in that statement. I think the social gospel . . . deteriorated because of poor theology. The sad thing is that those who have the right theology have not applied it to social issues.'[12]

Lausanne proved to be a turning point in evangelical thinking throughout the world, and greatly influenced evangelicals in Britain. At this time too, another focus of evangelical unity, and one which was deeply concerned about world mission, was emerging – the Evangelical Missionary Alliance (EMA).

The Evangelical Missionary Alliance

EMA exists to encourage co-operation and provide co-ordination between missionary societies and between societies, churches and colleges. Anticipated by the Fellowship of Interdenominational Missionary Societies, EMA was brought into being in November 1958 by EA, Gilbert Kirby serving as general secretary of both EA and EMA. The greater diversity and wider alliance that this involved posed new problems as well as fresh challenges. As Harry Sutton, general secretary of the Anglican South American Missionary Society, wryly observed:

Evangelicalism's emphasis on the priesthood of all believers meant that we were always in the position of having as many chiefs as there were Indians. This made life very difficult for the Evangelical Missionary Alliance designed to bring together missionary societies which in themselves had problems staying together ... It never ceased to surprise me, how we managed to get on together. But manage it we did!

From 1966 the leadership of EMA passed to Ernest Oliver, Gilbert Kirby becoming principal of London Bible College. Mr Oliver managed to combine this with his work as executive secretary of the Regions Beyond Missionary Union and chairman of All Nations Bible College, as well as later helping to set up and serve Tear Fund! One of the earlier and more significant things that EMA did through men like Ernest Oliver, Leslie Lyall (OMF), John Savage (EUSA), Len Harris (UFM) and Len Moules (WEC) was to draw up a syllabus for missiological studies in training colleges. In 1983 the EMA called its first full-time general secretary, Stanley Davies, and has since seen considerable growth and co-operation among various evangelical bodies at different levels. The changes over this period have been great and have demanded much flexibility and new thinking (not to mention a new humility) in missions strategy. The emphasis on Christian social responsibility highlighted by Tear Fund has increased greatly, though it was there before and has always been part of mission. There has been a greater commitment to partnership with the overseas churches and with new non-Western agencies. The growth of the non-Western missionary movement has been a major fact that many societies have had to come to terms with. New forms of partnership between agencies have been necessary, including relationships between 'vertically-integrated partnerships', for example in regard to work in North Africa involving radio, literature, correspondence schools, church planting, discipleship programmes and 'tent-making'.

The situation at present is in a period of flux and is complicated by independent churches sending out individuals to 'do their own thing'. This commendable vision and zeal can, in fact, cause unintended problems and difficulties for Christians 'on the ground' in those places. Movements such as Operation Mobilization have grown in maturity, widening missionary horizons. A significant recent development in the Evangelical Alliance is the new co-operation between EA and EMA to work together to bring the challenge of overseas mission to the local church. At present EMA has 120 member societies and 19 colleges in partnership.

Another major focus of ongoing evangelical unity in Britain has been the evangelical student organization, IVF/UCCF.

The Universities and Colleges Christian Fellowship

The history of the Inter-Varsity Fellowship of Evangelical Unions (IVF), which in 1975 became the Universities and Colleges Christian Fellowship of Evangelical Unions (UCCF), is well documented. Its strategic place and spiritual influence in Britain and beyond has been incalculable. As the student population in the country has grown (full-time students in 1968 numbered 460,000, in 1978 665,000 and in 1992/3 957,600) so the number of Christian Unions (CUs) has grown. In 1968 there were 52 university and 300 polytechnic and other college CUs; in 1978 54 and 500, and by 1992/3 148 (polytechnics having received university status) and 377. To meet and minister to this growth the number of full-time student/ministry staff workers also grew from 22 in 1968, to 54 in 1978 and to 51 in 1995 (assisted by 30–35 'relay-workers', young graduates working alongside staff workers in a voluntary capacity for one to two year periods).

Key features in the work of UCCF include the contribution of IVP (Inter-Varsity Press) to Christian literature which has produced hundreds of outstanding commentaries, theological works and books of practical help in the past thirty years and is now universally recognized as a major publisher of significant Christian and evangelical literature. These books have undergirded the life, thinking and ministries of evangelicals across all the divisions and have been a strong unifying force.

A further unifying element in the work of the IVF/UCCF has been the pursuit of an interdenominational approach to evangelism while maintaining a solid evangelical basis of faith. The work of the travelling secretaries in advising CU executives and the stature of IVF/UCCF's general secretaries, Oliver Barclay (1965–1981), Robin Wells (1981–1991) and Bob Horn (1993–) has been crucial in maintaining the essential character of a movement that serves the whole evangelical world and exists to promote the fundamentals of the faith in the student world.

Many evangelical Christians who now hold leading positions both in the church and in society at large have been affected deeply by their experience of CU life in their university or college. These are among its keenest supporters now, and many are members of its professional groups, such as the Business Study Group, Christians in Science, Association of Christians in Planning and Architecture, and affiliated associations such as the Christian Medical Fellowship and the Association of Christian Teachers. Such groups form valuable and effective networks of evangelical life and fellowship through the UK today. A notable feature of this period has been the growth and influence of national evangelical conventions and Bible weeks, which span many of the divides between evangelicals.

Spring Harvest, Keswick and other conventions

Clive Calver, one of its main promoters and leaders, has described Spring Harvest as 'the rebirth and renaissance of Keswick', the traditional annual summer gathering of evangelicals. However, the Keswick Convention (begun in 1875) itself has experienced a renaissance under the chairmanship of John Caiger, Alan Neech, Philip Hacking and Keith Weston, and with the ministry of such outstanding Bible teachers as John Stott, Eric Alexander, R T Kendall and Roy Clements. Numbers including children tend to be in the region of 8,000–10,000 over two weeks.

Still, it is beyond question that it is Spring Harvest that has been the more strikingly successful of the two in capturing the minds and hearts of a new generation and a great swathe of the evangelical world. Part holiday camp, part Christian convention, Spring Harvest has grown since its first gathering in 1979 to a multi-week, multi-venue Easter convention of up to 80,000 men, women and children. It combines Bible expositions, worship and preaching services, seminars for all ages and abilities on a huge range of subjects and issues. To service this it calls on a wide range of expertise drawn from evangelical organizations and leading evangelicals engaged in pastoral ministry, evangelism, education and social concern groups, missionary societies and Bible colleges. It began as a joint project involving British Youth for Christ, *Buzz* magazine and the EA, with Clive Calver, Peter Meadows, Dave Pope, Graham Kendrick and Doug Barnett among its first promoters and leaders. Regular speakers include Tony Campolo, Ian Barclay, R T Kendall and Ian Coffey.

Spring Harvest has swiftly come to involve figures from almost every major evangelical grouping and enterprise. Its stress on international mission has broadened the horizons of thousands, and many missionary societies have used the opportunity provided by its programmes and facilities. It has itself proved to be a major focus of evangelical unity at grassroots level and its influence has extended to Christians in many smaller and more liberal churches where there is often little Bible teaching and even less of contemporary styles of worship.

Its own style of worship and charismatic flavour have not commended it to all evangelicals. However, it has broadened and deepened its evangelical base over the years, for instance by the emergence of Word Alive which occupies one of its weeks and venues, and involves a coalition of Spring Harvest, Keswick and UCCF. This has been one of the most noteworthy developments of recent years involving teachers like Don Carson, Dick Lucas, David Jackman, Roy Clements and others.

A very successful and effective work has also been done by the Evangelical Ministry Assembly (meeting annually since 1984) and the Proclamation Trust (founded in 1986), whose goals are 'to teach the Bible to preachers in order that they in turn can teach it to others'. It seeks 'to provide a fellowship of like-minded evangelicals across denominational lines for encouragement in an exacting work'. Numbers at the assembly range from 700 to 800 ministers and leaders. Many other Bible Weeks (eg the Restorationist 'Downs' now 'Stoneleigh', 'Dales', 'New Wine', etc) and conventions (eg the Methodist 'Easter People') could be included here but are of somewhat more sectional interest.

The Evangelical Leaders Conferences and 'Leadership '84'

The period 1966–95 saw many attempts made to further *ecumenical* unity, including the Anglican/Methodist talks on unity in the 1960s and 1970s, Growing into Union (1971), the ARCIC Commission Report (1982) and, more recently, Churches Together (1989). In contrast with all this activity there have been few comparable efforts to further *evangelical* unity across denominations and groupings. In some ways this is understandable and even inevitable, since formal or institutional unity has not been on the agenda of most evangelicals. What they have sought is a greater demonstration of an already existing unity that seeks to be more recognized and more effective in the world at large.

However, there have been very many conferences, fraternals and public meetings set up to further mutual recognition of and co-operation between evangelicals of different backgrounds and constituencies. One such, on a national level, was the Evangelical Leaders Conference that met annually between 1983 and 1991. This was a small, by-invitation-only meeting of about forty to sixty leaders, serviced by though not under the aegis of EA.

This emerged from a conscientious attempt by the EA leadership to rethink its future and to reorder its present. Gilbert Kirby, Morgan Derham and Gordon Landreth wrote to about forty evangelical leaders across a wide spectrum to ask if they would be prepared to meet for three days to discuss both the present and the possible future of evangelical unity in Britain. The resulting conference, which met at High Leigh, proved to be the first of a series of such meetings, occurring annually, that brought together leaders from both separatist and denominational groupings, strong charismatics and equally strong non-charismatics. For some it was a new experience to be so close to people of such differing convictions. However, with participants sharing solid ground on evangelical fundamentals and showing a genuine willingness to listen to one another, it proved to be a source of increased understanding and mutual respect for many.

In the providence of God EA was to experience a dramatic upward turn in membership, visibility and nation-wide initiatives under a new general secretary, Clive Calver (1983–). The story of EA under Clive's leadership is told in a separate chapter in this book. Suffice it to say here that in his period of office the number of staff and personal members has increased dramatically, member churches to 5,000, with groups and organizations now numbering 800, including some which are very large such as Tear Fund, CARE Trust, the Shaftesbury Society, British Youth for Christ, Elim, and the African Caribbean Evangelical Alliance (ACEA).

One of Calver's first achievements was the major inter-denominational conference which took place at Bristol Sands, Leadership '84. This brought together about a thousand evangelicals in local church leadership to consider their response to the growing pressures of change both in the churches and in society at large, to issues of evangelism, involvement in society, international affairs, overseas mission, and other sometimes contentious but pressing topics. Those present came from very different backgrounds and constituencies, and were not always comfortable with each other's list of priorities, but it was a significant event in the deepening of evangelical unity.

Evangelical unity and co-operative evangelism

Between 1970 and 1980 it is estimated that the historic denominations in Britain lost a million members, two and a half thousand ministers and closed a thousand churches. This trend, as much as the biblical command and any spiritual compulsion, was to put evangelism on the agenda of all the denominations in the years that followed, culminating in the Decade of Evangelism in the 1990s.

The question has arisen, in consequence, whether evangelicals and their churches can stand alongside non-evangelicals in co-operative evangelism as well as in wider concerns such as social action. The responses to this question have been diverse, and convictions for and against run deep and sometimes divide evangelicals.

In 1968 EA published a book entitled *On the Other Side*, the report of its commission on evangelism. It sought to diagnose the state of Britain in the late 1960s, to work out the common ground British evangelicals occupied, and to point up the various opportunities that existed for relevant incisive evangelism. 'It never got the attention it deserved,' commented Morgan Derham long afterwards. It described as 'impossible' co-operation with those who falsified the essentials of the gospel by adding to them, subtracting from them or secularizing them. It left room in practice, however, for flexibility in more complex situations. In 1974 a self-consciously ecumenical attempt towards inter-church, co-operative evangelism was mounted, called the Nationwide Initiative in Evangelism (NIE). This failed in its main aim, however, principally because, as Gavin Reid has said, 'One thing we could never have done was to have agreed completely as to what the gospel was in the first place'.[13]

Ten years later, in 1984, Mission England marked a major success in what might be called limited co-operative evangelism. There were a number of reasons for this. First, while it incorporated as a central feature the ministry of Billy Graham, it did so in a series of multi-venue evangelistic campaigns in a number of regions outside London where Luis Palau and his team were conducting the parallel Mission to London. Second, it was determined from the outset that Dr Graham was not being invited to do evangelism *for* the churches but *with* them. Third, the gospel was simply but clearly presented with biblical integrity. Fourth, church relations were broad, with non-evangelical churches participating and converts being sent to those churches that took them to the meetings, whether Catholic or Protestant, evangelical or non-evangelical.

This compromise was acceptable to most, though not to all. Many of those who took a separatist and anti-ecumenical stand felt their participation would give credence, albeit unintentionally, to the equal Christian standing of those individuals and churches who did not believe some of the basics of the original, apostolic faith.

Mission England touched or tapped into a very large seam of 'religious sympathy' which exists even in our secular society and qualifies the sometimes glib description of Britain as 'post-Christian'. It brought a fresh sense of hope to a society increasingly disillusioned with secular materialism.

In 1987 the ecumenical British Council of Churches began the process of consultation about 'new ecumenical instruments' on the British scene, which was to end its former life as the BCC. In its place was promoted the Inter-Church Process.

EA's council of management responded to the proposals set out in the book *Churches Together in Pilgrimage* and to the Inter-Church Process as a whole, first of all in a letter written in February 1989 expressing both recognition of the importance of what was happening and concerns about (1) doctrinal ambiguity (even in central issues such as the Person and work of Christ and the inspiration and authority of scripture), (2) blurred relationships (in particular with the World Council of Churches) and (3) confusion about the Swanwick Declaration, a document of intent for a new ecumenical approach. This had been signed by conference members whose authority to speak for their constituencies was in some cases doubtful. It recognized that responses would vary in EA constituencies, affirmed its intention to stay in the ongoing discussion, but concluded: 'In our view, no wholehearted commitment can be given to the proposals as they stand.'

On Wednesday 14 February 1990 the full council of management of the EA met to debate the issue and to give a formal response to the invitation to become a participating member of the new Council of Churches for Britain and Ireland (which had emerged from the Inter-Church Process). After careful consideration of the issues involved, it concluded 'that it would be inappropriate for the Evangelical Alliance to accept the invitation'. Three main reasons for this were given. First, 'It was the unanimous view of the Council that it would be impossible for the Alliance which is based on a credal confession to enter into membership with a Body whose Basis of Faith was significantly different from our own'. Second, the fact was stated that 'we incorporate evangelicals who had differing views of the ecumenical debate which would make our membership of the new Council inconsistent'. Third, it also pointed out that 'The Evangelical Alliance has existed for 150 years seeking to draw together individual Christians, local churches, denominations and agencies, around an evangelical Basis of Faith which reflects Biblical, historic, Christianity', adding, 'For the majority of evangelical Christians in the UK we represent a parallel body to the Council of Churches for Britain and Ireland'.[14]

The growth of the charismatic movement

The period under review has also seen widespread proliferation and phenomenal growth in the pentecostal and charismatic movements in Britain and world-wide. Something like a quarter of the world church is now pentecostal or charismatic, and in Britain the evangelical scene has been notably affected by this movement with approximately 41% of evangelicals being charismatic or pentecostal.

The appearance of new churches in the House Church movement of the 1960s, their rapid multiplication in the 1970s and 1980s and, in particular, the growth of the 'restorationist' churches among them, has been a major event and force on the broader evangelical scene. While important differences remain, along with some suspicion on both sides, yet it is true to say that earlier antagonisms have gradually given way to a growing degree of mutual respect and recognition among churches generally. This can be seen, for instance, at local level in shared 'Bible weeks' and evangelistic events, and in national events such as Spring Harvest and Greenbelt, a Christian arts and music festival held annually over the August Bank Holiday weekend, attended by many thousands, especially young people.

In the older denominations, especially the Anglicans and Baptists, the growth of the 'Renewal', as it was commonly called, did much to increase the devotion and sense of calling of very many Christians, and affected many churches throughout the land. Furthermore, many churches not formally 'charismatic' have been affected by this movement in their songs, styles of worship and pastoral concerns.

The charismatic movement has been the occasion of considerable division among evangelicals in the past thirty years. Zeal and antagonism have often been equal and opposite forces in churches and between churches. There were and are lessons on both sides for the church as a whole, and much needed gifts and wisdom too. For EA to capture the minds and hearts of a new generation it was perhaps necessary, in the wisdom of God, for it to have, in recent years, an evidently pro-charismatic leadership and aspect. However, nothing is clearer to that leadership than the observation that all sections of the evangelical world need each other in worship and work in the world, in mission and ministry, in this life and the next. Theological depth and sound biblical preaching are crucial to the good of the churches in our day; the moral, social and political challenges we face need an informed Christian response, and very many of these elements are to be found scattered throughout the Christian community. Accordingly, no one section of the evangelical world has all the insight, understanding, expertise and zeal which evangelization needs at the end of the twentieth century.

EA exists to promote unity among, and effective Christian action by evangelicals of all kinds: charismatic and non-charismatic, paedo-baptist and credo-baptist, pro-ecumenical and anti-ecumenical, Calvinistic and

Arminian, from Anglican and from Free Church backgrounds. The Spirit of the ascended Christ is in us all, for us all.

Endnotes

1   I H Murray, *D Martyn Lloyd-Jones: The Fight of Faith, 1939–81* (Edinburgh, 1990), pp 427–429.
2   Murray, *D Martyn Lloyd-Jones*, p 499.
3   D W Bebbington, *Evangelicalism in Modern Britain* (London, 1989), p 249.
4   T Chester, *Awakening to a World of Need* (Leicester, 1993), p 23.
5   Chester, *Awakening to a World of Need*, p 23.
6   A McGrath, *Evangelicalism and the Future of Christianity* (London, 1994), p 40.
7   McGrath, *Evangelicalism and the Future* p 40.
8   Chester, *Awakening to a World of Need*, p 42.
9   Chester, *Awakening to a World of Need*, p 34.
10 Chester, *Awakening to a World of Need*, p 71.
11 Chester, *Awakening to a World of Need*, p 74.
12 Chester, *Awakening to a World of Need*, p 75.
13 G Reid, *To Reach a Nation* (London, 1987), p 21.
14 Letter of the Executive Committee of EA, November 1990, p 21.

Part 4
WHERE ARE WE HEADING?

Chapter 18

WORSHIP AND PRAYER

Dave Pope

To teach the human heart to respond to God is a very difficult task. Many large volumes have been written by some of the greatest authors and finest theologians covering areas of our faith and giving instruction for a life of discipleship, all to great effect. But actually to create the desire to worship, to engender a spirit of praise, to bring a sense of urgency to prayer, to instil a passion for intercession, cannot be achieved through words of wisdom, structured writing or human intervention.

There are those who have tried to elicit a heart response by moving from instruction to atmosphere or, to put it more crudely, from fact to feeling. Consequently, existential emphasis has crept into much of our Christian conduct. Create the right environment, and people will be moved to respond. Give people the right to trust their feelings, and their spirits will rise to the occasion. The last few years have witnessed some extraordinary growth in these areas; some of it has been a blessing and some a blight. But in it all, thankfully, God has re-emphasized the biblical basis for our response to him.

Nowhere is this more obvious than in Isaiah chapter 6, particularly as far as worship is concerned. Though this is well-trodden territory, it is nevertheless worthy of re-examination. Isaiah finds himself in the presence of the Almighty and recognizes the Lord of Lords and the King of Kings. The atmosphere is electric – an all-pervading sense of the overwhelming power of God with manifestations that deeply affect him (vs1–4). There is nothing clinical here. It is not the reading of Old Testament law with a three-point application, carefully alliterated, that drives Isaiah to his knees. Neither is it the heavily charged atmosphere. Isaiah's response (v5) is prompted by the presence of God himself – a confrontation with holiness, greatness, power and majesty – and his heart and spirit are deeply moved to such an extent that he expresses his worship in terms of availability and total commitment (v8).

Maybe this is where we have got it all wrong. It is only as we fulfil that divine appointment and allow ourselves to be confronted by God in all his fullness that our hearts will respond without human prompting and atmospheric manipulation. But we are all different, and God has given us the potential to respond in a variety of ways, sometimes in a manner that does not quite fit with others' expectations and understanding. We most probably would not be in the privileged position that was Isaiah's; some of us struggle to believe that *anything* can move in our worship services, let alone cherubim and seraphim cruising around the pews. But the power of God is as powerful today as it was in the year that King Uzziah died, so we need to be people of expectation and eagerness.

I would not want to convey the impression that I am ambivalent towards structure and atmosphere. It is when we get one out of line with the other that we have the potential for error. As the late David Watson said to me when I shared in a mission with him in Dublin many years ago, 'All Spirit, we blow up; all Word, we dry up; Spirit and Word, we grow up.' I will always value his wisdom.

But what is the implication here for worship and prayer? Surely it is that we take a biblical basis and allow the wind of the Spirit to blow, then find expression and interpretation which does not contradict the former or offend the latter. How easy it is to get all of this out of perspective, and even to elevate Christian conduct to such a high spiritual plane that it is devoid of sanctified common sense and practicality. History and scripture are littered with those who were so celestially minded that they were of little terrestrial value. Always trying to reach the zenith of spirituality can lead to total frustration and depression if it is not rooted in the practicality and normality of everyday life. One of my favourite illustrations is afforded by a story involving a doctor's family in Bristol. The senior man of the household was a minister of religion, and his son was a doctor. A visitor called one day and asked to speak to the man of the house. The person who opened the door to the unsuspecting guest had the presence of mind to ask, 'Do you want the one who preaches or the one who practises?' That says it all! As far as worship and prayer are concerned, is it not time we became more realistic and practical in our quest for that which is unattainable this side of eternity?

Let us apply this to worship. Paul was determined to encourage his readers and listeners to break from religiosity and high sentiment and to keep their feet on the ground. He emphasized that living holy lives was the bedrock of worship. A modern day Paul would say that if hands lifted in the air on Sunday are fiddling the books on Monday, they should not be raised the following Sunday! Holy lifestyle creates the real aroma of heaven. 'Gongs and pongs' may have their place for some as an aid to worship, but can never be a substitute for lives full of Christian integrity. In being slightly facetious here, I do not want to convey a negative or critical spirit. If formal tradition helps in worship, fine. If freedom and movements are aids, okay. If Wesley and Francis Ridley Havergal are an inspiration, hallelujah! However, if Kendrick causes the spirit to soar, so be it! Let us stop the comparisons and criticisms, and concentrate on the real issues. Worship comes from the heart, not from the lips.

The word 'worship' is derived from a Middle English word *wercscipe* which simply means 'to appreciate the worth of'. This is expanded in scripture by the Greek word *proskuneo* which means 'to approach with reverence, to kiss'. In the days of kings and courtiers, whenever a subject was ushered into the sovereign's presence, he would approach in an attitude of servanthood, with head bowed and eyes directed to the floor. The king would reach down, place his hand under the subject's chin and raise his face so that eye contact was achieved. Communication would then proceed. Maybe we have lost some of that reverence, awe and sense of occasion in our worship. How easy it is to race into the Lord's presence, launch into our favourite song or, if everything appears flat or tame, begin to count the preponderance of red hats or gents with pony tails! Surely the King of kings deserves more than this.

I mentioned servanthood. The spirit of the age and the secularization of our society has created an atmosphere in which egos evolve and are encouraged. Our education system is designed to produce self-sufficiency and a society that is in control of its own destiny. Increasingly, we see biblical values marginalized. A nodding recognition of our social ills and disgraces may well feature in a political party manifesto. But the reality often differs from the ideal. And the church has no right to criticize. We may drop a coin in the 'poor box' in the church porch or send a donation to the Shaftesbury Society, but unless genuine compassion is deeply ingrained in our lives we will never express Christ's love for the poor. It is easier to croon Kendrick's classic song that tells of 'clouds that are gathering' and 'bread being stolen' than to be part of the solution. Singing is always easier than serving!

Servanthood must be central to our response to God in worship and in prayer. To rediscover this emphasis is to find a new shimmering in what A W Tozer once described as the 'missing jewel' of evangelical worship. Like servants, worshippers should give as well as receive. To worship 'in spirit and in truth' (John 4:24) means that we are servants first and foremost. We live to worship, appreciating the worth of Almighty God. We serve to give him pleasure, not to increase our self-image or popularity stakes in the local community. We give him our heart's devotion and the service of our lives. We love him because he first loved us (1 John 4:19).

We should never change God's worship agenda. He jealously requires our adoration and praise in a spirit of love, commitment and servanthood. This gives him great pleasure and delights the hosts of heaven. But it is too easy for God's agenda to be distorted, for the Spirit to be organized out of worship and for frail humanity to usurp the place of Deity.

The last ten years has spawned an enormous increase in the number of celebrations, praise gatherings, events, worship bands, teams of musicians, worship leaders, product, songs and expressions of creativity. It has been like a river flowing through parched land. The United Kingdom is now viewed across the world as a place where God has achieved something very significant, as his people have come together in a variety of ways to express their unity and corporate worship and love for the Lord. Events such as Spring Harvest – often described as being 'pan-evangelical'

– have been used as catalysts in the process. But when process is taken over by product, when form becomes formality and when, more specifically, servants become masters, there are tremblings and tears in the heavenlies. Not that product, form or personality are wrong. But when the medium becomes more significant than the message, and when the support structure obliterates the Saviour, then it is time to rediscover Isaiah's worship experience.

God is a dynamic God, always doing new things and moving his people on. Lately, there have been some interesting manifestations in worship which have been warmly embraced by some and rejected by others. Change always has the potential for division, whether it be something as seemingly insignificant as introducing an overhead projector to facilitate worship, or allowing more freedom for the gifts of the Spirit to be exercised. Wisdom, explanation and pastoral back-up can help, but how often do you find those qualities of leadership readily available at local church level? A phenomenon, which has been loosely named the 'Toronto Blessing', has had significant but patchy impact on the British church. It cannot be described as revival or as a reawakening, but it can be described as a refreshing. It could be the prelude for a greater symphony, if God has his way. There must be no human manipulation.

Perhaps the greatest endorsement of the effectiveness of worship is when it leads to an emphasis on mission and Christian service. Lemonade fulfils its purpose when it is released from the bottle and enjoyed by thirsty people. If in our worship we only succeed in shaking the bottle and creating more fizz, we are likely to have some explosions to deal with. Introversion, strife, jealousy, personality-conflict are the heady gases that can blow a church apart.

However, it is different when worship is channelled into service. I long to see this happening more and more. Raised hands in worship applied to the plough, churches taking responsibility for social-action programmes, workers being sent out to plant churches world-wide, leaders giving time and commitment to taking on 'Timothys', church agendas incorporating community needs, churches becoming places for meeting and not just meetings! My heart is beating faster even as I write!

Perhaps the best measure of all of this is the quality of our prayer life. I would like to think that the days are rapidly disappearing when we are tempted to judge the effectiveness of worship by how many people attended the last celebration, or by how high people jumped off the floor! I have already indicated the importance of worship leading to work, but the latter can never be effective without the transforming and enabling power of prayer. Vehicles do not reach their destination if the fuel tanks are not loaded, and yet running on empty seems to be a growing phenomenon among church leaders.

The real situation surfaces when things go badly wrong; when there is a breakdown, moral failure or sheer inability to cope. Such is the time for repentance and a realization that God is in the re-creation business, but it is not the time for morbid introspection. Rather, wise counsel will draw attention to why things went wrong in the first place. Lack of account-ability, unwise practice and inability to cope with pressure may be partly responsible, but the lack of prayer and praying partners should not be minimized.

Maybe it is because we take things for granted that they go wrong so often. We have seminars on prayer, endless literature on prayer, prayer-tours and prayer-initiatives which are very good and positive. But unless all this connects with personal, disciplined application to lifestyle, then the outcome will never be any different. Malaise and apathy will continue to abound.

If there was ever a time for us to re-discover the importance of a disciplined prayer life, surely it is now when moral issues are being raised at all levels, which can only be confronted as we understand the dynamics of spiritual warfare supported by prayer. This reaches down into the heart of the individual. Of course we need corporate prayer. All credit to those organizations that God has raised up to present us with the relevant agendas and instructions on how to pray. But, for example, to pray for our education system at a national level may mean that we start to address how much time we spend with our children, our nephews and nieces, our godchildren or grandchildren, so as to have positive input into their lives. It is sometimes easier to mouth words to God about a current wave of legislation designed to modify an Education Bill, than to spend quality time with a child in the family, reading and explaining issues that under-gird family life. The heart of the human problem is the problem of the human heart, and if we can reach into young lives when they are tender and open, let us prayerfully take on that responsibility. We must never allow ourselves to think that legislation will provide the best protection.

In an essay of this kind, I do not want simply to state the obvious. Therefore, I am not going to attempt to pontificate on the frequency or style of effective prayer. I do not intend to deliver a homily on how to run an effective quiet time. I do not intend to attempt a theological analysis of the Lord's Prayer. All this has been covered elsewhere by writers far more qualified and experienced than I am. But I would value the opportunity of looking at some principles which God has etched on 'the tablet of my heart' and which I am currently thinking through in terms of my own spiritual development and application in ministry.

I have recently been greatly encouraged by considering how it is possi-ble to limit God! Initially, I struggled with this concept. We have a sover-eign, mighty, powerful God, addressed by the hymn writer as the 'Creator of the rolling spheres' and by the prophet Isaiah as being incomparably great. Such a God, by his very nature and title, is able to accomplish whatever he wants whenever it is expedient. Yet there is a sense in which there are limitations that *we* can impose on the effectiveness of his accomplishments. We read in the Gospels that, on one occasion, Jesus returned to his own home town and could do no great work there because of the lack of faith of the people there (Mark 6:5–6). The unique Son of God, great master and teacher, performer of outstanding miracles, seemingly immobilized by his own constituency. The clues are easy to discover. The 'prophet in his own country' syndrome is very relevant here, involving familiarity and even contempt. These are exactly the issues that some of us wrestle with when we are taken for granted and people's preconceptions blind them to the reality of who we are.

I remember an occasion, many years ago, when I presented to a church a strategy for an outreach programme in my local community. I have always lived and worshipped in the same area and am known by local church leaders. This proved to be a great disadvantage in progressing some of the ideas I felt God was laying on my heart. I was met by an almost condescending attitude that communicated a negative spirit which, I suspect, came from a sense of familiarity or, at worst, my being taken for granted. Perhaps God was trying to teach me a lesson in humility, but it illustrates the principle when it comes to examining the motivation behind our prayers. What do we expect of God when we pray? What do we expect him to do? What do we expect our prayers to accomplish?

The psalmist cried out, 'O my soul, wait only on God, for my expectation is from him' (Psalm 62:5). It will be easy to endorse this high sentiment, but what does this mean in terms of practicalities?

I remember some years ago being told a true story by a pastor whom I greatly respect. A lady, on leaving the church one morning, offered the information that she was praying that her next-door neighbour would become a Christian. The pastor asked how often she had spoken to her neighbour about the Lord, and was slightly taken aback to discover that no communication had ever taken place. He suggested the best route forward was to forget the conversion agenda for the time being and simply pray that God would grant an opportunity for a bridge of friendship to be built. A very puzzled lady left the church precincts that morning but agreed to follow through on the advice. Some weeks later the pastor was greeted by a very excited parishioner who told him how she had spotted her neighbour in the garden, had taken the bull by the horns and struck up a conversation, nothing spiritual, just chatter that focused on everyday matters. The pastor, I suspect, smiled wryly to himself, and suggested she should now pray that God would give the opportunity and courage to invite her neighbour in for coffee, without a spiritual agenda. Again, a somewhat bewildered lady agreed, and some weeks later returned in a very excited state to say that a wonderful thing had happened. Her neighbour had responded to her coffee invitation.

The pastor then suggested she should pray that next time her neighbour came in for coffee, God would give the opportunity for her to speak about her faith. When her neighbour next visited for 'elevenses', it was a Monday morning and she asked why her host always went out at the same time on a Sunday morning. 'Do you go to church, or somewhere like that?' she asked. This was the opportunity – not for a great exposition of

John 3:16 or an exploration of The Four Spiritual Laws, but simply to communicate why church was important to the family.

Note what was happening here and appreciate the profound wisdom of the pastor. It is easy to pray for the improbable! If you don't believe it is possible, don't pray for it! 'Lord, bring great revival to our nation' may be a very real prayer, but do we believe it to be possible? 'Father God, may there be a great outpouring of your Spirit in France.' But do we believe it can happen? The lesson in all of this is that we must be prepared to be part of the answer to our prayers in whatever way is appropriate. If we are praying for revival in our nation, how are we prepared to be involved? If we want to see God at work in France, that may have an implication as far as our cheque book is concerned, or in terms of taking an active role. Words directed heavenwards are one thing, but commitment to those words is another. It is the latter that causes the windows of heaven to open.

Note what else was happening in this story. Here was a woman who was learning what it meant to pray within her faith, and, as God answered, she went for something bigger. Her faith was being stretched, and she felt motivated and encouraged to ask for more. As she prayed, her faith grew and, as God met with her, her expectation was enlarged. Not only did she accomplish a work for the kingdom, but she also grew in her realization that God hears and answers the petitions of our hearts when we pray within our faith.

Perhaps the greatest excitement and deepest mystery of prayer is why God responds in some situations, yet is seemingly unresponsive at other times or in other circumstances. I am a great believer in the view that it is only when our wills and desires coincide with what is on God's heart that he draws alongside and ministers his goodness and grace. Of course, there is no way that we can determine where all this comes together. Man's curiosity and desire to explain the ways and purposes of God have led him on wild-goose chases, and we shall never fully understand the mind of the Almighty. His is infinite, ours finite. But this should not deter us from enthusiasm and determination in prayer, with the expectation that, where God's will coincides with what is on our heart, then great things happen.

Is there a place for excitement in our prayer life? I have to admit that, as a young person, my view of the church prayer meeting was that it would be the last place where the adrenaline would flow, where there would be the potential of a white-knuckle experience! Maturity, of course, tempers that opinion, but it is unfortunate that prayer meetings do get a bad press.

I have been enormously thrilled and encouraged by a number of initiatives that John Earwicker has taken. John currently heads the EA church-life team. He is wonderfully creative, particularly in encouraging people to pray. I have been in a number of prayer concerts he has organized, which use themes and prayer targets that inspire people to pray in different ways: sometimes in groups, sometimes as individuals, in quietness or speaking corporately, using overheads, facing north, south, east or west as geographical content and needs are addressed, and so on. This is a far cry from the prayer meetings that I remember where four people would meet together and employ the 'language of Zion' to beseech the Lord to work out his purpose across the world. Of course I need to be careful here, and I do not mean to belittle those who meet for prayer whatever the agenda. I am simply saying that if prayer is so important, let us pray creatively, imaginatively and with some structure; let us have particular prayer targets corporately and individually. I often find myself encouraging people not to give God the 'dog ends' of the day. It may be traditionally acceptable to pray as the last mindful thing we do before we hit the duvet, but may I suggest that if we are being honest, many of us are 'brain dead' before then. As long as quality time is given to prayer, let us allow ourselves the freedom to break free from some of the stereotypes.

I find a tremendous strength from prayer walks, when I go out alone or with others and talk to the Lord conversationally. The past few weeks have been particularly significant for me in a number of areas. Walking the Yorkshire Dales with a close friend, I found myself quite naturally breaking into prayer, thanksgiving and praise, at the sight of the beauty that God had set before us. It was a natural thing to do and an uncontrived response to all that God had been doing and saying. I often find myself talking to the Lord as I am driving. I keep my eyes open! But it is like having God in the car and feels perfectly natural, though I have received some strange looks from fellow road users at traffic lights who imagine that I am talking to myself!

I can almost hear some readers asking where reverence and respect fits into all of this. Talking to God in everyday circumstances does not mean that we take him for granted or demean his sovereign power. God shares his glory with no man, and he is awesome and powerful beyond description. Understanding this helps us to recognize the privilege of introducing him into ordinary situations, and knowing of his presence and influence in all that affects us.

For those of us who have any responsibility at leadership level, it is vitally important to communicate some of these principles. As the wind of the Spirit blows through our nation and our churches, God is doing wonderful things, though there are people who are still untouched by what is happening. God has ordained that if we who name his name are prepared to humble ourselves and seek his face, then he will be quick to answer. Some need to be taught to pray. Jesus did not perceive his duty towards his disciples as a kind of academic exercise that was part of a three-year training programme. They needed to learn how to pray. Today, we cannot assume that these principles are automatically picked up; they need to be taught.

I have recently been encouraged and challenged by discipling a very new Christian. His enthusiasm and love for the Lord have been a real tonic, and I have seen at firsthand what pastoral care and encouragement can accomplish. It has been a wonderful challenge to me not to assume automatic maturity in the Christian life but to take on the responsibility of teaching, training and developing another's potential. In turn, God has enriched me through the process.

As I draw to a conclusion, I would not want to gloss over the pain and difficulties in prayer. Ronald Dunn, who started one of the most effective intercessory prayer ministries in the USA, has covered this area in his book, *When Heaven is Silent*. His personal experience of tragedy and depression are woven into studies of Jacob's wrestling with the angel (Genesis 32:22–32), David's catalogue of depression and disappointment, and Job's trials and tribulations. It is essential reading. Perhaps I am drawn to this work because of my own experience when, in 1983, I found myself a victim in a horrendous road traffic accident in which there were two fatalities. For me, heaven appeared to be silent for a long, long time. With all the frightening scenarios and uncharted territory that I had to cover, I guess my maxim was 'Why pray when you can panic?' I have to admit that there was a significant passage of time when I simply could not pray. I did not have the faith to believe that God's heart was open, and it was in this situation that I proved that the powerful, steadfast and loving prayers of others carried me through.

It is when we do not feel like praying, for whatever reason, that we are at our most vulnerable. This is precisely why one of the best strategies to surface in recent years is that of prayer triplets. Three people commit themselves to each other and meet to pray for each other on a regular basis. Often the prayers of two will carry the third through. This principle provides an excellent structure for mutual support and accountability.

One of my favourite verses in the Bible is to be found in the Song of Songs: 'Awake, O north wind, and come, thou south! Blow upon my garden that the scents and the spices may flow out' (4:16). The warm winds of encouragement released in worship and prayer, alongside some of the bitter north-wind experiences of life, can, with mature understanding, allow the scents and spices of a Christ-filled life to influence and attract others. But, sadly, this is not always the case. Ego-centred theology – an emerging feature in some circles today – is an abhorrent aroma in God's nostrils. A concept of Deity that encourages us to follow God for what we can get out of the experience does not put a smile on his face. Quite the reverse, it brings tears to his eyes. Worship and prayer that is 'I'-centred is destined to be as effective as trying to empty the oceans with a thimble.

On the Day of Pentecost, preceded by one of the greatest prayer meetings ever recorded and accompanied by a powerful release of praise and worship, God launched a lifeboat. Down the slipway and out into the hurting world headed a bunch of the most unlikely people, who were destined to be used in remarkable ways to accomplish his purposes. Dare we ask God to do it again, even in these days! It is only as we embrace and endorse the power and potential in worship and prayer that we shall experience Pentecost revisited.

Chapter 19

INTO THE TWENTY-FIRST CENTURY:
FIVE PERSONAL VIEWS

Michael Baughen

United we stand; divided we fall. That familiar statement is poignantly applicable to evangelicals as we move into the twenty-first century.

On the one hand, we can see remarkable growth across the world: nearly all growing churches are evangelical; secular commentators are saying that 'born-again Christianity will be dominant throughout the church'; denominations like the Church of England have more than 50% of ordinands as evangelicals compared with less than 10% forty years ago. There is so much to encourage in evangelical life, mission strategy, media communication and relevant evangelism.

On the other hand, we have the spectre of evangelical history where ascendancy seems always to have resulted in break-up and division. Some would count five major times when this has happened since the Reformation. My heart is burdened with the rumblings all around, the sniping, the guerrilla warfare and the condemnation of evangelicals by evangelicals in the press and other publications, even though they are brothers and sisters in Christ. The individualism of evangelicalism is both a strength and a weakness, for it can pioneer imaginatively and it can endlessly split off into tailor-made segments.

Yet never in history have evangelicals had such an impact as today and, if we break apart now and lose the impetus God has given us for the twenty-first century, how will we be able to face him? It is a moment when the blessedness of peacemakers is essential. It is a time when we need to be more truly the people who stand under scripture in its fullness rather than its selected parts.

When Paul tackles unity in Ephesians chapter 4, he does so after the most glorious exposition of grace – grace lavished upon us, the grace by which we are saved, the grace that should abound in Christian lives. He focuses on Christ. There is no other foundation to unity. Are you in Christ or not? That is the fundamental question.

Paul presses this in Romans: 'If you confess with your mouth "Jesus is Lord" and believe in your heart that God raised him from the dead, you will be saved' (10:9). In the light of this, so many of our differences look utterly secondary. Are our different denominational emphases so important? Is not our unity in Christ vastly more important? Will it matter about modes of worship, modes of baptism, differences in church order, varieties of service, and so on, when we come before our Lord?

In Ephesians chapter 4, Paul insists that we are one in Christ, in his Body. This is a fact, not something to attain; but it has to be worked out. So he pleads, 'Make every effort', 'I urge you.' Maintaining unity is hard work, it needs deliberate action, it means going the extra mile and seeking to sort differences out.

However, unity in the faith and in the knowledge of the Son of God has to be attained, reached by the gifts and ministries that God has given for the up-building of the church. Too often, evangelicals require an exact agreement in every jot and tittle before they will have unity. This is what separates. Paul argues that it is from the basis of unity that we already have in Christ that we talk, share, listen, learn and adapt. We may still disagree with others in interpretation, but in Christ we still have unity.

Mission to the world is always damaged, even sabotaged, by disunity among Christians. We damage the gospel when our disagreements are paraded before the world. How our hearts cry within us when we hear some divisive statement on TV or radio. So, if we mean business for God as we go into the twenty-first century we must make every effort to be seen as truly one, even where we disagree.

We have so much to bring to the world. It is confused in its secular swamp, unsure of meaning and value, lost indeed without Christ. The twenty-first century will demand of us increasing skills in communicating Christ and his unchanging gospel – the power of God for salvation. We need the constant inspiration of the Holy Spirit in this challenging task – and he needs us to be in unity!

We also need to learn more from one another in the deepening of spirituality. Somehow we have not always seen this development in lives and churches. Converts have wandered off to find spirituality elsewhere. The quietness of meditation, of reflection, of growing into God have often been drowned by loudness, noise, activity and pressure. We must develop a fuller spirituality for the next millennium. Young hearts are seeking it. We must help them find it, not in the New Age confusion but in Christ and in the gracious work of the Holy Spirit.

Unity in social care, in caring for the sick, the imprisoned, the hungry, the thirsty – getting our hands dirty, as it were – also needs to grow. The spectre of the social gospel has no place in holistic mission – primarily to salvation but also to the whole person.

The more evangelicals increase in influence, the more we will be attacked, mocked and vilified, as is already the case over sexual issues and has been the case over scholarship until our large number of brilliant young evangelical theologians began to emerge. There will, no doubt, be attempts to make our views not politically correct. At least, persecution and opposition should strengthen our unity!

So, let us face the twenty-first century with realism about the dangers of division, with determination to keep the unity of the Spirit in the bonds of peace, but above all with our eyes on Jesus – as Lord, as Saviour and as Head of the church – so that his mission burns in our hearts and his kingdom extends marvellously, to his glory.

Gerald Coates

Looking into the future is like looking through the lens of a kaleidoscope. You can never be certain what is going to happen next! In fact, we have to ask how much of the future is left? For instance, our own deaths dramatically cut short the future for us all, and for some it may be shorter than we imagine! In the meantime, we are invited to hasten the future of another sort of age which will be preceded by the return of Christ (2 Peter 3:11–12). To do this we must invest our energies and our passion into networking the nation with the gospel – 'then the end will come' (Matthew 24:14).

In terms of life as we know it now, our 'journey with a purpose', as someone has put it (that is, our mission), must be our all-consuming goal. The reappearance of Jesus Christ at the end of this age will usher in another – one without crime, dishonesty, abuse, racism, sexism or nationalism. It is called heaven.

Meanwhile, how do we live?

Today we live in a liberal age which is awash with pluralism. 'Not knowing' has acquired a halo all of its own. Any one who claims 'to know' the meaning to life is looked upon as arrogant, narrow-minded, superior or slightly odd. Agnostic liberalism claims it is generous and non-judgemental. Nevertheless, it loathes evangelicalism and has a death-wish at its heart. It is destroying itself from the inside. It has emptied our church buildings.

By championing 'freedom of choice' and a 'don't-let-anyone-tell-you-what-to-do' philosophy, society has already begun to pay the price for the last forty years of abandoning God and his word. Liberals have been duped into believing we do not need the God of scripture. Medicine, science and humankind's innate goodness will take care of us, so we are told.

However, it is slowly dawning on parts of the population that this is not the case. For example, penicillin, one of the pillars of medicine, is failing. New strains of antibiotic-resistant bacteria mean that old, serious diseases are returning, some in lethal doses. Diphtheria, meningitis and pneumonia are back! The World Health Organization (WHO) estimates that thirty million will die of tuberculosis world-wide within the next decade. Sexual diseases, mainly caused through promiscuity (now called 'multipartner sex'!), are already at epidemic proportions throughout the world.

With little hope for a low-cost AIDS cure made available in our lifetime, the number of people already infected (17 million) will increase, and they will die tragic deaths.

Medicine is only one area of collapse in our sophisticated world. American's trillion-dollar debt, will, according to *The Sunday Times* colour supplement, create a 'third-world' economy within a decade or two. The breakdown not only of marriage but of family values throughout the Western world is damaging relationships on an unprecedented scale. Cynicism towards virtually all politicians and authority figures has seeped deep into the corporate social psyche. Without trust, progress is impossible. Television and tabloid newspapers trivialize the important and make headlines of absurdity and nonsense. The debilitating effects of mass and often continual unemployment for Europe's millions, plus addictions to sex, alcohol, drugs and gambling, do not make for a happy future.

We are witnessing a massive exodus from sanity. When will the reaction take place? As always, there will be one. How long will the responsible be willing to pay for the irresponsible? When will strong but silent feeling give way to the raised voice and the violent demonstration? The increasing population of retired, pensioned men and women, supported by a shrinking younger generation, will soon cost more than that younger generation can afford.

There are over two hundred nations in the world, though less than fifty are democracies. Our own democratic system has seen an increase in most types of crime; there is less safety on the streets; our prisons and hospitals are full to overflowing; and it is reckoned that by the time the average man reaches middle age, the vast majority will have at least one serious criminal charge against them. So, where do evangelicals fit into all of this?

If not *now*, then *when*?

Being meaningless (other than to yourself) in a meaningless time is being seen for what it is. The liberal mind-set has thrown up Don Cupitt and David Jenkins, Madonna and Michael Jackson, Michael Winner, Edwina Curry, Boy George and Prince Charles, Clare Rayner and Anne Diamond. These are the midget gurus who cannot see what is coming.

Evangelicals with the evangel are, in fact, the only hope for individual lives, families and society. The gospel gives birth to honesty in business and commerce, human care in art and architecture, medicine and education. Lives changed by Christ reflect the dignity, respect and values that are found in the Godhead.

Biblical Christians do not subscribe to the 'Mickey Mouse' theology or eschatology of gleefully rubbing our hands whilst a nation burns. To be sure, a disintegrating, nationalistic, sexist and racist world are some of the signs preceding Christ's return (Matthew 24:6). But this was so even when our Lord walked the earth.

This side of Christ's return we are not going to see a Christianized government and society. We are here to be salt and light, the former adding flavour and a preservative, the latter showing people a better way, a way out of their darkness. But we are not here to fight cynicism with cynicism, fire with fire, brute force with brute force. This is not what spiritual warfare is about. Might is not right, and God on our side does not give us the right to be rude, arrogant, superior and physically violent.

Evangelicals have got to wake up to the fact that they are the only hope for our nation. The alternative? A reaction that will lose us our liberty, our freedom and our much-cherished, if crumbling, way of life. What are we talking about here? Dictatorship? Well, they did that in Germany and they do it in China. They did it in the former USSR and they do it in Sudan. They did it in South Africa and they do it in Iran. For evangelicals, the search for pleasure must be replaced with a search for meaning. C S Lewis explained that pleasure is God's idea not the devil's. He added that pleasure and happiness come by seeking something else other than pleasure and happiness.

Power imprinted upon present-day emptiness may lead to fame and fortune. But for Christian people who have got their minds in gear, the twentieth century has been a study in the emptiness of power and the degrading nature of fame and fortune. Madonna and Michael Jackson have become the 'mother and father' of young adults – the 'walking wounded' – leading them into an unexpected nothingness devoid of reasonable purpose and meaning. Evangelicals have this purpose and meaning. Yet it is more than a message. It is *the* message. Our founder and leader is more than a vendor of words. He is a messenger who, through his miraculous birth, wonderful life, nation-changing ministry, death for us all and mind-boggling resurrection, became The Message.

Jesus the 'Message-Messenger' knew long before Marshall McCluhan that the medium is the message. So he embodied his message so that the evangel could be seen, heard, touched and understood. Christ was not only the signpost pointing the way but also the destination. Today Jesus Christ, the 'Message-Messenger', is not only admired but wonderfully loved by hundreds of millions of followers on this planet. Our role is to swell these ranks – 'then the end will come'. We do this by modelling grace and truth – the constituent elements of the glory of God (John 1:14). We facilitate this, not only by modelling grace and truth in our individual lives, but by allowing that grace and truth to permeate all our relationships at home, where we are educated, where we work, and throughout the church. This is life!

All living things grow. It is as we make Jesus attractive and intelligible to those around us, both spontaneously and in structured events, that the life of Christ touches others. This is why I am totally committed to church-planting, where bodies of people in every area of every city, town and village are living in such a way that people can see, hear, touch and taste the gospel, and experience Christ for themselves. The gospel is not merely a set of rational propositions and moral idealism: it is the power of God, allowing humanity to experience his love and forgiveness, his commitment and approval. This cannot be done merely through television and radio, but through 'bodies', individual and corporate, who in every locality and people-group are dragging the future into the present and declaring, 'the kingdom of heaven is here.'

The future depends on whether 'bodies', refreshed by God's Spirit, will pay the price. To be sure, 'bodies' blessed and refreshed are more likely to be challenging, developing and inspiring the future, than those that are discouraged, defensive and exhausted. The kingdom of God is not dragging our past around with us, but getting a hold of our future and aggressively pulling it into the here and now.

We must pray with humility and clarity, twins in the womb, as we step forward together. Soon we shall hear his 'Well done'. Until then, let us remember that our future and the future of people-groups in our nation depends on our being continually filled with the Holy Spirit, reading and bowing before scripture, and allowing for a release of God's Spirit and God's word through our network of relationships.

This is our future. What a future!

Rosemary Dowsett

A hundred and fifty years ago, Scottish Christians played key roles in the Evangelical Alliance's birth. Some of them, like Dr Chalmers, had played a decisive role in the Disruption that split the national church apart yet, at the same time, they longed to find ways of expressing the fundamental unity they believed to be God-given among true believers. Was it possible for Christians, united in commitment to the Lord and his word, to demonstrate some meaningful kind of unity even while respecting each other's conscientious distinctives? Was it possible to keep truth and unity together?

Further, in the light of the social upheavals caused by industrial expansion, Christians needed to work together, not just talk, to meet the urgent task of home mission amongst the unchurched urban poor. Further, waves of emigration from the Highlands, and the arrival of many Irish Catholics fleeing from potato famines, brought profound population changes. How could their generation be reached with the gospel?

These and many another questions forced Scottish evangelicals – ministers and laymen – to explore areas in which co-operation might be possible. Their debate, and the financial investment of wealthy Glasgow industrialist, James Henderson, in 1845 led first to the publishing of *Essays on Christian Union* and then to the calling of the Liverpool Conference out of which the Evangelical Alliance was born.

Now, a century and a half later, the details are different but the underlying issues may be intriguingly similar. Scottish Presbyterianism is still painfully fractured into many parts, and there are also many more denominations of other traditions, now than there were then. Emigration, especially of the young and the talented, is still a problem to the churches of the Highlands. The urban poor remain largely unchurched. Religious pluralism – Catholic and Protestant in Glasgow, 'Christian' and Muslim or Hindu in all the cities – presents more rather than fewer problems. Scotland may be a generation later than England in haemorrhaging its nominal church membership, but the crunch has now come. The issue of patronage, which precipitated the Disruption, has long since vanished. But the passionate desire for separation from English interference in any shape or form in the affairs of Scotland, which was part and parcel of that painful stage in Scottish church history, has largely crossed over into the political arena. Scottish evangelicals can be found on both sides of the nationalist debate, and it could well be explosively divisive in the future. Now, as then, it may be harder than we realize to disentangle personality and prejudice from truly non-negotiable biblical principles.

Today the tapestry of denominations is different from that of the past. There are many more independent churches, both those born of the charismatic renewal movement and those that have their roots in the Open Brethren movement. There is also a variety of Pentecostal denominations, a strong evangelical Baptist network, and some evangelical Episcopalian and Congregational congregations. All these are in addition to a *smorgasbord* of Presbyterian evangelicals. Is it possible for such a diverse group of churches, especially perhaps along the reformed/charismatic continuum, to find ways of working together? Surely we must. This presents a tough theological challenge if we are to engage in alliance with integrity.

Christian leaders in particular face a heavy responsibility. It is easy to guard our own patch, to stay in our own familiar ecclesiastical comfort zone and label it 'contending for the truth'. We need to work with great honesty at disentangling what is truly biblical from what comes from culture, temperament or history. In Scotland, many evangelicals, especially among the under-forties, have already experienced the enrichment that comes from worship and witness in an interdenominational setting. In the future, more grass-roots Christians will be increasingly impatient with maintaining denominational secondary distinctives. To do so represents an immoral wastage of limited resources of manpower and money. Are we prepared to find ways of burying at least some historical hatchets?

Whether or not some of Scotland's denominations will be able to move towards any kind of structural unity in the future is hard to predict. What is, I think, beyond question is the urgency of addressing the issue that taxed Chalmers: how can we co-operate in order to engage in effective mission, especially among the urban unchurched poor? A hundred and fifty years ago, it seems that the way that this was chiefly fulfilled was through agencies and mission halls, alongside the churches. If the churches could not act directly together, at least they could jointly finance enterprises one step removed from themselves. Again, today, large sections of the urban population are alienated from the churches and untouched by the gospel. How shall we reach them?

For a variety of reasons, most of the old mission halls have closed, and the compassion ministries petered out with the advent of the Welfare State. We need a new generation of pioneer missionaries in such communities, gifted and able, not to transplant a middle-class clone from the suburbs but, under God, to bring to birth a church appropriate for the context. There are already some brave attempts to do just that. In future, it may be that evangelists and pastors in such a setting will have to be largely self-supporting. This is the more likely, because often what is needed is a multiplication of small relationship-intensive fellowships where damaged people heal. Today there is, once again, both an urgent need for distinctively Christian compassion ministries and also the opportunity to establish them. Have we the courage – and the prophetic biblical insight – to develop radically different models of church that are both contextualized and faithful to the word? In a society of fractured relationships and broken families, can we be extended families of God's people, deeply bound up with each other and showing the reconciled community life that is God's design?

Change is always scary. There are many in Scotland today who pray for revival. Whether the church would actually be able to bear revival if it came, I am not so sure. I believe we would be changed out of all recognition, and would cry out with pain as well as ecstasy. Perhaps this is always true when we come face to face with God. However, unless and until the Lord sovereignly sends revival, we may not opt out of the here-and-now commitment to radical discipleship which is the demand of the gospel. If we were truly to follow Christ like that, Scotland might once more be confronted with her King.

Donald English

I would like to add the words 'with Jesus' to the title 'Into the twenty-first century'. This is not a pious correction of an over-secular title! Rather it suggests a model for our journey.

It seems an impossible task, trying to translate the ministry of Jesus into twenty-first century Western cultural terms. After I had finished giving 'Thought for the Day' recently on Radio 4, one of my colleagues remarked, 'You've just spoken to more people in three minutes than John Wesley addressed in his entire ministry!' How much more the case with our Lord himself. Yet it is not the details but the principles which matter, continuously applied in different situations.

First, Jesus presenced himself where people were. John chapter 1 is all about that. 'The Word became flesh and lived among us' (John 1:14). There is more here than simply 'being around', 'loitering with intent'. Perhaps it is because evangelicals have not emphasized incarnational theology that we have neglected its implications.

If we take the movement indicated in Philippians 2:5–8, we begin to get some sense of it. Try to imagine what it would be like to experience what Paul calls 'equality with God' or being 'in the form of God'; and then, by choice, 'taking the form of a slave, being born in human likeness'. It means accepting severe limitations on what can be attempted, because of the condition and limitations of those around one. In rightly emphasizing the need to be different as Christians, because of our fundamental experience of Christ and the consequent change of attitude to life, have we actually made ourselves different from everyone else in as many ways as possible? Has the church become a collection of ghettos, hidden away from the realities of our culture? At the simplest level it would be good to ask how many friends we have who are not Christians but whom we know well. Has our involvement in the cultural setting around us changed as that setting has changed? Or are our relations with the culture the same as they have been for a decade? Do we know what forces are driving our culture, and what the main elements in our cultural situation are in this country today? This is part of being in line with the model of incarnation of the one who called his people to be where he was.

Next, Jesus visited people in their natural context. He did not set up a conference centre and then gather people to him, though there were first-century models for this kind of activity. He walked or sailed from place to place, meeting whatever he found. He talked about what he found. Even his 'prepared' talks are full of the materials of everyday life, from building houses through sons and daughters, to sheep and goats.

This raises the question of how much we know about those who do not belong to the Christian church. Are we aware of their hopes and fears, their capacities and incapacities, their normal way of reaching decisions, the papers they read and the politics they espouse, what they want for themselves and for their families? These are not trick questions: they are about the very essence of life for other people. By going where people were and meeting them face to face, Jesus addressed such issues. He knew what was in people: we have to learn it. But this is our equivalent of walking from village to village.

Even invitations to come to him were in terms that they understood very well. Whether it was in terms of the yoke carried by the oxen, the water he offered to the woman at the well, the cross that he called all his followers to carry after him – the images were too relevant and meaningful for anyone to miss their point. Are we keen enough on mission, I wonder, really to learn the language and the concepts, the images and the communication patterns, that will enable us truly to meet people at those points of their lives where what we say and do makes sense?

Third, the challenge that Jesus offered was not an easy one. To seek to be intelligible, accessible and relevant is not the same as making the message easy. The method of the parable left it possible for people simply to walk away if they wished. But they had to *decide* to do so. The parable seemed, amongst other things, to offer a way in for those who were truly serious about what Jesus was describing and offering. It was certainly not highly persuasive, but its implications were deep and basic. What is more, whenever there were responses, and people showed any inclination to follow, it was not long before carrying the cross, denying oneself, eating his flesh and blood, came to the fore (Mark 8:34–38; John 6:44–58). Or there were warnings about builders who started and couldn't finish, or kings who began wars they couldn't complete (Luke 14:25–33). The challenge was not to give a little now and hope for more later. The challenge was to offer everything now. It sometimes appears as though Jesus' disciples gathered the crowds, and he dispersed them!

The danger for the Christian church going into the twenty-first century is not unlike the danger which chaplains discover when working in prisons. It is possible, as many chaplains will testify, to get easy responses to the gospel message. However, this can be done at an emotional and very thinly intellectual level that fails to come to terms with the true story of the life of the person concerned. This kind of shallow experience is not limited to prisons! It is clearly what Jesus had in mind in part of the parable of The Sower.

In the twenty-first century, we have to face the question of what it is that forms the lives of those whom we seek to win for Christ. This is about much more than personal, ethical and moral questions of faithfulness in marriage, proper care of children, doing a good day's work and seeking to say one's prayers. It has to do with the issues raised by the political uncertainty that is increasing around us, deeply disturbing issues raised by genetic developments, the kind of society we want, and the prevailing philosophy of unlimited self-development. The message we proclaim has got to show how following Christ relates to issues such as these. The questions we must answer are not originated by us nor within the Christian church. Many are not clearly referred to in scripture. But they are the questions of the day. They are the driving forces in the lives of people around us. And the gospel needs to be engaging with those particular issues if it is to reach the depths of the lives of those whom we seek to win for Christ.

Finally, Jesus gathered people into a community whose task was to tell others. Insofar as the first disciples are a pattern for us, they learned in order that they might share. They knew Jesus in order that they might help others to know him. They heard the message in order to pass it on. The driving force was being sent out into the world, under the power of the Spirit, to witness to the whole world. In many ways, if we take this message seriously, then the focal point of the church is not located within the church but beyond it. God's never-ending mission to the world will continue, with or without us. But he gives us the privilege of joining in his one mission to his world, requiring of us the necessary flexibility. We have to learn what it means to witness to a moving target, while running to keep up with a God who is the Lord of all the ages. There will never have been a more exciting time to witness than the twenty-first century. God give us grace to be ready for it by his strength!

Phil Wall

Premillennial investment

As a general rule, evangelical leadership has been appropriated as the result of revolution every third or fourth generation, as people have tired of the status quo and decided things needed changing. This tragedy has often caused much hurt and divisiveness, and has utilized some of our best creative passions and energies in trying either to protect or usurp leadership structures, instead of seeking and saving the lost. As we approach the next millennium, with a new generation emerging every seven years, it is essential that we address this particular issue of unity between the generations. This is imperative if we are successfully to face the challenges of a new day.

In 1993 *Time* magazine reported that the world was facing a leadership crisis as bureaucrats and managers rather than leaders exercised leadership. Management thinking, almost by definition, inhibits the development of a creative leader's potential, because its key focus is on the maintenance of what is as opposed to the creation of what could be. If this is a truism, it is a frightening mirror of much current leadership practice within the church. One of the key reasons for the significant haemorrhage of younger people from the church during the last couple of decades has been the inability and, at times, unwillingness for responsibility to be passed on into the hands of an emerging generation. This has created a bottleneck of leadership and left many disillusioned and frustrated. What our world desperately needs is not so much a new paradigm of leadership transference but, I believe, a fresh look at an old one. Only this will enable us continually to benefit from the strength and wisdom of the already established model as well as the power and energy of the new.

Biblically, we have numerous models of what is increasingly being known in both religious and non-religious spheres as the principle of 'mentoring'. To quote Paul Stanley, 'mentoring is a relational experience whereby one seeks to empower another through the sharing of God-given resources'. Examples such as Elijah and Elisha, Jesus and the disciples, Paul and Timothy provide solid ground for encouraging, theologically and pragmatically, a desperately needed investment of resources and partnership in leadership. Having the biblical ideal before us, we must move from the oft-repeated situation of evangelical disunity whereby one generation sits in authority, waiting to be ousted, as others had been ousted by them, whilst another generation squirms in a morass of frustration, desiring to take the reins.

The perfect example of this positive attitude is, of course, Jesus. In Philippians 2:5–11 Paul paints a wonderful picture of a majestic and godly

King who could have ruled his global subjects with an iron fist, but who chose instead to become the servant of all because there was a higher agenda. This is the principle of not being everything we could be because a higher agenda requires something else from us.

Those in leadership could choose to dig in and establish themselves in well-protected trenches of authority, vulnerable only to the bravest of the brave who, as in the tragedy of the First World War, dare to go 'over the top'. In both cases some make it to the opposing trenches and conquer, but many do not. Alternatively, established leaders could choose to be something different, because of a higher agenda, seeking to mentor, encourage, motivate, prepare and, where appropriate, step aside to establish a new generation of leaders.

The younger generation also, like so many of their peers, face their pitfalls. Driven by the culture of immediacy, they may, with immature impatience, dismiss that which is known and established as outmoded and irrelevant. Rejecting existing leadership and establishing their own structures and programmes, they inevitably build on the insecure foundations of inexperience and *naïveté*, which leads, eventually, to yet another insurgence and revolution. Alternatively, they could choose to be something different because there is a higher agenda. With a servant heart and a humble, teachable spirit, they could learn from and serve alongside those who can teach and model those principles which will establish them as mature leaders.

Without this shift in leadership development and transference, much of the evangelical unity that has been achieved over these last 150 years could be lost. Evangelicalism could become little more than a sterile and impotent creed to which different generations may assent with the heart, but which will leave the unbelieving world untouched.

My final words are a cry from the heart for my own generation and those that follow. We desperately need women and men of God who will take us under their wings and give us models of holiness and integrity that can help mould us into what we should be. We need people who will call us into a radical counter-cultural and sacrificial lifestyle from the experience of walking the paths of pain and hardship. We urgently want to learn from those who have lived the Christian life and who have survived through failure and frustration to establish ministries and lives of depth and substance.

Chapter 20

EVANGELISM TOMORROW

Steve Chalke

'Murder in the cathedral'

T S Eliot's play, *Murder in the Cathedral*, is the story of Thomas Becket, who was murdered in 1170 by King Henry II. Although it was his duty to defend the faith, instead, with the famous words, 'Who will rid me of this turbulent priest?', the king sent four knights to Canterbury to cut down his archbishop. God's voice was assassinated *inside* the cathedral by those who should have been committed to defending and proclaiming it.

It is always the church's task to be God's irrepressible voice to contemporary society. So when we look at the challenge of evangelism in the UK over the years leading up to the start of the new millennium and beyond, we are basically examining the task of the church to ensure that God's voice is heard outside its own walls and not simply 'murdered inside the cathedral'.

There are some exciting stirrings going on both inside and outside the church. Inside, God is bringing a freshness of vision and a renewed desire to serve him. Outside, in the wider society, the last few years have witnessed a growing sense of moral and spiritual hunger. But, unfortunately, these two worlds are in serious danger of not meeting. For whilst it has been encouraging to see the recovery of confidence in evangelism over the last twenty years, the uncomfortable truth is that we are still actually making little real impact on society in terms of our voice being heard or understood by those outside the church.

The truth is uncomfortable because, tragically, much of this lack of impact has been our fault. We have allowed God's voice to be silenced in the cathedral. The reasons for this are many and complex, like pieces of a huge jigsaw. I have chosen to focus on what I believe is the centre-piece of the puzzle: the church and 'the world' are just not hearing each other. When that happens you have a communication breakdown, making evangelism impossible.

The principles contained in Acts chapter 17 are key to a proper understanding of our evangelistic task. Whilst in Athens, Paul became distressed by the idolatry that he found. As a result, as well as preaching in the synagogue to 'the Jews and the God-fearing Greeks', he took his message to the 'secular' Athenians in their market-place, expressing it in their language, setting it within their cultural context, using an altar inscribed 'TO AN UNKNOWN GOD' – and poetry.

The market-place

In the Middle Ages, the church building stood in or near the market-place. Its physical proximity to the town centre symbolized the church's involvement in every area of personal and community life: work, family, education, entertainment; emotional, social and political as well as spiritual. But over the last century this relationship has changed completely. Banks and government buildings dwarf church spires as the influence of Christianity has diminished. At the same time, Christians have withdrawn from society into their own little ghetto and we have allowed ourselves to become consumed with our own concerns and ways of expressing them. Evangelical churches have emphasized an unbiblical distinction between 'temporal' and 'spiritual' concerns – and have given great priority to the 'spiritual'. As a result, we now find ourselves standing a small distance away from where most people are, concerned not with every area of their lives but to a great extent just with that small corner we call the 'soul'.

My own experience of training to become a Baptist minister is a symptom of this lack of 'holistic' thinking. When I, like many others, trained for what we termed 'the ministry', it was within an environment which taught me that I had been called to the highest calling of all – 'to preach the gospel'. It took me some time to work out how demoralizing, disempowering and marginalizing this message actually was for the majority of the church. I was encouraged, implicitly, to believe that, having been called to this 'highest' vocation, I was somehow operating on a higher plane than the banker, the plumber, the architect, the housewife, the milkman, the lawyer, the doctor, the carpenter, the shop assistant, the actor, the musician (to name but a few). The best they could hope for was to play a minor supporting role.

The truth is, of course, that God calls different people to do different things. Vocation – and the gospel – are far bigger than we give them credit for. God ordains *every* believer to serve him where they live and work, not just those the church chooses to accredit. To preach is not the ultimate vocation; to preach is simply to accept the huge responsibility of helping to equip the church for its calling to be God's voice in a world desperate for direction.

It is one of the greatest ironies that the Protestant wing of the church has, for the most part, lost sight of the very idea of the 'priesthood of all believers' which gave rise to its existence in the first place. We have entrusted the spreading of the gospel to an élite group of 'professionals', and perpetuated a false dichotomy between 'full-time Christian service' and 'secular work'. This has created generations of evangelicals who believe that their most valuable service for God is measured by their involvement within the local church – as an elder, deacon, Parochial Church Council member, youth leader, worship band member, sound engineer, and so on. The focus of their Christian service has become the church, not the rest of the world.

We need a new focus, in every local church, on what it is to be salt and light in the world, and how every church member can be salt and light. We need to move away from our cheap, rude and ineffective concepts of 'sharing our faith' and 'evangelizing' – based around bombarding the unsuspecting with our versions of The Four Spiritual Laws, the ABC of the Gospel, the Two Diagnostic Questions, and the like – toward a biblical understanding of incarnation and truth through relationships. As church leaders, we must grasp that it is not we who are on the cutting edge of evangelism but the rest of the church. Our role is to service them in this task.

Another symptom of our withdrawal from the market-place is that we have created almost a parallel society for ourselves, a mirror world. There are Christian radio stations, books, bookshops, schools, magazines, holidays, plumbers. At times, you get the impression that you could live your entire life without once having to come into contact with people who aren't Christians. There is a positive side to this, because every culture needs to feed and sustain itself, but we have withdrawn to such an extent that an entire subculture exists to service the church. This has become a massive barrier to evangelism, because it means that, generally speaking, we are living not in the real world we wish to see come to know Christ, but in a Christian ghetto entirely of our own making. In such a ghetto, it is too easy to lose track of the language and concerns of people outside.

Evidence of this problem is blazoned across the shelves of every Christian book store. For instance, within a few months of reaching the churches, what has become known as the 'Toronto Blessing' had produced a crop of books. Christian publishers tripped over themselves to get these out whilst the matter was still topical. Yet, at the same time, important issues, which were drawing much more attention within society as a whole, received little or no attention. Where was the rush of books at popular level analysing the introduction of the National Lottery and its implications for society and the church? Why were these not published in record time? Where are the books looking at the continuing deterioration of the National Health Service (NHS) in the light of the teaching of both Old and New Testaments? What are we saying about the provision of child care, or the development of education and housing policy? By the time this present volume is published, the government aims to have scrapped unemployment benefit and replaced it with an alternative system for 'job seekers'. How many books can we expect giving a biblical perspective on that and answering the question of what the local church should be saying and doing?

It's not that books on the 'Toronto Blessing' are ill-advised or unnecessary. It's just that we have become lopsided, totally consumed with what happens in the synagogue, not the market-place. We've locked God in the church, murdered his voice in the cathedral. And of course, the tragedy is that many people in the church are in the market-place, working in education, the social services, the NHS, industry, sales . . . even Camelot (the organization that runs the National Lottery)! But who has told them that they are on the front-line, let alone how they should face the battle?

Rwanda was one of Africa's most 'Christian' countries. Yet although 80% of Rwandans before the civil war called themselves Christians – thanks to concentrated evangelistic activity and the 'revival' that had swept the land in the 1930s – their superficial faith could do nothing to stop the 1994 blood bath. In the opinion of Roger Bowen of Mid-Africa Ministry (reported in *The Church of England Newspaper*, 27 January 1995), 'revival failed to equip the Church in Rwanda for the real world of politics and tribal differences . . . Church leaders had an unbalanced view of evangelism which, though effective in itself, precluded much teaching on social action and the practicalities of living out the Christian faith.' Unless we are involved in every area of society's life, our faith will be just as superficial.

The language

Having got ourselves out of the synagogue and into the market-place, there is more to do. Paul not only preached the gospel in the right area, he presented it in the right language – that of his audience. It is not just a case of going to market; it is a question of what we should be saying when we get there.

We often hear the cry of those who claim that it is our task to make the Bible relevant for today's culture. This is a mistake. The Bible is relevant. It has always been relevant. The problem is that the church has obscured this relevance by proclaiming it in language, terms and concepts that are not understood. And most Christians, especially church leaders, are so wrapped up in ghetto culture that they fail to realize that they do not speak the rest of the world's language or appreciate its concerns.

Imagine a person wandering into a shop in France, unprepared for a sales assistant who speaks no English. They place their order slowly, in carefully pronounced English with just a hint of a French accent. 'Have you got any bread?' The question produces no response. They try again, this time in firmer, slower and louder tones. 'Have . . . you . . . got . . . any . . . bread?' The assistant still looks blank, so the whole exercise is repeated again with even more volume, hand actions and a forced smile to cover the frustration. 'HAVE . . . YOU . . . GOT . . . ANY . . . BREAD? BRRRREAD?' The result, for all the energy used, is that the shopkeeper looks as bemused as ever.

Too often, our response when evangelism is not understood has simply been to shout louder. If 'the world' is not hearing us, it is because of their 'spiritual deafness', not our inability to communicate. We reassure ourselves with Bible verses which tell us that 'the god of this age has blinded the minds of the unbelievers' (2 Corinthians 4:4). However, without wanting to deny or in any way detract from the truth of Paul's statement to the church in Corinth, the clear implication of scripture is that God's word is only heard as God's word when it is both theologically sound *and* culturally relevant. One of its hallmarks is that it always makes sense and communicates to its target audience. If the church in the UK offers our society anything less, it is not being biblical – or evangelical, for that matter.

All too often our evangelism happens on *our* terms, on *our* territory and in *our* language. Whilst it fulfils the first qualification, that of being theologically sound, it falls short on the second, that of cultural relevance. And we are surprised when people respond to our message like it's double Dutch! For much of the time, we have effectively turned the gospel into something with which the majority of people cannot identify. One television producer put it to me this way: 'You evangelicals are always trying to answer Question no. 17 when we are not even sure what Question no. 1 is yet. In fact, some of you are worse than the politicians. It makes absolutely no difference what our question is, you always tell us what you want us to hear anyway.'

It is easy to reach the conclusion that the disciples were given the gift of 'tongues' so that those who had gathered in Jerusalem would be able to understand their message. The truth is, however, that many there for Pentecost, the Jewish Festival of Weeks – 'God-fearing Jews from every nation under heaven' – would have had at least one common language, Greek for instance. Instead, God chose to communicate with each individual in the crowd by using their 'native tongue', the language they had learned to think in, the one in which their parents spoke to them when they were children. Why? Because when God speaks to people, he starts where they are and speaks their language. He uses their mother tongue, their terminology and their thought patterns.

Although Paul was 'greatly distressed' by the number of idols in Athens, he explained the gospel to the Athenian people specifically by using their idols and their religious poetry. He started with what they knew and what concerned them, and moved from there to relate the gospel to them in terms and concepts they could understand.

'The Son of Man came eating and drinking, and they say, "Here is a glutton and a drunkard" ' (Matthew 11:18–19). Jesus came as a man of his time, in touch with his culture and a gifted communicator within it. He immersed himself so much in the culture of the world outside – in marked contrast with the Pharisees, who prided themselves on their withdrawal from the company of 'sinners' – that he was accused of being naive, unaware of the condition of those with whom he associated. Yet a properly incarnational theology requires this kind of immersion: John recounts that 'the Word became a human being, and made his home among us', literally, the Word 'pitched his tent among us' (John 1:14).

It is our responsibility as the church to 'speak the language' and address the issues and concerns of each social and ethnic group in our society, to see them as individuals rather than one mass to be addressed in our language from the security of our pulpits and buildings. We have to learn to declare 'the wonders of God' in a lot of very different cultures. Peter Wagner has identified over fifty separate ethnic groups living within the city of New York on the basis of country of origin alone. The King's Church in Slough recently identified over eighty different ethnic groups in their town!

It is encouraging to see the number of churches who are beginning to understand that being 'God's family' does not mean that we all have to do everything together, and who are developing different congregations to reach different nationality and ethnic groups within their immediate community. The whole Body of Christ is not an 'eye' or an 'ear' (1 Corinthians 12:17): there is room for considerable diversity. In fact, many Anglican churches have for years catered for different groups by having different services (such as an early morning 1662 Prayer Book service) throughout the day.

A good friend, who works with me in Oasis Trust, has developed two distinct congregations within his church in North London – one English-speaking and the other Turkish-speaking. These groups represent the dominant cultural split of the area. Other such experiments are well known. But we need to classify 'ethnic' groups by more than just language or country of origin. It is interesting, for instance, to see the growing number of youth congregations within churches around the country.

One of the most exciting recent developments in reaching people in their language has been inspired by the Willow Creek Church in Chicago, with the development of their 'Seeker Services' as an evangelistic tool. Though it has been encouraging to see the way in which the 'Church for the Unchurched' concept has been adopted by churches in the UK, one of the weaknesses in the way this idea has been taken up is in terms of a lack of targeting. Not all 'seekers' are the same. A lot more thought needs to be given to designing services or presentations aimed at specific groups defined by ethnic origin, age, interest, and so on.

When it comes to an evangelism which will have real impact, the big question is: 'Who are we trying to reach, and what will be relevant to them?' We need to become skilful interpreters of the gospel to a diverse modern culture so that it speaks to them in a variety of different ways as genuine good news.

As evangelicals, we are good at talking because we are people with something to say. Our weakness has been in terms of *listening* to others, which is why we sometimes appear to be arrogant. However, if we are to engage in evangelism in the market-place, in the language of those to whom we go, one prerequisite is that we first learn to listen and to understand. This is a painful experience for a brand of Christianity that has been so built around the ethos of the 'quick result'. Our arrival in the market-place must first be marked by listening rather than proclaiming.

Conclusion

It is said that Charles Spurgeon often looked out on the large Sunday congregation filling the Metropolitan Tabernacle and commented that, whilst he thanked God for the opportunity he was given to preach evangelistically in a church building, he believed 'this privilege to be extra-biblical'. For Spurgeon, the task of evangelism belonged 'outside' not 'inside' the church.

Today, in our post-Christian society, when our church buildings are rarely filled with those who do not know Christ, it is our task as much as it was for Paul in Athens to 'go', instead of expecting unbelievers to 'come' to us. We must radically rethink our models of church, the ministry and the process of evangelism and not allow God's word to be 'murdered in the cathedral'.

Rob Frost

Drama in outreach: speaking the gospel in the vernacular today

George Whitefield was in his twenties when he began to attract huge crowds to his open-air meetings in Bristol. However, he also held open-air meetings in Moorfields Park in London where crowds gathered each evening for bear baiting, wrestling, cudgel playing and dog fights. The account of his first meeting there reads:

> Public notice having been given . . . upon coming out of the coach he found an incredible number of people assembled. Many had told him that he should never come again out of that place alive. He went in, however, between two of his friends, who, by the pressure of the crowd were soon parted entirely from him and were obliged to leave him at the mercy of the rabble. But these, instead of hurting him, formed a lane for him and carried him along to the middle of the fields . . . from whence he preached without molestation to an exceedingly great multitude.[1]

The meetings grew more and more popular, tens of thousands of people gathering night after night to hear the preaching of this twenty-four year old parson. Soon the meetings were held in Kennington to provide more space. For Sunday 6 May 1739, his diary reads:

> At six preached at Kennington. Such a sight I never saw before. I

believe there were no less than fifty thousand people, and near four score coaches, besides great numbers of horses . . . God gave me great enlargement of heart. I continued my discourse for an hour and a half, and when I returned, I was filled with such love, peace and joy that I cannot express it.[2]

Occasional references from journals of the late 1730s give us an idea of what Whitefield's sermons were like. One day he preached to a vast crowd about an elderly, blind beggar being led by his dog on a lead and walking on the brink of a precipice. Whitefield described the scene in such graphic detail that one of the congregation, Lord Chesterfield, stood up and shouted, 'Good God! He's gone, gone!' 'No, my Lord,' answered White-field, 'he is not quite gone; let us hope that he may be saved.' He went on to describe the danger of trusting our own blind direction instead of trusting in the love of Jesus Christ. This sense of urgency, and ability to bring the dramatic into preaching was a hallmark of Whitefield's style.

John Wesley, invited by Whitefield to join him in open-air preaching in Bristol, was overawed when he witnessed the situation. 'Brother White-field expounded on Sunday morning to six or seven thousand at the Bowling Green, at noon to much the same number at Hanham Mount, and at five, to, I believe, thirty thousand from a little Mount on Rose Green.'[3]

Like Whitefield, Wesley was deeply moved by the prospect that such a ministry opened up. The opportunity to reach vast numbers of people in various parts of the country would give him a national platform from which he could expound his message of 'salvation for all'. No longer was he confined to small 'religious societies' – he could communicate with tens of thousands.

The field preachers of the eighteenth century used a high degree of dramatic content in their preaching, and one of the reasons for their effectiveness in reaching a secularized, unchurched culture was their ability to use visual imagery, exciting stories and dramatic delivery.

Is anyone listening?

Have you ever sat in the congregation whilst the distant echo of the preacher vibrated around the church and asked yourself, 'Is anyone listening?' There is no real way of knowing, but the distant eyes and stony faces are a fair indication that many are not really tuned in. I sometimes feel as if the preacher might as well be speaking in Swahili because the words are not reaching me.

It has been calculated that 23% of non-churchgoers do not read a newspaper at all, and 22% of the population never read a book. Yet congregations are often expected to use three different books during a one-hour service. The language of the pulpit often reflects that of the quality newspapers, but 19% of the population read the *Sun* and 18% the *Mirror.*

Those responsible for preaching need to learn what television chief, Sir Charles Curran, once described as 'an ability to convince the audience of their wish to expose themselves to what we want to say'. Preachers, however, often expect their listeners to understand 'Godspeak', to struggle with alien concepts, to comprehend religious 'norms' and to relate to archaic language. In our post-modern society it is the preacher's task to learn how to speak the language of the people. Preachers like to use a language all of their own, and some fail to see the need to learn the new vernacular. Philip Hawthorn writes:

> Just as ordinary people felt excluded by the Latin liturgy in the Middle Ages, so many people today feel excluded by the church's forbidding message buried in strange rituals and religious language. If God cares for all people then Christians must find ways to get out of their ghettos and into the modern market-place.[4]

Drama is one of the most important ways of communication, and it is time that preachers started to use it. Admittedly, some preachers have begrudgingly allowed it into services but usually in an embarrassingly patronizing way. They have simply permitted the 'young people' to 'do a skit' at the annual 'youth service'. But I would argue that the time has now come for drama to be taken much more seriously. After all, it is nothing new! In fact, the British theatre owes its historic roots to its life in the church.

Drama: the roots

Drama has been part of worship since the tenth century when the liturgy itself began to make use of dialogue, movement, gestures, impersonation, role-play and symbolism. A prime example is found in the tenth-century book *Concordia Regularis* which detailed a religious mime to be performed by the monks. By the twelfth century, liturgical drama was becoming popular. Playlets linked to Easter and Christmas were frequently performed.[5] One drama involved Rachel's lamenting the death of the 'Innocents' in the Christmas story, and another was about the three kings from the East.

Thomas Aquinas, by the direction of the Pope, developed an office for the festival of Corpus Christi in about 1264. Within fifty years this had become a popular festival, with religious processions as a central part of the festivities.

By the fourteenth century, a more extempore form of drama had evolved. The 'Mystery' plays were dramatic representations about the Creation, the Annunciation, the Passion, the Ascension and the Last Judgement. The words of the plays were expanded, utilizing the language and dialect of the people, and with interpolations from non-biblical characters such as 'The Spice Seller'. Around this time the laity replaced the clergy as the actors, craft guilds taking the responsibility for the production, fishmongers producing 'Jonah', carpenters 'Noah's Ark', and so on.

A primitive form of street theatre developed around these processions. These were based on history from the Fall of Lucifer to the Last Judgement, and different versions featured between twenty-five and fifty short plays. They were presented in major religious centres such as cathedral cities.

The Chester cycle of such plays was founded in 1328, and similar productions began in York in 1377 and Coventry in 1392. Many local parish churches copied the idea on a smaller scale. These cycles were major events and involved the whole community, including the clergy.

Next came the 'Morality' plays which developed in the fifteenth century. They depicted the story of man's journey from birth to the grave. At the heart of the morality play was man's choice between right and wrong. Characters in the morality plays were personifications of good and evil, vice and virtue.

R A Banks, in a historic review of fifteenth- and early sixteenth-century morality plays noted that: 'Preaching or didacticism seems fundamentally the main purpose of such plays; allegory is merely the manner used to convey the message.'[6]

Over the centuries, the church has used drama as an integral part of its communication. After all, it can be one of the most powerful and effective means of communication. Yet today it is often relegated to special 'guest services' or entrusted to groups of people in the church who have little skill or expertise.

Sadly, drama in church or evangelism sometimes reinforces the impression that we do not care about quality. Such an important and powerful ministry should not be entrusted to a group of untrained enthusiasts who convey little except their own inability to act. If only churches spent as much money, time and energy on church drama as they did on such things as worship bands, our communication in worship could be more effective. If only preachers would admit that in this televisual age it is not always easy to hold a congregation's attention for twenty minutes, and recognize that, when a message is spiced with drama, it can be much more compelling. It is time that more preachers dared to allow drama into the sanctity of their sermons. It is one of the best methods of storytelling and of bringing to life the amazing stories of Jesus.

I cannot believe that people looked bored when Jesus told the stories of The Prodigal Son and The Good Samaritan, or when he expounded the story of The Sower and the Seed, or talked of 'salt and light'. He understood that to capture and hold people's attention he needed to tell stories. Good stories can grip people's attention and communicate meaning far more powerfully than a series of abstract statements.

Drama is storytelling brought up to date, and over the last few years I have used it more and more in the course of my sermons, because I am committed to drama as the supreme method of storytelling. I work extensively with a drama company called Stripes. Time and again in schools, colleges, bars, cathedrals, at services and conventions, I have been able to 'preach off the back of' one of the stories they have told. Years later, people have reminded me of the 'prodigal son' clambering over the front of the church gallery as he returned home, or how 'house-builders' weathered the storm in the midst of a sermon about the 'Rock'.

I find that a sermon sprinkled with drama and illustrated by acted stories keeps people on the edge of their seats. Drama education expert, David Hornbrook, sums up how I feel when he writes:

Today, the pervasive presence of television in modern society has meant that we now have constant access to drama in ways never before possible. Drama has become built into the rhythms of our everyday lives, serving to confirm and reassure in a world in which active intervention in public life has come for many to seem futile and meaningless.[7]

Unfortunately, some Christian drama groups seem so intent on 'bashing the audience around the head' with the message that they fail to communicate. It is far more effective for drama to entertain and to raise the questions which the preacher will answer. Undoubtedly, comedy can be used in this way. One of the new 'Burning Questions' sketches features Adam and Eve in fig leaves. I use it to open up teaching about 'What's gone wrong with the world?'.

I do not believe that drama should replace the preached word. But I would argue that it should become a central part of it, either before or after the sermon. In the interests of communication, let it become a part of the preached word! Nigel Forde writes:

Prophetic Theatre is theatre which clarifies the word of God at a particular time; Evangelistic Theatre is that which clarifies the gospel in particular; Didactic Theatre – in this context – clarifies the teaching of the Bible and Entertaining Theatre is based on the nature of humankind and creation.[8]

Increasingly, educationalists are discovering that drama is not an isolated subject but is something at the heart of effective communication. Drama teachers are working with geography, history, art and religious departments in order to help bring ideas to life. Drama educationalist Betty Jane Wagner explains:

If we think of any material stored in books as an unpalatable beef bouillon cube, then some means must be found for releasing this dense mass into a savoury broth of human experience. In educational circles, this message has been called code-cracking, breaking the code so the message can be read.[9]

The primary role of drama in proclamation, therefore, should not be to 'hammer home the message' but to grab the audience's attention, to entertain, to tell stories, to raise questions, to hold up a mirror to human experience and to question people's presuppositions, so that the preacher has a listening audience waiting to make a connection. Gordon and Ronnie Lamont write:

We use drama quite naturally as a way of helping us to make sense of our lives, of understanding God and his world. This is not some trendy add-on to our Christianity, it is right there at the heart of our faith. We follow the example of Jesus who opened up difficult questions about God and his Kingdom by inviting his hearers into an 'as if' world.[10]

Drama is at its most useful when the viewers, empathizing with the characters, recognize some situation, some aspect of their lives or some burning question and, through this process of recognition, become riveted to the plot and open to the message. David Hornbrook explains:

We may therefore regard dramatic art not so much as another way of knowing, but rather as a way of participating in dramatic conversations which can lead to new perceptions, to us making better sense of things.[11]

I have been intrigued by the use of drama as a means of communication in Christian mission for over twenty years. And the national tours I have produced have been seen by literally hundreds of thousands of people. For example, speaking recently to some fifteen hundred people in Liverpool Cathedral, I chose the theme 'Who is Jesus?' The drama performed was not a religious diatribe but a conversation in a boat between two shocked sailors who wondered how someone could walk on the water.

It would appear that the church needs to discover new ways of communicating its message and making the gospel relevant and understandable to the younger generation. I would suggest that the use of multi-media means of communication, and especially drama, is one of the most effective means of doing this.

The use of modern media in evangelism is not religious entertainment or 'compromise with the world'; it is simply effective communication. The modern media do not change or cheapen the gospel. They do not replace preaching but complement it. The language of film, music, drama and dance is the vernacular of the new generation, and we must learn to speak it.

Endnotes

1   A Dallimore, *George Whitefield*, 1 (London, 1970).
2   Dallimore, *Whitefield*.
3   Dallimore, *Whitefield*.
4   A MacDonald, S Stickley and P Hawthorn, *Street Theatre* (Eastbourne, 1991).
5   E K Chambers, *The Medieval Stage*, 11 (Oxford, 1903), pp. 1–67.
6   R A Banks, *Drama and Theatre Arts* (London, 1985).
7   D Hornbrook, *Education and Dramatic Art* (Oxford, 1989).
8   N Forde, *Theatrecraft* (London, 1986).
9   B J Wagner (ed), *D Heathcote: Drama as a Learning Medium* (London, 1979).
10 G and R Lamont, *Drama Toolkit* (Buckingham, 1993).
11 Hornbrook, *Education and Dramatic Art*.

Chapter 21

GROWING A CHURCH

Roger Forster

Growth by faith

Many churches must be growing, since nearly 90,000 new Christians appear on the earth daily.[1] Ignorance of this fact can be one of the greatest hindrances to growing a church. Unbelief can also hinder growth: since the church is intended to consist of believers, unbelief must be precluded. I would go so far as to call unbelief a crime. It is by faith that we are saved, by faith we reproduce and by faith we grow. However, a faith in growth, it has been argued many times since the rise of the Church Growth Movement, is not necessarily faith in God and his Christ. The reply to this is that faith in Christ is trusting him as a person who is known through his words and his acts: 'for the words that you gave to me I have given to them, and they have received them and know in truth that I came from you; and they have believed that you sent me' (John 17:8). To trust Jesus is to trust his words which come from the Father. His last words to the apostles were that they should make disciples of all nations and teach others to do the same (Matthew 28:18–20). Jesus commanded, taught and expected church growth; he did not teach or anticipate church decline. To trust him as we obey his word, 'teaching them all things as I commanded you', is to believe in church growth. Confidence in Jesus is confidence in church growth. It is his idea and his command. Faith is essential for growing churches.

The massive expansion and growth of the Protestant church in the nineteenth century, and its temporary decline in the first half of this century, gave rise to a theologically scientific examination of church growth. The pioneering analysis and writing of men such as Roland Allen[2] led to the Church Growth Movement, fostered by Donald McGavran after his thirty years' missionary work in India. I have chosen to give an historical perspective of church growth in this paper, by quoting from significant works of the last few decades that speak to the closing years of this century.

McGavran's first book, *The Bridges of God* (New York, 1955), was an epoch-making contribution for our understanding of how people became Christians. Today, forty years on, with a massive decline in Western Christianity, his work continues to be relevant for a return to church growth. From his historical perspective, McGavran focused on what he called 'people movements' as opposed to the conversion of individuals that could isolate them from their culture.

Growth by 'people movements'

McGavran highlighted the advantages of 'people movements'.

- They are rooted in the 'home' culture and society, not imposed by outsiders.
- 'Spontaneous expansion of the church' occurs naturally, because national leaders rely totally on the Holy Spirit, missionaries being only advisers.
- They have enormous possibilities of growth.
- They provide a sound pattern for becoming Christians – primarily through an inner change by the power of God, and not a change in culture and living standards because of missionary influence.

Today, in a European context, we could understand 'people movements' as 'relationships', such as subcultures; ethnic groups or 'our kind of people'; 'lay Christianity' with non-clergy leaders, together with patterns of worship using contemporary language and music. 'People movements' still have relevance in post-Christian Europe.[3]

In a recent survey of the British people it was the sense of not owning the church that outsiders criticized. The cultural irrelevance of the church for the average outsider made the church not theirs. This was the main complaint. Our situation in the UK today is no different from the mission field of fifty years ago. McGavran answered the charge that the methods of growth would take the place of the message by saying, 'The message is the Lord and his chariot is the People Movement'.[4] In the same book, written forty years ago, he prophesied that 'the Great Century of the Christian Missions' may well be followed by a 'Greater Century of the Christian Churches'.[5]

As the churches of Christ all around the globe – the older churches and the younger churches – band together, recognizing the primacy of discipling those people who have been called of God, and resolutely refusing to be turned aside from this harvest, a century of expansion may result. From a human point of view, we advocate a 'winning strategy of missions'. From God's point of view, however, we are invited to 'march with him' down an ever widening avenue to the hearts of the nations.[6]

Growth in London

In 1974 two important personal things happened. First, our family moved into a new house. Second, a few months later, the Ichthus church plant began, with fourteen people meeting together in the room next to my study. As we began to grow, some members suggested that we should expand into my study and thus increase our capacity by ten. But I said, 'God is going to make us grow.' The faith-level required to sacrifice my study was, fortunately, too small for me. Instead, we went public and rented a senior citizens' club room on a local government housing estate where we could accommodate some fifty people. Later, we moved to the Friends Meeting House nearby which could accommodate eighty, then to the Lutheran building with the capacity to hold around 300 people; now there are thirty London congregations, over 2,000 adults and 800 children. There are also eighty people abroad planting churches with ten or so congregations, primarily in the Middle East. At each stage of our expansion there was resistance to the size of the proposed buildings. Faith was required to accept the vision of increased numbers of people.

God made human beings to know him. He wants us all to know Jesus Christ and be discipled. He desires the fulfilment of our beings in the relationships of the new society, the church. We should expect men and women who have been paid for through Christ's blood to become Christians. Everything but sin is aimed at this great objective. It is certain that God intended we should grow, and this by faith. A risk-taking faith is our first requirement. There are, however, other principles to help a growing church. Twenty-two years after *The Bridges of God*, McGavran published *Ten Steps for Church Growth*.[7] Here is a summary of those steps, together with later observations relating to them and their continuing relevance as we have pursued our work in London:

• Churches grow as they take the Bible as their final authority for their message, attitudes and practices. Bible-preaching churches grow.

• Churches grow when evangelism is top of the agenda and when members are seeking the lost. Commitment to global mission and God's purpose for all humankind is paramount. Evangelism, of course, means not simply to make converts but to fulfil the great commission by making disciples. Hardly a Sunday passes in our fellowship without reference to Christ's words of 'the gospel of the kingdom' being preached world-wide (Matthew 24:14). In this way the congregation is conditioned to think 'global mission'.

• Churches grow which offer 'Body' life of high quality. Converts will go elsewhere if the fellowship life of the church and its worship is not rich and meeting all the diverse needs of members. If we do not discern the Body of Christ – that is, recognize, love and enjoy it – how will anyone else? We must develop eyes to care for all people, particularly the new ones, so that love is demonstrated in our relationships. The sort of church where people say, 'I have come home at last' is the sort of church that grows.

• Churches grow which love their community and are involved in it.

This includes participating in neighbourhood life and events, prayer-walking, getting to know non-Christians and praying for their needs.

- Churches grow which are continuously starting new groups. We all grow stale by too much routine. Bringing something new into a church always stimulates growth. Finding social, ethnic or cultural groups in our communities that have never been touched by the gospel, and creatively 'invading' them, will keep the church alive and well.

- Churches grow that plan for growth and are prepared to take risks in order to grow. There should be faith-targets. Failure to reach these is better than never having them at all, as long as the aim is realistic. If one target is exceeded, so much the better. Church structures for training new leadership, home groups and new congregations must be incorporated into the programme. A church wishing to grow by bir-thing a new church must have a womb – a place where new life can be sheltered and nurtured.

Complaints are sometimes made that there are too many churches – generally meaning 'there are too many church buildings' – in our closely packed inner cities. I think the reverse is the case. We need about 20,000 new churches in England if there is to be a church for every 1,000 of our population. I do understand the reason for the complaints, with too many large and ill-attended church buildings so much in evidence. However, one answer for churches such as these, strangely enough, might be to plant a new church nearby.

At one time we had an old dog who became so dilapidated he was hardly a fit pet for my youngest child, the two older ones had so worn him out. So we promised her a dog of her own which was alive and well, and we got a young dog while we still had the old one. The effect on the old dog was remarkable. He began to have to fight for his food and not let himself be pushed around. It was not very long before a lot more life came back into the old dog and, of course, the new one did well too. This is what can happen when a new church is planted next to an old one. Of course, the new church needs to assure the old one that it does not want to take away its members. The new congregation should also spend time with the leadership of the old one and, if possible, pray with them; then they will know what the new church is really seeking and not assume the worst.

The result of a new church plant should be a supernatural break-through: the area benefits as a whole from increased spiritual warfare, strategic prayer and evangelism, and the old church begins to receive new power and people as well. If any are contacted who have connec-tions with the old church, they should be encouraged to go there and not to be part of the new one. In this way fear is avoided and a good relationship is born; both churches are stimulated into growth. Finally, the old church sees the new one growing and this reawakens faith to expect new things to happen to them too.

• Churches grow which pray and make room for the Holy Spirit. It hardly needs putting on record that churches need to put a high priority on prayer. The largest church in the world, under the leadership of David Yonggi Cho, in Seoul, Korea, has 'prayer mountains' where thousands pray throughout the week. Prayer saturates all that is going on and opens the door for the activity of the Holy Spirit. This sort of church is not only attractive because the presence of God is felt and seen, but also stimulates the ongoing process of reaching out to God to take more from him, for no church has got it all yet, and prayer is the way to receive.

Growth by cell groups in the city

Yonggi Cho has discovered that multiplying cell groups is the best means to evangelize and grow churches, even in the difficult cities that others have found so hard. He writes, 'Today, one of our greatest needs in the church is to evangelize our cities.'[8] He goes on to give the statistics for the growth of his own church, saying that it is the home cell that has proved to be the effective instrument in this evangelism growth.

It might be helpful now to define more closely what 'church' is if we are intent on growing it. The term is used biblically for the world-wide church (Ephesians 4:11–16) and the regional church (Acts 9:31). So global mission and local co-operation in a regional church-planting operation, like the Discipling A Whole Nation (DAWN) programme, should clearly be in our sights. However, it is in further definitions of 'church' that we have our prime responsibility to work out the Great Commission. A church may be city-wide (eg 1 Corinthians 1:2, Revelation 2:1), but could also be an area or a neighbourhood group, or even a small cell in a household (eg Romans 16:5). A 'house church' in the NT could be a fairly sizeable affair (*cf* Acts 16:14–15,40 – Lydia ran a business and retained staff; or Romans 16:10–11 where patrician households might be, in Paul's mind, almost a small village). On the other hand, 'church' could be something more modest: there is no reason to think that Aquila and Priscilla (Acts 18:1–3) had the means to buy sizeable houses with plenty of room or to have a whole household at their disposal. It seems more likely they would ply their trade of tent-making and maintain themselves on more average levels of living, with perhaps a small cell meeting within their home (Romans 16:3–5).

All these groups of varying sizes are called 'church'. To grow a church therefore must mean expanding home cells, as well as multiplying larger congregations and causing small congregations to grow bigger. Indeed, a combination of smaller units having local responsibility, with the backing of a large city-wide congregation, helps to overcome the difficulties of serious inner-city situations and ensures that a whole territory is covered with incarnations of Jesus. Eddie Gibbs makes this point when he quotes Windass in *Frontier* (Autumn 1973):

We need a boat to voyage in, we need a community, a man-sized community, smaller than a city, larger than the family. The 'progress' of economic man by tearing apart the social fabric in an economic liquidiser has done intolerable violence to human relations and we now have to heal the wounds.[9]

Seven steps to growth

Peter Wagner was a missionary in Bolivia where he witnessed the dramatic growth of the Pentecostal Church in South America (*Look out, the Pentecostals are Coming*, 1973). He studied church growth in North America (*Your Church Can Grow*, 1976). The seven vital signs of a healthy church, highlighted in the latter book, are still relevant twenty years later:

1   The pastor must be a person of faith, a 'possibility thinker', whose leadership can galvanize the church into action for growth; however, the leader must also be someone who is loved and appreciated. If there is team leadership, then the loyalty of the team to the overall leader is even more essential, especially where differing initiatives are taken by team members as they exercise their complementary gifts. In addition, healthy churches have leaders who are themselves engaged in many of the grass-roots operations of the church, so that they are seen to be fully involved in doing the things they are teaching. As demanding as this element might be, it seems essential if the flock is going to respect and follow their shepherd. Another essential is the shepherd's capacity to love his flock, leading from the front rather than driving them from behind.

2   Wagner states that a well-mobilized and trained laity, able to use all the spiritual gifts, is essential for growth. The use of spiritual gifts within the 'safe' environment of church life is a vital preparation for their use by an equipped laity in the more 'risky' area of evangelism. Until the laity is given opportunity to express all its abilities and gifts, as well as spiritual gifts themselves, we will not evangelize the world or indeed our own neighbourhood.

3   Healthy churches are big enough to provide the range of services, facilities and opportunities that meet the needs and expectations of their members. The quality of church life has already been mentioned. What about the issue of size? Is a cell or a neighbourhood group big enough? Is a major celebration too big? Whatever is decided, people must be able to relate together, giving and receiving, in a richness of community life. In a recent survey of non-churchgoers it was found that their greatest need was to be able to relate together in a community of meaningful relationships. The telling point was that they believed the church was the only instrument that could enable them to do this. We have a tremendous opportunity for evangelism in this area.

4   A balanced but dynamic relationship between celebration, congre-
    gation and cell characterizes a healthy church. There are those who
    will come to a knowledge of Body life through celebration where they
    can retain, due to the size of the meeting, a certain degree of anonymity
    and not feel threatened. There are others who will walk over the
    threshold of a cell group and immediately find the supportive relation-
    ships for which they are looking. Others will find that congregational
    life is more to their liking, with its looser social interaction and the
    security of a regular worship and teaching meeting. It is generally
    reckoned that a certain number of visits to a church or different sorts
    of evangelistic meetings is necessary for most, though not all, people
    to give their lives to Christ.[10]

5   Membership is drawn mainly from one homogeneous 'people move-
    ment' unit; Wagner quotes McGavran here: '[people] like to become
    Christians without crossing racial, linguistic or class barriers'.[11] Many
    of us working in the inner city find that this homogeneity is not
    quite so simple because of the complex racial, cultural and linguistic
    diversity that is present. We must learn to build integrated churches
    by using homogeneous 'entry points' (for instance enquirers' groups)
    rather than homogeneous congregations or celebrations. We find this
    is the most successful method, even though it may be slower than
    the total homogeneous church. Surely homogeneous units, meeting
    together as an integrated heterogeneous church, faithfully present the
    Lord Jesus – the one who reconciles all nations in himself.

6   Healthy and growing churches use evangelistic methods that have
    been proved to make disciples. For us, such methods centre around
    building relationships so that non-believers are drawn to the person of
    Jesus and into community with his Body. Having said that, less
    relational methods of outreach are also used, notably in breaking open
    new ground.

7   The final vital sign of a growing church is that its priorities are
    arranged in a biblical order. By this Wagner (writing nearly twenty
    years ago) means that social and political action is put below verbal
    proclamation of the gospel.[12] In our own fellowship, however, we
    conclude that evangelism is holistic, comprising the words of truth,
    the works of justice and mercy, and the wonders that demonstrate the
    risen Jesus. We would reverse Wagner's order: sometimes it is only as
    we 'invade' society with the salt and light of our Lord Jesus Christ
    that we gain credibility, preparing the ground for some people to be
    converted. Obviously, there are others whom the Lord already has in
    an area who will immediately come to faith. We encounter a variety of
    people who require a variety of forms of evangelism, so we aim to *be*
    good news as well as *speak* good news. Thus, with some qualifications,

Wagner's seven points could be applied universally for encouraging churches to expect growth either to continue or to begin.

Church growth by the Holy Spirit

Finally, it needs to be said that the provision which our Lord Jesus has made to fulfil his world evangelistic programme is the gift of the Holy Spirit. There will be no final conclusion to global evangelism, no final closure to the Great Commission, no final and glorious return of our Lord Jesus Christ without the continuing, ongoing waves of the Holy Spirit enthusing, inspiring and carrying the church on to its great destiny. It is with God that we walk through history: 'I am with you always, to the very end of the age'. It is with God that we will see the promise fulfilled, as he fulfilled the promise he made when Mary conceived and brought forth the Word of God himself (Luke 1:34–38). God does this in partnership with us as we call upon him to come into our midst: 'you will receive power when the Holy Spirit comes on you; and you will be my witnesses . . . to the ends of the earth' (Acts 1:8). The church that is a growing church will be a going church, continuously open to the Spirit of God and following him in the divine business of world evangelization.

I believe that the reluctance of the conservative church to receive the outpourings of the Holy Spirit in the first decade of the twentieth century resulted in a spiritual vacuum, two world wars and a deceleration in world evangelism. This must not happen again.

Tribute

Gilbert Kirby has served the cause of the growing church through the years covered by this survey. We thank God for his wise guidance and stewardship through EA of which he was general secretary, and his subsequent principalship of London Bible College. Thanks to men like him, biblical believers in this country have not been left behind and are overcoming a most serious church decline. Now, with all the encouraging signs of growth, we can look forward to a vibrant church once again in the United Kingdom, and also to playing our part in seeing the church worldwide come to its maturity. This is a vision to which Gilbert has clung and for which he has worked and inspired others through these difficult years, with long and loving service to his church and to his Lord.

Colin Dye

The story of Kensington Temple

In September 1849 Horbury Chapel, Notting Hill, was officially opened. Members of nearby Hornton Street Congregational Church had been deeply moved at a recent prayer meeting, and many had wept as they commissioned thirty-seven people who were to pioneer the new work in

Notting Hill. The new church, which soon grew to around 600 people, had both an effective local ministry and a strong missionary emphasis. Gladys Aylward, the great missionary to China, found Christ when she attended one of the services at Horbury Chapel, and Charles Spurgeon, the great Baptist minister, preached there.

It is interesting to notice the similarities between that Congregational chapel and the distinctive features of Kensington Temple (KT) – fervent prayer, vision for missions, social work and church planting. Horbury Chapel later declined, and was sold to a new and growing movement known as Elim. This was founded by George Jeffreys, whom the Lord had been using in a powerful revival of healing and evangelism. The building was renovated and renamed 'Kensington Temple'. The congregation grew to a regular 800 people.

However, George Jeffreys later resigned from the Elim movement. Shortly after this, in 1943, the majority of the congregation left KT in the hands of George Jeffreys' trustees and started a new church called 'The West London Christian Fellowship'. The new fellowship met in different venues under different pastors until 1958, when Eldin Corsie assumed the pastorate at Holland Park Mission.

Following the death of George Jeffreys in 1962, the trustees of KT offered to sell the building to Elim, and in 1965 Eldin Corsie led a congregation of around sixty people back into KT. His ministry in the Temple continued for a further 15 years. They were years of preparation in the spiritual life of the church. The congregation grew to 600. Eldin laboured effectively in every area that was later to bear fruit in the 1980s. He placed a strong emphasis on prayer, developed fellowship groups (the forerunners of today's satellite churches), welcomed members from the international community and exercised a strongly evangelistic ministry.

In September 1980 Wynne Lewis hit KT like a human tornado! His dynamic leadership style, together with his ability to hear from God and implement his plans, took the church forward by leaps and bounds. During his ministry at KT, which lasted over a decade, the church grew from 600 to 5,000 people.

In 1985 I joined the leadership team and founded the Bible institute and the first satellite church in Barnet. During the second half of the Eighties, the church's missions ministry assumed a greater significance when the entire leadership accepted responsibility for world evangelism. The church was now filled several times each Sunday, and there were up to forty different satellite congregations. In 1991 Wynne Lewis left KT for the post of general superintendent of Elim, and I was appointed senior minister.

The church today

The KT of today is building on all that has gone before. We currently reach up to ten times the capacity of the building. We are planting at the rate of one new church each week. The Bible institute has affiliated schools in a number of different nations.

We have a city-wide structure called the London City Church which links our churches together in a comprehensive strategy to win London for Christ. We have regular city celebrations that seek to bring together our central congregations and our satellite churches in a large venue on a regular basis. In 1992, 4,600 people gathered in the Royal Albert Hall, and in 1993, 10,000 came together in Wembley Arena. We are currently looking for a suitable building so that we can continue to grow. We strongly believe we have yet to see the full measure of all that God intends for us in London and our ministry to the rest of the world.

Growth factors

Dynamic life of the Spirit

KT was birthed through the moving of the Holy Spirit and continues to be carried along by his dynamic activity. The life of the church is saturated by his presence and we rightly feel that what happens has nothing to do with our ability – we owe it all to him. He moves in surprising and unexpected ways, arranging things as only he can. We often find that initially casual meetings between people prove to be divine appointments which lead to the development of new ministries. Frequently, combinations of people's spiritual gifts and interests coincide at a particular place and time, showing that the Holy Spirit is orchestrating everything according to his plan. Our role is to co-operate with the Holy Spirit, seeking to be sensitive to his leading and direction.

The gifts of the Holy Spirit are in operation at every level of the church's life. Revelation gifts and gifts of healing are particularly in evidence. Our meetings are lively with vibrant, Spirit-filled praise and worship, and they are designed to bring people into powerful encounters with the Lord.

Visionary leadership

Down through the years the leaders of KT have been known for their breadth of vision.

Plans are characteristically far-reaching, ambitious and all-embracing. Senior leaders refuse to get sidetracked or bogged down in detail. The day-to-day management and implementation of programmes is delegated to other staff. The major emphasis is on hearing from God and following these directives.

Evangelistic Emphasis

The vision is not narrow or inward looking. Rather the whole focus and orientation of the church's ministry is on outreach. We concentrate on the 90% of Londoners who are outside the influence of any church. We are constantly devising ways of reaching out to the lost. The church has a world vision, with up to 116 different nationalities present in KT. The mission statement is 'London and the World for Christ', and it is a reality as our people touch dozens of nations in regular ministry each year.

Training and mobilization

The leaders see their principal collective task to be that of equipping the saints and mobilizing them into ministry. The structured training ministry of KT (International Bible Institute of London) is not so much a separate division of the church as a strategy to fulfil this mandate. Every member of the ministry team is orientated towards training, and most are active within the institute. Many church programmes are designed specifically to mobilize the congregation into Christian ministry. The Ploughman (research), Watchman (intercession) and Fisherman (evangelism) programmes are current outstanding examples.

Prayer and intercession

The growth of KT has always been closely related to the prayer life of the church. During the late 1960s and 1970s, following the return to the KT building, there were many 'prayer warriors' who focused on the need for revival. During the early 1980s, small groups of dedicated women, mainly from Africa, moved the prayer life of the church forward with much fasting and nights of prayer.

In the early 1990s a new prayer initiative saw attendance at the Wednesday evening prayer meeting mushroom. The Watchman prayer programme was launched, with over a thousand people interceding according to a set agenda on a twenty-four hour rotation. There are daily early morning prayer meetings, regular periods of fasting and frequent all-night prayer meetings led by many different groups in the church.

Relevant preaching and teaching

A feature of the ministry at KT has always been the preaching. We are known for sound Bible teaching and powerful preaching popularly presented. The focus is on lifting people up through preaching rather than beating them down. People come with lives broken by the ravages of sin and the burdens of city life, and they find hope through the word of God.

Multicultural emphasis

There is a welcome and a place for people of all cultures in the church. We enjoy our unity in Christ expressed in the main central services and the great celebrations; but we also encourage the various cultures to develop their own homogenous fellowship structures and evangelistic programmes within their own ethnic groupings.

Caring church

Often larger churches are considered to be deficient in caring as the individual is lost in the crowd. This is always a challenge to us, but we find that the small-group programme enables us to care more personally for our members. Our people come to us on a Sunday because the whole ethos of the church, everything that we say and do, tells them that we care what happens to them the rest of the week.

Team ministry

We believe in encouraging the full range of ministries mentioned in Ephesians 4:11. No one leader can hope to carry all the gifts needed to build up a church. Team ministry is essential. Each team member is chosen for his or her particular strengths in ministry, and is given a clear area of responsibility in helping fulfil the overall goal of the church.

Flexible structures that promote growth

Churches can easily be either over-structured or under-structured. It is hard to get the balance right, particularly in a large church. If the church is under-structured, it loses focus and becomes fragmented. If it is over-structured, the life of the church is stifled.

We have found that flexibility is the key. Nothing is set in concrete but, like the new wineskins that Jesus spoke of, our structures can be constantly shaped and adjusted in order to keep pace with what the Holy Spirit is doing. One of our greatest challenges is to develop and adapt our church structures in ways appropriate to our size and progress.

Growing a growing church

The church has six main initiatives in order to fulfil the vision.

Planting churches: building a city church

Planting new churches is the most effective way of evangelizing London. Local people are reached by new, culturally relevant communities of the kingdom meeting in their area. We have a vision to plant 2,000 churches in and around London by AD 2000. These will not simply be independent churches each doing their own thing, but will interlock as a 'city church'.

The New Testament describes the Body of Christ in a city as the church of that city. Obviously, KT is only one part of what God is raising up in London today, so a more technically accurate description for KT would be a 'city-wide' church, working with other church streams in the city. We could plant 2,000 churches all over the capital and still make little substantial impact in London for Christ. Thousands of individual churches will not pull down the strongholds of Satan. It is only when the parts come together as a co-ordinated whole, rising up as the Body of Christ in the city, that the church becomes a force to be reckoned with.

In 1985 the first official KT satellite church was launched in Barnet. The nuclear group had been meeting for ten years as the 'Barnet Nurses Fellowship'. Beginning in a member's front room, the church moved finally into a community hall in the locality. Now over forty strong, the church functions fully in its own right while maintaining strong links with the main central church.

The Ethiopian church met for many years in the basement of KT. Rapid growth led to their moving to a nearby Baptist church. They hold Sunday services in their own language, with over four hundred people celebrating their own culture in Christ.

Now, in 1995, we have over eighty fully-fledged churches, averaging around 45 attendees, with over 3,000 people meeting in London city churches and KT satellites across London. Ten per cent of the KT congregation is actively involved in church-planting. We recruit leaders for the satellites aggressively, mainly from within KT. We strive to ensure that satellite leaders are trained for their work by offering a practical course tailored to the specific needs of satellite church leaders.

A new research department facilitates the task of planting. Borough representatives gather details of population, people groups, openness to the gospel, availability of halls, and the spread of KT membership and existing local churches for each area of London.

Our churches have been planted through a wide variety of means including: key leaders from KT planting out; existing fellowship or international groups growing into satellites; churches being founded by student church-planting teams; London city churches planting their own satellites; and leaders recruited from outside KT coming to join the church-planting programme.

Discipling: making each one count for Christ

Large churches are often criticized for a perceived lack of discipling. Some believe it is all too easy for an individual's gifts and potential to be lost in the crowd. But with up to 116 nationalities in attendance and worshippers coming from a vast geographical area, we have developed numerous strategies for releasing each person into effective discipleship.

Each person counts for Christ. Through our cell group programme, counselling ministry and outreach teams, and specialist groups for specific professions or ethnic groups (such as Media Arts Fellowship and a Caribbean Fellowship) we seek to place every person in a structured environment where they can both give and receive.

As one of many churches around the world which are growing in depth of response to God, we have developed an appreciation of the power and purpose of praise and worship. KT's worship life has been shaped by recognizing that praise declares God's purpose. It builds an environment of expectation and faith, releasing the power of God. It should reflect our specific situation, and good music is a 'gathering factor'. Praise is certainly more than a programme filler!

Training at the cutting edge: the International Bible Institute of London

Our in-house training programme releases a workforce that can affect every area of church and community life, which maximizes the resources of the local church, and which produces leaders and people with a unified history and vision.

KT's training programme grows out of and focuses on KT's vision-prioritizing church-planting, evangelism and world missions. We have developed specialized faculties for concentrated training. We have schools of church-planting, prophecy and creative ministries. We create an environment of faith where ministries are nurtured under anointed leaders. We make training available at every level: occasional, part-time or full-time studies, complemented by flexible departmental and church-wide programmes.

Evangelism: London and the world for Christ

Our Missions department exists to recruit, train and mobilize the whole church into evangelism. Evangelism is a part of our daily church life and every Sunday we see people commit themselves to Christ. Our aim is to make the gospel as accessible as possible through our meetings. Different services are used to reach different kinds of people. The Fisherman programme, launched in 1993, has more than a thousand people committed to a lifestyle of evangelism and involved in a specific outreach activity. Teams regularly minister on the streets, in schools, hospitals, prisons and old people's homes.

The nations of the world have come to London. God has spoken to us that KT would touch many nations throughout the world! Increasing numbers of people from within KT are exposed to short-term missions work where many amazing healings and deliverances take place. We want every member of KT to go on a short-term mission at least once during their time in the church.

One of our secretaries went on a mission trip to Kenya where, in one of the first services, she was part of a team praying for the sick. A blind lady was completely healed as the secretary laid her hands on her and prayed in the name of Jesus. The secretary came back radically changed and sold on mission.

Recently, God has highlighted the needs of the French-speaking world. We have now targeted France and the Republic of Benin as long-term missions projects.

Caring: total care for the total person by the total church

No member in our church family or beyond should have basic needs while someone in the Body can meet them. A ministry is being pioneered which, when mature, will not only demonstrate our care for each other but also change the atmosphere in the community.

One recent breakthrough occurred when the Social Services Department approached KT to find out if we could help place Eritrean and Ethiopian teenagers in foster homes. The youngsters are being brought into the country, given some money and left to fend for themselves with no understanding of English. Our Eritrean and Ethiopian churches were happy to become involved. So we are already on our way to working with and in the community.

Communication: proclaiming the vision

Vision must not only be received from God but also communicated to the whole church. We seek to use a variety of contemporary means to share what God is saying and doing. Our publications department uses high quality journalism to produce our magazine, *Cutting Edge*. In a creative and relevant way it gives the congregation and interested outsiders an overview of the moving of the Holy Spirit in and through the church. We also have a regular newspaper, *City News*, which covers evangelism and mission reports, stories and events. We are also careful about how we publicize the church's activities. Our image must represent our identity, that of joyful, caring people.

The Rose of Sharon Theatre, launched in May 1992, provides not only a platform for our school of creative ministries' students, but also an excellent evangelistic tool. People who feel uncomfortable in a church will often sit quite happily through a high-quality performance with a Christian epilogue.

Technology has helped us deal with the problem of overcrowding at services! These days it is relatively cheap and amazingly simple to provide a simultaneous relay of a service at another venue. This gives sound and vision to people who are located any distance away.

As we face the future, we are convinced that God wants us to continue to grow. We have no upper limit as to the size of the church. But our principal focus is to reach out to those without Christ and disciple them in a network of small-group fellowships and ministries across the city. We are on target to reach our goal of becoming a fully-functioning city church by the year AD 2000.

Endnotes

1 US Centre for World Mission Mobilization Division (1994).
2 See for example R Allen, *Missionary Methods: St Paul's or Ours?* (London, 1912).
3 Perhaps 'post-Constantinian Europe' would be better.
4 D A McGavran, *The Bridges of God* (London, 1955), p 93.
5 McGavran, *The Bridges of God*, p 158.
6 Perhaps a lovely preview of this is 'March for Jesus' across the world.
7 D A McGavran and W C Arn, *Ten Steps for Church Growth* (New York, 1977).

8   D Yonggi Cho, *Successful House Cell Groups* (New Jersey, 1981), p 61.
9   E Gibbs, *Urban Church Growth* (Nottingham, 1977), p 12.
10 J Finney, *Finding Faith Today* (Swindon, 1992).
11 D A McGavran, *Understanding Church Growth*, (Grand Rapids, 1970), p 198.
12 P Wagner, *Your Church Can Grow* (California, 1977), p. 156.

Chapter 22

FORWARD TOGETHER

Ian Coffey

In 1971 a new Bishop of Norwich – Maurice Wood – was about to be appointed. The label for his churchmanship was given as 'conservative evangelical'. Her Majesty the Queen, never having heard the expression before, asked for it to be explained to her.[1]

Over the last quarter of a century the scene has changed considerably. Evangelicals are known, seen and (increasingly) heard. Whether they are understood is another matter. Their profile is considerable. The English Church Census (1989) revealed a landscape of evangelicals within English denominations. Peter Brierley, the author of the report, cited the following facts:

- 34% of churches in England were evangelical
- These represented 28% of adult churchgoers
- Charismatic evangelicals were the fastest growing section
- There were an estimated 1 million evangelicals in England
- The Methodists were one-third evangelical
- One-quarter of URC Churches were evangelical
- Over three-quarter of Baptists, Independent, Afro-Caribbean and Pentecostal churches were evangelical
- One-sixth of Anglican churches were evangelical[2]

Within the international scene, the evangelicals have experienced growth in numbers and influence. As one respected commentator has noted:

> Evangelicalism is one of the powerhouses of the modern Christian Church in the Western world. Evangelicalism, once regarded as marginal, has now become mainline . . . [It] is generally accepted to be well on its way towards becoming a major constitutive element of global Christianity.[3]

Not everyone is thrilled at the rise of this particular star within the solar system of Christendom. There are plenty (both within and without the church) who would share the distaste for evangelical Christians expressed by Lord Salisbury, the Conservative Prime Minister, at the end of the nineteenth century. He wrote of its 'reign of rant', its 'nasal accents of devout ejaculation' and its 'incubus of narrow-mindedness . . . brooding over English society'.[4]

With its new-found strength and influence, surely the evangelical movement world-wide has cause to feel comfortable. As one writer described it, 'Evangelicals have the ball at their feet'. It remains to be seen if they can resist the temptation of turning around and putting it into their own net. In his incisive book, *Evangelicalism and the Future of Christianity*, Alister McGrath sounds a long, loud warning bell:

> Evangelicals are sinful human beings like everyone else. And the sheer humanity of evangelicalism may easily eclipse whatever within the movement is of God. It needs to learn from its own history, which alerts it to the errors of the past. Without this perspective, it may do little more than repeat yesterday's mistakes, resulting in tomorrow's decline. Above all there is the danger that evangelicalism may break up into mutually suspicious splinter groups, each claiming to be the only representatives of a 'true evangelicalism' which others have 'sold out' or 'betrayed'.[5]

Increased media attention – in part the result of a skilfully orchestrated campaign of persuasion carried out by the revitalized Evangelical Alliance – carries with it a down-side. Family rows can so easily become headline news. Late in 1994 controversy was stirred by an EA statement over daily worship in schools. The denominational weekly newspaper, *The Baptist Times*, cited the public argument that followed as evidence of the growing reputation of evangelical Christians:

> News of the controversy . . . was extensively covered on BBC radio news bulletins and was the lead item on Teletext. A few years ago it would have been unthinkable that such a dispute within the evangelical constituency would have merited any coverage at all.[6]

Perhaps more than at any other time in the last fifty years, those Christians who would call themselves evangelical – both in the UK and around the globe – need to co-operate, basing that mutual commitment on those essential truths of the Christian faith which are the warp and woof of the movement.

But what shape should such co-operation take? What obstacles does it face? How can it be achieved? And, perhaps most important of all, does it really matter? We cannot afford to ignore such questions.

Is co-operation a priority?

The fact that there is not time to do everything is not a discovery peculiar to the modern world, but the development of technology which has given us the fax machine and cellular phone has lent new meaning to the phrase 'the tyranny of the urgent'. We so often live as slaves to whatever dumps itself on top of the pile. And in a world of sophisticated electronic information highways, the pile changes by the minute.

It has been pointed out that in the UK alone, someone may lead a local church yet only attend on Sundays. There are conferences running almost every week of the year on prayer, evangelism, 'signs and wonders'. As one Christian leader has remarked, the next few years will probably see conferences for leaders on time management, which include seminars on 'How to attend conferences'.

For local church leaders with strong denominational ties – or, in the case of newer churches, networking links – there are meetings, boards, synods, committees and ... more conferences. Whoever christened St Vitus as the patron saint to the twentieth century was right. With a myriad of meetings and endless challenges, why add another layer of busy activities labelled 'evangelical co-operation'?

In the closing decades of this century evangelicals have:

- gained ground (grown in numbers)
- gained recognition (within the wider church)
- gained a voice (with governments and media)
- gained a family (by discovering other evangelical Christians)

With all these gains, is it not time to concentrate on other matters?

The reason why those who call themselves evangelical Christians should be concerned about co-operation is intimately bound up with their understanding of the kingdom of God. If we are concerned to see the kingdom of God advancing, then co-operation with others who share that same vision is not a luxury with which we can dispense. It is a vital necessity.

Co-operation is not to do with advancing a particular theological party or lobby group. It is not to do with building up this organization or that. It is a kingdom goal and, as such, is worthy of our best attention.

Over against this noble task lies an uncomfortable truth. Protestant Christians have proved themselves wonderfully adept at fragmentation born of a 'we're the only ones here, so let's go it alone' mentality. History demonstrates that whenever evangelicals have become strong numerically, break-away groups form, caused by a variety of issues. Disputes over doctrinal interpretation, personality clashes between strong leaders, and disagreements over methods are just a few examples of how polarization, and ultimately fragmentation, can occur. There are sufficient indicators in the early part of the 1990s that warn of the danger of history repeating itself.

Perhaps it is a feature of our fallen human nature that we focus more readily on the grey clouds above our heads than on the green shoots beneath our feet. There are plenty of areas where evangelical co-operation has started to achieve results, and it is surely here that the building blocks of co-operation should continue to be laid.

Mapping the territory

There are several key areas where strong evangelical teamwork is called for over the coming years. Some of the more obvious ones are:

Evangelism and social action
John Stott, writing in 1984, made this telling comment:

> One of the most notable features of the world-wide evangelical movement during the last ten to fifteen years has been the recovery of our temporarily mislaid social conscience.[7]

The evangelical movement continues the struggle to get its house in order in this crucial area of Christian mission. Some still see evangelism and social action as either/or options, rather than as a both/and concept. Reflection and engagement are required if we are to achieve a more balanced approach to mission. We have begun, but there is a lot more ground to be claimed.

Stemming the tide of secularization
Many have identified this as an area of primary concern for the Christian church. The influences of secularization are keenly felt at almost every level of life in the United Kingdom. Others have written with skill and insight, analysing the trends, warning of the dangers and highlighting some answers.

One thing seems to stand out in sharp outline: divided, insular and uninformed Christians will make no impact on a world without room for God. If we are to stem the tide of secularization, it will come through the type of effective co-operative networks that draw Christians together in education, politics, the performing arts, the media and other spheres.

The battle for the mind
The American academic, Mark Noll, has written about *The Scandal of the Evangelical Mind*. Although, primarily, it offers a critique of the evangelical movement in the USA, he touches on issues that closely parallel the church in the UK. He quotes an interview with the British writer, Os Guinness:

> Evangelicals have been deeply sinful in being anti-intellectual ever since the 1820s and 1830s. For the longest time we didn't pay the cultural price for that because we had the numbers, the social zeal, and the spiritual passion for the gospel. But today we are beginning to pay the cultural price. And you can see that most evangelicals simply don't think. For example, there has been no serious evangelical public philosophy in this century . . . It has always been a sin not to love the Lord our God with our minds as well as our hearts

and souls ... We have excused this with a degree of pietism and pretend[ing] that this is something other than what it is – that is, sin ... Evangelicals need to repent of their refusal to think Christianly and to develop the mind of Christ.[8]

The rise in the number of credible evangelical theologians in the later years of this century is notable. Their ranks look likely to be swelled in the future, too. But Noll pinpoints the need for Christian thinkers, 'across the whole spectrum of modern learning, including economics and political science, literary criticism and imaginative writing, historical inquiry and philosophical studies, linguistics and the history of science, social theory and the arts'.[9]

If ever an area cried out for evangelicals to work together it is the battle for the mind. Part of the ongoing task of evangelization is to see the Christian gospel released into every area of society, challenging thought-forms and ideas and pointing to a kingdom which cannot be shaken. The definition of that task is summarized by Charles Malik, a Lebanese diplomat, scholar and Eastern Orthodox Christian:

The problem is not only to win souls but to save minds. If you win the whole world and lose the mind of the world, you will soon discover you have not won the world. Indeed it may turn out that you have actually lost the world.[10]

The ecumenical minefield

In the early 1990s the ecumenical landscape in Britain and Ireland underwent a transformation. So-called 'new ecumenical instruments' came into being with the aim of securing greater dialogue and partnership between those who live in these islands and consider themselves to be Christians.

At that time I was serving as a member of the leadership team of EA, and was asked by its council of management to take responsibility for the many months of discussions surrounding the Alliance's response to these changes. I quickly discovered that within the broad evangelical constituency there were, broadly speaking, four viewpoints.

First, were those who believed evangelical Christians had a duty to be involved in ecumenical relationships. They took the view that evangelicalism had things both to give and receive through these wider links.

Second, were the group that firmly believed that any linkage with non-evangelicals would be an unacceptable compromise of the gospel.

A third section (not insignificant in terms of size) believed, with varying degrees of tolerance, that ecumenical structures were a waste of time.

A fourth grouping was made up of those evangelicals who had not the faintest clue what was happening. For many of them an ecumenical structure might well mean a large church building such as a cathedral. They neither knew nor cared about relationships with churches of different traditions.

In the years that have followed, the Council of Churches for Britain and Ireland (CCBI), with their national counterparts, have continued their work. The EA, having declined the invitation to join CCBI, has maintained contact with the ecumenical bodies, believing that they are best able to represent evangelical concerns from outside these structures. However, some evangelical Christians in the many denominations that belong to CCBI are working vigorously within the system and contributing to many of the important discussions taking place between Christians of widely different traditions.

It is my firm conviction that those evangelicals who take such opposing views on matters ecumenical must continue to talk and listen to each other. Rather than engage in the fruitless exercise of trench warfare, we should be mature enough to respect the integrity of those who do not share our particular outlook.

March, sit or kneel for Jesus?

The history of the evangelical movement reveals that prayer has been a vital component in its development. In recent years a broadening appreciation has grown towards non-evangelical approaches to prayer. For example, evangelical writers such as Richard Foster and James Houston have popularized the spiritual disciplines, including contemplative prayer.

At the same time the 'March for Jesus' movement has made a remarkable impact around the world. Thousands of Christians have taken to the streets of their cities, towns and villages to sing and pray. They have done so with the firm conviction that the church needs to be on the streets of local communities praying, praising and declaring the kingdom of God.

Inevitably, not all evangelicals have greeted the 'Marches for Jesus' with enthusiasm. It seems that, when it comes to the subject of prayer, if there are four evangelicals, there will be five different opinions.

Once again, there is a need for honest, open dialogue and a humble searching of the scriptures. If prayer is as important as the Bible suggests, then matters such as the nature of spiritual warfare, forms of prayer in relation to other cultures and traditions, the place of spiritual gifts and the role of signs and wonders are all areas where some common understanding needs to be found. And beyond the discussion, we need to engage in some serious praying, as Derek Tidball suggests:

Given the secular atmosphere in which we now live, and the pressure many endure in their jobs and family life, how much praying, of any kind, is still done? Prayer meetings are now less well attended than they were, family prayers rare and individual quiet times often cut short. Prayer marches take place but are, in practice, more committed to singing than praying. Housegroups include prayer, but not in the concentrated form of the prayer meetings . . . the doubt remains as to whether evangelicals pray as once they did. Will the evangelical enterprise of the next generation be sustained by prayer as that of previous generations has been?[11]

The next generation

The evangelical movement has the inbuilt propensity to become exclusive, and history records how often splinter groups have formed on matters which, with hindsight, have proved to be inconsequential. One of the safeguards against what has been described as a 'ghetto mentality' is for younger leaders to be allowed to emerge and flourish. One has only to look at the ruling élite of countries such as China or the former USSR to see the results of an ageing and defensive leadership, steadfastly holding the reins of power.

A healthy evangelical movement in the early years of the twenty-first century needs a new generation of leaders, spiritually equipped, theologically experienced, culturally adaptable, politically aware and streetwise.

They are there, within the ranks of traditional denominations and the new church groupings, but it is a case of identifying and nurturing them. This reveals the need for close co-operation between evangelical leaders within the various streams. The EA, already aware of this need, has initiated a Younger Leaders Consultation. Such a grouping can only achieve its full potential when younger leaders are given the room to grow.

It remains to be seen if the current evangelical leaders in the UK will grow into a geriatric 'mafia', or pass on the torch of leadership to a new generation.

Through many dangers, toils and snares

As John Newton realized when he wrote his classic hymn, 'Amazing Grace', the path of Christian discipleship is not an easy one. Each generation faces its own particular challenges that call for wisdom, skill and, above all, the grace of God.

As the world-wide evangelical movement contemplates the arrival of the twenty-first century, we recognize that the return of the Lord Jesus Christ is nearer now than it was when he urged his disciples:

> Therefore keep watch, because you do not know on what day your Lord will come. But understand this: If the owner of the house had known at what time of night the thief was coming, he would have kept watch and would not have let his house be broken into. So you also must be ready, because the Son of Man will come at an hour when you do not expect him. (*Matthew 24:42–44*)

What does this readiness entail for our generation at this particular period in the history of the Christian church? I believe there are four cautions that need to be sounded as evangelicals look to the next few years.

We are not good at learning from our past

Derek Tidball has traced the growth of the evangelical movement through the nineteenth century until, in a relatively short space of time, ground was lost and retreat set in. What were the reasons? He cites weak leadership, energetic but unproductive activism, fragmentation in its ranks, and dilution of evangelical theology. He comments:

> The history of evangelicalism suggests that whenever success is experienced care needs to be exercised . . . Positions of strength carry with them the inherent seeds of decline. Perhaps the position of weakness is not such a bad location after all. Evangelicalism at the turn of the twenty-first century needs to read its history with care and take note.[12]

We are not good at co-operating when we are strong

One of the lessons of history is that when evangelicals are weak they make attempts to group with others who share their outlook. Conversely, when they are strong they tend to pull apart. In the early 1990s groups such as the World Evangelical Fellowship (WEF), which is the umbrella body for the world's EAs, identified fragmentation as a major threat to the international evangelical movement.

The council of management of EA (UK) has begun to give serious consideration to this challenge. At a meeting of the council held in February 1992, several potential areas were identified where fragmentation between evangelical groupings could occur:

Ethnocentrism. This is the belief in the intrinsic superiority of one's nation, culture or group, often accompanied by feelings of contempt towards other groups. The pull of nationalist aspirations in various parts of the United Kingdom may well impact the evangelical churches in those places most strongly affected.

Isolationism. With the growing strength and influence of evangelicals within their denominations, the tendency may be to concentrate on in-house concerns, leaving little time for broader contacts.

Pluralism. When WEF surveyed its global membership in 1991, it discovered that, 'There appears to be a strong agreement in different parts of the church around the world that *the* most important issue . . . is pluralism and the uniqueness of Christ'.[13]

Such a challenge will inevitably prompt varied responses from the evangelical community. One person's tolerance can be seen as another's compromise. Could this prove to be a potential flashpoint?

Extremism. Any false teaching, whether it is misguided enthusiasm or rank heresy, is off-centre in regard to biblical Christianity. The approach of the year AD 2000 could bring a fresh crop of new eschatological views, which may polarize some sections of the evangelical movement.

Ecumenism. As we have already identified, evangelicals have widely vary-ing views on the ecumenical movement. It is possible that gaps could widen in the coming years, particularly as evangelicals who have opted-in become more involved in ecumenical structures.

Schism. Evangelicals have, sadly, demonstrated that schism is not all that difficult to achieve. A list of current issues where evangelicals disagree includes: the role of women, the nature of prophecy, signs and wonders, eternal punishment. On the other side of the Atlantic a 'Battle for the Bible' still rumbles on with heated debates over the distinctions between words such as 'inerrancy' and 'infallibility'. Alister McGrath expresses the view shared by many when he writes:

> Evangelicalism faces so many challenges and external pressures that the last thing it needs is a protracted civil war, which can only lead to fragmentation, bitterness and a negative public witness. 'See how these Christians love one another' was the public reaction to faith recorded by Tertullian in the second century. Is it too much to hope that a similar response might be evoked by evangelicals today?[14]

We are not good at listening to each other

The epistle of James passes on some timely advice: 'Everyone should be quick to listen, slow to speak and slow to become angry' (James 1:19).

As evangelicals we need to listen carefully to each other. The existence of bodies such as EA allows our legitimate differences to be recognized, while at the same time we learn to work alongside others. This can create a safe environment where dialogue can take place. It also opens the way for God to bring about new partnerships that otherwise would not exist. Not to co-operate with others in the Body of Christ is foolish. Not to listen to them is arrogant.

We are not good at listening to those who are outside us

Can you be a Christian without being an evangelical? I happen to think you can. Many of us recognize the godliness of other professing Christians who themselves would be uncomfortable with the theological definition 'evangelical'. We have much to learn from those beyond our ranks in the realms of theological reflection, spirituality and mission.

The ecumenism of relationships is a potent force. As an evangelical movement we must increasingly be open to learn from those of different traditions. This does not mean that we dilute our essential convictions or compromise our standards in any way. But we affirm that for Christians the world over:

> We limit not the truth of God
> To our poor reach of mind,
> By notions of our day and sect,

Crude, partial and confined,
No, let a new and better hope
Within our hearts be stirred;
The Lord hath yet more light and truth
To break forth from His Word.[15]

Towards a new dawn

Just recently a telephone call came through to my office asking if I could verify the credentials of a Baptist group in Cleveland, Ohio, USA. As I tried tactfully to point out to the caller, there is more than one Baptist denomination in America! Historian David Bebbington has reported that: 'By 1980 there were forty-six separate Baptist denominations, not to speak of such robustly independent congregations as the "Rock Solid Baptist Church Affiliated to the Lord Jesus Christ" in the village of Tiger, Georgia.'[16] Evangelicals on this side of the Atlantic suffer from the same spirit of division. There are wounds in the Body of Christ that are self-inflicted and that need healing. Is this an unrealistic dream, this side of heaven?

In January 1995 a significant meeting took place in Chicago between the leaders of the two main evangelical groupings in the USA, the National Association of Evangelicals (NAE) and the National Black Evangelical Association (NBEA). The very fact that the two organizations exist, (one white- the other black-led) underlines the extent of the problem. The objective of the meeting was pure and simple – reconciliation. If necessary, the leaders affirmed, they were willing to abandon their respective organizations. It was an honest and painful time. Executive director of NAE, Don Argue, publicly confessed and repented of racism within evangelical ranks. As he knelt, three senior African-American church leaders laid hands on him and offered prayers for the breaking down of racial barriers in American society. Argue has been quoted as saying, 'The National Association of Evangelicals is too old, too white and too male . . . The evangelical table is broad and wide and long.'[17] One of those present at this historic meeting was George D McKinney, a bishop of the Church of God in Christ, a fast-growing African-American Pentecostal denomination. He commented, 'We are getting the house in order. Billy Graham is right: racism is a major obstacle to revival in this country because it's sin.'[18]

Here is an example of evangelical co-operation at its finest: addressing deep issues in a biblical way, recognizing that in real life problems are not solved with sound-bite solutions. It is the message of the cross of Christ that makes forgiveness, reconciliation and a new start possible. This is the historic, biblical, apostolic faith. It is the evangel of evangelicalism, not simply to be preached but most of all to be practised.

Here is the bread a hungry world needs.

Endnotes

1 O Chadwick, *M Ramsay: A Life* (Oxford, 1990), p 142.
2 P Brierley (ed), *Christian England* (Bromley, 1991).
3 A McGrath, *Evangelicalism and the Future of Christianity* (London, 1994), p 9.
4 Quoted by D W Bebbington, *Evangelicalism in Modern Britain* (London, 1989), p 276.
5 McGrath, *Evangelicalism and the Future*, p 191.
6 *The Baptist Times*, 22 December 1994.
7 J R W Stott, *Issues Facing Christians Today* (Basingstoke, 1984), p xi.
8 M A Noll, *The Scandal of the Evangelical Mind* (Grand Rapids, 1994), p 23.
9 Noll, *The Scandal*, p 7.
10 Noll, *The Scandal*, p 26.
11 D J Tidball, *Who Are the Evangelicals?* (London, 1994), p 207.
12 Tidball, *Who Are the Evangelicals?*, pp 237–238.
13 Report of the World Evangelical Fellowship's Long Range Planning Team, Manila, 1992.
14 McGrath, *Evangelicalism and the Future*, p 155.
15 G Rawson (1807–89).
16 M A Noll, D W Bebbington, G Rawlyk (eds), *Evangelicalism* (Oxford, 1994), p 371.
17 *Christianity Today*, 6 February 1995.
18 *Christianity Today*, 6 February 1995.

Chapter 23

FACING CONTENTIOUS ISSUES

Derek J Tidball

It is ironic to be asked to contribute a chapter on 'Contentious Issues' to a volume in tribute to Gilbert Kirby, since he has spent his whole ministry as an evangelical statesman seeking to reconcile evangelicals who disagree with one another. As general secretary of the Evangelical Alliance his eirenic character must have been tested to the limits, whilst as principal of London Bible College, during days of rapid social change and the heady days of charismatic renewal, his skills were employed to the full. If students, myself among them, sometimes accused him of being a fence-sitter, it was because, in their youthful immaturity, they had not yet caught Gilbert's passionate commitment to a biblical vision of unity. It would be a fantasy, I fear, to think that all of them had caught it since.

Two books, written by Gilbert Kirby, demonstrate his commitment to interpret evangelicals to one another. *Too Hot to Handle* (Lakeland, 1978) set out to discuss thirteen controversial issues that have generated misunderstanding among evangelicals in the belief that 'nothing does more to harm the spread of the Gospel than bickering between Christians, so often caused by ignorant prejudice'. *All One in Christ* (Kingsway, 1984) explored the theme of spiritual unity, recognizing that it was a difficult goal to attain but one worth pursuing with all our strength.

Evangelical divisions in context

Evangelicalism has never been anything other than an alliance of churches, groups, parties and individuals who coalesce around a few major issues.[1] The issues, however, are so significant that what unites evangelicals is far more vital than what divides them. The issues are also sufficiently weighty to distinguish evangelicals from others in the church and to give rise to a distinctive spiritual ethos. David Bebbington has recently sought to distil the essential features of evangelicalism in these terms: a high view of scripture; the centrality of the cross; a belief in the necessity of conversion; and, consequently, energetic activism in the practice of their faith.[2] But although there is agreement on central issues, the issues are few and leave plenty of room for disagreement among evangelicals. Consequently, the history of evangelicalism has been dogged by division about lesser things.

Disputes have arisen over most other topics. Wesley and Whitefield had a celebrated dispute over Arminian (which stressed free will) and Reformed (which stressed the sovereignty of God) theology. Anglicans and Dissenters differed over churchmanship, baptism and communion. Keswick may have advocated that we were 'all one in Christ', but Bishop John Ryle, a doughty evangelical leader in his day, was an ardent opponent of Keswick theology from a more traditional puritan perspective. The rising interest in premillennial views of the Second Coming caused conflict in the nineteenth century. And attitudes towards biblical criticism or evolutionary teaching were far from united. In our own century there have been major divisions over the pentecostal and charismatic movements, Campbell Morgan, the great Keswick Bible teacher and minister of Westminster Chapel, London, calling it 'the last vomit of Satan'. Likewise, churchmanship has continued to cause friction, especially after the celebrated call of Dr Martyn Lloyd-Jones, in 1966, for evangelicals to leave their mixed denominations and form a pure church. Whilst evangelicalism has always contained points of tension and disagreement, these issues vary over the years. A glance back at the issues Gilbert Kirby wrote about as contentious, only as recently as 1978, illustrates how rapidly things change. Whilst many of the issues may still be with us, such as those of Christian Involvement, the Arts, and Sunday, the steam has gone out of the debates. Other issues, such as predestination and free will, the way of holiness and interpreting prophecy, have almost receded over the horizon, perhaps not altogether helpfully.

Contemporary issues

What, then, are the contemporary areas of division? The landscape of the church has changed almost beyond recognition since the 1960s, and virtually every feature of change has been contentious.

The Holy Spirit

The chief theatre of war (and that, sadly, has not always been too strong a word) in recent years has been that of the Holy Spirit and, as a result, what evangelicals along with others now call spirituality – that is, forms or styles of spiritual life. Whilst pentecostal teaching and experience was largely confined to historic pentecostal denominations, which had originated in Great Britain during the 1920s, evangelicals could, in great measure, tolerate it chiefly through strategies of avoidance and because it was safely contained. However, from the 1960s onwards, people within historic denominations began to have fresh experiences of the Holy Spirit leading to the renewal of their spiritual lives, and that was another matter altogether. It was too close to home to countenance with polite silence.

Sides were taken and, for all the good charismatic renewal did, divisions ensued.

Charismatic renewal has undergone a number of developments since its inception in the 1960s. Its initial phase of personal renewal evolved into a phase of tension and division within numerous local churches and between key evangelical leaders. The tensions were resolved in a number of ways. Some churches settled on an identity that was either charismatic or anti-charismatic. Others eventually decided there was little hope for existing churches and left to form new churches, initially called by the misnomer, 'house churches', and later often identified as 'restoration churches' (because of an emphasis in their theology that God was restoring the pristine church ready for the end times).[3] It is more accurate to describe them, diverse as they are, simply as new churches but to recognize that they cannot remain new for ever, and several of the 'streams' involved are already showing signs of developing denominationalism. At the same time most, but not all, evangelical churches within traditional denominations were showing signs of being affected by a diluted form of charismatic renewal, as patterns of worship and ministry began to change in ways to which we shall return later.

To the first wave, of pentecostalism, and the second wave, of charismatic renewal, some claim there needs to be added a third wave, which originated around 1980.[4] This wave derived its energy from John Wimber and the Vineyard Fellowships that he led, and manifests itself in a much greater emphasis on and acceptance of the element of the miraculous, including healing, words of knowledge, being 'slain in the Spirit' and prophecy, than had hitherto characterized the charismatic movement. Subsequently, various phases have emerged which have led people to focus on prophecy, revival or, most recently, on phenomena such as laughing, weeping, roaring or resting in the Spirit, which have become known as the 'Toronto Blessing'. Since, at the time of writing, this phase is still relatively novel, it is difficult to assess whether it is a significant third wave or a less distinct development of charismatic renewal.

Whatever the historical evaluation of elements of this movement prove to be, there is no doubt that the charismatic movement has caused major realignments in the church in recent decades, which has had a vast impact on evangelicalism and caused numerous divisions. Perhaps the crucial division has been on the different status accorded by evangelicals to the authority of scripture and the authority of experience. Whilst all would agree on a high view of the Bible, they have differed over the actual place it has in their theologies and practice. A caricature of two very different positions on the spectrum might read like this. Some have argued strongly for the Bible alone as our authority and guide and granted little place to contemporary experience. These have tended to stick doggedly to Bible teaching, expository sermons and the daily 'quiet time' as the core of evangelical discipleship. Such evangelicals are not particularly interested in one's feelings, doubts or the emotional dimensions of faith. Faith tends to be a cerebral exercise, and the disciple is encouraged to 'simply trust' what the word says, whether it matches their experience of God or is contradicted by it. In gatherings and worship, it is the word that predominates, other matters being merely the preliminary. It is not that God cannot speak today, but when he does, he does so through the teaching of the Bible. All is tested by scripture which is listened to again and again, even if it is never translated into experience.

At the opposite end would be those who believe strongly that our experience matters. So what a person 'feels' like in themselves, what they 'feel' of God and what they 'feel' in worship becomes more central. God communicates with them in a more direct way, without necessarily using the intermediary of the Bible. The Holy Spirit is a living communicator who can speak today, post-scripture if not on a par with scripture, through prophecies, dreams, visions or pictures. The sermon, as a means of deductive teaching from the Bible, will therefore not dominate in their gatherings. Expressive elements in worship become more crucial, including the repetitive use of songs, drama, movement and dance. The test of God's presence will not be the quality of the exposition but the manifestation of phenomena associated with the Holy Spirit. Old routines and disciplines are discarded as legalistic and are replaced by a search for a living and warm sensing of God. To these evangelicals, belief is not a matter of mental assent to a set of doctrines but of trust through a living relationship. Whether something is true is not considered the key issue (it may be true but irrelevant or lifeless). Whether it works and can be felt is more crucial. Personal issues are frequently the focus of ministry with people being set free from a range of problems (from demons, past hurts and abuse, to coldness, fear and inhibitions) by a range of techniques (from words of knowledge and prophecy, and slaying in the Spirit to exorcism).[5]

The picture is deliberately drawn in stark terms to highlight the areas of tension. In practice, there would be some merging between these two positions, and both would acknowledge strengths in the opposite camp. Even so, to the former group, the latter are dangerously undisciplined and self-indulgent. They have devalued the Bible and only resort to it as an occasional prop rather than their vital foundation. They have put themselves in the centre of the picture, which is a very narrow focus and shows little concern for truth. By their emphasis on experience they open the door to heresy and antinomianism. To the latter group, the former are sound but lifeless, correct but ineffective. Whilst they believe in the Bible they do not seem to believe that the Bible works in a contemporary way.

This general picture enables us to list a number of specific areas of division more briefly:

1 Is the Bible our only source of God's authority, or can it be supplemented by God speaking in a direct way to his people today?

2 What is the nature of Christian initiation? Is it repentance and faith in Jesus Christ alone, albeit expressed in water baptism, or is it

repentance and faith in Jesus Christ, expressed in water baptism and baptism in the Holy Spirit? What, to use David Pawson's expression, is the 'normal Christian birth'?

3 Are all the spiritual gifts mentioned in the Bible (Romans 12:6–8; 1 Corinthians 12:8–10, 28–30; Ephesians. 4:11–12), including the more 'supernatural' ones of prophecy, tongues and healing, still to be practised today? Or have the gifts now been reduced largely to those of pastoring and teaching?

4 Is prophecy an inspired and immediate word for the church, or is it preaching, an exposition of the word by another name?

5 Is holiness a matter of steady progression and effort on the part of the believer, aided by the Holy Spirit and assisted by the teaching of the word, which results in a sense of continuous spiritual conflict? Is it a matter of the believer yielding his or her self to God, in a manner taught traditionally at Keswick, which results in a sense of peace? Or is it a matter of meeting with God through more dynamic encounters, of exercising spiritual gifts and so being lifted to a different level of spiritual existence, which results in a sense of power?

6 Should worship be well prepared in advance even if not liturgical, and be led by a few people who perform to a largely passive audience, using traditional hymns and concentrating on the sermon? Or, is worship to be more spontaneous and more expressive, giving room for the Spirit to do what is unplanned, in which all participate using their gifts and exploiting a variety of media but especially using (often repeated) contemporary songs?

7 Is the church being prepared, through the rediscovery of the pattern of the early church and the place of apostles, prophets and elders, for the end times? Or are these developments a distraction from the ongoing mission of the church in the community and world?

8 How are present phenomena, which some claim to be manifestations of the Spirit, to be evaluated? If they are from the Spirit, what is their significance? If they are not, does their origin lie in human aspiration or devilish counterfeit?

9 Is faith a commitment to believe, regardless of what one feels, or a means by which the living God should be experienced?

10 Is salvation restricted to dealing with sin, or does it relate to physical and emotional ill-health as well?

Denominations

Other divisions are of longer standing but are being expressed in new ways. Churchmanship has never been an issue on which evangelicals have agreed. From earliest days, there were some strong tensions between evangelicals in the established church and those who were Dissenters (later known as Nonconformists). The issues were not unimportant, but they were not considered so important as to prevent fellowship. They related not only to matters of worship or baptism, but also to whether the church was to be allied to the state and inclusive of all who lived within a given geographical area, or whether the church was a community composed only of believers who would stand separate from, and sometimes over against, the state. These differences have meant that most evangelical statements of faith contain little reference, if any, to the church,[6] leading the critics of evangelicalism to believe that they have an underdeveloped doctrine of the church.

Today there are numerous, and inconsistent, tendencies evident among evangelicals regarding the church. Traditional divisions regarding baptism or the state still matter to some, whilst others, regardless of denomination, demonstrate a growing *rapprochement* on matters such as believers' baptism. Some evangelicals have undertaken a new engagement with their denominations. It has been noticeable that, in recent days, a number of evangelicals have assumed positions of leadership within their denominations, whereas previously they may have been indifferent to such responsibilities (or perhaps denied them). For many, however, denominations are simply irrelevant, a relic of the past. In days of increasing mobility and consumerism, people join the church that suits their needs best or matches their style most appropriately, regardless of a denominational label. Some would go further and argue that denominations are a hindrance to the spread of the gospel and a means of disunity for which we should seek repentance. The newer churches were born in the hope of escaping the denomination trap and becoming pan-evangelical communities which would lead to the doing-away of denominations as far as Spirit-filled evangelicals were concerned. But this was not to be. The existence and distinctive ecclesiology of these churches has caused further fragmentation in the evangelical family.

Whilst these things cause disagreement, greater division is evident between those evangelicals who belong to comprehensive denominations and those who belong to homogeneous evangelical fellowships. The latter, being separatist in character, find it hard to understand how the former can belong to denominations which embrace those who are liberal in theology and who seek unity with, for example, the Roman Catholic church. Those in mixed denominations are often concerned, for all their evangelical commitment, that the latter are in danger of having too narrow a perspective, judging everything from their own limited experience and missing out on the richness of the history and breadth of the church.

Differences between old and new, established and non-established, separatist and ecumenical may often be disguised in some of the great evangelical gatherings, such as Spring Harvest, but nonetheless continue to cause friction and frequently prevent evangelicals from expressing greater public unity or even evangelistic harmony.

Evangelism and social action

Evangelicals are supposed to have rediscovered their social consciences at the Lausanne Congress on World Evangelization, held in 1974. Evangelicals had a creditable record of social and political action in the eighteenth and nineteenth centuries but, for various reasons, their social conscience was 'mislaid' at the beginning of the twentieth century. For most of this century, evangelicals displayed a somewhat narrower concern with evangelism and the need for personal conversion. Their social conscience, never quite lost to view, showed signs of stirring again in the 1960s and, at Lausanne, a more holistic approach to mission – one that brought evangelism and social action back into relationship with each other – was advocated, whilst maintaining a careful distinction between the two. The more holistic emphasis was enshrined in clause five of the Lausanne Covenant which affirmed that both were part of our Christian duty and that salvation should transform the totality of our personal and social relationships.

The delicately worded position of Lausanne has, however, been a further cause of division. Some would argue for a much more radical position, as some did at the congress itself. They would argue that evangelism is impossible if separated from social action. Illustrations such as two blades of a pair of scissors do not adequately express how integrated social action and evangelism must be. Some would even say that evangelical mission is not primarily about personal conversion but social transformation resulting from the preaching of and hastening in of the kingdom of God. To others this is all dangerous nonsense and symptomatic of the sort of thing said earlier this century, which led to the preaching of a social gospel and proved so inhospitable to vital evangelicalism. What is needed, they argue, is the simple old-fashioned preaching of the gospel, the warning of judgement, the calling of sinners to repentance and their personal conversion.

Hell

A recent debate that has caused sharp disagreement is the debate about hell. The traditional evangelical view of hell is that it is a place of punishment where the damned will experience unending and conscious torment. This view is captured in some celebrated events hallowed in the evangelical memory, such as when Jonathan Edwards preached a sermon during the Great Awakening, in 1741, on 'Sinners in the hands of an angry God' with such electrifying effect.

More recently, some have questioned whether the Bible does, in fact, intend to teach endless conscious torment and whether other interpretations are not more faithful to its teaching. Hell as endless conscious torment raises moral questions about the goodness of God since, some would argue, everlasting punishment of this kind seems disproportionate to the finite crime of sin. They have opted, therefore, for a view of conditional immortality (related to, but not to be confused with, annihilationism) which states that since immortality is the gift of God (2 Timothy 1:10) who alone is immortal (1 Timothy 6:16), those who die in impenitence are refused that gift and only those who believe receive it. The view, it is said, that each person has an immortal soul derives from Greek philosophy rather than the Bible and, once that is acknowledged, some of the incentives to believe in hell as everlasting punishment are removed. Those who argue for conditional immortality argue that to be denied eternal life is an awful condemnation which is both eternal in its quality and in its duration. There is no second chance.

There is evidence that evangelical publishers have engaged in a conspiracy of silence over this issue, and that serious works of evangelical scholarship might have been published on this topic earlier this century but for the exercise of gentlemanly censorship. The views are now, however, in the open and have been put forth by many respected evangelical statesmen like John Stott, John Wenham and Roger Forster in the United Kingdom, and Clark Pinnock in the United States. But their views have met with sharp reactions and called forth lengthy rebuttals by those, like John Blanchard, who fear that such views are a dilution of biblical teaching and a dangerous compromise with contemporary culture which is characterized by easygoing tolerance. They fear that a lesser view of hell will rob unbelievers of an incentive to believe the gospel and believers of an incentive to preach the gospel.

Women
One of the most contentious issues has been the role of women in the church and in society. The history of evangelicalism regarding women is more ambiguous than many are prepared to admit. Even so, the dominant evangelical perspective was that, for all women had to offer in Christian service, they were not to assume leadership responsibilities and should principally care for the home and the family. Recently, many evangelicals have reassessed key texts on the place of women, and women have had greater freedom to work, lead and minister. This shift of viewpoint by evangelical Anglicans was responsible, in a large measure, for the General Synod of the Church of England voting in 1992 for the ordination of women to the priesthood. But the issue remains controversial, with some evangelicals maintaining, on the basis of 1 Corinthians 14:33–35 and 1 Timothy 2:11–15, that women should not lead, teach or preach and should be content with the role of home-maker. They argue that changing attitudes among evangelicals is purely a reflection of changing public opinion. The issue has divided both evangelical groups and many local churches.

Ethics
During the early and mid part of this century evangelical ethics were relatively straightforward. The ten commandments, including Sabbath

observance, were beyond dispute; the sanctity of family life and marriage was observed; authority was respected; and several *mores* of the evangelical subculture (like no smoking, no drinking, no dancing and no theatres!) were frequently preached. The 'swinging Sixties' put paid to all that and, together with growing prosperity and the advance of the genetic revolution, ushered evangelicals into a bewildering ethical jungle for which they were ill-prepared. So this area, too, has become the scene of some sharp divisions.

The list of topics is long, from genetic engineering to modern entertainment, from homosexuality to environmental issues, from nuclear energy to euthanasia. A common issue which has touched many churches at a pastoral level is that of divorce. Some still firmly hold to the idea that divorce is never right and that the person who does divorce should remain single and never be allowed to remarry or else they would be guilty of committing adultery in God's sight. Failure results in church discipline. Others, however, have relaxed that line and not only welcome into their fellowships those who have been divorced, but are also willing to remarry them, believing that biblical law permits divorce and remarriage. The degree of readiness to remarry those previously divorced varies from place to place. Whatever the solution adopted, most churches find themselves caught in the tension, on the one hand, of upholding the holiness of God and the purity of the church and, on the other hand, of ministering the grace of God and the acceptance of the gospel. But differences between them have caused evangelicals to be suspicious of and argumentative with one another.

Causes of division

Whilst it would be possible to continue to list 'issues that divide' evangelicals, it might not be profitable to do so and space does not permit. Rather, it might be helpful to our understanding of the contemporary scene to comment on *why* such divisions exist.

Doctrinal

Doctrine matters to evangelicals and undoubtedly exercises a major influence on what is believed. Belief is not merely an outward expression of the other factors mentioned below. Sometimes, as in the debate about hell or views on the baptism of the Holy Spirit, the division is a conscious doctrinal disagreement. At other times, doctrine is less consciously recognized but still exercises a great influence. Behind much of the debate about the Holy Spirit and his work today, for example, lie different views of God. A doctrine of God which stresses his transcendence or which tends towards deism will distance God from his world and his people's experience, and will see him operate indirectly through the word of God and within the 'laws' of nature. A doctrine which stresses his immanence brings God close to people, involves him intimately in their experience and allows for his operating more on a supernatural plane.

Behind many other debates lies the key issue of the inspiration of scripture. All evangelicals believe that scripture is divinely inspired, but some will take that to mean it is a divine book which is to be believed and obeyed in the most obvious and direct way; whilst others will see divine inspiration as channelled through specific human beings who lived at particular historical times and in distinct cultural settings, and our interpretation of scripture needs to take that into account. These positions, crudely expressed, lead to some very different understandings of the meaning of the one text to which all evangelicals wish to be loyal.

Culture

Evangelicals have never lived in a cultural vacuum but have, inevitably, been children of their day, however much they wished to be separate from it in their loyalty to God. The history of evangelicalism shows how cultural forces have shaped and reshaped evangelicalism, determining its various emphases and expressions as culture has changed. In the days of Wesley and Whitefield, evangelicalism was very much an enlightenment religion and has remained such with its emphasis on the word, its individualism and its concern that conversion or the Holy Spirit should be experienced. But the subsequent culture of romanticism has also had its influence, and can be seen in much of the holiness teaching that was added to the evangelical galaxy through movements such as Keswick. In our own day it is tempting to identify the expressiveness of the charismatic movement and its preoccupation with looking inwards with the wider cultural movement of modernism. As modernity gives way to post-modernity further changes are afoot, as can already be seen.[7]

The difficulty is that evangelicals often confuse cultural changes with theological changes. The impact of culture is often subtle and unconscious and thus, not surprisingly, difficult to discern. Consequently, evangelicals often resist change as spiritually dangerous when it is nothing of the sort. So, out of a desire to remain faithful to truth, many evangelicals rigidly maintain old patterns, forms of expression and lifestyles, and resist the new. The evangelical stage, therefore, gets more and more crowded and, as time goes by, there are ever new causes of fragmentation and division.

Personal and generational

To the list of factors that contribute to our divisions we must add those which are to do with our personal backgrounds, denominational loyalties, family experiences and social class. Evangelical Anglicans from public school backgrounds who are 'well-connected' differ remarkably from salt-of-the earth Pentecostals and provincial, middle-class Baptists. Then, too, the time at which we were born and the particular experience of our society during our formative years tends to shape the way we subsequently think and behave. The generation to which we see ourselves belonging probably has a distinct outlook that influences our practice of the evangelical faith. None of this implies that our lives are fixed and we cannot change. Nonetheless, such factors tend to exercise an enduring influence on us and make us different from one another – so different, that for all we share in an evangelical gospel, we sometimes find it hard to understand one another. All of this suggests we have a marvellously inventive Creator who can think of endless permutations, and a wonderfully powerful Re-creator who can take our diversity and make us one.

The answer to divisions

Granted that evangelicals will often differ from one another, two questions need to be asked. What are the limits to legitimate disagreement? And what is the correct way to handle disagreement? Space will only permit some hints being given at this stage. The limits to our disagreements are surely defined by scripture, particularly in Acts chapter 15 and Galatians chapter 1. There must be agreement on the gospel of grace, made available through Jesus Christ and received through faith. Any other gospel is 'no gospel at all' and leads to eternal condemnation. We must be careful not to add to this gospel either with well-meaning rules or by imposing cultural conditions on those who believe. All would agree that this centre must be held, but we differ over where the circumference of the gospel is to be drawn. How much is to be included as one spells out the central gospel?

Many issues will divide. Again, scripture tells us how we should handle such divisions, in Romans chapter 14, Philippians 2:1–11 and Ephesians 4:1–16. Where there are disagreements we must first look afresh at scripture and see where we can make progress in agreement on matters of principle. Whether we can do so or not, we must at all times have the mind of Christ among us, which will be characterized by humility, love and non-judgementalism. These will lead us to accept one another, knowing that we are each answerable to our own Master.

Our evangelical history contains some excellent examples of ways in which our forebears have sought to grapple with those scriptural injunctions and apply them to the issues of their own day. Richard Baxter wrote, in 1670, *The Cure of Church Divisions* which is full of pastoral wisdom and, sadly, is not as well-known today as it deserves to be.[8] It is a marvellous application of the spiritual principles we have mentioned and takes account of what happens when Christians cannot reach agreement and must separate from one another. In 1741 Jonathan Edwards wrote *The Distinguishing Mark of the Spirit of God*[9] which contains much of worth for contemporary discussions and divisions about revival. In 1846 the Evangelical Alliance not only adopted a statement of faith but also some 'Practical Resolutions', an eight-fold statement of how to maintain and advance good relations among evangelicals, especially in times or areas of dispute. The present general director of EA is seeking to rehabilitate those resolutions, and rightly so, for they are sorely needed.

Conclusion

It is foolish to pretend that evangelicals will agree on everything this side of heaven. As a faith that calls for personal commitment, it is inherently likely to cause strong opinions to be expressed and strong convictions to be held. What we must acknowledge, however, is that we are 'one in Christ'. This is not only for the sake of the world which we seek to win for the gospel, but for Christ himself. To do otherwise would be to suggest that he died in vain and his cross has failed to break down the walls that people love to erect which divide them from one another. We must be united around the cross not only because we are a showcase of the gospel but because we ourselves want to be recipients of grace. Nothing that divides evangelicals is at all significant in comparison with the cross that unites them.

Endnotes

1 For an introduction to the complexities of evangelicalism, which makes use of a Rubik's Cube as a means of explanation, see D J Tidball, *Who are the Evangelicals? Tracing the Roots of Today's Movements* (Basingstoke, 1994), pp 19–24. All the issues raised in this paper are dealt with in greater depth in that book, and the reader will find there signposts to the appropriate literature in each area.

2 D W Bebbington, *Evangelicalism in Modern Britain: A History from the 1730s to 1980s* (London, 1989), pp 2–19.

3 The history of these churches is documented in A Walker, *Restoring the Kingdom: The Radical Christianity of the House Church Movement* (London, 1985).

4 The phrase 'third wave' was coined by P Wagner in 1986. See K Springer, *Riding the Third Wave* (Basingstoke, 1987), p 31.

5 Some of these issues are helpfully explored in D Pawson, *Fourth Wave: Charismatics and Evangelicals, Are we Ready to Come Together?* (London, 1993).

6 This is not intended to suggest, of course, that some evangelical statements of faith written by or subscribed to by those from within particular denominations may not have a clause about the church.

7 This is a much debated and complex concept. The best introductions are to be found in D Lyon, *Post-modernity* (Buckingham, 1994), and *Faith and Modernity* (Oxford, 1994).

8 A discussion of it, together with a précis of its contents, can be found in D J Tidball, *Skilful Shepherds: An Introduction to Pastoral Theology* (Leicester, 1986), pp 301–305.

9 Reprinted and published by Banner of Truth in *Jonathan Edwards on Revival* (London, 1965).

Chapter 24

THE ROLE OF SEPARATION

Alan Gibson

Jesus Christ is into separation. He once said, 'I did not come to bring peace, but a sword' (Matthew 10:34). Our difficulty is in integrating this negative dimension with our Lord's positive purpose of reconciliation. This humanist age abhors absolutes, especially those religious principles so deep as to justify people separating over them. Many evangelical Christians, and not a few church leaders, feel the same. They dislike any talk of separation and will find this subject a turn-off.

Jesus Christ is also into co-operation. The Three Persons of the Holy Trinity work together, they co-operate. It was our Lord's prayer that their united action should be the pattern for our co-operative task in witnessing to the world (John 17:23). Christian unity is not a theoretical concept. It must be expressed in practical and regular Christian co-operation. The Bible does not condone today's fashion to 'do our own thing' rather than our making the effort to work with others.

At first sight, then, there may not seem much hope for a clear programme of principled separation and co-operation among today's churches. To view the prospects for the future we must first go some way back into the past.

Separation from the world

Salvation is Christ separating us from the world into the church

Outside the liberal fantasy of universalism, separation is an essential dimension of the biblical doctrine of salvation. We are saved out of something dreadful into something wonderful. Our rescue is from the dominion of darkness and into the kingdom of light (Colossians 1:12–13). Just as 'a great chasm has been fixed' between heaven and hell (Luke 16:26), so it is the Christians' confidence that they have been separated once and for all from their guilt, from their former destiny and consequently from all the lost who have not been saved.

However warm our friendship with our colleagues, our neighbours or even our family, our spiritual relationship with them depends on this crucial reality – if they are not saved, they are lost. Paul insists that 'from now on we regard no one from a human point of view' (2 Corinthians 5:16). The Bible is full of these polarized terms. We are in Adam, or we are in Christ; we either remain children of Satan, or we have become children of God.

The essential gospel call is for those still in the world to come to Christ, to move from the one realm to the other. Although regeneration is God's work, conversion is man's work. While only grace can enable us to do so, it is we sinners who are called to repent, to believe, to turn to Christ and to save ourselves from this corrupt generation' (Acts 2:40). God's people were chosen to be separated from the world to him, which is the basic meaning of the New Testament (NT) term 'sanctified' (1 Peter 1:2).

The moral implications of separation

The NT calls upon those who are so separated to recognize this spiritual reality in their moral life. This is the force of the much-misunderstood call of the apostle Paul: 'Therefore come out from them and be separate, says the Lord' (2 Corinthians 6:17, quoting Isaiah 52:11). It is a call to separate from the wickedness of the unbelieving world (6:14) and everything that contaminates body and spirit, and to live in holiness (7:1). The other apostles make very similar appeals (*cf* James 1:27; 1 Peter 4:2–4; 1 John 2:15–17), because the world, the flesh and the devil oppose holiness every step of the way.

While all evangelicals would nowadays affirm this call, there are widely different applications of it. The old shibboleths of drinking, dancing and premarital sex have all been eroded in practice, with Christians arguing for involvement in contemporary society as a mode of witness. At the same time the NT concept of 'soundness' has been eroded to the point of ridicule, as if doctrinal orthodoxy is inevitably doctrinaire and wooden. Paul, however, uses the adjective 'sound' in a moral context, of teaching which promotes godliness and God-honouring behaviour (1 Timothy 1:9–11). If evangelicals today were a little more concerned about being biblical in their teaching than being exciting in their presentation, then perhaps we would see fewer moral aberrations to bring dishonour on the name of Christ.

The religious implications of separation

It is remarkable how soon the first believers became a distinctive body in Jerusalem. Immediately after Pentecost they 'were together' as a sharing community, meeting, worshipping and growing daily (Acts 2:44–47). Initial persecution only served to strengthen their common identity and, although highly regarded by the people, 'no one else dared join them' (Acts 5:13). How over 3,000 could do so we are not told but, 'all the believers used to meet together in Solomon's Colonnade' (Acts 5:12). At this stage of the church's infancy, the only separation mentioned was that between the community of born-again believers and the unconverted society of Jews from which they had been saved.

Two different events were to change all that.

Following the martyrdom of Stephen, the Jerusalem congregation was 'scattered throughout Judea and Samaria' (Acts 8:1). Although this separation of the first church into congregations in different towns was prompted by the devil's opposition, it was overruled by God. The subsequent evangelistic activity of the scattered believers led to further evidences of the Spirit's power, along with baptisms in Samaria. Congregations, one in their faith, now began to be separated by their geography. Philip's dramatic interview with the eunuch from Ethiopia sent the first known Christian convert into Africa. Not just towns but continents now separated the congregations. Such dynamic expansion was soon to explode into the whole Mediterranean world. Before long, the conversion of Saul of Tarsus was followed by the church at Antioch sending out the first missionary team across national and natural boundaries into Turkey. Subsequent journeys planted congregations in Greece and Italy, until the physical separation of the church became a considerable international reality.

The second catalyst for separation was culture. It had reared its head before the scattering of the believers, whilst they were still one congregation in Jerusalem. Acts chapter 6 records the dispute between those converts from the Jews of Hellenistic background and those Jews who had retained their predominantly Hebrew culture. The difficulty was amicably settled, but it presaged the much deeper problem which even the apostle Peter found hard to grapple with. Should the social outcasts of the Gentiles be received as full members of the church without first becoming proselytes to Judaism? Following the interview that the messengers from Antioch had with the apostles in Jerusalem, the Holy Spirit's wisdom enabled the apostles and elders to prevent these deep cultural differences hardening into a schism and creating two church bodies, one Jewish and another Gentile (Acts 15:18–29). Later the apostle Paul could write so movingly of the Body of Christ, separated into disparate congregations but not divided in its faith and purpose (Ephesians 2:11–22). The rest, as they say, is history. And most of it is downhill.

Separation within the church

East and West

Reasons for separation between churches began to multiply. Persecution by the Romans led to serious differences about who should be re-admitted to church membership and on what terms. Emerging heresy brought the need for doctrinal clarification, not least over the sensitive issue of the Person of Christ and later over the relationship of the Holy Spirit to the Father and the Son. The most profound changes arose, however, following the conversion to Christianity of Emperor Constantine in AD 313. Christianity now became socially acceptable and officially recognized. There were enormous positive benefits. Persecution came to an end, church property was restored, clergy were exempted from taxes and the Christian Sunday was recognized. But it was not all gain. Once it became common for people to associate with the church for social reasons, without the life-changing experience of the new birth, there was a fundamental shift in its character. The previously clear separation between the church and the world became blurred. In NT times it was the gospel which created the church and which separated it from the world. Now those who were strangers to gospel experience and lacking faith in Christ, the gospel's moral dynamic, were no longer outside the church but within her community. The primitive church's principle of separation from the world became irreparably compromised.

The concept of separation came to mean something quite different. In AD 324 Constantine laid the foundation stone of the new city of Constantinople on the shores of the Bosporus, a city to rival Rome as the centre of a new Christian empire. The divergence between East and West, involving political as well as theological factors, only intensified. In the eleventh century the eventual split between the Roman and the Eastern churches became the first major denominational separation.

Recovering the gospel

The Western church had become notoriously corrupt by the start of the sixteenth century. Although the essence of the gospel had been kept alive in some missionary communities, the church itself, from the Pope downwards, was preoccupied with personal, financial and political power. God's gracious revelation of justifying righteousness to Martin Luther did not initially lead him to contemplate separation from Rome, but later events made that inevitable. Ecumenical theologians in the twentieth century have tried to represent the Reformation movement as an unnecessary misunderstanding about semantics, but that is far from the case. What such reinterpretation does demonstrate is that the Reformers had a much clearer view of the nature, ground and significance of justification by faith alone, in Christ alone, through grace alone, than most evangelicals do today.

Whilst the shape of Reformed churches varied in the different countries throughout Europe, the invention of the printing press facilitated a rapid exchange of pamphlets and books, giving doctrinal coherence to this remarkable movement of the Holy Spirit. For Calvin and others, the break necessitated by the Reformation was not a schism of the true church but a separation from a spurious church, which was no more than a religious institution of the fatally deluded, to restore the integrity of the genuine church.

Denominations multiply

For some, however, the Reformation did not go far enough. The Continental Anabaptists were critical of the Reformers for accepting the support of the secular powers and retaining infant baptism. In sharp contrast, the Anabaptists witnessed to the principle of the gathered church. Like most church upheaval, concern over these spiritual principles was intertwined with social and political factors. Such, for instance, were not absent from the excommunication of Henry VIII and, with the Elizabethan settlement, the eventual separation of the Church of England. The subsequent concern of the Puritans to effect further reform of the state church from within, and the Separatists to do so from outside, had historic political consequences. It is no exaggeration to say that the English Civil War and the sailing of the Pilgrim Fathers for America were the fruit of these concerns. Whilst the separation of Presbyterians and Independents (later known as Congregationalists) from Anglicans had profound theological convictions at their roots, both movements were shaped by the social conditions of the day.

Intellectual influences too were at work, profoundly affecting the life and character of the churches. Rationalism had become the prevailing ideology, and congregations were being fed sterile doctrine rather than living truth. It was against this that the Continental Pietist movement reacted, which in its turn influenced eighteenth-century revival leaders and led to the separation of Methodist churches from the parish structures of Anglicanism. The nineteenth century saw further separation from the established church by the leaders of the so-called Plymouth Brethren. It also saw the emergence of evolutionary naturalism, providing the background to the German Higher Critical theology and the growth of Arminianism. As a protest against these trends, first the Particular Baptists separated from the General Baptists, and then the 'Down-grade Controversy' led to C H Spurgeon's dramatic resignation from the Baptist Union.

With the birth of the twentieth century, Pentecostalism emerged on both sides of the Atlantic, and new denominations were formed to maintain a witness to these distinctive teachings and experiences. Much nearer our own day, some found it necessary to separate from Brethren assemblies and denominational churches in order to express the 'new wine' of charismatic renewal in 'house churches' (now preferring to be known as 'new churches') free from traditional constraints.

The situation today

Few evangelicals do not practise some kind of denominational separation. If it is a biblical responsibility for individual believers to commit themselves to membership of a local church, then that commitment is some kind of separation from those who choose to become, or to remain, members of a different church. This does not mean they will never cooperate with members of a neighbouring evangelical church of a different denomination, but it does mean that they have chosen to meet regularly with their own church and not with the other.

The question is, where do we draw the line? A religiously sincere but unregenerate and heretical group may use the word 'church' to describe themselves, but they are not part of the genuine church. They remain part of 'the world' and, since there is a biblical duty to be separate from the world, then we should also separate from them. There is also a duty for churches to bear witness to the gospel, not only by their preaching but also by the company they keep. 'Joe Public' sees our public image, even if he never comes inside to listen to our preaching. Consequently, some evangelical churches believe that the only way to remain loyal to the gospel is to demonstrate their uniqueness in their church relationships. They do that by formal church separation from churches which deny that gospel; it is a matter of conscience and loyalty to the Saviour himself. It is unhelpful for the pejorative term 'separatist' to be used of these churches, for they may be in the very forefront of co-operation with genuine gospel churches beyond their own group.

Not all evangelical churches today, however, agree about those from whom we should validly separate. None would hesitate (I hope!) in remaining formally separate from the Unification Church (the Moonies). But what about the Roman Catholic Church? Does its acceptance of the historic creeds mean that it really is part of the true church whilst in error on some matters? Or do the additions to the faith required of its members forfeit its right to be regarded as a genuine church in the biblical sense? Many Bible-believing, gospel-preaching and world-denying churches today belong to comprehensive denominations which employ ministers who deny there is only one gospel that saves and which contain 'churches' obsessed by a 'feel-good' liberalism strongly opposed to scriptural absolutes. Some evangelical congregations in these bodies hold an ecclesiology more strongly committed to the church and its catholicity than to the responsibility of expressing their local autonomy in separation. It has to be admitted that the issue is so low on their agenda that they have never taught it to their people. As a result, a call to separate from false churches to join more closely with the true churches of other denominations would not persuade their congregations. For many it would also cost them their buildings. Those outside these denominations must not be surprised that most within them have no compelling conscience on the issue and prefer to remain where they are.

Co-operation in the church

Co-operation is an acknowledgement of common goals

Since the Trinity of the Godhead is the biblical model for Christian unity, there ought to be a constant readiness for members of the one true church to work together in the common purposes of God. This is exactly what we find in the NT. From the embryonic Jerusalem community on the Day of Pentecost to the international fellowship reflected in Paul's epistles, God's new Israel did not serve Christ in the atomized isolationism which bedevils some evangelicals today.

The churches co-operated in prayer for each other, in exchanging news, in sharing ministries and in sending gifts of money. In an age without jet travel, fax machines or electronic mail, they kept in touch and seemed to have a knowledge of one another, whether in Rome or Caesarea, which today is not always reflected in single congregations. This they did because they were still aware of the one purpose for which Christ had redeemed them – to be his witnesses to the ends of the earth.

Of course there were problems. After all, they were only human. John Mark came between Barnabas and Paul (Acts 15:36–41), Euodia disagreed with Syntyche (Philippians 4:2) and Diotrephes 'refused to welcome the brothers' (3 John 9–10). Even the apostles Paul and Peter had their differences to overcome (Galatians 2:11). But overcome them they did, and the work of world evangelism went forward.

It should involve the whole church

Ideally, every Christian in a local church has a gift which should be used in co-operation with all the others (1 Corinthians 12:12). Within the church catholic there should be co-operation between congregations, each aware of its own submission to the one Head (Revelation 1:12–20). Today, however, churches have multiplied in geographically widespread continents, let alone countries and villages. Within those countries they have been separated into a variety of denominational organizations, all claiming their first loyalty. The last century has also witnessed the proliferation of para-church organizations. Most of these are specialized in their aims and pragmatically effective, especially where they bring together Christians committed to a specialized ministry such as Bible translation, student evangelism or the provision of homes for elderly believers.

Such worthy organizations both assist and hinder co-operation at the same time. They facilitate individuals from different churches sharing their interests as one aspect of the overall ministry of the Body of Christ. Their particular character, however, is limited to people in those churches with that gift, or burden, or calling. For example, compassion for people living with Aids is an essential element in the church's witness today, but it is not the only thing local churches should be doing. Other elements are also essential if evangelical churches are to present an all-round ministry and to support each other in fulfilling it. Furthermore, a case can be made for arguing that the one area of co-operation we are in danger of undervaluing today is the church itself. Yet this is the Body that Christ founded, and its microcosm in the local congregation is not to be relegated to insignificance. It is in the church that the complementary functions of worship, edification, evangelism and social witness are to be held in balance.

If we are to avoid harmful divisiveness in the whole Body, then humility and mutual respect are called for among good para-church organizations. Sadly, this has not always been evident, with competition for limited resources and personality conflicts afflicting our relationships. It ought to be self-evident that any personal empire-building can only detract from the work of the Master-builder himself. It is nothing short of tragic that this truism is so widely overlooked in our publicity-hungry age.

Are there specifically evangelical hindrances?

Bible-believing churches are right about the gospel, about the final authority of scripture and about the provisional character of all church structures in this world. The problems arise when they extend that list to include matters not essential to salvation. Take bishops, for example. If the monarchical episcopate were a development of church order after the close of the NT canon, then no matter how long its pedigree, however valid a deduction from scripture and, whatever its usefulness, its acceptance cannot be made a pre-condition of church co-operation. Before all my Anglican readers give me up as a bigoted sectarian, however, let me hasten to say that there are many other current examples of the same principle. Some churches today require an independent church order, others baptism by immersion, others the exercise of charismatic gifts, some even the use of the same Bible translation as a condition of unconditional co-operation. Should this be so?

The situation is confusingly complex. In a laudable attempt to bring some order to the varieties of evangelicalism today, Derek Tidball has recently proposed the model of the Rubik's Cube.[1] He suggests that the three most important dimensions of evangelical relationships are their attitudes to the church, spirituality and the world. In respect of the church, he lists a local congregation's options as Established, Pentecostal, Ethnic, and so on. In terms of spirituality he suggests they may be described as Reformed, Holiness, Renewal, Radical, and so on. Following the sociologist Bryan Wilson, he then analyses the way they relate to the world as either Introversionist, Conversionist, Transformationalist, and so on. I have given only examples here. His point is that local churches do not all display the same mix of options. Some parish churches in the Church of England are closer in profile to a Conversionist, Reformed Baptist church in the next town than to a Renewal, Transformationalist Anglican parish next door. And the permutations are almost infinite. We are into a pick-and-mix ecclesiology.

If only it were that simple! A recent English church census invited congregations to choose from a number of adjectives those which best described their overall style. Hundreds chose more than one label, some even opting for what the compilers of the census thought were mutually exclusive alternatives. Tidball's model is seriously limited. It may help to show the range of attitudes on various topics held by a church. Where it fails is in unravelling the threads of relationship networks churches build up over the years. This nexus looks more like a kitten let loose in granny's sewing basket than anything as stable as a Rubik's Cube!

Conduits for evangelical co-operation

These come in all shapes and sizes. For personal co-operation there are para-church agencies for (almost) every special interest imaginable. A glance at the main index of the UK *Christian Handbook* is mind-blowing in its range, from the 'Abbey Missionary School for the English Language' to the 'Zambesi Mission'. On offer are conferences (congresses, forums, holiday-weeks, seminars, week-ends, events, celebrations . . . of such there is no end) which individuals may attend. We are introduced to new friends, all sharing our vision, eager to keep in touch and for us to co-operate with them. Many of these occasions are immensely useful, although some do claim too much for themselves.

Where they are wholly evangelical groups, denominations do at least have the advantage of retaining the biblical perspective of the church. Those who conscientiously separate from churches which preach another gospel give pointed witness to the fact that it is the gospel that makes the church. Some independent congregations are sensitive about the word 'denomination', fearing its centralized connections, and refer to their group as an 'association' or 'fellowship'. However they are 'denominated', they can act as a corrective to the hobby-horses of individual Christians and the isolationism of some congregations. At their best they can also help to reflect the range of Bible duties that local churches should be fulfilling together. A number of these evangelical groups relate together for mutual support in the British Evangelical Council, a body open to congregations and groups that stand aside from comprehensive ecumenism. The 'new churches' often have a structural relationship with other churches in their own 'ministry' but without the formal transdenominational links with which they relate to other renewal ministries, through their leaders. Evangelical churches in doctrinally comprehensive denominations are faced with another range of issues. While some are militant about gospel distinctives in their own local witness, they are committed to membership of a group with its own obligations. For example, the Presbyterian in Scotland may regard the term 'church' as applying primarily to his denomination and only in a subsidiary sense to the local congregation. Incidentally, some of them also regard their own as the True Church in Scotland from which other churches are historic aberrations, a feature which does not always help creative congregational relationships at local level. For the genuine evangelical congregation, however, relationships are complex. Their buildings are often held in trust by the church, their ministers are trained by the church, their offerings are administered through the church. Decisions are made by an assembly in Edinburgh or a presbytery in Glasgow which include some strongly opposed to evangelical absolutes. Yet this is the context in which they have always worked and in which they have found it possible to retain a good conscience. Far from being restless about it, some can envisage no other way and maintain that churches without such structural strength are inherently unbiblical.

Similar attitudes are displayed by many gospel ministers in the Church of England and in other denominations. Through their denomination they co-operate with other evangelicals, but also with non-evangelical churches. They maintain that a Christian who is not an evangelical is no less a genuine member of the Body of Christ, deserving of their love and encouragement to a more biblical position. Rather than speak of evangelical unity they prefer to emphasize the hard realities of Christian unity to which evangelical churches must make a vital contribution. The question, however, is not whether individuals can be Christians and not evangelicals but whether, in Luther's words, justification by faith remains the doctrine of a standing or a falling church. We must also ask whether in such dual loyalties these individuals are failing to separate from the baptized world of spurious churches and failing to co-operate adequately with those who are their true brothers and sisters in the genuine Body of Christ.

The present writer is grateful that the officers of the Evangelical Alliance have invited someone outside its membership to contribute to this symposium. I need not add to the positive commendation that appears in this book of EA's work in promoting co-operation between individuals, agencies and churches, nationally and locally. Perhaps I may, however, add this cautionary comment from a respectful observer. One reason why some evangelicals cannot associate with EA is their ambivalence over separation. EA itself has no direct association with comprehensive ecumenism, but it does not require its members to separate from it. Some churches and individuals prominent in EA and its leadership are also strong advocates of evangelical involvement in bodies and activities where the Bible's authority is entirely bypassed. While respecting their sincerity, it must be asked whether this is not a distortion of the gospel's trumpet sound which our generation so desperately needs to hear.

Future prospects

So much for where we are; but where are we now going? Let me suggest some of the more significant factors that will influence evangelical separation and co-operation in the foreseeable future.

Confusion over justification

Recent scholarship, professing to be biblical, has profoundly affected evangelical perceptions of the doctrine of justification. The 1992 Anglican-Lutheran Porvoo Common Statement uses the concepts and the language of the ARCIC II in failing to treat justification as a distinct and forensic act. This is not the way the Bible treats justification, and is highly dangerous. It opens the way for a wholesale review of the Protestant Reformation. While many evangelicals had previously been ready to co-operate with the Roman Catholic Church as co-belligerents in social witness, they are now being told that formal church separation from it is no longer necessary. From being the objects of evangelism, Roman Catholics are being portrayed as our partners in mission. In some quarters this has already become the orthodox evangelical view, and those who dissent from it are regarded as unfortunately stuck in a sixteenth-century timewarp.

The 'open' evangelical

Correspondents in the *Church of England Newspaper* in the early part of 1995 reflected on the Evangelical Leaders' Conference held in January of that year, when the definition of 'evangelical' was raised once again. Those committed to the inerrancy of scripture were criticized, and it was insisted that the true evangelical must leave room for the humanity of the biblical writers. It was a controversy sadly reminiscent of the separation of the Inter-Varsity Fellowship from the Student Christian Movement in the 1920s. The so-called 'open' evangelical is apparently ready to accept not only errors in the Bible but contradictions between Jesus and Paul, together with serious ambiguities about moral guidance. This is not a domestic controversy among Anglicans, for it goes to the very heart of our gospel authority. To say the least, co-operation between those wearing the same 'evangelical' label, but at loggerheads about their basic source of authority, will become increasing hard to achieve. It is not impossible that these strains will prove too strong for some Anglicans, resulting in a reluctant evangelical secession.

The uncertainty over the lost

Hell is an emotive subject. Its character is real and awesome. Our Lord himself repeatedly spoke of it in the most solemn terms. The 'eternal punishment of the wicked' used to be a common element in evangelical statements of faith. Today's evangelicals, however, are not so sure about hell, as more and more question hell's unending duration and prefer to speak of some kind of annihilationism. A few highly respected evangelicals hesitate to be dogmatic about this. Then there is the question of those who have never heard the gospel. Can they be saved without having heard the name of Jesus and consciously believed on him? The principals of two leading independent Bible colleges suggest that they can. By no means all evangelicals would agree, with some having genuine fears about the implications of their arguments for the exegesis of scripture. The growing popularity of these views cannot but impact on missionary relationships.

A sense of proportion

Evangelical worship culture has gone through considerable changes in the last three decades. Since these changes reflect the context of contemporary society, they are unlikely to lessen. What is called 'post-modernism' refuses to adopt one overall style. The implications of this 'free for all' are especially painful for the serious-minded evangelical church committed to the centrality of preaching, and refusing to dispense with what has stood the test of time. Few features of evangelical life, however, are more likely to cause separation within churches and between churches than forms of worship. The exercise of charismatic gifts and the accompaniment of physical phenomena are almost universal in some sectors of evangelicalism. If we cannot pray together, how can we work together, since prayer is itself the essence of our work? Co-operation in evangelism, youth work and leadership training happens in the context of corporate worship. Without a sense of proportion about these very fundamental questions, further separation between gospel churches at different points on this spectrum seems inescapable.

Ecumenism and world faiths

Canberra was the setting for the seventh assembly of the World Council of Churches in 1991, and the evangelical responses were decidedly cool. What disappointed them was not only an absence of a real theology of the Holy Spirit but the presence of so much overt syncretism, denying the uniqueness of Christ.[2] As ecumenism becomes more free from its biblical moorings we must not be surprised that the ship is sailing closer to the rocks. Contemporary theology in the secular universities reflects the dominant world-view of humanist subjectivism, where every person's god is as good as the other and every person's truth is as valid as the other. Ironically, this very threat to biblical absolutes has driven some evangelicals to co-operate with any who stand for an objective Christian theology and has led them into a new *rapprochement* with Roman Catholics.

No wonder other evangelicals believe it is time to get the kitten out of the sewing basket and set to work unravelling these threads.

Endnotes

1   D J Tidball, *Who are the Evangelicals? Tracing the Roots of Today's Movements* (Basingstoke, 1994), pp 20ff.
2   *Beyond Canberra* (Oxford, 1993).

Chapter 25

EVANGELICALISM, CEREBRALISM AND UNITY

Robert Amess

David Gillett, principal of an evangelical Anglican theological college, says in a helpful book (*Trust and Obey: Explorations in Evangelical Spirituality*) that 'Charismatic renewal has challenged an evangelicalism which, in some instances, has revealed an excess of cerebralism and legalism in its spirituality'.[1] This article is not concerned with charismatic renewal, and the danger of 'legalism' is incidental to what I am seeking to convey. It was the word 'cerebralism' in the above quotation that caught my attention. Perhaps, unwittingly, Gillett has presented us with the nub of the evangelical dilemma.

Evangelicalism is by definition cerebral. Its adherents believe that the faith they hold is biblical truth, inspired by the Holy Spirit. This faith has been codified in the great credal statements of the church, including the confessions of the Puritans, and in 'statements of faith' like that of EA. These are unashamedly 'of the mind' and require mental assent.

Yet here in this essay the word 'evangelical' is being used in a different, broader sense. I am writing about the 'new' evangelicalism that began in the early years of the eighteenth century and from which, in large measure, modern evangelicalism has sprung. Though it was an expression of biblical faith, it taught us no new doctrine save in emphasis. Yet it brought such fresh emphasis and vigour at a time of spiritual decline as to be described by some as a revolution.[2] It was never purely cerebral. John Wesley (1703–91), one of its key leaders, has been described by E J Hobsbawm, though with some exaggeration, as 'intensely emotional' and 'irrationalist'.[3]

To be sure, modern evangelicalism must hold fast to the verities of the faith, for it is unashamedly and inextricably part of biblical Christianity and, divorced from it, ceases to be evangelical. In an age when the term 'evangelical' has become respectable this needs to be underlined. Put negatively, there are things that an evangelical cannot say or write – think is another matter – and still be regarded as an evangelical. To this extent, evangelicalism *is* cerebral. And yet, from its inception, modern evangelicalism has been something more than and slightly different from a systematised statement of faith. This is why, though evangelicalism differs little from orthodoxy, not all orthodox Christians can be described as evangelical. Those who hold fast to the Thirty-nine Articles or the Five Points of Calvinism or the Westminster Confession are not necessarily evangelicals since their confessional statement pre-dated the birth of modern evangelicalism. The new evangelical differed from his predecessors in that his mind was touched by his emotions and his faith was worked out in experience. Being an evangelical affected not only the mind, but the heart and then almost everything else. Subjectively, mind and conscience became aligned with emotion; objectively, faith affected lifestyle, politics, one's view of society and the church. The new evangelical looked at the world in a different way from that of members of other sections of the true church of which he was a part and, at first, a very small part.

Evangelicalism did not, and does not, respect confessional and denominational boundaries. In certain respects it differs from Calvinism which it initially rejected but subsequently digested by a process that involved considerable pain; witness the tension between Wesley and Whitefield. Eventually, as in the case of William Carey and others, Calvinism, baptized into evangelicalism, became a powerful force to take the gospel to the world. Thus the new evangelicalism, even in its more Calvinistic expressions, ceased to be of the mind only and expressed itself with great vigour in its evangelistic outworking.

This bringing together of heart and mind is demonstrated perfectly in the conversion of John Wesley at the very beginning of the evangelical movement. Wesley was cerebral through and through, and totally orthodox in his beliefs and convictions. Many of his hymn translations from the German, which we treasure and sing, pre-date his conversion experience. Some have even doubted whether, in fact, Wesley's Aldersgate Street experience was his conversion, being rather some 'second blessing'. But we have no option other than to accept Wesley's own understanding of the event. On 24 May 1738, while listening to a reading from Martin Luther's preface to his commentary on Romans – an exercise of the mind if ever there was one – he had an experience of which he wrote subsequently, and which is now seen as the essence of modern evangelicalism:

> I felt my *heart* strangely warmed. I felt I did trust Christ, Christ alone for my salvation and an *assurance* was given me that He had taken away my sins, even mine . . . [4]

Modern evangelicalism had been born. It was not just a 'warmed heart' that Wesley experienced – something which, by itself, would have been acutely dangerous – but a warmed cerebralism. Wesley always possessed a mind of the highest order, but, as with everything else, one that changed when he became a new creation.

In some respects the new evangelicalism differed from the Puritanism that had preceded it and which influenced it. Men such as George Whitefield and Jonathan Edwards espoused their doctrines, yet both differed in certain respects from what had gone before. They were part of the new movement, that of the warmed heart. And evangelical 'experience' made them unequivocally different. Their evangelical faith was in the finished work of Christ. However, this faith had to be worked out and brought to bear on a wide range of practical concerns. Wesley fulminated against the slave trade; Whitefield founded an orphanage; Wilberforce and the Clapham Sect became involved in almost everything! There was hardly a social concern that these evangelicals did not address, a social malady they did not endeavour to reform or a secular issue they did not feel free to concern themselves with. The warmed heart led to committed activity for Christ. Evangelicalism could not live in a vacuum. What they did was important, though sadly it is the only thing for which they are acclaimed by most secular historians. In fact, it was almost incidental to their overriding passion – the gospel.

Evangelicals were by definition *evangelistic*, to a greater degree than the Puritans. As D W Bebbington indicates, 'activism' was one of their salient features;[5] and their primary thrust was the proclamation of the 'Good News' at home and abroad. From them, through the Spirit, revival came to this country; by them the modern missionary movement blossomed.

Whenever evangelicalism has become purely cerebral, it has ceased to be evangelical, for it has lost its evangelistic edge. This is why some argue that certain sections of the charismatic movement and the Separatist and Reformed traditions within the church need not be regarded as evangelical, despite their claims or the 'soundness' of their beliefs. Some charismatics, on the other hand have to be reminded that the 'warmed heart' is not all there is to evangelicalism.

This leads to another key feature of the true evangelical, which is vitally important today. Modern evangelicalism was not only credal and activist; it also discovered and recognized a basic unity amongst people of like faith and experience. Since their origin in the eighteenth century, evangelicals have discovered that their various distinctives are transcended by their common features, and that their party characteristics are secondary to their common experience of Christ. Evangelicalism is the parent of true ecumenism. In this regard it is arguable that Richard Baxter was the first evangelical,[6] or at least stands in a direct line with modern evangelicalism. Becoming a Presbyterian minister after the Great Ejection of 1662, Baxter formed the Worcestershire Association, a local ecumenical venture, bringing together men of like mind from the Presbyterians, Congregationalists and Anglicans. This was not a seeking for doctrinal convergence but a natural demonstration of unity in 'the Body of Christ'. Often, but wrongly, attributed to Baxter, though a true reflection of his spirit, is the slogan of all true ecumenism:

In things essential – unity;
In things doubtful – liberty;
In all things – charity.

Baxter has been described as 'the first exponent of Ecumenism in England'.[7] He claimed that all who accepted 'the Creed as a summary of belief, the Lord's Prayer as a summary of devotion, and the Decalogue as a summary of duty, were truly Christians and members of the Catholic or Universal Church of Christ'.[8]

Baxter's theological and spiritual convictions involved him in the Great Ejection, yet his heart recognized the true church as wider than his conscience and convictions. He said, 'Of the multitude that say they are of the catholic church, it is rare to meet with men of catholic spirit.'[9] Speaking of the disunity of the church, Baxter said, 'How rare is it to meet with a man that smarteth or bleedeth with the Church's wounds, or sensibly taketh them to heart as his own, or that ever had solicitous thoughts of a cure.' This was a rare, if not unique, sentiment for the age. But to say that this equates with modern ecumenism is too simplistic. When Baxter says he could accept as members of the universal church those who 'accepted the Apostles' Creed', he assumed that it was sincerely believed. Although he would not have taken the term to himself, Baxter was an evangelical first and foremost in that, for him, the verities of the faith were absolute. However, there is a true element of *rapprochement* in Baxter's thinking. He lays down six principles for the peace of the church:

1   Do not stress 'controverted' opinions which divide churches.
2   Do not stress philosophical uncertainties such as 'free will'.
3   Do not stress verbal controversies that if 'anatomized' would disappear.
4   Do not stress items of faith that are not owned by the whole church of Christ.
5   Do not stress doctrines of which a previous and purer church was ignorant.
6   Do not stress anything that is non-apostolic.[10]

Here was the very epitome of a warmed cerebralism leading to mutual recognition of the people of God though widely separated by doctrine and denomination. It was what Wesley described as a 'catholic spirit'.

This is an emphasis that needs to be stressed and a conviction that needs to be recovered by evangelicals today. When modern evangelicalism has become overtly cerebral, it has inevitably become once again subject to party spirit. Instead of the essentials being the basis for unity, the distinctives have become the cause of separation.

Where the mind, applying a doctrinal system, is the sole criterion, then evangelical unity is a pointless task and a dangerous pipedream. The code, once established, must be enforced, while those outside the system are exactly that – outside. From such reasoning (and 'reasoning' is the operative word) have come the notions of 'guilt by association' and 'second-degree separation'. The reasoning is cogent and the result inevitable; but this is not evangelicalism in the historic sense.

The history of evangelicalism therefore is the history of the warmed heart and mind. It is also the story of the essential but elusive search for unity amongst people of like experience, bound by common distinctives and biblical convictions. The quest for unity must start here before it looks for something wider. We must learn to walk before we can run, but sadly, with regard to unity, evangelicals are barely beyond the crawling state.

John Wesley preached a famous sermon on the 'catholic spirit' (no. 39 of the 53 sermons that Methodist lay readers are still required to read). He describes what a 'catholic spirit' is not, saying that 'It is not an indifference to all opinions'; nor is it indifference to public worship, nor the outward performing of it. Using one of those words typical of him, he says that it is not 'latitudinarianism'. Rather, a man with this 'catholic spirit' 'is fixed in his congregation as well as his principles'.

How does Wesley characterize a 'catholic spirit'? It is possessed by one 'who gives his hand to all whose hearts are right with his heart' and who 'with the strictest care', while retaining the blessing of his convictions, 'at the same time loves – as friends, as brethren in the Lord, as members of Christ and children of God, and fellow heirs of his eternal kingdom – all, of whatever opinion or worship, or congregation, who believe in the Lord Jesus Christ'. His brother Charles puts it supremely well in the hymn appended to the sermon:

Redeem'd by Thine almighty grace,
I taste my glorious liberty,
With open arms the world embrace,
But *cleave* [sic] to those who cleave to Thee.

The outworking of this amongst the first evangelicals was a self-recognition that transcended denomination, built bridges across class divisions and subsequently led to the formation of EA in 1846.

It is often forgotten that, in the middle of the last century, pressures to break evangelical unity were more intense than they are today. Fierce arguments raged between Anglicans and Nonconformists. Feelings ran high regarding access to Parliament and university education, and emotive subjects like the right of Nonconformists to be buried in consecrated ground.[11] The birth of the so-called Plymouth Brethren, Irvingism and the Oxford Movement[12] heightened the tension.

Yet in several instances the heart overruled the mind and caused people diametrically separated by intellect, class and experience to seek an expression of their common experience of Christ. They were evangelicals.

This is what made the early Brethren leader, A N Groves (1795–1853), a true evangelical. Groves withstood the 'exclusive' tendencies that were beginning to appear in the teaching of J N Darby (1800–1882), declaring, 'I would not by joining one party, cut myself off from the others.'[13] He added, 'Should it be asked what are to be done with errors? . . . so long as Christ dwells in an individual, or walks in the midst of a congregation, blessing the ministrations to the conversion and edification of souls, we dare not denounce and formally withdraw from either, for fear of the awful sin of schism, of sin against Christ and his mystical body'.[14]

Admittedly there are dangers. It is true that an evangelical heart must not override an evangelical mind. When this happens, it can cause much difficulty and even error. Pendulums, though necessary for the clock to run, should never swing too far. The warmed heart must not overrule the mind at the expense of truth. Properly warmed, however, the mind is humble and open, in contrast to the cold mind which is analytical and hard, yielding its own distinctive fruit.

Evangelicalism has always been unashamedly credal, but when it has been nothing more than that, it has lost its edge, codified its vision and dissipated its energy. Evangelicalism, when it has combined biblical conviction with evangelical 'experience', has moved mountains. As with John Wesley, the world becomes its parish. However, there is little room for manoeuvre between the twin poles of evangelicalism: they belong together. Evangelicals do not imagine that they are the sole recipients of all truth, or that their number encompasses the whole people of God. They might wish that were true – but clearly it is not! But the corollary is also true and has to be underlined. To hold to the evangelical doctrines in a purely intellectual sense is not to be an evangelical, or John Wesley would have been one prior to his conversion. Calvinists can be evangelicals, but Calvinism is not evangelicalism. Arminians can be evangelicals, but Arminianism is not evangelicalism. Neither, for that matter, is being orthodox or 'sound' or 'charismatic'. What motivated the first evangelicals, and caused EA to be formed at a time when evangelical unity was under severe strain, was a vision for unity. Men and women with similar convictions on a core set of fundamental truths wished to demonstrate their unity. With convictions 'warmed' by an 'assurance' that made them intensely personal and deeply experienced, these men and women actively strove for a tangible unity with others of like experience.

This is why, today, evangelicals are the despair of some denominationalists. When an evangelical seeks a spiritual home, the labels are secondary: thus an evangelical Baptist family, moving to an area where the Anglican church is a 'gospel' church, make their home there despite some hesitancy over certain doctrines; a young evangelical Methodist, attending university in a town where the Bible is preached systematically and experimentally in a Baptist rather than Methodist church, makes that church his spiritual home; and so with other denominations. Evangelical ministers frequently find that their churches contain people of wide-ranging backgrounds and church sympathies. If the church is evangelical, then the fellowship of those of like mind and experience overrides all other considerations.

Evangelicals are a difficult people to deal with. Whereas classic ecumenism debates the intricacies of authority, churchmanship and tradition, evangelicals have little interest in such things. Their concerns are being part of the people of God and sharing with others a personal experience of faith in Christ through the Spirit. This is why in both EA and the British Evangelical Council there are disagreements over baptism, church government, the place of the sacraments, eschatological considerations and other doctrinal nuances; but these are transcended by a tie that binds stronger than any of the things that would separate. As their titles indicate, they are evangelicals.

The writer is *not* arguing that convictions do not matter. The common evangelical experience has been testified to in the scriptures and has been codified. As indicated above, evangelicals disagree on some fairly major issues. Nevertheless, they have had common distinctives for 250 years on doctrines such as the person and work of Christ, on the concept of biblical faith, on a common experience, on motivation for mission and on recognisable spirituality. When some, if not all, of these features are recognized in others, evangelicals have built bridges towards them. This is an evangelical ecumenism. For some, though not all, it has become a divine imperative.

Differences between evangelicals there most certainly are. Given the time, and with patience, these can be articulated, for we are by definition people with convictions. Yet, with the exception of those things we would die for, peripheral issues can lose some of the importance that has become attached to them.

This is wonderfully illustrated in an old, important book, *The Churches at the Crossroads*, by J H Shakespeare who was general secretary of the Baptist Union at the beginning of the century. Writing of the various shades of difference between the then disunited Methodist churches, he says:

> The two largest and most powerful [forces] in our English religious life today (after the Wesleyans) are the Primitive Methodist and the United Methodist Churches. They differ little in any respect. It is said that a Primitive Methodist officer in France was asked to explain the difference, but he replied that, though he had understood it when he left England, he had now forgotten what it was.

This is how it must be with evangelicals in the climate of spiritual warfare that we face, both in the world and in our churches. We can articulate the differences between us, but as time goes by and our eyes become increasingly focused not on ourselves but on the task in which we are jointly engaged, these differences lose some of their importance. When we discover that others share our fundamental beliefs and warmed personal experience, and are engaged in the same spiritual battle, we begin to forget what the differences are. This is called evangelical unity.

Endnotes

1   D Gillett, *Trust and Obey: Explorations in Evangelical Spirituality* (London, 1993), p 12.
2   See, amongst others, E J Hobsbawm, *The Age of Revolution* (London, 1962), pp 266ff.
3   Hobsbawm, *The Age of Revolution*, p 277.
4   A S Wood, *The Burning Heart: John Wesley, Evangelist* (Exeter, 1967).
5   D W Bebbington, *Evangelicalism in Modern Britain* (London, 1989), pp 10ff.
6   Bebbington, *Evangelicalism*, p 34.
7   H Davies, *The English Free Churches* (London, 1952), p 79. Quoted in R Rouse and S C Neill (eds), *A History of the Ecumenical Movement 1517–1948* (London, 1954), p 146.
8   Rouse & Neill, *The Ecumenical Movement*, p 143.
9   Rouse & Neill, *The Ecumenical Movement*, p 157.
10 R Baxter, *The Reformed Pastor* (Edinburgh, 1656, 1989), pp 162f.
11 O Chadwick, *The Victorian Church 1829–1859* (London, 1966), pp 370f.
12 Bebbington, *Evangelicalism*.
13 *Memoir of the late Anthony Norris Groves Containing Extracts from his Letters and Journals*, compiled by his widow, 2nd edition (1857), p 36. Quoted in F R Coad, *A History of the Brethren Movement* (Exeter, 1968), p 23.
14 Coad, *The Brethren Movement*, p 127.

Chapter 26

MAINTAINING NEW TESTAMENT UNITY

R T Kendall

Recently out on the streets with the Pilot Lights, Westminster Chapel's street evangelism team, I had a conversation with an Indian medical student from a Hindu Brahmin background. I was trying to lead him to the Lord, but he kept asking me about the various divisions in the Christian church. 'Why can't the Roman Catholics, Jehovah's Witnesses and you get together?' he asked. He thought such were all Christians, and yet he knew there was some division. 'Why all the different churches?' he enquired.

Of course Satan delights in any division in the church of God. He will do anything to achieve it. And it is something that he can do quite easily, because Satan has going for him already the fact that each of us is anxious for self-esteem, honour and glory. It is so easy for every one of us to claim we are right and find evidence to prove it.

Unity at any level is very hard to achieve, even in politics. Back in the 1980s in the Labour party there was Neil Kinnock on one side, Arthur Scargill on the other. The two Davids – David Owen and David Steel – the leaders of the Social Democrats and the Liberal parties could not make their pact work. In the Conservative Party Margaret Thatcher had her battles with the 'wets'.

So unity is always difficult to achieve, especially in the church, because there the devil is truly threatened. Jesus' desire in his high priestly prayer in John chapter 17 is 'that all of them may be one, Father, just as you are in me and I in you. May they also be in us so that the world may believe that you have sent me' (John 17:21). Evangelicals seem to be very uneasy about the subject of unity. Some of us would rather not talk about it. But this feeling is wrong and is (I suspect) often motivated by pseudo-guilt and fear, as Dr J I Packer has put it.

Paul instructed the Philippians to live lives 'in a manner worthy of the gospel of Christ' and went on to say, 'Then, whether I come and see you or only hear about you in my absence, I will know that you stand firm in one spirit, contending as one man for the faith of the gospel.' In my contribution to this book I will look briefly at a number of New Testament passages with special reference to Philippians 1:27: 'that you stand firm in one spirit, contending as one man for the faith of the gospel'.

Where does one begin in order to achieve unity in the Body of Christ? Many of us who are evangelicals have a very quick answer: we tend to begin with doctrine. I am prepared to say, however, that this is not the right order; it is not the biblical way. I think the reason many of us have taken this stand is because we are reacting against the absence of sound doctrine in the ecumenical movement. And I sympathize with this reaction. We must oppose any denial of the virgin birth, the infallibility of scripture, the deity of Christ and the view that faith alone in the blood of Christ is the only way we are saved. Because of such denials many good people have said, 'Well then, the only way toward unity is that we get our doctrines right first.' In taking this approach, laudable though it appears, we are usually not aware that we are being motivated by a spirit of fear, and there are several things wrong with it.

First, saying that we must begin by getting the doctrine right tends to result in an intellectual unity, not a Holy Spirit unity. We sometimes think we are being theological when actually we are merely being cerebral. The result is often smugness and snobbishness, and unity is postponed indefinitely.

Second, it tends to result in a limited number of people deciding what the faith of the gospel is. For example, those of us who are Reformed often want to superimpose a Calvinistic view of election on all Christians. In America some fundamentalists put premillennialism side by side with Christ's virgin birth! The result is that unity is postponed indefinitely.

Third, doctrinal unity is always a superficial unity, an anaemic unity. For those who generally agree on doctrine have it only at one level, and that is on paper. They say, 'This is what we affirm.' But I know from personal experience that they still do not have unity! They quarrel with each other and are prone to rivalries, jealousies and factions; and they are usually making no impact on the world. They are no threat to Satan. It is almost always a small minority who stress getting doctrine right.

It becomes a satanic ploy to keep us from going out into the world. Many fall for the devilish trap, 'Let's get our doctrine right first.' And you know what? Years later they are still trying to get it right, attempting to dot every 'i' and cross every 't'. Before it is over they are like the two Quakers, one of whom said to the other, 'All the world is queer but me and thee, and sometimes I worry about thee!' This is invariably the consequence of beginning with doctrine, unless the group is very small.

So, where do we begin? Where Paul began, where he told the Philippians, for example, to begin – namely, in the Person of the Holy Spirit.

The problem with Philippians 1:27 is that in both the Authorised and the New International Versions, and in some others, the word 'Spirit' is printed with a small 's', and this prevents our realizing that Paul really meant the Holy Spirit. In the original Greek they did not use capital letters. The translator has to decide whether to use a capital or not, and he is not always right.

When I began reading Philippians 1:27, I assumed that Paul was talking about the human spirit. I consulted the Greek and a wide range of commentaries, but it was only the evangelical ones that suggested it might refer to the Holy Spirit. Having pondered long, it began to grip me that Paul must mean the Holy Spirit. For one thing, every time he spoke on this matter in Corinthians and Ephesians, he clearly meant the Holy Spirit. Second, I began to realize that when he used the expression 'one Spirit' he usually meant the Holy Spirit. For example, in 1 Corinthians 12:13, Paul says, 'For we were all baptized by one Spirit into one body – whether Jews or Greeks, slave or free – and we were all given the one Spirit to drink.' See also Ephesians 2:18 and 4:4.

If the reader will bear with the alliteration, in Philippians 1:27 I suggest we have four natural divisions. Paul begins with a *request* for unity – 'whether I come and see you or only hear about you in my absence, I will know that you stand firm in one Spirit'. He describes the *recipe* for unity – 'that you stand firm in one Spirit'; then its *reality*: – 'contending as one man'; and finally its *reason* – 'for the faith of the gospel'.

Note that Paul ends where some would want to begin! He concludes with 'the faith of the gospel'; this unity is for the gospel's sake. If we begin with the gospel, we may be protecting ourselves, hiding behind our doctrine, using it as a camouflage to protect ourselves. Our action may appear to be valiant, noble or God-honouring, but Paul starts by being self-effacing so that the gospel may be set free.

I need not write in detail on this point about Paul's *request* for unity: his point is clear. He refers to it in 1 Corinthians 12:13: 'For we were all baptized by one Spirit into one body'. And in Ephesians 4:1–4 he says, 'As a prisoner for the Lord, then, I urge you to live a life worthy of the calling you have received. Be completely humble and gentle; be patient, bearing with one another in love. Make every effort to keep the unity of the Spirit through the bond of peace. There is one body and one Spirit . . .'

We are all agreed on the need for unity. How do we get it? What is the *recipe*? As I have already said, Paul explains it in Philippians 1:27 in exactly the same way that he does in Ephesians and Corinthians: he emphasizes the one Spirit – the Holy Spirit. I think the reason is very simple. The Holy Spirit in *me* will not fight the Holy Spirit in *you*. If I truly seek and honour the Spirit and do not grieve him, he will work through me in an unhindered manner. If you truly seek and honour the Spirit and do not grieve him, he will work in you in an unhindered manner. It is impossible therefore for us to quarrel bitterly with each other and be Spirit-filled, for the Holy Spirit in you will not fight the Holy Spirit in me.

However, if I grieve the Spirit, my flesh will prevail. 'All is yellow to the jaundiced eye', as Alexander Pope put it. The trouble is, when I grieve the Spirit, I do not always know then and there that this is what I have done. I may only realize it later, since at the time it seemed right to assert myself. If I grieve the Spirit, I am left on my own and I just carry on. However, a grieved Holy Spirit will not operate through me, unless he chooses sovereignly and graciously to overrule. Yet I could maintain the 'truth' of the gospel with great vigour, eloquence and zeal – with or without the ungrieved Spirit. I could become very self-righteous, hiding behind this most noble enterprise – the integrity of the gospel. But my own heart would be cold and out of sorts. This cannot be so if I am on good terms with the Holy Spirit.

> And do not grieve the Holy Spirit of God, with whom you were sealed for the day of redemption. Get rid of all bitterness, rage and anger, brawling and slander, along with every form of malice. Be kind and compassionate to one another, forgiving each other, just as in Christ God forgave you. (*Ephesians 4:30–32*)

'The fruit of the Spirit is love' (Galatians 5:22). The essence of the Spirit is love. When the ungrieved Spirit of God works in us, I am going to love and accept others: 'But the wisdom that comes from heaven is first of all pure; then peace-loving, considerate, submissive, full of mercy and good fruit, impartial and sincere. Peacemakers who sow in peace raise a harvest of righteousness' (James 3:17–18). I used to sing a little chorus: 'Jesus, be Jesus in me.' When the ungrieved Spirit works in me, I am going to be like Jesus to you.

This is what Paul knew. It was the only way that those Philippians were going to have unity. In Philippians 2:1–11, he gets to the heart of this matter. The famous verses, 5–11, are introduced by verses 3–4: 'Do nothing out of selfish ambition or vain conceit, but in humility consider others better than yourselves. Each of you should look not only to your own interests, but also to the interests of others'.

In Philippians 1:27 Paul says, 'Stand firm in one Spirit.' Why 'stand'? Several things are suggested by this word. First, we can 'stand' to love one another. We can pause and ask, 'Do I really love my brother or sister, or do I feel hurt by them?' If I feel hurt, I may harbour a grudge. Then the problem is me. I may find I want to punish that person either by judging or putting them straight. This shows I am not made perfect in love. 'There is no fear in love. But perfect love drives out fear, because fear has to do with punishment. The one who fears is not made perfect in love' (1 John 4:18). When I seek to punish someone with a cutting word to or about him or her, I betray that I am governed by a spirit of fear (2 Timothy 1:7) and am not made perfect in love.

If we really love someone, we will want God to bless and prosper them just as they are, regardless of what they have said or done to us. Jesus said, 'Love your enemies and pray for those who persecute you' (Matthew 5:44). After all, there are times when we are in the wrong and yet we still want God to bless us. Parents know of times when their offspring quarrel, and maybe one child will say to Mum or Dad, 'Well, I hope you won't let him/her do that'; but the parents love their children all the same. Similarly, in the Body of Christ, God loves every one of his children as though there were no one else to love, as St Augustine put it. Here is the test of love: do

I want God to bless the person who hurt me? If so, I will not avoid that person or say anything about him or her that would not make them feel good if they heard it.

A second thing we can do when we 'stand' is listen. For instance, we may hear the wind and sense the direction in which it is blowing. The Holy Spirit is like the wind according to Jesus (John 3:8). One of the best things I ever heard Arthur Blessitt say is this: 'People talk about waiting for the Spirit to move. The Spirit is always moving, because the wind is always blowing.' We need time to listen to what the Spirit is saying. Jonathan Edwards taught us that the task of every generation is to discover in which direction the Sovereign Redeemer is moving, and then to move in that direction.

How do we know it is the Holy Spirit who is giving us the impulse to move? The answer, I believe, is whether that impulse encourages or degrades someone else. If I give someone a feeling of heaviness by my words and my attitude, I am not acting in love and the impulse is not of the Spirit. However, if the impulse is of the Spirit, people will know that they are loved by me. They will feel it. This is Paul's recipe for unity, by which we may live together.

Next, we turn to the quality of the unity – 'contending as one man for the faith of the gospel' (Philippians 1:27). He uses a Greek word here that literally means 'supporting each other side by side'. Here is the *reality* of unity. When unity is a reality, two things occur. First, grace, by which I mean the fruit of the Spirit: 'the fruit of the Spirit is love, joy, peace, patience, kindness, goodness, faithfulness, gentleness and self-control. Against such things there is no law' (Galatians 5:22–23). This produces a consensus not on details, such as the choice of my tie or the colour of my suit, but on the things that matter, because there is joy, peace and liberty. The greatest liberty is having nothing to prove, so that we are not suspicious of another. That is grace.

Second, gifts emerge. Every Christian has one or more gifts. Each of us is unique, since God threw away the mould when he made us; it is no accident that we are alive. Moreover, he has brought us into the Body of Christ, partly for fellowship and partly because he wants us to be identified with him. There is something therefore for each of us to do that nobody else can do.

Two things militate against the use of our gifting: fear and pride. The fear is that my gift will not be noticed, the pride that someone else may be exalted more than I. This is why Paul's 'body' analogy in 1 Corinthians 12 is so vital: hands and feet, eyes and ears are all part of the body and equally important. Likewise, each of our gifts has its place in the Body of Christ.

I may wish I had another person's gift. I may wish that I could be a better preacher than I am, that I had a better mind, that I could be like someone else. I may wish that my opinion would be more widely heard. But, where grace and the ungrieved Spirit are at work in me, I find it easy to let the one who does have the gift for a particular task get on and use it. In the flesh, I could have said, 'Move over, I'm going to do that.' But, controlled by the Spirit, I say, 'You're the one to do it.' As I honour the Holy Spirit, I will want him to work in another person unhindered and allow my gift to remain in suspension until God is ready to use it.

What is the *reason* for unity? The answer is found in the words of Jesus: 'My prayer is not for them alone. I pray also for those who will believe in me through their message, that all of them may be one, Father, just as you are in me and I am in you. May they also be in us so that the world may believe that you have sent me' (John 17:20–21). This is why Paul ends with the gospel; unity is for the sake of the gospel.

Jonathan Edwards once said, 'The one thing that the devil cannot successfully counterfeit in the life of the believer is a love for the glory of God.' In the Spirit you just want the gospel of the glory of Christ to advance. What hinders unity every time is when 'I' want 'my' opinion asserted and vindicated first, with the result that the gospel never advances. The proof that we are Spirit-filled is when we are willing to say, 'I want to get out of the way – let the gospel be heard.' This certainly is what Paul wanted. The gospel's advance is more important than who is proved 'right'. He wanted them to stand fast in one Spirit, working side by side with one mind, for the faith of the gospel.

The reason for such a united stand, according to Paul, is the lost. The Philippians should contend for the gospel 'without being frightened in any way by those who oppose [them]' (Philippians 1:28). There is no need to be terrified by unconverted people. If there is love, there will be no fear of the unsaved. But if fear and pride become more important than the advance of the gospel, Satan has gained a victory.

Are we willing to lose face for the gospel so that people will be saved? Or are we more concerned to be proved right? The real proof that we are 'right' is that we are willing to go without vindication in order that the gospel advances. Take the story of Solomon and the two women who came to him with one live baby, both claiming to be the mother (1 Kings 3:16–28). Solomon said, 'Well, now I don't know whose it is, so bring the baby to me.' Then he said, 'Cut the baby in half and give half to each.' At that point the real mother said, 'Don't hurt the baby! Let the other woman have the baby.' Solomon recognized this woman as the mother. She was willing to forego her rights as a mother for the sake of the baby. Likewise, our love for Christ and the gospel should take precedence over all personal ambition. In this way we honour the Holy Spirit.

I was named after my father's favourite preacher, Dr R T Williams (who was known by his initials). He was general superintendent in his denomination, and one of the things he often did was to preach ordination sermons for young ministers. When he ordained a young minister, he made two statements for which he was famous. The first was 'Young man, beware of two things in your ministry: women and money', adding, 'If you ever get involved in a scandal in either of these two areas, God will forgive you but the people won't.' The second was 'Young man, honour the Blood and honour the Holy Ghost.'

'Honour the Blood' (that is, the work of the Lord Jesus Christ on the cross) will keep our doctrine intact. If anybody does that, there will be little need to worry about in the rest of their theology or their attitude to the Bible. 'Honour the Holy Ghost' is what Paul is saying when he urges us to 'stand fast in one Spirit.' If we honour the Spirit, he can work unhindered in us.

How do we define the 'gospel' if that is where we end rather than begin in our approach to unity? The person in whom the ungrieved Spirit works will not have a defective gospel: it will be the true gospel of Christ – that the God-Man died on the cross to pay the debt we owe to a righteous God. Why is this so? Because only *this* gospel paves the way for the ungrieved Spirit to indwell a person richly. Nothing but the true gospel will produce this quality of self-effacing love.

Chapter 27

LOOKING FORWARD: MISSION

Peter Cotterell

Perhaps because of the generally negative and sometimes apologetic attitude towards mission now common even amongst evangelicals in Europe, it is extremely difficult for most Christians to appreciate the transformation of the world church since 1800. The world population has increased by some 530%, from 903 million to 5,673 million, but the world-wide church has grown by an astonishing 816%, from 208 million to the present 1,905 million. What is equally striking is the world-wide distribution of the church. Whereas in 1900 the vast majority of Christians, some 91%, were from the North Atlantic areas, with only 3% in Africa, by 1994 the figure for Africa had risen to 20%. For all the admitted shortcomings of the early European missionaries, for all their paternalism and their lack of strategy, the statistical evidence is utterly clear: the missionaries went out to make disciples and to plant churches, and they did so.

The advance of the world-wide church

The generally negative view of mission is explained both by the decline of Christianity in the North Atlantic region, and also by the realization that the percentage of the world's population that is Christian is actually falling, by something like 1% per decade.[1]

Kenneth Scott Latourette has divided the history of the church into four periods: 'The First Five Centuries', 'The Thousand Years of Uncertainty', 'The Three Centuries of Advance', and then 'The Great Century' from 1800 to 1914.[2]

If we make use of David Barrett's statistical surveys, published annually in the *International Bulletin of Missionary Research*, Latourette's four periods represent:

1   An initial growth of the church to the point at which more than 20% of the world's population made some claim to a Christian commitment.
2   A long period when that figure very slowly declined to less than 18%.
3   Three centuries in which, painfully, the figure rose again to some 23%.
4   A striking advance to almost 35%.

In 1888 there was an innovative missions conference in London's Exeter Hall: 1,579 delegates were present, from 139 mission organizations. Not only was the conference itself innovative – perhaps the first expression of unity in mission in modern times – but it also marked the end of an era: 'London 1888 marks the coming of age of North American foreign missions after a century of decided British leadership'.[3]

And so we come to the modern period, characterized by a continuing expansion of mission activity (there were some 600 missionary societies in 1900, more than 4,000 in 1994) and the massive growth in world population from 1.6 million in 1900, doubled by 1960 and expected to exceed 6 million by the turn of the century. The consequence is that statistics are confusing: on the one hand, there are more missionaries than ever before and there are more Christians than ever before; but, on the other hand, the percentage of the world's population that is in some sense Christian has marginally fallen, from 34.4% in 1900 to 33.5% in 1993.

Other religions have also been expanding. From 1900 to 1994 Islam world-wide has grown by well over 400%. Religions that once appeared to be remote and exotic, and essentially the province of the specialist missionaries, are now to hand, open to inspection. Their adherents live, travel, work alongside us, and they appear to be very little different from the generality of people. Some clearly better, some perhaps worse, but not the curiosities we had expected them to be. This fact directs attention to a new fundamental division within the Christian church, between those who continue to believe in the historic Christian mission and those who no longer do so. Followers of other religions do not appear to be necessarily either deprived or depraved, and their need of salvation is consequently less obvious. In the past a principal division on this issue in Western Christianity has been between the conservatives and the liberals, but now, even amongst conservative Christians in Europe, there is a loss of certainty, reflected in declining attendance at missionary meetings and in the financial support of missionary societies. Must we believe that a good neighbour, a respected colleague who happens to be a Muslim needs something added to his religion to assure access to heaven?

Of course there is a sense in which all that we have is the same division but determined by a different issue: not the issue of biblical inerrancy but the issue of biblical authority – the authority of a New Testament which is unequivocally missiological. As Gilbert Kirby has neatly expressed it:

Neither indifferentism nor syncretism is new to the religious scene. They are continually recurring phenomena. We are constantly being told that there are many ways to God and that God is too great to reveal himself in a single revelation once for all. Yet that is the historic Christian position. We believe that the incarnation was a unique historical event in which God has intervened decisively in the world.[4]

We would, of course, be quite wrong to suppose that the loss of certainty which characterizes North Atlantic Christianity is also characteristic of the world-wide church. The fact is that there are four times as many indigenous workers and five times as many missionaries today as there were at the turn of the century. And although the world's population has more than tripled in that period of time, the actual space to be occupied remains constant: we do have a significantly higher density of Christian witness world-wide. And there is a clear rationale for the missionary task to be shouldered by the witnesses.

Mission must always be related to the immanence of God, to the idea of the kingdom of God, to an awareness that God created the world, was incarnate in the world and has an eschatological goal for the world. Mission in advance must be mission ushering in the kingdom in the expectation of the *parousia*; mission must be missionaries (and this does not imply merely those who are professionally missionaries, members of mission sodalities) living under the constraints of a present King and an imminent kingdom.

Mission in advance will, it seems to me, require a greater honesty in the evangelical understanding both of the King and of the kingdom. As I have argued elsewhere:

> Mission will always be a power confrontation which includes those signs of the presence of the Kingdom so confidently announced in the New Testament. Mission is more than the multiplying of missionaries or even of churches. It is rather the confrontation of the human condition, of human meaninglessness, and in the name of God so resolving it that God's Kingdom comes. The Kingdom is the entelechy of the church. The mission of the church is to be that entelechous flower out of which the perfect will come.[5]

It is accepted that the church is the imperfect entelechous[6] flower that will, in its eschatological future, be made perfect, but its present imperfection is part of the unredeemed imperfection of the whole world, part of the reality of the dethroning of God. Although evangelicals speak enthusiastically of the reign of God ('God is on the throne'), this is not the present reality. Mission in advance will become a reality in so far as his right to rule is acknowledged, first in the church, and particularly by the individuals who constitute the church, and then through the church, in the world.

The naive adoption of the phrase 'God is on the throne' has certain consequences. It inevitably leads to the concept of God that is appropriate to the Muslim world but not to the Christian one. For the Muslim, God is directly responsible for all that happens. It is Allah who positively wills fire and famine, flood and earthquake, rape and murder. There is, for the Muslim, no second kingdom to blame for these events. It is the responsibility of the Muslim to submit to these events which are precisely that: events, not calamities. How can an act of God be at the same time calamitous?

In fact, the adoption of the phrase 'God is on the throne' leads to the fashioning of a god who is a moral monster. It also makes nonsense of the focal prayer of Christianity which pleads with God:

Thy kingdom come,
> thy will be done in earth, as it is in heaven.

The kingdom has not yet come, and God's will, while done in heaven, is not done on earth. God is not on the throne here. Indeed, few Christians would claim to have him enthroned in their own lives, directing their decisions, determining their goals, still less that he is on the throne of government, of the business world, of the lives of motorists, of drinkers, of drug pushers. It is the task of the church to expand the area of the world over which God is enthroned. However, without the recognition that God is not on the throne, it is simply impossible to explain to the suffering world around us – the victims of famine, of war, of illness – that this is not the perverted will of a monstrous God but the consequence of a fallen world, a world into which God has stepped in order to redeem it. The greatest event in world history is not that man once stood on the moon, but that God once stood on earth.

The eight collections of Proverbs express a consistent and genuine insight into both poverty and prosperity. On the one side, there are people who prosper because they are obedient to Torah, and there are people who are poor because they disregard Torah. On the other side, there are people who prosper because they are disobedient to Torah and there are people who are impoverished as a consequence of that disobedience; there are good landowners and there are oppressive landowners; there is poverty that results from oppression, but there is also poverty that is the reward of the 'slothful man' (Proverbs 20:4; 24:30–34).

David's complacent observation in Psalm 37 – 'I have been young, and now am old; yet I have not seen the righteous forsaken or his children begging bread' – represents a striking example of the importance of a proper hermeneutic. To deduce from his statement that the situation he describes is the norm for the Christian, or even that it was the norm for David's own time, or that it was even the case for David's own life-experience, would lead to a very strange perception of life. Uriah was not alive to present his case against the king! The canonical understanding of poverty and prosperity, or righteousness and wickedness, is much more complex and at the same time much more realistic. It is by ushering in the reign of God – in the lives of kings and governors, of the law-makers and landowners, of the moguls of the business world – that, proportionately, the potentiality of righteousness may be realized.

David, in fact marks out two linguistic domains – the domain of the good and the domain of the wicked. The first domain includes such words as trust, faith, righteousness, justice, patience, hope, meekness and peace. The second domain includes violence, wrongdoing, wrath, anger, folly, perishing, plotting. The distinction between the two groups is seen in terms of eternity, 'for ever' (vs18,27,28,29), and this, in turn, is associated with 'dwelling in the land', a sense of permanency over against the admitted prosperity of the oppressor who, nonetheless, has no assured future to look to:

> Yet a little while, and the wicked will be no more;
>> though you look well at his place he will not be there.
> But the meek shall possess the land
>> and delight themselves in abundant prosperity. (*Vs 10–11*)

An expanded hamartiosphere (or world of sin)

Mission in advance is far more than adding numbers to congregations. It involves challenging the 'second kingdom' (ie the devil's), refusing to accept the exploitation of the poor, the widow, the orphan, the stranger. Mission advance will recognize that we have been given new perceptions of the extent of the kingdom and thus new responsibilities as we seek to bring this kingdom in. The reality of this process can be seen in the emergence of specialist missions dedicated to new expressions of the kingdom: The Leprosy Mission (1874), Tear Fund (1968), Christian Aid (1950). Nor is it only in such specialist missions that compassion is being expressed in the name of God. Most mission societies today are putting very large resources into relieving physical human misery. Our understanding of the concept of sin has broken free from its classical theological setting and has become biblically holistic, seeing sin as both personal and societal (as traditionally, theologically formulated) but also as political, economic and sociological. Salvation is now perceived to be not only future but also present, and in all of this mission has advanced.

In his invocatory address to the Lausanne Congress held in Manila in 1989, Jovita Salonga, President of the Philippines' Senate, painted a picture of his country that could describe many other countries equally well:

> The Philippines is a country where your prayers and discussions will sound familiar. As far back as I can remember our people have been described as 'the only Christian nation in Asia' . . . but sometimes I wonder whether that is a compliment or a cause for continuing reproach. During the twenty year rule which ended in February 1988, we were also described as the most corrupt nation in Asia. The roots of . . . insurgency may be traced in part to our massive grinding poverty and the host of injustices poverty breeds . . . Italy was once described . . . as 'a poor country full of rich people'. The Philippines, by contrast, is a rich country full of poor people.[7]

The fact is that the presence of the Christian religion (I use the word advisedly) is no guarantee at all of freedom from that corruption which is present in the rest of the world. But we can now see that whether in Italy with its context of poverty, or in the Philippines with a potential for abundance, sin destroys authentic human living for the multitude. And, at the same time, sin provides an anodyne – in wealth, in hedonism – for the sheer loss, the loss of true humanity, the degradation, of their oppressors. As has been well said, wealth cannot make you happy but it can enable you to endure your misery in comfort!

We have been able to advance mission as we have seen sin in harsh human statistics. In the fact that each year 14 million children die from treatable illnesses merely because they were born in the Majority World, and each year 250,000 children lose their sight simply because of their inadequate diet.[8] And at last Christians, evangelical Christians, are expanding their hamartiosphere, their concept of the domain of sin, to see these who die and these who are blind as God sees them, to see our own wealth as God sees it, to see our indifference through the eyes of a crucified Christ.

Authentic human living

As it advances toward the twenty-first century Christian mission has an expanded view of salvation. This can be seen in its present as well as in its eschatological perspective. The concept of our being created in the image of God has been beautifully explored by John Macquarrie.[9] Authentic human living involves a recognition of unique individuality, a relationship to a community, a proper perception of creation and a submissive God-awareness.

The recognition of unique human individuality militates against the view of humanity that dismisses the individual through an obsession with the abstraction of the masses. But we are each of us unique: the destruction of one person is the irrecoverable loss of a unique creation. And thus God incarnate can spend infinitely valuable time talking with blind beggars and sufferers from leprosy, and prostitutes and extortioners, and see each of them as uniquely valuable and so worth salvation.

I am still haunted by a photograph I have, from the days of the holocaust, showing nine women lined up above a mass grave, waiting to be shot.[10] The photograph is so framed that the bodies of those already executed can be seen. This photograph speaks more powerfully than all the statistics: *there* are nine unique individuals, Jews, dismissed from life by men who might even have thought themselves to be Christians.

Surely in any real expansion of Christian thinking there must be a recognition, a recovery, of this uniqueness of each individual. As Graham Kendrick, the twentieth century's greatest hymn writer, has so artlessly expressed it:

The King is among us,
His Spirit is here,
Let's draw near and worship,
Let songs fill the air.

He looks down upon us,
Delight in His face,
Enjoying His children's love,
Enthralled by our praise.

For each child is special,
Accepted and loved,
A love gift from Jesus,
To His Father above.

(Extract taken from the song THE KING IS AMONG US by Graham Kendrick. Copyright © 1981 Kingsway's Thankyou Music, PO Box 75, Eastbourne, E Sussex, BN23 6NT, UK. Used by kind permission of Kingsway's Thankyou Music.)

However, salvation must involve a restoration of a true humanity in community. On the one hand, there is the imperative of a constructed Christian community, the church, and, on the other hand, there is the *philanthropia* (love for others) required, which looks beyond the church to the hurting world which cannot heal itself. And the problem here is that the church we have commonly constructed in the past has been a congregation, directed by a presidential minister, rather than a community, shepherded by a pastor, a congregation which of set purpose produces a dichotomy of clergy and laity which is entirely foreign both to the NT and to the early church.[11]

A divided church in permanent conference

By its many divisions the church is diminished. We have advanced in our divisions even as we have declined in our numbers. David Barrett's *World Christian Encyclopedia* lists some 200 denominational groupings in the United Kingdom including, for example, the Apostolic Church of God, the Apostolic Church of Great Britain and the Apostolic Church of Jesus Christ, as well as the Church of God Fellowship, the Church of God in Christ Pentecostal, the Church of God Pentecostal, the Church of God Anderson, and the Church of God UK. These absurdities stand in stark contrast to the assertion of Christian unity expressed in Ephesians chapter 4. The fact is that, with the exception of Eastern Europe, we have fewer Christians, but in every sector – Scandinavia, the United Kingdom, the Catholic South, Central Europe – we have fewer Christians but more congregations, more divisions.

C S Lewis saw very clearly the value to the 'second kingdom' of division in the kingdom of God, and at the same time the absurdity of most of the divisions. Screwtape is represented as instructing his student Wormwood:

I think I warned you before that if your patient can't be kept out of the Church, he ought at least to be violently attached to some party within it. I don't mean on really doctrinal issues; about those, the more lukewarm he is the better. And it isn't the doctrines on which we chiefly depend for producing malice. The real fun is working up hatred between those who say 'mass' and those who say 'holy communion' when neither party could possibly state the difference between, say, Hooker's doctrine and Thomas Aquinas', in any form which would hold water for five minutes.[12]

The Christian church does present to the outsider a totally bewildering confusion of denominations and doctrines, so that it becomes almost meaningless to speak of 'Christians' without adding some denominational label: Catholic, Orthodox, Lutheran, Anglican, Reformed, Methodist, Pentecostal, Baptist, Brethren, Mennonite. In one sense the labels are unimportant, to the younger generation increasingly unimportant, but the conflict carried on between them is important.[13] Perhaps the conflict in Ulster, which has been a reproach hurled at Christian witness all over the world, is the best example. Few of the vocal protagonists bother to attempt to understand the other side, and the intemperance of the language, still more the violence of the conflict, has shocked the world. If we cannot resolve the doctrinal differences between Rome and Protestantism, it should, at least, be possible to accord to one another some measure of respect at least equal to that we are prepared to show to those who make no pretence of being Christians.

The North Atlantic churches seem to have an almost insatiable appetite for conferences. Karl Barth wrote, 'The true community of Jesus Christ is . . . the fellowship in which it is possible for one to know the world as it is.'[14] It appears that it is this knowledge of the world that has become a priority for the church rather than the task of witnessing to it. In his 1988 *Annual Statistical Table on Global Mission*, David Barrett wrote:

There is a multiplicity of planning going on. This can be illustrated by two current massive mega-trends:

1 Since 1948 there has been a vast mushrooming of 5,300 significant congresses or conferences – Catholic, Protestant, Ecumenical, Evangelical, Charismatic – dealing with evangelization at national, regional, continental, or global levels.

2 The last 100 years have seen an unprecedented rash of new publicly announced plans, proposals, and strategies for accomplishing and completing world evangelization. The grand total of these since AD 30 now stands at over 680 distinct and separate plans. Four hundred of these 680 had fizzled out by the year 1960, but 250 are still in existence today, though 100 of them are clearly moribund and about to fizzle out.[15]

It is probably significant that in the earlier years of the modern missionary movement the conference and planning activities relating to world mission were very largely the concern of the more liberal wing of the church. As Stephen Neill once wrote, 'Protestant missions have never been distinguished by having any plan at all.'[16] But in recent years, arguably starting with the 1974 International Congress on World Evangelization held in Lausanne, the evangelical world seems to have been obsessed with congresses and conferences to the detriment of mission action. To quote David Barrett again:

> With this vast proliferation of planning, and with such massive resources of personnel and finance available, one would have expected the total of persons who have never heard the good news of Jesus Christ to fall dramatically each year from 1900 to 1988. But this is not happening. Something has indeed gone wrong.[17]

So far as can be seen, no notice has been taken of David Barrett's observation. The Manila-based Second International Congress on World Evangelization took place in 1989 and duly produced its Manila Manifesto to be added to the Lausanne Covenant. But still the percentage of the world's population that is Christian has continued to decline, to 33.5% in 1993.

It is certainly arguable that the tolerance (one might equally say indifference) experienced by the North Atlantic churches may be partly responsible for its divisions and ineffectiveness. In a video presentation at the Manila Congress the narrator comments:

> When the task is hardest, when the forces are most united against Christianity, when talking about Christ is illegal, when money is scarce, when time is short, then certain words are heard over and over: unity, co-operation, and collaboration.[18]

It may be that any significant advance in mission within Europe and beyond Europe from Europe must await the time when the church is once again taken seriously by secular society, when the present uncertainties of that secular society become certainties of impending eschatological disaster. It may be that at such a time the church itself might abandon its modern obsession with its 'daisy-chains'[19] and take seriously its mission.

Endnotes

1   See D Barrett's *World Christian Encyclopedia* (Oxford, 1982), p 3, and his annual statistical table in *International Bulletin of Missionary Research*, 18 (1, January 1994), pp 24–25.

2   K S Latourette, *A History of the Expansion of the Church*, 7 vols (Chicago, 1972).

3   T A Askew, 'The 1888 London Centenary Missions Conference', *International Review of Missions*, 18 (3, July 1994), p 113.

4   G W Kirby, 'The impact and influence of non-Christian religions', in P Sookhdeo (ed), *Jesus Christ the Only Way* (Exeter, 1978), p 18.

5   F P Cotterell, *Mission and Meaninglessness* (London, 1990), p 278.

6   Definition from the Collins Dictionary: '**entelechy** n. *Metaphysics* **1** (in the philosophy of Aristotle) actuality as opposed to potentiality; **2** (in the system of Leibnitz) the soul or principle of perfection of an object or person; **3** something that contains or realizes a final cause, esp. the vital force thought to direct the life of an organization'.

7   J D Douglas (ed), *Proclaim Christ Until He Comes* (Minneapolis, 1990), p 46.

8   Douglas (ed), *Proclaim Christ*, p 156.

9   J Macquarrie, *Principles of Christian Theology* (London, 1966), chapter 3.

10 M Wurmbrandt and C Roth, *The Jewish People* (London, 1974), p 417.

11 See P Beasley-Murray (ed), *Anyone for Ordination?* (Tunbridge Wells, 1993), especially chapter 6, by A Kreider, 'Abolishing the Laity'.

12 C S Lewis, *The Screwtape Letters* (London, 1942), p 84.

13 See, for example, L Samuel's chapter 'Has Rome changed?' in *Time to Wake Up* (Welwyn, 1992).

14 K Barth, *Church Dogmatics*, IV, 3, p 769.

15 *International Bulletin of Missionary Research*, 12 (1, January 1988), p 16.

16 S C Neil, *Salvation Tomorrow* (Abingdon, 1976), p 129.

17 *International Bulletin of Missionary Research*.

18 Douglas (ed), *Proclaim Christ*, p 209.

19 With acknowledgements to A Carmichael's dream.